oots and Jim Hunter leaving for a trip "outside", 1931.

Margaret Jackson and Emma MacDonald saddled up with Bob Jackson looking on.

ck horses ready to leave Chinchaga for traplines.

Chinchaga River from the air.

epee at Paddle Prairie.

Halabisky dog team, Keg River village in background.

e Mike Papirny family.

Harry Bowe and Louis Jackson on Harry's steamer.

"WAY OUT HERE"

HISTORY OF CARCAJOU, CHINCHAGA, KEG RIVER, PADDLE PRAIRIE, TWIN LAKES

ISBN 1-55056-194-4

Published by
Keg River History Book Committee
Keg River, Alberta
T0H 2G0

First Printing, 1994

Printed and bound in Canada by
Friesen Printers
a Division of D.W. Friesen
Altona, Manitoba R0G 0B0
Canada

Great meeting you Carl.
Hope you enjoy this.
Linda Halabisky / 9/12/99 -

ACKNOWLEDGEMENTS

ACKNOWLEDGEMENTS
Alberta Provincial Archives
The Peace River Record Gazette
MacKenzie Regional Planning Commission
New Horizons
Alberta Historical Resources
United Grain Growers, Keg River
Stittco Energy, Calgary
Manning Motor Inn
Daishowa Marubeni, Peace River
Manning Diversified Forest Products
Creeman Logging
Carson Lein Services, Manning
Manning Elks
Mr. and Mrs. Dave Befus
Shelly Pawlowich
Bev's Crafts and Creations
Houlder Automotive, Grimshaw
Royal Canadian Legion, Manning
Credit Union Manning
Michalchuk Construction
United Farmers of Alberta (UFA), Manning
K. R. Vreeling
Vos Family
Keg River Community Library
Keg River Community Hall
Keg River Ladies' Club

KEG RIVER HISTORY BOOK COMMITTEE
Dr. Mary Jackson
Margaret Befus
Anne Vos
Janice Freeman
Sarah Price
Joyce Vos
We also appreciate the assistance given by:
Mary Lou Ng (typing, researching)
Bobby Ng (proof reading)
Donna Kuhl (proof reading)
Nora Petersen (researching)

NEW HORIZONS COMMITTEE
Dr. Mary Jackson
Margaret Befus
Anne Vos
Janice Freeman
Sarah Price
Bill and Elsie Halabisky
Ted and Muriel Stigsen
Bill Brick
Mabel Omoth
Bertha Parenteau
Bill and Gladys Tkachuk
Vic and Delores Zatko
Annie Michalchuk

TABLE OF CONTENTS

WAY OUT HERE

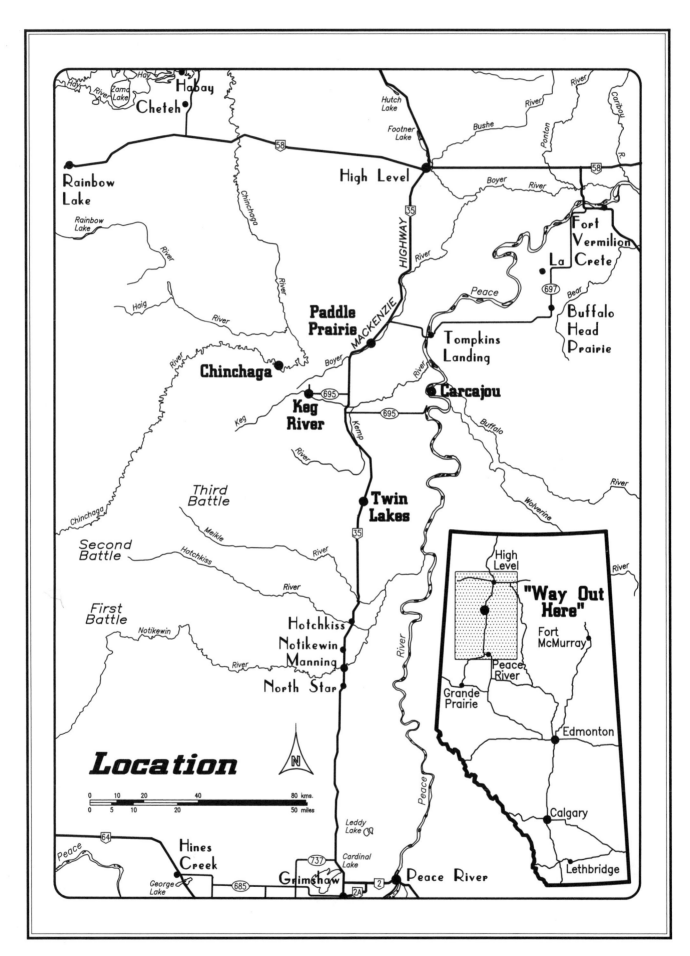

Hay River
Zama Lake
Habay
Cheteh
Hay River

Hutch Lake
Footner Lake
Bushe River
Ponton River
Caribou River

Rainbow Lake
58

High Level
58
Boyer River

Chinchaga River

Rainbow Lake River

Fort Vermilion
La Crete

Haig River

Peace River
697
Bear River

River

Buffalo Head Prairie

Paddle Prairie

Boyer River
MACKENZIE
HIGHWAY
35

River
Tompkins Landing

Chinchaga

695
Keg River
695
River

Keg River

Buffalo River

Kemp River

River
Carcajou

Keg River

Third Battle

River

River

Wolverine River

Second Battle
Meikle River
Hotchkiss River

River

Twin Lakes
35

First Battle
Notikewin River

River

River

Peace River

Hotchkiss
Notikewin
Manning
North Star

Location

N

0 10 20   40   80 kms.
0 5 10   20   50 miles

Leddy Lake

64
Peace

Hines Creek

George Lake

737
Cardinal Lake

685
Grimshaw
2A
2
Peace River

Inset map:

High Level
River

"Way Out Here"

Fort McMurray

Peace River

Grande Prairie

Edmonton

Calgary

Lethbridge

Way Out Here

In days of yore
To the westbound shore
Where factories now pollute,
The pioneers of this great land
Journeyed – way out here.

On train, on foot,
On horseback, too,
Through open fields and plains,
God only knows why they left their homes
To venture – way out here.

With all the perils, toils and strife
These pioneers once faced,
They had courage to keep up the pace.
That lured them – way out here.

Now the days of axe and cabin
Like the people have all gone.
Without the dreams of the pioneers,
For us who follow on,
We wouldn't be – way out here.

Anne (Wevik) Oystryk

Chapter I
History of Our Area

My Home on Buffalo River
by John M. Okerholm

On the bank of the Buffalo River,
Stands a cabin I call my home;
For here I feel free to go and to come.
In the woodland about I go roaming,
Where the moose and the deer make their
  stay;
And here many a drummer is drumming,
When the springtime is well on the way.

In the springtime the songbirds are coming,
And the hillsides will ring with their song,
The robin and the sparrow and the redwing,
Are all singing their loveliest song.
And often I sit and listen in the evening;
With the sunset aglow in the west.
And the hillsides around me are ringing,
With music I consider among the best.

The stream just below this little dwelling,
Is gurgling his simple little song,
I go there with bucket for filling,
Of a morning as the sun comes along.
Quite often I meet there my neighbor,
The beaver that lives around the bend;
He is on his was from his labor,
To spend the day in his riverbank den.

Often to the hilltop I go roaming,
And from there I have a wonderful view;
For miles I can see chokecherries growing,
As will as saskatoon bushes, too.
There are places where black bear is feeding,
When the berries are ripe in the fall;
And often I sit and watch their proceeding,
And this I always love most of all.

Often I see the deer in their feeding,
They are the most beautiful of all;
I found fawns that lay, pretended sleeping,
And refused waking up if I call,
The moose seem rather shy by nature,
And do not care to trust anyone,
And to this end take very strict measure,
And choose mostly to feed when alone.

And there are a few of my neighbors,
They are all of the four-footed kind;
Here I do my play and my labor,
And my payment is a contented mind.
My fate may change in the future,
And my mind wander back to this home.
Where I lived my life close to nature,
When I was young and enjoyed to roam.

A HISTORY OF OUR AREA
by the History Book Committee

In this summary of the history of the Carcajou, Keg River and Paddle Prairie area, meet some of the colorful people of this region! Then read on in this book for further fascinating stories about these pioneers.

CARCAJOU

Originally called Wolverine Point, the first settlement in our area was inhabited by Beaver Indians.

The settlement was situated on the east bank of the Peace River, about 200 miles upstream from the current site of Fort Vermilion and about 150 miles downstream from the current site of the town of Peace River.

The first white man known to have been at Wolverine Point, Alexander MacKenzie travelled up the Peace in 1792, exploring for the North West Company. He mentions Wolverine Point in his diary.

The river was a major transportation route for the native Indians and the fur traders. Wolverine Point became the location of a North West Company trading post in the early 1800's.

Archibald McDonald accompanied by George Simpson, explorers for the Hudson's Bay Company, recorded that they dined below Wolverine Point on August 22, 1828.

The name of the community is believed to have changed as French fur traders began to use the name Carcajou for the area. Carcajou means Wolverine in French.

The area was also called Fort du Tremble. This name is believed to have originated because of the trembling aspens that surrounded the region.

The Carcajou village site was surveyed in 1916 by J. W. Pierce, who made this entry in his diary: "(We found) at Carcajou Point a small settlement of Indians and half-breeds. These people have a few cattle and horses for which they produce feed from the prairies nearby, but apparently hunting and trapping is the chief source of their living. Across the river, we found an English-speaking family who came in here a year ago (the Rankin family) with some stock and they were erecting a house and buildings."

Some villagers were also mentioned: Sarah and Olivier Hamelin, Xavier Sowan, Mrs. Norbert Wanuch, Louis Wanuch and Captain Smith. There were nine houses, three stables, a barn, four gardens, two storehouses (one belonged to the Hudson's Bay Company), a Roman Catholic church and a graveyard in Mr. Pierce's survey of the Carcajou village.

Mr. Pierce also mentioned the first known flood in Carcajou, thought to have occurred about 20 years prior to his survey and caused by an ice jam. This flood in the late 1800's destroyed the houses on the flat. Damage to trees was still visible in 1916.

Chillaway Wanuch and Benjamin Cardinal were trappers who arrived in Carcajou prior to 1920. Charlie Gram was a fur trader in this area, using a post built in 1920 which is still standing and continued to serve as a warehouse for years. Other traders in the 1920's were Charlie McLean, the Hudson's Bay and Revillon Freres.

Martha Rankin worked hard to establish a post office in 1927, then served as postmistress for 33 years. Mail was delivered to her by boat, dog team, horses, or by plane.

Early transportation in and out of Carcajou was by way of the river. Many boats travelled between Peace River town and Fort Vermilion and stops were made in Carcajou. Depending on how heavy a load they were carrying and the water level in the river, the upstream trip to Peace River took two to three days. The boats generally did not travel at night. Winter trips, usually by dog team on the ice of the river or rough pack trails through the bush, would take much longer.

In the 1930's a few Mennonite families moved to Carcajou with plans of settling in the Buffalo Head Hills area (close to the location of the Tompkins Landing ferry today). The Wielers, Unrahs, Friesens, Brauns, and others stayed in Carcajou for up to 10 years. Most then moved on to settle in the La Crete area. But some found the hardships of the North even greater than those they had left on the dusty, depressed prairies, and returned home.

Many of these families were caught by the flood of the Carcajou flats in the spring of 1934. As the ice was breaking up, it jammed and huge chunks of ice simply choked off the flow of water, causing the river to rise quickly. The families on the flat were forced to scramble to higher ground, losing many possessions including animals and household items. It was many days before the water receded.

The first school opened in 1934 with Agnes Thompson as the teacher. It closed in 1938. It was not until 1960 that the area had another school. Northland School Division built a one-room school on the west side of the river with Mrs. Edna Kiselczuk as teacher.

Carcajou Settlement

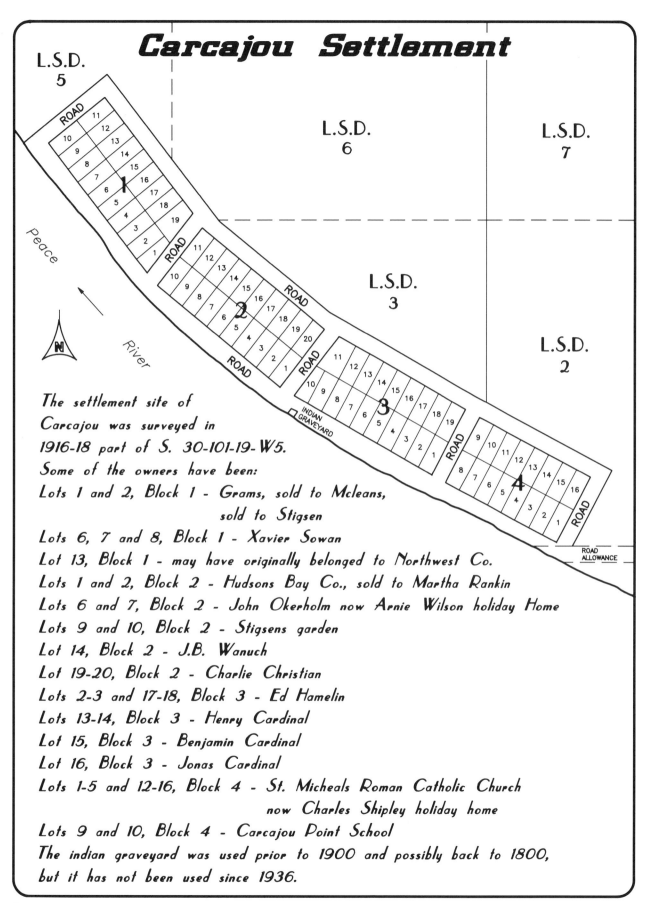

L.S.D. 5

L.S.D. 6

L.S.D. 7

L.S.D. 3

L.S.D. 2

Peace River

N

ROAD

INDIAN GRAVEYARD

ROAD ALLOWANCE

The settlement site of
Carcajou was surveyed in
1916-18 part of S. 30-101-19-W5.
Some of the owners have been:
Lots 1 and 2, Block 1 - Grams, sold to Mcleans,
            sold to Stigsen
Lots 6, 7 and 8, Block 1 - Xavier Sowan
Lot 13, Block 1 - may have originally belonged to Northwest Co.
Lots 1 and 2, Block 2 - Hudsons Bay Co., sold to Martha Rankin
Lots 6 and 7, Block 2 - John Okerholm now Arnie Wilson holiday Home
Lots 9 and 10, Block 2 - Stigsens garden
Lot 14, Block 2 - J.B. Wanuch
Lot 19-20, Block 2 - Charlie Christian
Lots 2-3 and 17-18, Block 3 - Ed Hamelin
Lots 13-14, Block 3 - Henry Cardinal
Lot 15, Block 3 - Benjamin Cardinal
Lot 16, Block 3 - Jonas Cardinal
Lots 1-5 and 12-16, Block 4 - St. Micheals Roman Catholic Church
            now Charles Shipley holiday home
Lots 9 and 10, Block 4 - Carcajou Point School
The indian graveyard was used prior to 1900 and possibly back to 1800,
but it has not been used since 1936.

Carcajou Village site.

A proper, graded, gravelled road connected Carcajou to the MacKenzie Highway in 1963. One reason for its construction was to allow trucks to haul gravel from natural deposits on the banks of the Peace.

With better roads and the Keg River School being relocated to near the Cabins on the highway, Carcajou students began being bused to Keg River in 1968, a practice that continues to this day. The Carcajou school building was moved to Keg River to serve as an extra classroom.

Telephones were installed in the district in 1974. Electrical power was late to arrive in Carcajou because of its great distance from the main power line. The line was finally built in the 1980's when right of way was granted by the Paddle Prairie Metis Settlement, and the expense of the installation was shouldered by the community members.

Carcajou is prime agricultural land, but it was struck with yet another devastating flood in 1974. Again during spring break-up, the ice jammed and houses were flooded. Grain bins full from the previous harvest were under five to seven feet of water. In some cases, the grain swelled so much that steel bins burst!

Some of the land in Carcajou is made up of rich river silt which was moved up through floods and as the Peace changed its course. The river tends to moderate the temperature and delay frosts in the autumn.

Carcajou began as a settlement on the east side of the Peace River but with the connection to the MacKenzie Highway, its population of 16 now lives on two flats along the west side with 2000 to 3000 acres of land under cultivation.

CHINCHAGA

A small group of native people lived along the Chinchaga River around the turn of the century. The area was then referred to as Hay River. These were migratory people and Hay River was a summer home for them. Today a public campsite is found by the river as the river itself offers good fishing and swimming. It is a shallow, winding river with sand bars and nice beaches when the water is low.

KEG RIVER

According to tales passed down through generations, Keg River received its name from kegs of brew found in the river. Small barrels used to store liquor could have been put in the river to keep them cool. Baril River was also used as a name for the Keg River. Speculation is that Baril River was changed to Keg River because "baril" meant "barrel" or "small cask".

Catholic Church records refer to a River Barree in 1910. It is not known if this was a tributary or yet another name for our river. Keg River is 700 kilometres northwest of Edmonton and 200 kilometres north of Peace River.

The area referred to as Keg River is quite large, extending from the boundary of the Paddle Prairie Metis Settlement in the north to the Naylor Hills in the south, to the Chinchaga River in the west and towards Carcajou in the east. Prior to the formation of the Metis Settlement in 1939, the people of what is now Paddle Prairie also considered themselves residents of Keg River.

The Slavey and Cree Indians were the first people to live in this area. The village was originally located where the church, hall and library now stand on open prairie near the banks of the Keg River. Those early residents lived in teepees as Keg River was only a summer home. They trapped for a living and moved to their traplines during the winter. They originally travelled to Fort Vermilion to make purchases and sell their furs.

The overland route between the Peace River and the village of Keg River was recorded in 1894 by Clement Paul. He came by boat to the mouth of the Keg River with one dog and 1300 pounds of grub. Others followed this route but it was later changed: instead of ending at the mouth of the Keg, it continued south to the bank opposite Carcajou settlement.

Permanent log buildings for the Hudson's Bay Company were built in Keg River in 1896 by Clement Paul and his crew from Fort Vermilion. (One of the buildings is still standing today.) The Hudson's Bay operated a fur trading post and store from 1896 to 1970. Clement Paul was also called upon to build the Revillon Freres post in Keg River. They began buying furs in the early part of the century.

Many baptisms and marriages were performed in Fort Vermilion but Father Joussard held the first Mass in Keg River at the home of Clement Paul on March 26, 1904. It was also at this time that he married Clement Paul and Eliza Chalifoux, the first recorded wedding at Keg River. Father Dupin and Father Joseph Habay continued regular visits to the area after 1904.

In his journal in 1908 Alexander MacKenzie (not the early North West Company explorer but a Hudson's Bay post manager) wrote of the prairie where Keg River is situated. The Cree phrase was "Kisikow Muskotayo" or Day Prairie.

"It is a long, narrow stretch of prairie running upwards 40 miles to the head waters of Keg River. This Kisikow Prairie continues on eastward to the head waters of the Paddle River. Then the prairie continues over 90 miles to near Fort Vermilion.

"At the forks of Keg River is to be found a small settlement possessing a few head of horses, cattle and hogs. They raised some barley and vegetables, but outside their immediate wants, no other cultivation has been attempted. The Hudson's Bay Company and Revillon Freres have trading stores here. The provincial government made an appropriation towards having a wagon road cut out from Point Wolverine on the Peace River direct to this settlement, via which supplies are taken as far as Hay River (Chinchaga), which is about 20 miles west of Keg River."

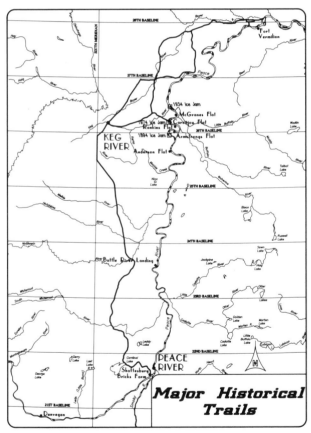

Historical Trails.

By the time of the 1916 land survey, pack trails had been established from Keg River to Fort Vermilion, Fort St. John, Notikewin, Carcajou, and the Chinchaga River. The Keg River village site was surveyed at that time. A survey crew member, Dick Hutchings, later ranched near the Chinchaga River.

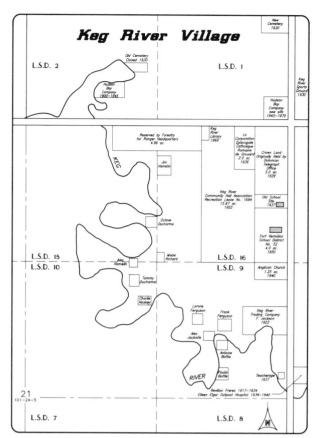

Keg River Village.

Two other original white settlers in the district were Carl Norquist and "Peg-Leg" Morris. Later settlers included Albert Trosky (1919) Harry Bowe, and Frank Jackson (1920). Many new settlers travelled from the town of Peace River to Carcajou by boat, then across country on the pack trail.

Frank Jackson opened the Keg River Trading Post in 1921. This meant that Keg River was the home of three trading posts and stores. The 1920's was a busy time for Keg River, mainly because of fur trading.

Each of these trading posts brought supplies in on the Peace River during the summer. Warehouses were built on the west bank of the river across from Carcajou to store these supplies until they could be brought overland to Keg River by horse and wagon.

In the 1920's Harry Bowe had some livestock, and also into ranching at this time were Peg-Leg Morris, Albert Trosky, Dick Naylor, and Isabelle Chalifoux.

Clement Paul did some cultivation as early as 1913. In the 1920's Harry Bowe, Albert Trosky, and Frank Jackson began working up the prairie. Today there are approximately 20 000 acres under cultivation in this district. Most of the land now being farmed was once covered by heavy timber.

There was a strip of prairie which appealed to the first native settlers as well as the first white settlers, it made for easy travelling and provided immediate food for any cattle brought into the area.

Mail was delivered to Carcajou by boat and brought overland to Keg River in the 1920's and 30's. For a brief time in the 1940's an airplane made regular trips with passengers and mail for Keg River and Carcajou. During this time, mail was delivered to Peace River in one day, even faster than service today. But it was not to last. As roads improved, mail came directly into Keg River by truck. Harry Bowe was postmaster for years.

The Dominion Telegraph line and office were built in 1930. This was an overland communication link with Peace River and Fort Vermilion. A trail was cut along the telegraph line but was passable in the winter only by sleigh and in the summer only by saddle horse.

Until 1929 the nearest medical aid was in Fort Vermilion, a distance of 130 miles which took two to three days of travel. In 1929 Dr. Mary Percy arrived at the cabin provided for her on the bank of the Notikewin River, halfway between Notikewin and North Star, to treat the influx of settlers. She had accepted a one-year contract with the provincial government, planning to return to her home in England at the end of the year.

Fortunately for Keg River residents, she married Frank Jackson in 1931 and moved to the community. Here, without a government contract, she continued to practice medicine until her retirement in 1974. In the 1940's, with the help of the Anglican Church, she operated an outpost hospital.

Dr. Jackson has received many awards for her lifetime of service to the district. Most recently, in 1990 she was named an officer of the Order of Canada.

Construction of the Roman Catholic Church was begun by Father Habay of Fort Vermilion in 1934 with help from local people as well as others from Fort Vermilion. Completed in 1936, this church building is still in use some 60 years later!

The first school in the area, opened in 1937, was built by community volunteers. Winifred Lawrence came from England to be the first teacher. Prior to the opening of the school, some children had attended the Catholic residential school at Fort Vermilion.

Today, just south of Keg River Cabins on the highway can be found the Dr. Mary Jackson School, built in 1963 with additions in the 80's.

The building currently accommodates about 80 students from kindergarten through Grade 12.

In 1936 Cat trains began the job of building a winter road to the Yellowknife gold mines. By 1942 there was an even more important goal, the Canol Project. The American Army arrived and in record time built the road north to the MacKenzie River and the oil fields at Norman Wells.

After the Americans left, the Alberta Government continued to upgrade the road and turned it into the MacKenzie Highway.

It was rebuilt and widened between 1957 and 1961. From where it begins at Grimshaw all the way north past Keg River it is now paved, as is the Keg River Post road from the highway to the church, hall and library.

In 1945 a forestry station was set up in Keg River with Frank Lafoy as the first ranger. It has since closed and the area is now served by the Manning Ranger Station.

There was a local single-wire telephone system set up by Glady Harrington in the 1940's. Later, this was made into the Keg River Mutual with 20 members and connections to Paddle Prairie, the Naylor Hills tower, the Forestry office and local farmers. This system was replaced by Alberta Government Telephone party lines in 1969.

The Keg River Cabins were originally opened in 1946 by Glady and Eva Harrington on the MacKenzie Highway at the Keg River. They have been flooded by the river and closed from time to time, and have had a number of owners. Currently these owners operate the only local store and also serve as post office, gas station, restaurant, and motel.

Homesteading was a popular reason for people moving to the Keg River area. Many people took out homesteads, but with the need to clear and break the land, it was expensive for the first few years. Homesteaders had to find work off the homestead in the winter to pay all the bills from the homestead!

Two sawmills operated in the area in the late 50's and early 60's. These offered new jobs for homesteaders and another reason for people to move into the district. In the 60's the discovery of oil at Rainbow Lake, some 100 miles away, fuelled new economic activity.

As farms were established in the district, the improved roads meant quicker delivery of products to markets. Horse teams were replaced by trucks. Grain and stock were generally taken to Grimshaw (120 miles) for sale.

A rural electrical association was formed in 1961, bringing power for the local families.

The Great Slave Lake railroad was built north from Roma in 1963 at the urging of the member of Parliament for the area, the late Ged Baldwin. What a boost for the district! It was followed in 1965 by the United Grain Growers Elevator. Farmers now truck their grain to the local elevator or load their own rail cars with grain.

The residents of Keg River have volunteered to build the two halls for the community. The first was destroyed by fire at Easter in 1978. The community library was also built by volunteers. These buildings and the local cemetery are maintained completely by volunteers.

The population of the Keg River district in 1973 was 393 but by 1993 it decreased to 203.

PADDLE PRAIRIE

by Susie (Parenteau) Fischer

According to legend, the Beaver Indians came to the area by canoe and hung their paddles in the trees. When the first settlers arrived, they found the paddles and called the area Paddle Prairie.

In 1930-32 the half-breeds of Alberta formed an association known as "L' Association des Metis D'Alberta et des Territories du Nord Quest" (The Metis Association of Alberta and the Northwest Territories).

The Metis people and the government did not want to make the same mistakes as were made with the land "scrips" (certificates of a right to receive payment later in the form of cash or land). The Metis were to either go on the reserves with the Treaty Indians or to live like the white people. Since the Metis chose not to do either, Metis Colonies were set up through negotiations between government and Metis leaders.

Some of the leaders were Joseph Dion of Gurneyville, Malcolm Norris of Edmonton, Felix Calliou of St. Paul, Jim Brady of St. Paul and Peter Tomkins of Grouard. These men volunteered their time and travelled many miles on foot and drifting down rivers looking for good land. As a result of these meetings, in 1938 the Government of Alberta passed a law known as the Metis Betterment Act. The land at Paddle Prairie was set aside as a Colony and permanent land base for the Metis people and could not be sold.

Some of the original families known to have lived on this land were the three Bottle or Chalifoux families: Louisa and Paulis and their children: Antoine, Joe, Peter, Margaret and Clara; Louise and Archie and their children Walter, Edwin, Arthur, Malcolm, and Jeanette; Isabella and Alphonse and children Archie, Frank, Clemence, Henrietta, Thomas and Donald.

When the Metis Settlement was established in 1939, the white people needed to move. Some of the people that moved off land that was included in the Metis Settlement were John and Marie Rose Christian and their children Lucy, Annie, Jean, Charlie, Joe, George, Archie, Elaine and Malcolm; Jim Hunter and his three sons Leonard, Norman and Earl; Manilla and Lonnie Root with their daughters Ethelyn and Alma; Mr. Coleman; the Bindle brothers; Dick Hutchings; Fitz Simmons and Bob Bodz.

Records have been kept as families have moved to the Settlement at Paddle Prairie.

1939 The first settlers arrived by wagon and team with some cattle and chickens.
   1. Elsie and Adolphus Ghostkeeper with their children Annie, Ivy, Margaret, Norman, Mary, Ralph and Hazel.
   2. Josephine and Samuel Johnston and Matilda.
   3. Rose and Sam Johnston – Patsy, Jim and Rose.
   4. Mary and Jean Cardinal – Margaret, Florence, Madeleine, Ida, Rita, Alice, Matilda and Eliza.
   5. Margaret and Jean Felix Ghostkeeper.
   6. Grace and Joe McGillivary – Clifford and Margaret.
   7. Madeleine House – Peter, Joe, Henry, Jerome, Dan, Katherine, Alvina and Jack.
   8. Bella and Napoleon Auger – Margaret, George, Silvester, Adolphus, Charlie, Mary, Sammy and Jimmy.
   9. Maggie and Joe Calliou – Johnny, Mildred, Joseph and Marie.
   10. Peggy Belcourt and Louis Calliou – John, Betty and Violet.
1940 Sarah and Fred Martineau – Mabel, Bertha, Louis, Mary, Norma, Shirley, Lyle. (Fred was the first Supervisor of the Colony.)
1941 Eva and Ambrose Nooskey – Joe, Rose, Julia and Lloyd.
1942 1. Lucy and Henry Calliou – Malcolm, Johnny, Louise, Mary.
   2. Emilie and Louis Houle – Bertha, Betsy, Stella, Florence, Raymond, Thelma, Velma, Clarence, Flavian and Jeannette.
   3. Mary Ann and Roger Wanuch – Albert, Bertha, George, Stella, Charles and Ralph.
   4. Helen and Ed Wanuch
   5. Johnny Wanuch
   6. Paul Wanuch
1943 1. Laura Clark-Mitchell – Henry and Jean.
   2. Julia Ross-Parenteau – Delorme family.
   3. Flora and Sam Parenteau – Leo, Ernestine, Eddie, Tommy, Robert, Susie, Ambrose.
   4. Marion and Louis Lariviere – Marion, Jimmy, Lawrence.
   5. Alice and Teddy Martineau – Lloyd, Frank, Burniss, Raymond and Hazel.
1944 1. Josephine and Frances Poitras – Rita, Elziar, George, Emery, Joan and Beatrice.
   2. Mary and George Gaucher – Pat, Walter, John, Wilson and Alice.

1945 1. Marie and James Bellrose - Marjorie and Leona.
   2. Flora and Alexis Supernault - Silvester, William, Jimmy and Jon.
   3. Jonas and Lavicy Supernault - Mary, Malcolm and Clifford.
   4. Delphine and Daniel Supernault - Doris, Florence, Vina, Billy, Lester and Sadie.

The current population of Paddle Prairie is approximately 600. Many large, new homes have been built in the last few years. Paddle has a store, gas station, fire hall, and large office building. The Paddle Prairie Recreation Complex was opened in 1993 with a community hall, arena, and tennis courts. The Paddle Prairie School has 120 students in kindergarten through grade 12.

TWIN LAKES

Thirty miles south of the Keg River Cabins on the MacKenzie Highway is a service station, restaurant and lodge owned and operated by Rod and Mary Roth. Across from their business is a beautiful lake which has a public campsite for overnight camping. The lake has a twin further from the highway, thus the name TWIN LAKES. Fishing and boating are popular activities during the summer months on the lake.

Our Life in Carcajou (1933 to 1940)
by Mary Braun

(Editor's Note: We thank Mary Braun for consenting to have this article published in our book. She wrote this story for her family in 1981. Mary was ten years old when she arrived in Carcajou with three older sisters and her parents.)

In the latter part of October, 1932, the first Mennonites arrived at Carcajou. There were three families: the Jacob Unruhs with four children; Rev. and Mrs. Isaac Wieler and seven children; and the Isaac Hieberts with four children.

These three families came down the river from Peace River to Carcajou, in an open scow propelled by a motor boat. At the mouth of the Wolverine tributary their craft ran onto a rock in shallow water. Ice was already beginning to form. The men on board carried bags of flour and grain through the water to the shore until the load was light enough to allow the scow to float again. They then made the last 12 miles to the landing at Carcajou. The goods piled on the shore had in the meantime become wet by the rising water of the Peace and were retrieved only after freeze-up, when the men were able to drive to the site on the ice with horses and sleigh.

In September of 1933, we arrived at Carcajou, also in an open scow propelled by a motor boat.

This outfit was owned and built on the banks of the river at the town of Peace River, just south of the old Railway Bridge, by a man named John Natzler who was freighting store goods down river.

On this particular trip Mr. Natzler was taking a load down river to O'Sullivan and Stigsen's Trading Store at Carcajou. The building of the scow took about two weeks. He agreed to take us along if he had the available space to pack our meager amount of household effects.

These effects consisted of bedding, at least one old wire-framed bedstead, a kitchen table, a large chest which our grandfather had made and given to Mother as a bridal gift (incidentally, this prized old relic is still much in use though well over ninety years old now), a small cook stove that was bought in Peace River, as well as a few other things that I have now forgotten. We also had our winter supply of flour, a large metal container of lard, and some salt and sugar among our possessions. These goods had been taken in trade for the old Model T Ford and trailer in which we, a group of seven people including driver Abe Wieler, made the trip from our farm home north of Osler, Saskatchewan, to Peace River town.

I recall that we all lived in a tent with the cooking and eating done out of doors, waiting out the day when the scow would be ready for the downstream trip. The trip itself was uneventful but thrilling to us prairie-dwellers.

At one point we received a shock when Father, who was not adapted to walking along the narrow edge of the scow, suddenly lost his balance and nearly fell over backwards. He managed to swing forward, landing with both hands in the bread pan of dough which Mother had placed in the sun to rise.

On arrival at Carcajou, our belongings were unloaded and we then walked a mile or so to where the Hieberts and Wielers lived. The three families were living on land owned by C. W. McLean in the river flat. The fourth family, Elder Mr. Frank Dyck, his wife and small son Frank, had arrived in the spring of '33 and had a tiny shack close to the Hieberts and Wielers. Like ourselves, all these people came from the Osler area in Saskatchewan at the beginning of the dry '30s. The Hieberts and Wielers lived in the same yard. Hieberts had built a neat little log house of peeled spruce logs with sod roof and dirt floor. Nearby was a larger log building in which both families stayed the first winter. We always referred to it as the big granary.

This home was partitioned off into three bins, or should I say rooms - the walls were only level with the top of the outside wall, leaving the gables open. It even boasted a real roof and a board floor. What they did with a granary at that time I don't know, as to the best of my knowledge there was no threshing machine, so what methods or means, if any, were employed for threshing grain, I would not know. Let that be as it may; it was now used for a dwelling.

The two families had their quarters in two of these bins which were very cold that first winter. The Hieberts had built their own that summer, so now there was room for us and we promptly moved in. Here we stayed till our own house was finished just before winter set in.

Our new house was located about a quarter-mile distant, very near the edge of the spruce bush running the length of the flat along the river bank. It was a beautiful setting indeed and to us, who knew only the open prairie, those lovely big evergreens with which the river bank was lined from one end of the flat to the other, were right out of this world.

Meanwhile we set up housekeeping in our new quarters. We had some bedding, and with straw spread out along the floor to serve as a mattress, then covered with this bedding – we had a bed ready for all six.

As far as I remember, our cooking utensils and dishes – what there was of them – were kept in boxes under the table. The cramped space was not cluttered with furniture as we did not even own a chair.

The board wall separating us from our neighbours had as many cracks as it had boards. The young fry on both sides were not long in discovering this. Simply to hear what was spoken on the opposite side was not enough to satisfy us; our prying eyes had to see as well! This was especially so on rainy days when we were indoors much of the time. We usually approached our post of observation with caution since a fairly steady vigil might be held on the other side as well.

The Dycks had a tiny shack close by, which they heated from a fire pit. The sidewalls were made of mud with something placed over top from where a stove pipe led through the sod roof. The front was open much like a fireplace but the place was always smoky.

The Dycks had been given a couple of hens and the natives had given them a dog; these shared the tiny dwelling with them. On one occasion a hen fluttering about the room, flew into the open fire, burning off its feathers. Unhurt it still strutted about – somewhat naked.

We four families had one thing in common – we were all desperately poor. When we left Saskatchewan, Father traded our milk cow to Isbrandt Friesen for two heifers that they had bought along with other cattle the winter before from Mr. McLean. He was a trader and farmer at Carcajou when the Mennonites first arrived there but he sold the store to O'Sullivan and Stigsen, the cattle to the Mennonites and then went downriver to Fort Vermilion to set up a trading business there. He kept the half-section of land for a number of years after leaving and rented it to three of the families.

They all had a few head of stock and each had a cow or two to milk. Our two heifers were out on the range with the other cattle and we did not get to see them till the first snow drove them homeward. Someone must have owned a binder, as the fields of grain were in stooks and it was apparent that a good crop was realized.

Mr. Wieler and Mr. Hiebert did all the hauling work together as each only owned one horse and harness. A half dozen or so oat sheaf stacks were made near the yard. These stacks served another purpose for us kids – we used them in our games of hide and seek or tag and with about ten kids in the same yard, there was a lot of activity.

Every second Sunday morning, church service was held and attended by the small group in the Wielers' small room. Mr. Wieler had much trouble with his eyes as he suffered from trachoma, which made things rather trying for him, especially when working in dust and bright light. He always wore dark glasses.

These three families had a large garden and as I remember a very bountiful vegetable crop that first year, even ripe beans and lots of delicious muskmelons! We had none of these things since we had come too late in the season. Mother was a great worker and with our help she dug potatoes for Unruhs and received potatoes as payment.

In Saskatchewan we had seldom seen sheep but here it seemed to be the rule that everyone had a few. As it turned out, the wool was a much needed article as this was the only kind of footwear one could come by.

Mr. Hiebert made spinning wheels as well as a few other household necessities such as a table for themselves and one for the Wielers. The material used was birch, sawed into boards with a handsaw; when dried and planed it was quite durable. The spinning wheel made for us gave us many years of service until it was lost in a fire. In time we had all learned the art of spinning.

Unruhs lived on the same land but about half-a-mile away. They were better off though, having owned a good-sized farm in Saskatchewan and not having come into this country penniless, as for instance did my parents, who had one dime left in their pocket.

The Unruhs had two shacks instead of one, as well as a few barns for their stock. Isbrandt Friesen also owned some horses and cattle which were kept at the Unruhs' as the Friesens planned to come to Carcajou in the spring of '34. One of their sons, Abe, was staying with the Unruhs that winter to help care for the livestock. Jake Unruh Jr. and Abe Friesen stayed in the old bunkhouse next to the one in which the Unruhs lived in.

This old bunkhouse, like the big granary we lived in, had been there many years before and also had a floor, though splintered, broken and rough. Under it was a small cellar used for potato storage space. The roof was of sod, but then all log buildings had sod roofs and dirt floors with the exception of the two just mentioned. These were chinked with mud or moss and in some cases even manure.

The mud chinking was prepared with great care and lots of hard work. Fine short straw and water were mixed with clay, and we kids were assigned the job of trampling in this mixture with our bare feet till it was nicely mixed and of the right consistency for smearing into the cracks between the logs. It made a fairly wind-and frost-proof building. This was an annual fall job, and the more buildings, the more mudding we had to do – how I always hated that chore!

One of my sisters worked at the Unruhs' most of that first winter, for which she earned one sheep. To our joy, this sheep presented us with a lamb in the spring – the first that we kids had ever known. Sheep at that time were worth about four dollars.

Very soon after our arrival Father went to work cutting down trees for our own log house, which had to be ready for winter. He borrowed a horse from Mr. Unruh with which to skid the logs out of the nearby bush, then started the process of logging up the walls of green spruce. Once the walls and low gables were up, log beams were placed the length of the house from gable end to gable end. Spruce poles were placed over the beams ready for the sod cover.

Incidentally, the roof poles or rails were also green, unpeeled and to our dismay the bark on them later produced an enormous variety of bugs and beetles - you name it - that were continuously dropping down on us. There were three small windows that let in precious little light even in summer, let alone in the short winter days, when they were so thickly frosted over, one could see little more than where the windows were. This was our house, we had toiled hard to make it what it was, and once it was ready, we eagerly moved in – lock, stock and barrel.

Next, a small addition was built onto the end. This was to house the two heifers, four hens, one rooster and of course, the one sheep. Where we got the hens, I don't remember but that rooster was a very spunky fellow. I remember his crowing was the best alarm in the dark mornings and also days, as the only light to enter that windowless barn was through the door. This was soon too warped from the steam on the inside and the cold on the outside, to close completely. Every time one dared to go through that door, we'd be met by the fury of that rooster's beating wings and clawing feet. We were never long in retreating from that cave-like barn.

Father and one of the girls earned oat sheaves for our winters feed supply by hauling oat sheaves for the Unruhs. They had left a field of stooks standing, and since there was now very deep snow and the stooks were also frozen to the ground, this was very hard work. Each one had to be pulled and pried loose, then hauled to their place where they were piled in a stack. Our sheaves had to be put on the roof top, as rabbits were everywhere – one stumbled over them coming out of the door. It soon became apparent that they were sick and that winter, the rabbit population decreased to a very small number. The snow was nearly three feet deep and our low log structure was buried to the windows.

Our cellar, if one should call it such, was a hole dug in back of the house over which a shelter of logs, poles and sod roof was erected. This was entered through an opening sawed through the bottom logs and from the inside of the house, with steps dug down into it. It wasn't frost-proof, however, and we used only the small entrance to keep a few pails of carrots that were given to us by the Wielers and Hieberts. These were frozen solid but as long as they did not thaw, they did not spoil. We often chewed on frozen carrots and found them very sweet due to the freezing.

Our furniture was a laugh! The one table brought from Saskatchewan was truly a prize in that time, but chairs were all blocks – logs sawed off to the right height measuring over a foot in diameter and just the right size for a seat - of these we had no scarcity. The cupboard was a large plywood packing box which was placed on woodblocks. The big chest, and I must not forget the new Williams sewing machine, one wire-framed bedstead for the parents, the small cook stove and two double beds for us four girls made up the furnishings of our home. These beds were a picture of real workmanship; the frames nailed together from sturdy peeled spruce rails with lighter rails of the same kind forming the bottom. A generous layer of straw covered this and over this came the bedding – what there was of it.

Quite often, due to the rough makeshift beds, holes wore in the cloth, leaving the sleeper to snuggle in the bare straw. Something that stands out in my mind concerning those beds was that when we wriggled around too much, some of the rails under us would suddenly drop out with a clatter or in some cases even break through. We never troubled ourselves to repair such damage in the night.

There was something else equally provoking of despair, or should I say of humor, for I don't recall that we were given to despair very easily. When the house (or what-you-may-call-it) was built, it never occurred to us that green logs should be peeled and allowed to dry. This was not done and when the cold weather came, the one cook stove, though placed in the middle of the room, could not offer enough heat to keep the whole place reasonably warm and also dry, so the walls became dripping wet. We were alarmed and went to work ripping the soaked bark from the logs. They still would not dry. Instead, with the weather becoming colder, the dripping wet walls were soon sheathed in ice. Our stalwart rail beds were securely frozen into the corners of the igloo-like house.

For Mother it was a struggle to keep us supplied with footwear. She spent hours by the feeble light of a small coal oil lamp making heavy knee-high woollen socks for us, with which we wore wooden shoes. The soles were made of wood with the toe end enclosed with moose hide (Heldtschoren). We became quite adept at walking in them.

When my brother made a pair of skis, my sister and I even wore these wooden shoes on skis. This was our greatest outdoor pastime. We'd mount the skis together and run all over the chinook-hardened surfaces. Then on a sunny day, we skied down to the boat landing at Carcajou. For the first time since freeze-up we saw the river. The huge chunks of ice that had been forced together by the fall breakup looked monstrous to us.

Here we met Nellie Stigsen and her mother. Though our English was very poor, we soon became friends as Nellie was near our age. They doubtlessly found our outmoded dress somewhat strange, especially our clumsy wooden shoes. We often noticed the sly glances they cast at our feet. Nellie, in contrast, was wearing a pair of cute-looking beaded moccasins. Later on, we took to wearing this type of footwear over our home made woollens.

The Stigsens had come to Carcajou from Calgary and jointly owned the store with Jack O'Sullivan. Though store and house were both log structures, their house was beautiful compared to ours. The store was mostly a fur trading business.

The four Mennonite families did not patronize their business much, being too poor to buy – credit was then also out of the question. In fact, Mr. Stigsen was not a man with much feeling toward his prospective customers. When the parents tried to trade some woollen socks or mitts for a few necessities, he would consent only if a trapper happened to be coming in to whom he could sell them, but this was usually on very short notice. Poor Mother sat up late and early by that feeble light, plying her birch wood hook, for she surely must have them ready by the set time. She would receive one dollar's worth of groceries for a pair of large knee socks, but a dollar was of course much more than five are now.

That first winter, our food fare was of very poor quality and plain enough to make it rather tiring at times. We had white flour and a few other things to go with it, but we had no meat other than a few times when we were given a piece of moose meat or liver. This was greatly appreciated.

I think we ate more flapjacks or pancakes than anything else. We sometimes called them bannock though later we learned that ours was far from the real thing. We made them simply from flour, water and salt to taste and fried them. We had no milk, cream, butter or eggs.

The white bread wasn't satisfying, so we began grinding wheat in a small coffee grinder. This was held between the knees and steadied with one hand while the other hand turned the crank. A drawer in the tiny box-like grinder held less than a pint of flour at a time so it was repeatedly emptied into the bread pan. Since the flour was put through two or three times to make it fine enough for bread-making, this was a slow process.

Sometimes, to speed it up a bit, we borrowed the Hieberts' coffee grinder (when they weren't using it for the same purpose). The coarse part of the flour was cooked as cereal.

Our threshing methods were as primitive as the flour milling was. The wheat sheaves were placed on the floor of the granary and the wheat pounded out of the heads with a flail. It took a bit of practice but after a while, even a child could master this mode of threshing. A hand-cranked fanning mill was made, with which to blow the chaff out of the wheat. Weed seeds were not much of a problem as yet, hence the wheat needed only to be separated from the chaff.

I well remember how my friend Katherine Hiebert and I were sent to the task of flailing wheat for bread-making. How fed up we used to get! We'd pound and pound.

As for myself, I cared not in the least how the floor underneath was knocked to splinters or the leather thongs with which the flail end was fastened to the handle, twisted into knots and broke. It was explained to me time and time again: if the flail was swung properly, the leather would not twist off. Of course I knew this all too well from experience and oddly enough we never seemed to run out of flails. To help break the monotony, we would often stop for a bite to eat. Our lunch was a head of raw cabbage which was near at hand; so we'd take a bite, then chomping, we flailed away.

It was fortunate for us that this means of wheat threshing was used only for the purpose of bread-making. Cattle were fed on the oat sheaves and the pigs and chickens were given wheat sheaves.

Abe Wieler, who had come into the country with the first families, had been working for the Unruhs and also at Charlie Rankin's. When Charlie went to his trap line, Abe joined him. In the summer of '33 he had returned to Saskatchewan but came back with us to Carcajou by fall.

As Father had not driven a car until we got the Ford (which incidently we traded for a wagon shortly before leaving for our new destination), Abe undertook to drive us to Carcajou. He went back to Rankin's again then, and as far as I remember, he and Mr. Rankin trapped together once more. On coming out of the bush he stayed at the Wielers a while (Mr. Wieler was his uncle) but they had very little room – still living in the granary.

Before winter's end Abe started work on the building of a small cabin for himself. The snow was very deep, so not far from us, he shovelled out a clearing big enough for a cabin. The logs were prepared in the nearby bush but had to be brought out with a team and sleigh, and this was no simple task.

Because of the deep snow, the only way the horses could move forward was in leaps but the one horse was extremely lazy. Mr. Wieler meant to break a trail with the sleigh before attempting to take on a load, but old Dan just would not consent to leaping along in that deep snow with the sleigh floating behind and no amount of persuasion could make him budge. Mr. Wieler asked Abe to go ahead and make a trail in hopes of getting Dan to move. Abe started off into the snow, pulling up one leg, pushing it ahead, pulling up the other one and so on. It was a laborious way to break trail, but it worked – Dan finally followed through. The logs were deposited around the clearing and by spring Abe had his first cabin completed.

In the same fall as we came, only much later, four more families left Saskatchewan with hopes of reaching Carcajou for winter. They hired a man at Peace River to pilot their scow down river. They even had a few head of livestock with them. It was too late, and ice in the river put an end to their journey.

At one of the Battle Rivers near Notikewin, they were able to make a landing and here they spent the winter. These were: Isaac Doerksens, David Peters, Abram and Isaac Fehrs (the latter two were brothers). My brother, who'd come to Peace River in a freight car taking care of livestock for these people, was also on the boat and as a result he spent part of the winter with them. In the middle of the winter he set off on foot intending to walk to Carcajou.

I do not recall whether he walked all the way from Notikewin to Keg River. Nevertheless he reached Keg River and spent a night with Harry Bowe. He had little more than the clothes on his back with him and being very inexperienced at travelling such distances in the bitterly cold weather, it was a wonder that he reached Bowe's safely.

From there it was only thirty miles to Carcajou, but Mr. Bowe thought it risky for someone so unfamiliar to the country to walk it. He knew it could be disastrous so he warned my brother not to stop in case he became tired, cold and sleepy but to keep moving. At one point he made a little fire to warm up and to keep from falling asleep, he kept walking around the fire. By the light of the morning he walked the rest of the way to

Carcajou. We were more than a little surprised to see him suddenly walking in. Mother worried about him a great deal but of this we'd had no inkling and we were overjoyed at this sudden homecoming.

Concern was expressed by the non-Mennonite people that the late fall break up could result in spring flooding. To the Mennonites who were unfamiliar in the ways of the country, this did not pose any real problems, but they were soon to learn the hard way.

While the ice-choked river finally came to a breakup in the last part of April, it was closely watched by the natives who were well acquainted with the Old Peace. Our parents were all warned of the flooding possibility. An ice jam soon took place, causing the water to rise rapidly. They were advised to move to higher ground. So when Mr. Unruh came along asking Father if we'd like to go along, he jokingly referred to it as going for a picnic. They did not want to believe what they were told. It seemed our parents were willing, so we got on the wagon with the Unruh family taking only the bare essentials with us, as they naturally expected to be back by nightfall.

With me it was less of a joke and I could not understand their uncaring attitude. We now also owned a pig which was left in its pen; the sheep and its lamb were likewise shut up in their little pen in the barn, given feed till we returned. The hens were also left behind and to me this caused concern. We drove through Carcajou, a little village of about half a dozen native families and the storekeeper, following the wagon trail along the river bank perhaps a mile or so uphill, where we had a high clear view of the tumultuous ice-choked river. The water was very high and fast-moving.

We stopped, unhitched the horses, tied them to the wagon, then we sat on the edge of the hill watching as huge slabs of ice were forced upwards and then crashed down into pieces. It was an awful turmoil, the likes of which we did not see in later years, but of course fall breakups seldom occur. Before nightfall we returned to our homes.

As we drove back, Xavier Sowan, an elderly Indian who with his wife lived near the boat landing, was carefully watching the rising water. When he saw us going back into the flat he tried hard to make Father and Mr. Unruh understand the danger of flooding. He had markers to show the rapid rate the water was rising and just how little more was needed before it would run over the banks at the lower end of the flat. Talking in Cree and motioning with his hands he tried to explain the matter to them, but they couldn't understand a word of it and merely said "yes" to everything and went their way. He must have been frustrated at the ignorance of those strange Mennonites. Later we were told just what the old man had said to them.

We were soon to learn what we'd been warned of! Later the same evening Father and Mr. Unruh were driving along the wagon trail past Dycks when they heard someone nearby. It was Mr. Dyck sitting on his sod roof keeping watch on the rising water. He told the men he'd soon get down and go inside. This he did, closing the door and going to bed.

In the meantime we'd all gone to rest too. At midnight a horse and rider pulled up at our door calling out, "The water is coming!" What a rude awakening! We were all on our feet, rushing about wildly, for we knew not what.

The lone pig was set free to go its way while two of my sisters had the sheep on a leash with the lamb following, running for the low hills rimming the flat on one side. Here it was tied to a tree. The hens were left behind, as was most everything we owned. We were now in a hurry!

Soon the Unruhs drove up and we were off once more – all kidding aside this time. Now we were in great earnest. Again we drove up the high river bank to where we'd been earlier in the same day. Here we camped in the open and tried to get some rest but this was not easy as we were somewhat shaken up. We lay on the ground listening to the rumbling of the ice below.

At the Wielers' and Hieberts', excitement ran as high as elsewhere but they had taken cattle and feed up during the day and were more ready to go when they saw the water rolling toward them. When the last trip was made, the wheels were half under water.

Mr. Dyck had shut himself in and gone to sleep but his wife and son had left with the others earlier. They now banged on the door from the outside. He finally woke up and they all got onto the hills in time. Had the old Indian's warning been heeded we could have spent the whole day getting everything to safety.

The following morning the men went back into the flat using a row boat. At our place, which was at the upper end from where the river burst its banks, they found the lone rooster standing on a floating log crowing to his three drowned hens floating nearby. One hen was sitting in the nest and was saved. Our pig, as well as the neighbour's, had swam to safety. As far as I remember, all the cattle were driven to the hills.

When the men rowed their boat to Unruh's, they went right into the house. A pan of milk had been placed on a cupboard for thickening and this was still afloat so the men took it down and enjoyed a lunch of 'thick milk'.

Potatoes stored in the bunkhouse cellar were all in the water. The Unruhs had stored salt blocks for the cattle in the bunkhouse as well, and these had dissolved in the water, making the potatoes worthless. Our own potatoes were stored in the same cellar.

Charlie Rankin, our neighbour, remained at home as his buildings were all on higher ground with a ravine running along either side of the yard. Their flock of about a hundred sheep stayed right in the corral, where over the years a heavy build up of manure left them high and dry.

In our house the water was about 2 1/2 feet deep. Though the water receded fast, the low lying places provided us with lots of rafting and boating for a good part of the summer. A large slough in the lower end of the flat became a deep lake and as the level of the water fell, fish about four inches long were found in the pools of water. They had washed over the river bank with the flood water. The Hiebert girls gathered pails of little fish in these pools and carried them to the lake but for some reason they could not survive in the lake water. When the water fell farther, the shore at one end of the lake was strewn with dead fish.

The little lake was a real haven for cold water fowl. Rats were also plentiful and of course we tried our hand at rat-trapping. I'm sure the rat population did not decrease because of us, as our trapping efforts were usually in vain.

Across the river to the north side was another large flat. The Okerholms lived on that bank near the landing which had been known as Bottlers Landing years before. The Dick McGranes occupied the entire flat and they owned a number of cattle, horses, goats and a flock of sheep. This flat too was under water, forcing the McGranes to retreat to higher ground.

We remained on the hilltop a few days, then came down into the village where we lived in what they called the schoolhouse for a few weeks. This was the largest building at Carcajou, so we and the Unruhs stayed here until the water fell far enough for us to get to our places with the wagon. Meanwhile, one of our cows had a calf in the bush, so when she was found, she and her calf were brought to the barn at Stigsens.

We then had lots of milk, which helped a great deal as far as our diet was concerned. Mother sometimes took milk to the Indian couple since we now had more than we needed. Mrs. Sowan, like her husband, spoke only Cree. One day as Mother brought her milk, she eyed Mother's bare feet, chattered in Cree and shook her head. The next time Mother called on this kind hearted lady, she had a neat pair of moose hide slippers made so Mother need not go barefoot any more.

Our wooden shoes were soon discarded, once we discovered that in return for milk we could earn moccasins. I later carried many a pail of milk to different native families in trade for moccasins. My first pair was adorned with a bright red felt patch on top of the foot. I was ever so proud of them and wore them only on Sundays.

My brother and Abe Wieler had gone rat-trapping before breakup and on their return were quite surprised to find the watery conditions. I don't remember if they had any pelts with them.

Following close behind the ice were the four families who had wintered at Battle River. We were still in the schoolhouse as it was much too soft in the flat. To improve this and give us some solid footing, we carried in lots of straw and trampled it in with the mud.

We also were to discover some other discomforts. It seems that when the water came in at the down stream end, an awful lot of waste, whatever could float, and bugs of every description were washed along with the rushing water to the upper end of the flat where our house was located. The place was crawling with insects and we moved right in with them.

Every night before retiring, the beds and walls had to be carefully inspected for bugs, which were destroyed. It made one shudder to think of the possibility of bugs getting into our ears, nose or mouth while we were sleeping. Eventually they became less but the mosquitoes were another first for us! The others had found this out the summer before and we'd heard lots about the 'skeeters'. The stories were not overdone. It seemed we were always in a cloud of smoke, trying to ward off the little pests.

Three of the families who came that spring were not long in deciding that this was not the right place for them. The two Fehr families soon made haste to depart. Selling what they had, they returned to Saskatchewan, where the raging dust storms of the 30's were in full swing. The letters received from our relatives there always spoke of the drought and how some people had gone on relief.

The land Mr. McLean owned was rented to the Hieberts, Wielers and Unruhs. The part the Unruhs rented was then rented to us by Mr. Unruh on a fifth crop share – he supplied the machinery such as he had and four horses. Father, with the help of our brother, had built a bigger barn and now we had room for the four-horse team. Once the higher-lying land was dry enough, it was plowed and seeded, but the wheat froze before it matured, thus there was no flour in the kernel. Flour we had to have and it could not be bought, so we had no choice – the frozen wheat had to be used for bread making.

The Rankins across the river owned a small-hand operated grinder which they loaned to us. It was hard work but faster than the coffee grinder we had used last winter. The immature wheat kernels produced a soggy dough that would not rise even with yeast and it soured quickly, forcing us to bake every day. It had no nourishment whatever, though it was heavy.

This summer we, too, planted a large garden and the vegetables were good. Once we were able to use potatoes again, we relied on them more than the bread. This was a great improvement in our diet as we had milk products to go with it.

The summer brought other changes. The Isbrandt Friesens were moving to Carcajou and with them came several other families. Their own family of six sons and one married daughter – Mrs Frank Martens, her husband and two children; and David Fehrs with a family of ten including three married ones: Isaac Fehrs and two children, Abram Bergens with four children and John Martens with two children.

Mr. and Mrs. D. Fehr with their youngest son Peter came ahead of the others on one of the river boats as Mr. Fehr was anxious to find a place in preparation for his families. He rented the farm from Wilfred Rankin on the Rankin Flat across from Carcajou. The rest of the families were waiting in Peace River while I. Friesen with the help of others, built two large scows to carry the passengers, a lot of freight and some livestock down river. A threshing machine, tractor and some horses were transported by other boats as they could not load all on their own scows.

These people had misfortune on the river. When they undertook to pilot their own scows downstream, they ran on to a rock, knocking a hole in the bottom of the front scow. They had no choice but to cut it loose to save the rear scow

on which the passengers were carried. The scow sank taking with it the freight and some livestock. Some animals drowned while others escaped swimming to shore. A lot of these goods were retrieved by people who kept a lookout for them downstream. The first notice of this to reach Carcajou was a desk belonging to one of the families, floating in the river. It was now obvious that something had gone wrong up river. Eventually all of them reached Carcajou, though much the worse and poorer for the experience.

The Dick McGranes were planning to leave Carcajou to make their home in B.C. Mrs. McGrane left on the boat in the summer while her husband stayed for another season of trapping. He sold all their belongings, cattle, horses, sheep and goats to the Unruhs and Friesens.

The same summer these two families and the Frank Martens moved across the river. Martens remained only one winter before returning to Saskatchewan. With foresight, these families built their log structures on the low hills to avoid getting flooded out as we had. When the Unruhs went across we moved into the place they vacated and this was to be our home for the next six and one half years.

The Wielers then moved into the place we left. The Stigsens and Okerholms were also leaving to make their future homes in southern B.C. Abe Wieler bought the cabin along with some home made furniture, traps, snowshoes, toboggan, motorboat and trap line from Okerholms. This was the life for Abe – he now had his own place – a 'home' he called his own. In December of 1937 he and my sister Susie were married. This was the only wedding to take place among the Mennonites and I'm sure the smallest in Carcajou.

When the Stigsens left on the same boat with the Okerholms, son Ted Stigsen stayed on to take over the store.

The summer of '34 the David Peters returned to Saskatchewan and the Isaac Doerksens alone remained of the last four families to come. They built a house not far from ours. Here they stayed one winter before renting the farm in the Rankin Flat from Jack O'Sullivan, who was now operating a boating business between Peace River and Fort Vermilion.

No more Mennonites came to Carcajou after that because of the lack of land. At the outset they had hoped to settle on land east of Carcajou and west of Buffalo Head Hills.

It was here that a delegation of men from Manitoba and Saskatchewan came to look at land for Mennonite settlement. Carcajou was to be the stopping place only but there was no access to this land other than on horseback, and further more it was unsurveyed. As a matter of fact, some 40 years later it still remained unsurveyed. No one ever settled on it, so it is not quite clear to us now what far flung plans were in the minds of those first settlers.

The Isaac Wielers were not long in following the Friesens and Unruhs to the McGrane Flat, where for a few years, they made their home. Times were very difficult; food and clothing were scarce and often because of our ragged appearance, we were embarrassed to meet strangers. Of our small group the Wielers, Hieberts, Dycks, and ourselves were the hardest pressed but none yielded to the temptation of asking for government relief.

Another stumbling block was transportation. If a church gathering was to take place or visiting outside of our own flat, the river had to be crossed. This wasn't so bad in the winter but river crossings in the summer were a different story. In time we became accustomed to canoeing over the river.

Because of the lack of farming land the Mennonite families soon became restless and began searching farther afield, moving to La Crete and Buffalo Prairie area. Mr.Friesen's health was failing and he was not to live through another move.

The winter of '37 was difficult for the Friesens. Mr. Friesen became seriously ill and was bedridden for the last few weeks of his life. As it became too hard for Mrs. Friesen and the boys to carry on alone, my Father and Mr. Wieler took turns staying with him during the night.

Dr. Jackson was sent for once but his condition was not to improve and at the beginning of February he passed on. The funeral was held in the Friesen home with burial in the native cemetery on the river bank at Carcajou. Father, with the help of Mr. Doerksen, made the coffin from rough boards planed by hand and Mother, with the help of the Friesen boys and Mr. Wieler, prepared the deceased for burial.

As the other Mennonites left one by one, we remained a few years longer renting land from Mr. McLean. He now allowed us a third share – this included butter and eggs from the livestock. We now milked several cows and had a fair number of hens. The butter and eggs were all sent by boat to McLean's store at the Fort, where we also got our groceries. Our living conditions improved a bit with the years but our workload did not become lighter.

I remember one year when we had no seed drill and the seeding was done by hand. Sacks of grain were loaded on the wagon or stone boat and with Father facing the rear, he grasped hands full of grain and scattered it over the field as we drove along. It was then harrowed. Oddly enough, we had a good crop that year.

Our flails had also been replaced. Mr. McLean sent us an old threshing machine and grinder. Both of these were powered by a car engine. The thresher had no feeder or straw blower, so the sheaves were tossed onto a small platform, Father cut the twine and pushed them into the teeth of the separator. The straw dropped out at the rear, where two or three of us were armed with pitch forks, pitching it and trampling it into a large stack to be used by the cattle during winter.

One fall we even shipped a little wheat on the boat to Peace River. It had to be sacked for shipping. The soil was very rich and the flood water had made it even more fertile. Grain, especially oats, grew to such heights that it bedded down very easily when sudden rainstorms came. One year we had to leave large patches of oats in the field because it was bedded down so badly it could not be cut with either binder or mower.

The years became drier and our little lake again became a slough. Forest fires, which were new to us, gave us many a scare. Our neighbours and the natives had been here many years before us and were not as easily given to fright as we – they knew the country's ways, whether wet or dry.

We stayed here until the spring of 1941, when we made our home at the Fort (Fort Vermilion).

The seven and a half years beginning in the fall of 1933 represent a brief summary in the lives of the Jacob Braun Family. It is written as simply as we lived it. Should someone read this, I ask the reader to please excuse the spelling errors made throughout this writing.

Fort du Tremble
by Margaret Befus

Fort du Tremble was the original trading post on the Peace River between Fort Vermilion and Peace River. Why it was abandoned and Carcajou became the place of trade no one really knows. Alexander MacKenzie mentions Carcajou Point and the natives there, yet it is probable that his men built Fort du Tremble.

Fort du Tremble was on the Hudson's Bay portion of the east bank of the Peace River, 60 miles above Fort Vermilion, near the mouth of the Keg River. It is shown on the Hudson's Bay map of 1857 and map of the North West Territories of 1877. This fort was originally built by the North West Company about 1800 or earlier, and is called "old Fort du Tremble" by David Thompson in 1804.

Muriel Stigsen remembers stopping there on a return trip from Fort Vermilion and finding a rock chimney and part of a fence. Trees were beginning to grow up in the chimney. She remembers it being on the west side of the Peace.

Ted Stigsen says he never saw the fort but recalls hearing that Fort du Tremble was not far from the old Tompkins Landing, which was south of the Tompkins Landing we know today. Whether the chimney is still standing today is unknown. It is possible that the ice jams and floods have removed all traces of this fort.

Firsts at Carcajou
by Margaret Befus
First white man:
> Alexander MacKenzie on his trip upriver from Ft. Chip in 1792

First trading post:
> Fort du Tremble, built by North West Company about 1800

First privately owned trading post:
> Charlie Grams – before 1920

First Post Office:
> 1927, Postmistress – Mrs. Martha Rankin

First automobile:
> Model T Ford owned by Charlie McLean. Sold to the Rankin family when he left for Fort Vermilion in 1933. The Rankins made a stationary engine of it. Are parts of it still around?

First sawmill:
> Rankin's. The saw was run by a White engine. The governor did not work. Ted Stigsen had to act as governor. This engine was also used for threshing.

First grain separator:
> Bought by Charlie McLean after he went farming. Brought to Carcajou on a boat. It was wooden and had to be hand-fed only half a bundle at a time. No blower was attached, so the straw had to be forked away.

First radio:
> Owned by John Okerholm, about 1928. It was a crystal set with earphones.

First snowmobile:
> Owned by John Okerholm in the early 1950's.

Ted Stigsen store and warehouse, 1990.

Back, L-R: Abe Wieler, Dave Fehr, Ollie Olson, Bob Hardy, Muriel Stigsen, John Okerholm, Dorothy Rankin. Middle L-R: JoHanna Stigsen, Louis Bourassa, Lillian Green. Front, L-R: Olive Okerholm, Isobel Rankin, Mary Ware.

Hans Leu in the foreground, at the Carcajou settlement, 1953.

First combine:
> A Massey Harris, pull-type, owned by Elmer Dovey.

First power saw:
> A McCullough, owned by Edna Kiselczuk.

First grain auger:
> Owned by Ted Stigsen. It was a 4-inch auger that was not very reliable!

First outboard motor:
> Owned by Hudson "Bay" Bruce, 1948, a Johnson 4-H.P. motor.

Carcajou ladies. Back, L-R: Laura Christian, Sandra Sivertson, Muriel Stigson, Aurora Tupper, Margaret Befus. 3rd Row, L-R: Eugenie, Merry, Janette Tupper. 2nd Row, L-R: Sharon Tupper, Harriet Befus, Doris Christian. Front, L-R: Beth, Jan Befus, Barbara Christian, 1971.

THE PEACE
by Margaret Befus

Wide and smooth between its banks
The river flowed with peaceful thanks,
That we treated it as a true friend.
No garbage dumped at every bend,
But now to some a refuse dump;
Tailings, tin cans, juice from the sump.
Worst of all, effluent from the mill
With brownish bubbles makes its spill.
Now when I go down for a swim
I look for foam along the rim,
Man's trademark on this stream
That once was sparkling clear and clean.

O Come To Keg River
(This was written as a tribute to Frank Jackson and sung to the melody of "This Land Is Your Land, This Land Is My Land" by the students from the school. The actual author or authors have not been identified.)

O come to Keg River –
We will tell you a tale

Of Mr. Frank Jackson
And the Carcajou trail.

How our forefathers came
To this land of peace
With its beautiful hills
And its wild grey geese.

Jackson was a trader
In the days of old
For that's the story
That we were told.

He loved this land
Where the Keg meets the Peace
With its misty hills
And its wild grey geese.

When our forefathers came
In 1910
They settled this land
From glen to glen.

They built this town
In the valley of the Peace
With its beautiful hills
And its wild grey geese.

They were hardy folks,
These ladies and men,
That came to Keg
In 1910.

They had plenty of guts
And a worn-out plow,
A vision of the future,
Two horses and a cow.

The cabin was built
And the land was broke
And in no time at all
The mighty Keg awoke.

They built this town
In the valley of the Peace
With its beautiful hills
And its wild grey geese.

We'll make you welcome
With our big centennial smile
And northern hospitality
That's never out of style.

When you come to Keg River,
When you come, 'when you come,
When you come,
When you come.

CHAPTER II
THE WORLD AROUND US

Moose
By John M. Okerholm

I sat one day on the bank of the Peace,
Though this was done quite often before;
But this time I watched a moose through the
    trees
That were shading the little island shore.

She swam to the island 'fore break of day,
To give birth to her two little calves;
And now she prepared to be on her way,
For she never done her things by halves.

She stepped in the water and swam away,
And left the island and calves behind;
She did not return till the very next day,
As if her calves were not on her mind.

She swam to the island only once a day,
To bring food to her fast-growing young,
An hour each day was all she could stay,
But they did fine on the milk she had brung.

I'd visit them there in their island ground,
Whenever I was out in my little canoe;
In two weeks time they were playing around,
The way little calves will usually do.

Moose calves when born have no animal scent,
The wolves cannot smell them if left alone;
That was the reason she came and went,
She protected her calves by her being gone

These calves were happy at their island home.
They'd run and play on the island shore;
They were never afraid whenever I'd come,
But each time more curious than before.

But then one day on her usual round,
She thought that they were now plenty smart;
They were now a good size and how they
    could run,
They were a real joy to their Mother's heart.

She now decided to bring them along,
To her feeding ground which was her home;
She stepped in the water and coaxed them
    along,
They waded right in and so left their home.

She started to swim with her two little sons,
It was a beautiful sight that I could see;
She never stopped to hesitate, not once,
I am sure her heart was plumb-full of glee.

She took to the bush which was her home,
Where she could raise her darling little sons;
She went just as quietly as she had come,
And I applauded her good luck, there at once.

For me the show was over for one more year,
The moose-crop had once more come and gone;
But I remember them little darlings there,
On their Peace River birch island home.

Animals and Birds

by Frank Jackson

(These stories were written by F. Jackson, but were not used in his books.)

OWLS

There was a great horned owl making a good living taking our little pigs. We did not suspect this until our young son, John Robert, saw the carcass of one of the little pigs about 15 feet up in a tree.

Clemence Sinclair had a very frightening experience with a great horned owl out at the Chinchaga. She had been visiting Mrs. Chalifoux, and was walking the half-mile home, carrying her baby, wrapped in a white shawl. The owl flew down and tried to pull the baby out of her arms. She said it was an enormous bird, and she couldn't fight it off. Luckily the owl finally flew away without the baby after she yelled at it.

Owl.

SWANS

I met old Joe Lizotte of Fort Vermilion once, when he first went to Great Slave Lake. On the north side of the lake, he said, there were swans nesting so close together you could hardly walk between them. Now there are none, but I remember the first spring after Mary and I were married, calling her outside one night to see a great flock of swans flying north by the light of the full moon.

COUGARS

There was great excitement in the village in 1940, when cougars were heard. They have a cat's yowl, magnified 100 times! We owned the tanned skin of a cougar that had been killed about 10 years before. It was regarded by everyone as a great curiosity. I bought the skin from Larone Ferguson, who'd shot it and brought it to me, saying he thought he'd killed a tiger! Mountain lions are common in the Rockies, but they were unheard of here.

We heard the strange howling across the river, and I fetched Mary out to listen. All the Indians heard it and they were so scared that they all crowded into one little house for the night.

The next night we heard two of them howling just across the river. They were making a noise like courting cats, but much louder. Then all the sleigh dogs in the village started to howl as if they'd heard wolves. I hoped the natives would go out and hunt the cougars.

ANTS

When I dug the dirt for my garden on the north side of that bluff, I opened up an anthill. It went five feet down, and you could see where they had their passageways. It was wonderful, just like streets with cross sections. I got a matchstick and put it into one of these runways and watched a dozen of them trying to haul it out. I caught a grasshopper and put it in there, and they killed it.

There was an ant's nest out here by that big tree I planted. They would dig holes right up into the tree and the sap would run out and they would feed on it. They were killing the tree, so I cut it down. I can't see the use of ants, but they are industrious little creatures.

WOODBORERS

There was a farmer in North Star who built a house of green lumber. It was full of woodboring beetles. The noise the beetles made got so bad that the people could not sleep at night. Ted Whitney, the sanitary inspector, was up here and he asked me if I knew of anything that would kill these beetles.

In the old house, I had them in the windowsill. You could hear them in there, grinding away. Finally they came through a little hole, so I poured coal oil down it. They just thrived on it! You cannot fumigate them, because they just back up into their burrows. I filled that hole up a half-dozen times with coal oil and they just kept boring! Then I blocked the hole with glue and they didn't come back!

SLEIGH DOGS

Sleigh dogs are not to be trifled with. I have never heard of a wolf attacking a person, but sleigh dogs have. They did not kill any children at Keg River, but in the 30's at Fort Vermilion they killed two children who were crossing the river on the ice. Sleigh dogs also killed a mounted policeman's wife at Lower Hay. They were loose in a pen, and I guess she did not feed them quickly enough, and one of them pulled her down.

Harry Bowe was bitten on the cheek by a dog in Keg River. While my wife Mary was walking to see one of her patients, a sleigh dog broke the chain with which he was tethered and lunged at her. He was up to her in one bound, with his mouth wide open. She was wearing gauntlet fur mitts and as the dog grabbed for her, she withdrew her hand from the mitt and left it in his mouth. This gave her just enough time to get inside the house.

Dog teams waited in front of my store while their owners were inside. One day as Mary was passing Trosky's sleigh, one of the dogs jumped up and bit her arm. She was wearing a very heavy coat, so his teeth did not break the skin. Her yell brought men out of the store to help. She learned to never walk too close to a dog team.

MOOSE

One time I was coming from Carcajou to Keg River Crossing. I was going up the hill at Steep Creek just where all the little spruce were, when

Moose.

I saw a great big bull moose standing right on the brow of the hill. He was buckskin-colored, the only moose of that color that I had ever seen. He must have heard me, and was watching to see what was coming. As I came over the brow of the hill and he saw me on horseback he headed for the spruce. He went through there just like a bullet. How in the world he got through there I don't know, the spruce were so close.

FISHERS

The fisher is another animal that is scarce now. A few were seen here in the early 70's but there used to be hundreds of them. They lived on squirrels.

The man who opened the first Hudson's Bay Company Post at Upper Hay River (now known as Meander River) had just a little shack there. He told me that he used to have an awful time with fishers that used to try to get down his chimney. If he was not there to stop them, their weight would bring down the stovepipes, and everything in the shack would be ruined by the fishers. He said they were worse than squirrels.

A Martin wondering what kind of tree he's in.

WOLVERINE

Out west where Dick Hutchings lived, at Chinchaga, there used to be lots of wolverines. You cannot fool wolverines; they were the devil on the trapline. If you had a wolverine on your line, half your fur would get torn, or they would rob the traps. If they did not eat the animal they would pack it off and bury it somewhere.

Trappers used to clean a limb off a tree, and hang their cache from the limb on a wire. The wolverines got wise. They could not pull the cache on account of it being on wire, but they would get far enough out of the limb to weigh it down, and another wolverine at the bottom would catch it.

I was in Edmonton one time and bought a bunch of great big fishhooks, as thick as a pencil. I told Frank Smith to put his cache on top of a tree stump, six to eight feet high, and put these fishhooks pointing upwards and spike them to the post. He caught two or three that way, caught up on the hooks, but they got wise to that, too.

The skins used to be worth $20 or $30 even in the early days. They made good parka hoods because they don't frost up. They also make a good robe to throw over your knees when you are travelling by sleigh.

WOLVES

I haven't the least sympathy for wolves. In my opinion they are the most cunning and determined predators in the bush. Some people say they kill off the sick and old game animals, but this isn't true in my experience. They size up an animal before they attempt to kill it and they look for ones that will make a good meal. Ask any trapper.

One time I was riding out to Battle River over the telegraph line, on my way to Edmonton. I had no bed or anything, because I figured on riding right through. It started to rain heavily, and was dark, so I decided to quit. I picketed my horse Dan on a rope to a big bunch of willows. I took the little piece of tarp that was over my saddle blanket and put it over my shoulders to keep dry, then I got in under the willows. It wasn't too bad.

It was just getting daylight, and Dan must have been humped up fast asleep when all of a sudden he gave a snort and took off down the trail. Right behind him there was a moose and right behind the moose were four wolves. They were all going hell bent for leather back the way I had come.

It was no use going after Dan. We were 40 miles from home, so I left my saddle and blankets and walked to Bill Reed's at Notikewin. (My horse reached home safely at noon, but I don't think the moose had much hope against four wolves.)

Wolves were very much in our conversation when the Hague children arrived in 1940. There were lots of wolves around, close to the edge of the settlement. They had recently killed a calf. One night I had to get out of the car and chase a big old wolf off the trail. He just sat there and looked at me.

We used to hear wolves howling away across the Keg in the hills at night, but then they started to come around the settlement and killed pigs and calves. One winter they packed the snow down, making a trail hard enough to walk on. We knew the packs of them must be killing a lot of moose and deer, but when the Doveys moved in with sheep, the wolves really were doing great damage. The winter that Frank Lafoy was the game guardian he shot 13 of them, but there still seemed to be lots more.

Eldon Tupper at Harrington Farm with wolf pelts.

One morning just as we were getting up, Milton Rudy came in and said, "I went out of my house and heard pigs squealing. I ran back to get my rifle and I was just up to the pen when a wolf jumped out over the fence with a pig in its mouth. I shot at it and missed. It dropped the pig and beat it across the river."

I went with him to see the pig. It weighed about 80 pounds, and had big holes in its back where the teeth went in. The backbone had been crushed. Milton was still carrying his rifle, so I asked him to shoot it. It was of no use to anyone after a wolf had bitten it.

We had been losing pigs, too, so Milton's discovery solved our mystery as well. Shutting them into their pen was no good when a wolf could jump over the fence. It was a slab fence, the slabs standing on end, about five feet high. Wolves destroyed over 50 head of livestock about that time also, as is confirmed by this *Peace River Record Gazette* report from October 8, 1941.

KEG RIVER AREA SETTLERS PAY BOUNTY FROM OWN POOL

"Over 50 head of livestock were killed in a six-week period by timber wolves, according to information brought in from the area by settlers. Animals destroyed included cattle, hogs and sheep. In addition, settlers claim a considerable quantity of wild game is being destroyed.

"The provincial department responsible for game regulations does not pay bounty on wolves in the Keg River area, the boundary line for the bounty-paying area being about halfway between Hotchkiss and Keg River. Despite this, the settlers of the area are paying bounty for wolves. A pool having been formed by the settlers themselves under the plan the bounty for females is $25, $10 for males and pups."

GRIZZLY BEARS

Grizzly bears were not common around here, but occasionally one has been seen. They are always dangerous. There was one killed near here by a man who had only a .22 and two shells with him. Suddenly the grizzly charged him. Luckily he shot right into her open mouth and killed her instantly. He didn't wait to see if he had killed her. He made for the nearest tree and sat up there for an hour or so in case she came to.

The *Manning Banner Post* of October 11, 1981 ran the following story:

GRIZZLY BEAR ATTACK

"The Petro Canada gas compressor station 20 miles west of Keg River was the location of a grizzly bear attack. Employees Allen Maloney of Fort St. John and Louis Pawlowich of Keg River were in the residence on site at 11 P.M. when a grizzly bear was sighted in the yard. Louis Pawlowich used the 303 British rifle and wounded the bear, which immediately ran away and was lost in the dark.

"The next morning Robert McBain, another employee, arrived from Keg River with a dog. The three men with two rifles and the dog went looking for the bear they believed to be dead.

"The dog ran up to it barking, the bear jumped up and charged immediately. Louis dropped his gun and began climbing a tree. The bear started mauling him and pulling him back down. The other men were afraid to shoot but finally got a chance and shot the bear in the neck. The bear dropped away. Robert got Louis into a vehicle and departed. They phoned for a helicopter to meet them on the MacKenzie highway. Louis was taken to High Level hospital where 56 stitches were required in his face, shoulders, arms, and legs."

SKUNKS

One year in the 30's, when I hayed on the Paddle, I remember seeing hundreds of skunks. It was always dark when I left on my saddle horse to come home. The road was always full of skunks; there were hundreds of them that year going up and down the road eating grasshoppers. There were a lot of grasshoppers that year, too.

Charlie Ireland, who was there that year, used to round up skunks with a saddle horse. He had a whole barn full of them. He was going to kill them in the winter when the fur was prime.

We were getting about two dollars apiece for them, but then they dropped to fifty cents. When I was in the Edmonton Fur Auctions there was a whole stack of them in the corner where they'd thrown them because they were worth nothing.

Years afterwards they started bleaching them and dyeing them. They made a marvellous job of it. One day I was sitting talking to a man who was running the Edmonton Furriers on Jasper Avenue and he showed me a fur cloak. He had half a dozen of these cloaks made of skunk pelts selling for $500 each. They were beautiful things, a kind of roseate pink in the centre that went out to a yellow. They had been dyed in Montreal.

GRASSHOPPERS

In 1932 and 1934 we were plagued with grasshoppers. They were so abundant that a person could not walk without stepping on them. The July 27, 1934 *Peace River Record Gazette* told of our plight.

GRASSHOPPERS ARE DESTRUCTIVE IN KEG RIVER COUNTRY

"A repetition of the grasshopper plague of two years ago in the Keg River district is reported by R. Hutchings, prominent farmer of that district, who was a business visitor in town this week. Mr. Hutchings states that the weather has been entirely favorable to the hoppers, with a brief shower each day washing away the poison bait that has been set out, a mixture of bran, molasses, and strychnine.

"Mr. Hutchings declares that grasshopper eggs remain in the soil four to five years, only hatching when conditions are favorable. He believes breaking up the prairie and planting brome grass would eliminate the problem.

"This season the Keg River district suffered rather heavily from summer frosts in June and the first week of July, and what was not destroyed by the frost is fast disappearing before the onslaught of hoppers."

The Beavers
by Joseph A. Denman (1946)
Amphibious, industrious,
Shy furry pioneers:
Our Canada's proud emblem they
Efficient engineers.
Intrepid architects of dam,
Of reservoir and mirror;
Our pride is somewhat shaken as
We watch them persevere.
Blithe, busy beaver tribes, along
Meandering creek and stream,
Exemplify the Utopian State,
Of which men only dream.
Expert they toil with humble tools,
With stone, and mud, and wood;
With all for each and each for all,
They practice brotherhood.
No clamour theirs, no wage dispute,
No wealth, no poverty,
But each one works and shares alike,
In his community.
With neither axe nor adze, they hew
The trees, and peel the bark,
With equal zest they frolic forth,
These folk of Lilliput,
To dam a dancing mountain stream
Or build a winter hut
Unlike the more ambitious ants
Who grudge the time for fun;
Our beavers gambol in the pond,
When all their tasks are done.
The lucky stars observe, just when
The revelry begins;
As the beavers splash, and frisk about
In bright brown glossy skins.
A splash! A dive! Then plop, plop, plop!
"You can't catch me," they brag,
As from the bank, they dive into
A glorious game of tag.

Beaver.

When winter roofs their toy lagoon,
They sleep together curled;
A frugal eat, in sweet content,
At peace with all the world.
Such is the beavers' moral code,
So simple, yet so grand;
Which men might copy, were they not
TOO DUMB TO UNDERSTAND.

Woodpeckers and Squirrels
by Anne Vos

Woodpeckers are noisy little fellows who like to bang their heads on trees, either looking for food, sending out Morse Code messages to prospective mates or possibly making a hole for a nest.

The power companies who bring in the towering cedar poles to build power lines have found out how destructive the woodpecker can be. Whether the pole makes a nice echo or if there is a tasty type of beetle living in the wood, we don't know. The pesky birds drill so many holes the poles are weakened. The power company has had to install wire to cover many of the poles.

Another woodpecker story involves 400 hives of honeybees. The colony was all packed up for the winter in groups of four and wrapped with insulation and plastic. Some smart woodpecker with a love for fresh bees and larvae drilled a hole through all the wrapping into the hive. He then told the rest of the birds about this convenient winter food supply.

The squirrels also found this mecca (the beehives) and they loved the honeycomb. Together they destroyed 200 hives before they were discovered! Fish and Wildlife was called but they would not accept responsibility for these feathered and furry creatures.

A squirrel certainly has a mind of its own. One time a mother squirrel had her family of five babies in a combine. It was a safe, dry place until the farmer started up the combine and moved it a short distance.

There was only one thing for the mother to do. She moved her babies to the bush. A human would probably take the most direct route, but not this squirrel. She carried each baby up to the top of a granary and down the other side, repeating the process with each baby.

Cheaky

by James Tupper, 1969

Cheaky was a coyote,
He was long and lean,
People often tell me;
He was seldom seen.

He liked to visit all the farms
On his nightly round.
The farmers never heard him
For he never made a sound.

They say all good things must end
And likewise do the bad.
So it was with Cheaky
When he met with Tommy's dad.

Now Dave was out a-milkin'.
When Cheaky came along,
And Cheaky went into the barn,
From whence there came a song.

Now Cheaky got suspicious
And turned about to run;
He should have started sooner
For Dave now had his gun.

The shot sped straight and true
And Cheaky dropped right there,
The chicken roost no more to rob
For he was dead
For he was dead beyond repair.

A Stuck Skunk

by Bertha Parenteau

A skunk was seen scavenging in the scrap pile. Shortly after, he was backing up wildly all over the yard with his head tightly stuck in a tin can! Now everybody knows about the wrong end of a skunk, so all we could do was watch, well out of his way. When he finally tired, someone bravely grabbed the can and pulled it off. The skunk left immediately!

Bears

by Charlie Christian as told to Doris Christian

I was one of eight children born to John and Marie Christian on their farm in Paddle Prairie. I was about 12 years old in 1934 when I used to go trapping with my Dad a lot of the time. We used to walk many miles on snowshoes to check our traps.

One day we stayed late and it was getting dark as we made our way home. Dad couldn't see at night so I had to help him. I used to either lead him on a short piece of rope or, if we forgot the rope, we used a short stick. When I saw a hole in the cutbank with a lot of dry grass sticking out, I asked Dad what it was. Dad said it was likely a bear den and we should kill the bear. We only had an axe and a knife.

Dad said he would stab the bear or hit it with the axe. He crawled a way into the den and stabbed the bear. We pulled the bear out and gutted it, but it was too dark to skin it. Dad said we better camp for the night. We decided to sleep inside the bear den because it was warm in there. The den was

Black Bear.

in a cutbank, so we had to climb up a way to get in. Dad told me to go up first, then he would give me a push to help me up into the den. When I crawled in I saw eyes staring at me. I tried to back out but Dad kept pushing me in. I was getting so scared I finally kicked Dad in the chest and he went rolling down the bank. He wanted to know why I had kicked him. I said there was another bear in there because I had seen his eyes. Dad asked, "Are you sure?" We decided to walk home.

The next morning Dad went back on horseback with a gun. He found TWO more bears in the den! Dad killed them and brought all three of them home.

Ethelyn Root with baby bear, April 24, 1933.

Our Encounter with Grizzly Bears
by Sherry Halabisky

Our whole family loves fishing, no matter what the weather. Once when we were camping with relatives near Moosehorn on the Chinchaga River, Dad asked my brother Shawn and me if we wanted to go fishing with him upstream. We went happily, taking only our fishing rods and of course Dad's cigarettes.

Along our trek we stopped several times to try our luck but to no avail. At one of these stops we found some tracks and some fish bones. I asked Dad if we could turn around, but he said the rapids were just a bit further and we could cross there and then go back towards camp on the other side of the river. We decided to do that because Dad "used" to be bigger than us and MOST of the time we did what he said!

Once we got to the rapids, Dad took my hand to help me across the river, Dad and I were looking down at the rocks because we didn't want to fall and do damage to our cute faces when Shawn called out, "Bears!". Dad and I both figured out he didn't mean specks in the distance. BUT neither of us figured he meant there were bears directly in front of us either – but when we looked up we saw them – pretty big specks! We stopped dead in our tracks, balancing on the rocks in the middle of the river. Ahead of us were three GRIZZLY BEARS – two young ones and MAMA!

Mama bear was at the edge of the trees and the two "little" ones kept charging at us as far as the edge of the water where they would turn around and run back to Mama bear. They repeated this "charging" a few more times, and every time they came Dad would yell "HEY" (which was the only word he could remember at the time)! The mother bear only growled or swatted them as if she were scolding them. I think in some way both the mother bear and Dad had some sort of respect for each other. They were both trying to protect their "young 'uns" and neither wanted any trouble.

Dad finally told Shawn and me to get back across the river, but Shawn wasn't going anywhere without me and Dad couldn't pry my fingers off his arm, so we all started to back up. It was about then that Shawn disappeared under the water. He emerged a few seconds later; he had fallen into a hole between the rocks. We finally got to shore and started up the big bank (at least it was big to a seven-year-old). Shawn and I were both worried about our fishing rods. Dad said, "Drop the damn things!"

We got on an animal path, Shawn and I ahead of Dad, when Dad saw a tree six to eight inches at the base and called to us to come back and get up the tree. Shawn was up like a squirrel and then there was ME! Dad kept trying to shove me up the tree and like a non-squirrel, I kept sliding back down! After a few tries, I finally grabbed a limb and got up under Shawn. (The tree was fairly wet and I'm not sure if it was water dripping off Shawn or "something else".

Dad was still on the ground when we heard the bears coming across the river. Shawn and I could see the water splashing everywhere. Dad finally started to climb up a small tree beside us. We could now hear the bears snorting and growling, then all of a sudden they went running by us on the animal path.

We were probably in the trees for a half hour.

Dad kept yelling during this time, hoping someone back at the campsite would hear him. All this time the bears were still wandering around in the bush. Shawn and I both wanted to take off for camp but Dad said we should wait for someone to come with guns, just in case the bears were circling around us. Finally a bunch of guys showed up, calling for us. When they got close we climbed down and were glad to see the guns!

Mom came running behind in rubber boots that were much too big for her and I remember thinking it was totally hilarious. She didn't even look at Dad, she just grabbed Shawn and me and took us back to camp.

The bears did some damage to our fishing rods but what made Dad really mad was the fact that they had broken some of his cigarettes! We still love fishing but I for one am always looking over my shoulder with my eyes and ears alert.

Treasures
by Helena Peters

Think of me when the sun turns snow into
    fields of diamonds,
When Northern Lights dance in the darkened
    sky,
When softly falling snow caresses your cheek
And all the world turns into a wonderland.
These are things I love,
And more:
The ever-new sunsets and sunrises,
The moon in all its stages shining through the
    night,
The stars with their mysteries
And all the hoary frost after a fog,
Dressing everything in sparkling white.
I love the trees in all their splendor
Before they lose their leaves;
The mountains, too, they beckon and call,
Saying, ''Come here, come up here.''
I love prisms and rainbows in their primal
    colors,
The clean air, fresh and crisp;
These are my riches, my wealth.

Thunder and Lightning Storms
by Mary Jackson

When a man came around selling lightning arresters, I had him install one on each corner of the roof. They were connected to heavy copper cables which were embedded in the ground. July had been a very bad month for thunderstorms.

There had been five lightning strikes within a mile, three of them within 24 hours.

In 1953 one of the strikes hit the Fergusons' house. This house had once been our home. The lightning ran in on the aerial wire and the electric light wire. It burnt the insulation off all the wires and filled the house with smoke. It smashed all the windows on the west side of the house and tore a hole in the pantry ceiling.

The girls had just prepared sandwiches and cakes for the dance that evening, and had stacked them on a shelf in the pantry. They were thrown all over the place. Ernie Ferguson was playing the guitar and it shattered into a thousand pieces. The little six-year-old girl was knocked out, but it did her no lasting harm. It was amazing that nobody was killed and that the house didn't catch fire. It might well have, if it had not been a log house.

Another time lightning struck the Rudys' home. It ran down the aerial wire, blew the radio into atoms, tore the curtains to shreds and blackened the wall, but didn't set the house on fire.

In 1965 or 1966 the Galandys' clothesline was struck. From the clothesline the lightning came into the house along the exhaust pipe of the washing machine. Their little dog, Bullet, slept by the machine and was electrocuted right there.

Allan and Eugene were playing with a mechano set in the bedroom which adjoined the room with the washing machine. There was so much electricity in the house that their hands tightened on the metal parts and later had to be pried open. Luckily no one was hurt.

The most amazing thing was that the clothesline had been full of washing and everything was burnt off and the remains were lying on the ground!

One time Dan Mudry was in the bush cutting firewood. He was sawing with a power saw when lightning hit the very tree that he was falling. The bolt knocked him flat on the ground, but miraculously he was not otherwise injured.

Lightning struck the Vos' home just as my daughter Anne was about to put wood in the cookstove. It must have come down the chimney through the stove as she lifted the lid with a metal lifter. She received a shock. Luckily she was wearing runners and she suffered only with a stiff thumb.

Archie Chalifoux rode to Chinchaga to check on his cows that were pasturing there. A storm approached quickly, so he checked the cows and ran for his teepee after tying up his saddle horse. Just then there was a huge flash of lightning and a crash of thunder together. The horse whinnied and reared up. Archie looked to where the cows were in the pasture, surrounded by a barbed wire fence, and two of them were lying dead by the fence. It happened just that quickly.

In 1987 my grandson's home was struck. Henry and Anne had a large mobile radio antenna that the lightning hit first, then travelled along. The radio was on the top of the refrigerator, as the radio melted, it burned a hole in the fridge!

The wiring in every electrical appliance in the house was "cooked" and thus the appliances were ruined. The radios, water pressure system, television and other appliances needed to be replaced, but again the house itself was not destroyed.

The Broadhead home was hit by lightning in 1990.

In 1993 the Bricks had a strike in their yard that broke the large windows of their home. This was another close call. For a small community we seem to have had our share of lightning strikes. It is too bad lottery winnings haven't occurred with the same frequency!

Northern Lights
by Anne Vos

Northern lights often light up our nighttime sky. They are a joy to watch as they change colors and move. They often appear to be dancing. They are particularly beautiful on very cold winter nights.

To the natives of the north the lights were considered to be a mystical gift provided to bring messages from the dead. They were also thought to foretell the future. The older natives were firm believers in nature.

The red northern lights were considered to bring a dire warning of a coming catastrophe. The atmospheric conditions which cause the red lights mustn't occur often because red northern lights are very rare. Local old-timers tell of brilliant red northern lights on the eve of the declaration of the First World War.

The only other time the red northern lights were known to have been seen locally was February 18, 1953. The natives believed the end of the world was imminent. There were gatherings of families and much distress. When nothing happened everyone went quietly back to a normal life.

It is a very eerie feeling when you look out your window in the middle of the night and there is a bright glow as if there were a fire close at hand.

When you go outside you are totally engulfed in a shimmering blanket of light.

The Lonesome Pine
by Ellen Bouma

I saw a tree so straight and tall;
Arms outstretched, it seemed to call
A passing bird to cradle in his arms.

But the bird flew on;
It had no time
To stop and chat
With the lonesome pine.

Squirrels, rabbits scurried by;
Robins, whisky-jacks soared on high
And even they had no time
To stop and chat with the lonesome pine.

Then winter came
And the winds grew chill;
The only sound that broke the still
Was a woodcutter's axe
On a faraway hill.

And the pine played tricks;
There was magic in the air
And he thought he heard singing
And children everywhere.

He woke with a start
For he could hear
The sound of laughter
And sleigh-bells near.

He shook his needles
And ruffled his cones,
Made all kinds of noises
To make himself known.

"Oh look at the pine!
What a beautiful tree!"
"Oh," thought the pine,
"Do they really mean me?"

The lonely pine felt sheer delight
When they took him home that very night
And when the children's prayers were said
They placed a star upon his head.

And Oh how he felt so very proud
And he stood himself extra tall
As everyone gathered around him
To sing Merry Christmas to all!

Floods

by Anne Vos

The area has had a number of floods through the years we remember.

The Keg River is usually a meandering, narrow, deep creek that begins west of the village and flows east into the Peace. A number of small creeks join in along the way. Some of the larger ones are Blackbirds Creek, Smeaton Creek and Kemp Creek.

In 1955 the Keg poured over its banks, filled up the sloughs and then followed the draws across farmer's fields towards the northeast, eventually joining the Boyer Creek.

June 30, 1962, was the first flood after Keg River Cabins was established. What a shock to find the river coming through the yard! The cause this time was the constant rain for most of June.

Keg River Cabins first flood, 1962. The Dupruis children playing in the water.

In 1972 the spring runoff out of the hills was very rapid due to warm weather. The river went over and with new roads the water followed road ditches in another direction, heading through the north fields and over to the Boyer, causing plenty of trouble along the Boyer at Paddle Prairie.

On April 27, 1974, the Carcajou flat on the east side of the river was not completely underwater – but almost! The flat on the west side was not so fortunate. There was an ice jam in the river and the river rose 30 feet in a few hours. The huge blocks of ice made a tremendous noise. As the ice pushed higher, it began shearing off trees along the banks while the water pressure built up.

The water poured into the flat from the lower end to a depth of at least 20 feet. Since the flat has the shape of a bowl, there was no way for the water to get out until a ditch was dug. To prevent back flow should the river be high again, a one-way valve was put in.

The Befus farm site was inundated, being situated at almost the lowest point in the flat. No cows or horses were lost but Dave Befus had a very scary experience. The mother cat, kittens and canary all drowned. The water was up in the second floor of the house and the family lost everything.

Dave Befus house after the water had receded some in the flood of 1974.

At the Wim Vos farm, one and a half miles from the river, the water came from the east first, then from the west. The trees along the bank held the big ice blocks close to the river. There wasn't much time to plan – within two hours of the first warning signs, there was water everywhere.

Wim decided to move his trailer home out first. He hooked it on to a winch-truck and dragged it to high ground. Then tires, propane bottles, even Befus's empty granary floated by. Tractors were driven up the hill, but no one could guess how high the water would come before the ice jam broke.

The water was up three feet on steel granaries full of grain when the bolts started popping or breaking as the grain expanded with the moisture. The whole side split out of one bin, spilling canola into the water. Darkness arrived, but there wasn't much rest and with all this water there was NONE to drink.

Aftermath of 1974 ice jam at Carcajou, Wim Vos' yard.

Morning light brought an unbelievable sight of water wherever you looked and plenty of sightseers. Then to add to the misery it turned cold and snowed and the Carcajou road was washed out!

Peace River in flood. Notice the line of driftwood, June 14th, 1990.

Not many acres of crop were planted that year because the flat was wet most of the summer. A ditch had to be dug to get the water back into the river. The ice blocks took nearly two months to melt where they lay along the bank with the smashed trees. Clearing the debris out of yards and fields took much longer. The Befus family home was damaged beyond repair. They rebuilt at the top of the hill overlooking the flat.

Once again in 1977 the Keg River Cabins were flooded. Bob Riczu was the owner and this time the Petersen place went under as well. They had a foot of water swirl through their front room and three to five feet through their farm yard.

Flood at Ted Peterson's place.

The first week of August 1987 brought the worst flooding we have ever seen. The entire length of the district was affected with the river overflowing its banks and covering hundreds of acres of farmland on either side of the river.

The cause was one of several storm cells.

Another from the same disturbance created a deadly tornado in the Edmonton area. One of these storm cells hit the Simonette area, dumping 11 inches of rain.

Nine inches were dumped on the Naylor Hills at the same time. In a few short hours this water made its way into the Smeaton Creek and Keg River.

At one o'clock in the morning the Smeaton turned into a raging torrent tearing down the stream bed like a freight train. The noise woke up the Batchelor family. They rushed down to their stock and managed to get them out of the water and to safety. The main road along the 26th baseline was washed out and the huge culvert was parted and stood on end.

Culvert that washed out where the road crosses the Smeaton near Ken Batchelor's, 1989.

26th Baseline road, west of Ken Batchelors, 1987.

30

By six in the morning the upper end of the Keg River prairie was rapidly being flooded. Dennis Halabisky's and Gary Galandy's farms on the south side of the river were under water. Bill Halabisky had a D-9 Caterpillar and tractor in the field and the water rose to six feet on them.

Gary Galandy's, right center. Hall, left center, 1987.

Bill Halabisky's, right center, 1987.

The water kept coming out of the hills with tremendous force. The water monitoring station on the Keg River near the Cabins was totally waterlogged with five feet of water in the building!

The flooding Keg River. In the foreground is the water measuring building, which malfunctioned due to high water, 1987.

The Keg River Cabins underwater in 1987.

This was August and the farmers were due to start swathing in a week or so. The sight of barley ready to be cut, standing in two feet of water will not soon be forgotten by area farmers.

The aerial photo taken from Vos' plane by Dennis Halabisky on August 2, 1987, shows how much water there was. Normally no water would be visible – it is usually down under the trees in the bottom of the river!

The new Cabins had a huge crew filling sand

Dave McDonald's and Bill Halabisky's, center, 1987.

Ed Aabak's field, Sec. 29-30-101-24-W5, 1987.

MacKenzie highway, Keg River Cabins, 1987.

bags. The buildings were spared due to all this work and cutting the old road with the highway backhoe. The salt in the sand did more damage than was expected – the well was ruined for some time.

In 1991 there was another flood at the Cabins but this one wasn't as severe. Now a levee has been built so hopefully there won't be any repeats.

The new Keg River Cabins and the flood of 1991.

Chinchaga River at Ridsdale's

Hay River west of Meander River beyond junction with Chinchaga.

CHAPTER III

COMMERCE AND DEVELOPMENT

Reminiscing on the Bank of the Peace
by John M. Okerholm

Today I went out to this beautiful stream
Like I used to do so very long ago.
Here I have dreamt many a secret dream
While I padddled my canoe to and fro.
Here I am sitting and looking back on a life
That I will remember and love to the last.
Where life was lived without too much strife
But those days are far in the past.

And today the song-birds are a busy lot.
The Henbirds are tending their nest.
The Malebirds are singing and flying about
And far too excited to stop and rest.
The young ones will need oodles of feed
But yet there is time to sing if they choose
And tend to their individual need.

In bushes not too far away I heard
A drummer that drummed all day.
He gave fair warning to a neighboring bird
That he is King of all his survey.
A Prairie Chicken came and passed on the
   wing.
She cackled "good morning" as she gave me a
   glance.
Then she flew straight as a pebble from a
   string
For yonder hill where the Prairie Cocks dance.

Wild flowers too are a beautiful sight-
Buttercup, Daisies, Crocus and Rose.
Some stay open all through the night,
Others that sleep in the softest of moss.
Beautiful colors that gladden the eye
Stand in profusion wherever I look.
They just like I will wither and die.
The place we knew, will in vain for us look.

This morning the River is beautiful, too.
Impatient it seems and eager to pass.
It may be having a secret rendezvous
Like a lover and his beautiful lass
And thus it has run through long forgotten
   past
And so it will love, like I, to the last
Who have on its bank maintained their home.

But before long I will take my last look
   around
And hang my cane in some nearby tree
And here then will mingle in this well known
   ground
The dust that at one time was me,

And the song birds will sing the same as today
From the top of the very same trees
And wild flowers, too, will blossom in May
And happily dance in the morning breeze.

Fur Trading
by Mary Jackson

Clement Paul of Fort Vermilion built a log trading post for the Hudson's Bay Company at Keg River in 1899. He built another one for Revillon Freres about one and one half miles from the Hudson's Bay in 1911.

Hudson Bay Post at Keg River after a summer of fixing up and painting by Harry Borbridge.

Keg River was very good fur country, and some of the trappers travelled long distances to trap, as there were no registered trap lines at that time. Trappers from Keg River went as far as Rainbow Lake, Hay Lakes, Bistcho Lake, out towards Fort Nelson, and towards Lower Hay River, as the boundaries of Alberta, British Columbia and the Northwest Territories had not yet been surveyed.

The trappers would take their supplies out by pack horse in the fall, and be gone for two or three months. When they went out on the spring hunt they took pack dogs.

Frank Jackson and John Brown started the Keg River Fur Trading Company together in 1924. Frank built a store halfway between the Hudson's Bay and Revillons. This was in the native settlement and Moise Richards was the chief at the time.

Local trappers at Jackson's trading post, Dan House in centre.

Supplies had to come down the Peace on the *D.A. Thomas* during the summer and were then hauled the 40 miles to Keg River by wagons. Warehouses were built at the Peace, across from Carcajou, to store the freight, as the teams could only haul about half a ton per load because of the steep hills at the Peace and the Keg Crossing.

Usually several freighters went together, so they could double up their teams to pull the hills, but the round trip usually took three or four days. Hauling freight for the three posts kept quite a number of men busy through the summer.

Albert Flett and freighters travelling from Peace River to Fort Vermilion.

Trappers sold their furs wherever it was convenient for them, so some of the Keg River men sold at Fort Vermilion, Hay Lakes, or Upper Hay (now Meander River), while some of the Battle River trappers sold at Keg River. The following is a list of those who sold fur to the Keg River Trading Company between 1924 and 1930, and the summary of the furs purchased.

Johnny Arnault	Charlotte Hamelin
John Brown	Olivier Hamelin
Blackbird	Alec Hamelin
R. Butler	Edward Hamelin
Burgo	Ambrose Hamelin
Napoleon Blue	Joseph Hamelin
Mrs. Blue	Joe Hale
Harry Bowe	Charlie Ireland
Alphonse Chalifoux	George Jones
Archie Chalifoux	Alec Jacknife
Emlieu Chalifoux	Alfred Law
Georgie Chalifoux	August Lizotte
Henry Chalifoux	August LaFleur
Paulus Chalifoux	Joe Lafferty
Peter Chalifoux	Daniel McGlure
Isidore CapotBlanc	D. J. MacLeod
Narcisse CapotBlanc	Monias
Napoleon CapotBlanc	Hilaire Minault
Aquanesi CapotBlanc	Eli Minault
Conajay CapotBlanc	Harry Minault
Bissima Cardinal	Magloire Mercredi
Richard Cardinal	Carl Norquist
Jean Marie Cardinal	Charlie Noskey
Clement Cardinal	Wilfred Rankin
John Christian	Moise Richard
David Centerno	Adele Richard

Edward Chittaway
Octave Ducharme
Celestin Ducharme
Emile Ducharme
Joe Ducharme
Emile Desjarlais
Johnny Elson
Frank Ferguson
Larone Ferguson

Jimmy Richards
Frank Smith
Mrs Stoney
Maria Stoney
Thomas Stoney
Hume Stewart
Ed Trosky
Edward Wanuch
Adam Wanuch

Lynx pelts on Trappers cabin built by Slim Hansen, 1960.

Revillons Freres Trading Post, 1933.

Dan Gray's dog team on the trap line.

Because of the Depression, fur prices went down rapidly in the 1930's. Revillon Freres closed their trading post at Keg River in 1935. The Keg River Trading Post closed in 1948. The Hudson's Bay Company built a new store in 1939, but it was finally closed in 1970.

Larone and his beaver pelts from the spring hunt.

Furs Purchased by Keg River Trading Co. (1924-1930)

	1924-25	1925-26	1926-27	1927-28	1928-29	1929-30
Wolf	48	75	26	14	4	9
Weasel	72	54	92	319	664	522
Mink	74	69	15	8	3	9
Skunk	37	12	1	6	1	1
Lynx	99	87	44	39	48	26
Beaver	88	141	139	72	-	-
Bear	3	4	13	23	10	16
Red Fox	63	89	60	11	25	10
Cross Fox	63	78	40	8	19	7
Silver Fox	13	14	13	2	1	-
Marten	11	16	18	60	33	11
Otter	-	1	-	-	-	-
Fisher	1	1	1	1	-	-
Wolverine	-	8	1	2	1	1
Muskrat	112	33	120	335	429	1053
Squirrel	-	535	1581	12!5	2482	3514

ALBERTA

№ 5148

DEPARTMENT OF LANDS & FORESTS

Certificate of Registration of Trap Line

(RESIDENT)

SUBJECT TO THE PROVISIONS OF "THE GAME ACT"

Dan Gray of Keg River, Alberta.

Is Hereby Granted the Sole Right to *hunt, trap and kill Fur-bearing Animals during the Open Season, and as permitted under existing Game Regulations, on the following described Registered Trap Line, No.* but not elsewhere.

Area consists all of Twp. 101 - Range 12 - Twp. 100 - Range 11-12. All West of the 6th Meridian. Excluding from the above all Privately-Owned or Leased Lands excepting those of the Licensee. and all twp 99 ranges 12 all told

Issued this 18th day of June 1957

(signature)

Dan Gray's Registration of Trap Line, 1957.

Dave McDonald and his fur catch of 1950. L-R: Lynx, Mink, Martin, Beaver and Wolf.

(Editor's Note: For interest we have included the average price paid per skin by the Hudson's Bay Company in early winter (October) 1922 and late winter (April) 1923. This information is courtesy of the Hudson's Bay Archives in Winnipeg)

	1922	1923
Black Bear	8.79	11.10
Brown Bear	8.40	9.50
Beaver	14.15	17.89
Ermine	.58	.72
Fisher	52.20	54.29
Silver Fox	125.20	119.77
Cross Fox	37.82	40.95
Red Fox	16.92	16.76
White Fox	26.65	33.49
Blue Fox	60.00	40.00
Lynx	18.02	19.71
Marten	20.23	25.18
Mink	8.28	8.73
Musquash	.97	1.56

Otter	18.54	23.34
Skunk	1.78	1.72
Prairie Wolf	12.00	10.00
Timber Wolf	14.00	16.11
Wolverine	12.75	14.60

The Hudson's Bay Company
by Mary Lou Ng

This is the history of the Hudson's Bay Company in the Keg River area, based on research done in 1993 at the company archives in Winnipeg. Unfortunately, many records were not available and it was impossible to fill in all the details.

The Northwest Company formed in 1783 was the first reported fur trader in this region. Fort du Tremble was located on the east bank of the Peace River, 60 miles above Fort Vermilion, near the mouth of the Keg River. The fort was built by the Northwest Company before 1800 and operated as a trading post for at least 15 years. (See the area map with this article.)

The post was called Old Fort du Tremble by David Thompson when he visited the area in 1804. Other names used were De Tremble and Des Trembles. The name is believed to have originated with the trembling of the leaves of the aspen trees in the region. The Hudson's Bay Company took

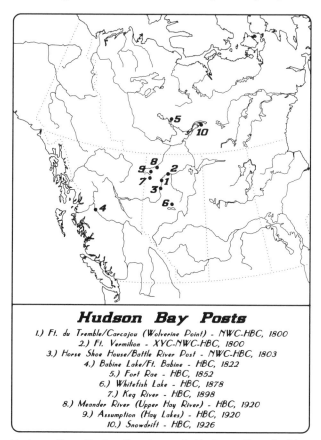

Hudson Bay Posts
1.) Ft. du Tremble/Carcajou (Wolverine Point) - NWC-HBC, 1800
2.) Ft. Vermilion - XYC-NWC-HBC, 1800
3.) Horse Shoe House/Battle River Post - NWC-HBC, 1803
4.) Babine Lake/Ft. Babine - HBC, 1822
5.) Fort Rae - HBC, 1852
6.) Whitefish Lake - HBC, 1878
7.) Keg River - HBC, 1898
8.) Meander River (Upper Hay River) - HBC, 1920
9.) Assumption (Hay Lakes) - HBC, 1920
10.) Snowdrift - HBC, 1926

Hudson Bay Posts. Courtesy of Hudson Bay Archives, Winnipeg, Man.

over the Northwest Company in 1821, but HBC records do not include Fort du Tremble.

In 1885 a Hudson's Bay Post was operating on the Peace River at the mouth of the Battle River. This post operated outposts at Keg River and Wolverine Point, but these were closed in 1885 due to starvation among the Indians. By 1887, however, Battle River had experienced flooding for three years and the post there was closed permanently and the goods were transferred to Wolverine Point.

Wolverine Point is sometimes referred to as Keg River and the exact location of this post is not known, although it was believed to have been on the Peace River between the mouth of the Wolverine River and the Keg River. It is also possible that it was this post that later became known as Carcajou Point because Carcajou is French for "wolverine". The length of time that this post operated is not known.

It is believed that during this time William John "Billy" Grey was one of the Hudson's Bay employees who looked after these posts. He came to Canada from Scotland in March, 1888. He immediately went to work for the HBC in the Athabasca District in the Northwest Territories serving in many capacities for 30 years.

Grey looked after the Keg River and Carcajou Point posts at the same time! He travelled the 35 miles between the posts by dog team or on foot. This was an unbelievable feat, especially in the bitter cold of winter or during spring breakup. Billy certainly lived up to his contract with the HBC "to devote the whole of his time and labor in their service by day or night".

In 1914 a trading post was operated in Keg River as an outpost of Fort Vermilion. As the district manager for the HBC noted: "It is necessary to keep outposts open because of the great distances between Fort Vermilion and the other posts in the district. In good years, all outposts have shown good profits."

In 1918 Keg River began to operate as a post in its own right, no longer an outpost of Fort Vermilion. It continued this way until its closure in 1970.

The first records of post managers are from the 1920's. From 1920 to 1922, Joe Kemp was the manager of the Hudson's Bay Trading Post at Keg River. He recorded buying two-thirds of the fur in the district, with his competition, Revillon Furs, buying the rest.

In 1922, Mr. Kemp was replaced by J.S. Mooney because the district manager found an "unsatisfactory condition of affairs" during his inspection of the post. Later, with Mr. Mooney in charge, the district manager reported that everything was in A-1 condition. Even the debts were reduced! This referred to the practice of granting grub stakes to the trappers and then attempting to collect by buying their furs at season's end.

Mr. Mooney reported that he experienced strong opposition from another fur trader at Carcajou Point. In response to the opposition at Carcajou Point, the Hudson's Bay opened an outpost there under the management of A. Tennant (a clerk who was paid $480 for the year).

By 1924, Fred Clarke was the manager at Keg River. One district manager's report indicated that competition for fur was intense at this time. "Mr. Clarke is a keen and zealous trader, but due to competition in Keg River from Revillon Furs and the Keg River Trading Company and at Carcajou by McLean, he is not buying all the fur in the district."

The following table shows the types of furs and the number of each purchased in the Athabasca District in 1924 and 1925. It is based on information found in the Fur Journals of the Athabasca district in the Hudson's Bay Company Archives.

TYPE:	1924	1925
Bear – Black	366	386
Brown	30	45
Grey	4	3
Beaver	5348	4990
Ermine	5484	3301
Fisher	56	80
Fox– Silver	284	466
Cross	1655	2460
Red	2420	4172
Lynx	3028	2974
Marten	1924	1626
Musquash	43102	22590
Otter	47	61
Skunk	1010	831
Wolf – Timber	9	10
Prairie	853	1595
Wolverine	31	35
Castorium	72.5 pounds	54.5 pounds
TOTAL VALUE:	$463 323	$481 832

The praise of Mr. Clarke by the district manager was not to last. "The post staff probably did what they could, but in several instances especially Messrs: Larry Clark at Upper Hay River, A. Tennant at Carcajou Point and Fred Clarke at Keg River have shown distinct incapability and disregard of instructions and consequently were removed from their charges."

That brought Thomas Clarke to Keg River as post manager. He was provided with a bookkeeper

in the hope of having better management. At this time the horses that were owned by the Post were sold and the freighting from Carcajou was contracted out.

During this time the transportation of goods into Keg River from Edmonton was done by ED and BC railway to Peace River, then by steamer down the Peace River to Wolverine Point and from there to the Post (35 miles) by wagon or sleigh at a rate of two cents per pound. Because of the condition of the road and having to ferry supplies across the river, very little was freighted in the summer.

From 1927 to 1931, Fred Young was the Keg River post manager. In 1928 he reported a bad year for fur traders. The opposition (Revillon and Keg River Trading) took the lead all winter, paying higher prices for furs. Keg River Trading had even set up a temporary post at Hay Lakes to secure the collection of furs with Allie Brick as the trader.

The Hudson's Bay Post at Carcajou Point was located on Lot 1, Block 2-30-101-19-W5. Both a store and a house were owned by the Bay in this location in 1927 when C.G. Rankin was in charge. In 1928, J.G. Murchison took charge of the post. In 1929, Fred Young was Post Manager at Keg River and he oversaw the operation at Carcajou Point also. By 1931 the Carcajou post was closed permanently with the buildings left unoccupied.

A Hudson's Bay Company district manager commented on the late 1920's in this way: "Severe losses were experienced in the 20's due to a failed hunt and were aggravated by several post managers who exceeded their authority in granting unwarranted advances, for which they were severely admonished."

In 1931, James Smith became the post manager at Keg River. Mr. Smith was born in Scotland. He was 20 years old when he joined HBC in 1926. He spent the first summer as a purser on the Hudson's Bay boat. Then he went to Hay River as an apprentice clerk for two years.

In 1932, Smith reported his opposition in Keg River continued to be Revillon Furs and Keg River Trading. The latter continued to operate an outpost at Hay Lakes in the midst of the Indian hunting grounds. A post was also being operated at Rainbow Lake by McLeod.

James married Annie Yurkowski in 1932 in Keg River and remained until 1938 when they were transferred to Little Red River. Later they went to Atikameg (White Fish Lake) where he retired after serving the Bay for 45 years. He and Annie had a family of six children.

Annie Smith washing clothes by hand with daughters Patsy and June.

In 1938, Jim Smith was replaced at Keg River by Harry Borbridge. He started with the HBC as an apprentice clerk in Fort Vermilion. He recalls writing daily in the post journals which were checked by district managers during post inspections and left for the next manager to continue. Unfortunately, none of these journals for the Keg River Post have been found.

Furs at Hudson Bay Post, Keg River, 1936.

It was in Keg River that Harry Borbridge met Isobel Moulton. They were married in 1939. Harry and Isobel now live in Winnipeg, where he retired after 47 years with the Hudson's Bay.

Clarence Douglas (Doug) Stevens was post manager from 1939 to 1943. While Stevens was here in Keg River a new Bay store and house were built (1942).

New Hudson Bay buildings, 1950's.

He was born in Amherst, Nova Scotia, in 1914 and joined the Bay in 1934. Immediately before coming to Keg River, he was a clerk in Old Fort Babine. Doug Stevens was another long-time Bay employee. He spent a number of years in Fort Rae, NWT, after leaving Keg River. His retirement came on February 1st, 1979. Doug has been an avid ham radio operator and is currently living in Cold Lake.

In 1942, the Post reported a profit of $6,161 on fur purchases of $18,635. The Post paid wages of $1,550 and had a total operating expense of $2,852.

Jack Kerr replaced Doug Stevens as an acting Post manager in Keg River in 1943, coming from Fort St. John, where he had been a clerk. He remained at Keg River until 1944 and with the HBC until his retirement in January, 1974. In 1944 Wm. Yurkowski began working as a clerk in the Keg River store.

On the departure of Mr. Kerr for holidays, R. E. Howell came to Keg River directly from the Fur Training School. In June, 1946, Mr. Howell left Keg River for Sturgeon Lake. By 1969, Mr. Howell was a district manager and on June 20, 1970, he was honored for 40 years of services to the Bay.

Following Mr. Howell as post manager was Foster Raymer (Ray) Ross. With him came an unusual era of stability in post managers. Mr. Ross and his family remained in Keg River from 1946 until he retired on October 31, 1958, after 33 years with the Bay.

Mr. Ross had been hired in Edmonton on June 1, 1925, and served as manager in Tree River, Bernard Harbour, Reid Island, Coppermine, and Holman Island before Keg River. During the Second World War, Mr. Ross was given a leave of absence to take up a special assignment as purchasing agent with the Air Observers School in Edmonton. After he returned from that assignment to become post manager at Keg River. Mr. Ross died on October 26, 1976, at 84 years of age.

During his 12 years at Keg River, Mr. Ross reported a variety of experiences. The district manager for the Athabasca District made a late fall inspection of the posts at Upper Hay River and Keg River in 1946, His excursion from Athabasca was completed with the help of a plane, canoe, horse, car, truck and train! Transportation was always an opportunity for excitement. He arrived in Keg River in -40° temperatures.

Raymer Ross on MacKenzie Highway.

By 1953, rabies in the district was a great concern. "We have hopes that the worst is over and that the foxes and wolves of the district will once again become the hunted, not the hunters." In fact, the rabies epidemic was devastating to trapping in the district. The skunk disappeared completely from the district and the fox have only begun to return 40 years later. The wolf population didn't completely die out but their numbers were drastically reduced.

A district manager visiting on an inspection tour in the 1950s, when welfare was just beginning at Keg River, remarked, "It's a hell of a way to run a Government, but it is good for business!"

In 1958 Mr. Ross reported the only direct account of crime at the Keg River Hudson's Bay. "Last evening about 1:00 A.M. when I answered a knock at the door of the dwelling. I was ordered outside by a masked man with a rifle. I hastily backed into the house. After going into the kitchen for something to use as a weapon, I returned to the door and the man had apparently left after poking the rifle through two of the small windows in the storm door leading into the house. Apparently no attempt was made to enter the store. Nothing was missing and the only damage was two broken window panes in the storm door.

However, when a boy went to the Post Office at 8:00 A.M., he found the postmaster, Mr. Harry Bowe, tied up in a chair where he had been all night and the money in the Post Office had been cleared out. The Police and Postal Authorities were notified and the police have been in. I saw only one man, a stranger, but Harry Bowe said there were two, possibly three".

A 1948 report from Keg River was about the highway. "Good progress is being made on the Grimshaw – Hay River highway and all the Alberta portion should be finished this summer. Upper Hay River and Keg River will then have a gravelled highway from Edmonton."

In January, 1949, the Hudson's Bay Company publication *The Moccasin Telegraph* included the following stories: "The Egg and I has its counterpart in Ray Ross at Keg River, where dozens of hens are cultivated by Ray in his spare time. Ray thinks the sound of hens cackling is wonderful music after so many years in the Arctic. The hens lay, too!" (The Egg and I was a best-selling book at that time.)

"A road has now been graded between Grimshaw-Hay River and North Vermilion. Some gravel would be a great improvement, but local residents are thankful for small mercies because even the graded highway is a vast improvement over the former bush road."

Mr. Ross was helped in the store by local clerks during his time as post manager. Some of these clerks were: Miss A. Lorenz (1947), Mrs. P. Rudy (1948), Albert Wanuch (1948), Miss Ivy Ghostkeeper (1949), Miss A. Jackson (1950), Mrs. R. Lambert (1951) and Mrs. V. R. M. Jacob (1951).

The Hudson's Bay Company's desire to have each post manager grow a garden, was promoted through a garden contest in *The Moccasin Telegraph*, and Mr. and Mrs. Ross grew some winning gardens in Keg River. They won:

1949 – Best Garden, Zone 6
1950 – 2nd Best Garden, Zone 6

1953 – Best Garden Snapshot

There were not many reports of vacations taken by the Ross family, but in 1949 Mr. Ross paid a brief visit to Edmonton, and Andy Stewart looked after the post in his absence.

With Ray Ross' retirement in October, 1958, Norman Tuck moved to Keg River as the post manager. Two children were born to the Tuck family while they were in Keg River. Lloyd Lawrence was born in 1959 and Marianne Elizabeth in 1960. Two clerks who helped in the Bay store during Mr. Tuck's time were Miss V. J. Ferguson (1960) and Eugene Tywoniuk (1960).

Norman and Beth Tuck. Hudson Bay manager.

In 1961 Andy Reid had a relief assignment at Keg River as Mr. Tuck left. Mr. Reid was assisted by clerk Miss D. Galandy. The foundations of the store and the house were replaced in 1961.

Later in 1961, Harold C. Poole transferred from Waterways to Keg River and became post manager. in 1962 while Mr. Poole was manager, Northland Utilities supplied electric power to the post.

Post managers changed quickly in Keg River over the next few years:

1963   Ben N. H. Hunter (Delores Galandy was clerk)
1963   Art J. Sparks (won Best Garden, 1963) Dale Hagel (relief assignment while Mr. Sparks was on holiday)
1965   W. N. G. Scott (Stewart Sowan was clerk)
1966   Harmel Rivet (reported 400 construction workers completing the Rainbow Lake pipeline a quarter-mile from the store.) Harmel (Mel) married Lily Michalchuk.
1968   D. Osmond
1968   Bob Walker (Graeme Smith was clerk)

1968   Garth Yeomans
1969   Peter Martel (reported a very dry summer and fire destroying a sawmill)

On August 29, 1970, the Hudson's Bay Store at Keg River was closed. The buildings and land were sold.

COMMUNICATIONS
by Mary Jackson
TELEGRAPH AND TELEPHONE

The deaths of three women in childbirth in northern Alberta in 1929 hurried along the building of a telegraph line from Peace River to Fort Vermilion by the Dominion Government. It was in use as far as Notikewin by 1930, and reached Keg River by 1931 and Fort Vermilion by 1932. The line was cut through the bush just wide enough for wagons or sleighs to haul the poles and wire. Wooden bridges were built across the creeks and the Kemp and Keg Rivers. A telegraph office was built at Keg River on NE-20-101-24-W5.

Keg River Alta

Dec 3rd 1939

To The Minister of Public Works
Edmonton Alta

Dear Sir
        We the undersigned petitioners of unorganized territory
of Keg River Alta do humbly pray of you to give us the Provincial
aid in construction of roads and bridges between Battle River Alta,
and Keg River Post.
The transportation is so crippled in this locality that half the
homesteaders have already left their good places through lack of
good roads;
We therefor pray of you to give grant on the following roads and
bridges:- A bridge between Carcajou and Keg River Post, Township
101 Range 21 W.5 Second road between Keg River Post and Notikewin
Alta.
        We hope that you will look into this matter at once.
        We the undersigned are yours truly.

#	NAME	OCCUPATION	POST OFFICE ADDRESS	REMARKS
1	Mike Rudy	Farmer	Keg River Post	S.34 T.101 R.24
2	Harry Wilson	Farmer	Keg River	"
3	Nick Tomlaw	"	Keg River Post	S.24 T 101 R 24
4	H Bowe	"	"	SE¼ S24 T10 R24 W5
5	H. C. Bost	"	Keg River Post	NS. 28-T14 R24
6	H. Son	"	Keg River Post	SE 4 28 T 101 R24
7	M. Yurkowski	"	"	S 27 T.101 R.24
8	L. Fryteiuk	"	"	S. 27 T.101 R.24 M.5
9	P. Fryteiuk	"	"	NE¼ 22 T101 R24 M5
10	W. Walalitchey	"	"	S.W. ¼ 28-T101 R24
11	S. Gardob	"	"	S 48 102 R 24
12	F. Young	Manager HBC	"	S. 28 T.101 SE22
13	A. H. Thorburg	Rancher		S 32-101-24
14	L McMillen	"		S 32 101 24
15	Harry Jacobson	Mgr Keg River Trading Co		S.W. 33, 10.1. 24
16	George C Jones	Rancher	Hay River	
17	H Power	Farmer	Keg River	NW¼ 13
18	R C Rankin	Fur Trader		
19	Alex Rudy	Farmer	Keg River	Sec 13, 101. 24
20	Wm. Rudy	Farmer	Keg River	Sec 4, 102. 24
21	D S McLeod	Trader Keg River		Sec 4
22	Luis Bourassa	Farmer		Sec. 33, 101. 24
23	J Ternawski	"	"	29 -101 -24
24	A Ternawski	"	"	34 -101 -24
25	Nik Zemeluk	"	"	27 -101 -24
26	L. Fedowchuk	"	"	2 -102 -24
27	Peter Rudy	"	"	3 -102 -24
28	S. Romanchuk	"	"	14 -101 -24
29				
30				
31				

Petition for roads. Document courtesy of Alberta Provincial Archives, No. 67303 3520.

The telegraph line gave Keg River a trail that was very wet, and even though detours had been cut around the worst of swamps and muskegs, it was only possible to travel it on horseback.

The telegraph operator, Glady Harrington, used to make one trip a year, late in the fall, to do maintenance work on the line. There were two small log cabins built for his use, one at Goffit Creek and one at Shaganappi. At times he had to make emergency trips when the line went dead because of lightning strikes, wet snow, or ice storms, but this didn't happen very often – usually the line gave very good service. The power for the line was a basement full of big glass batteries with zinc and copper sulphate and a wind charger that Harrington had to maintain.

Cabin on telegraph line, 1936.

Messages were sent in Morse Code by key from Fort Vermilion to Keg River, to Notikewin, to Peace River. From Peace River to Edmonton the telegraph line of the Edmonton Dunvegan and British Columbia railway was used, so that by the fall of 1932 it was possible to send and receive messages by telegraph from Fort Vermilion to Edmonton. There were telephones in the offices and the operators sometimes used to talk to each other instead of using the key, but phones were not available for public use. The telephones were magneto-type with batteries, but the power was produced by turning the handle very vigorously.

A line was built to Carcajou connecting with the main line in 1932. There was no Morse key, just a telephone. In the winter they also ran a line across the Peace River ice to connect with the people on the east side of the river.

These telegraph lines were abandoned in August 1957 with a promise that Keg River, Paddle Prairie, High Level and Meander River would all be connected by microwave. Until the microwave system was installed, radio-telephones were put in these places.

After the old telegraph line was abandoned, it was put up for sale by the Crown Assets Disposal Corporation. A good deal of the line was impossible to salvage since trees had grown up in the 30 years since the line had been cut. The Keg River Chamber of Commerce offered to buy it, so that we could have our own telephone line built at Keg River. We were able to purchase that part of the line from Manning to Keg River for $150 and the Carcajou line for $96.

The company was incorporated as the Keg River Mutual Telephone Company, certificate #25160, on June 2, 1959. By July 1959 the following people had joined: Harry Bowe
Dave McDonald
Nick Tomilou
Peter Rudy
 Bob Peel
Johnny Vos
J. H. Patterson
Harry Wilson
 Ernie Brick
Louis Jackson
Arthur Jackson
Del Weber
Frank Jackson
Dr. Mary Jackson
C. A. Isaac (Keg River Cabins)
Paddle Prairie lines to the store, the nurse and Fr. Jean. Keg River Forestry also had a line.

A single-line phone line was built by the local people. This was a very valuable service for families who had no vehicle or were snowbound. A series of long and short rings identified each customer.

A pair of thieves was caught when they made the mistake of playing with the phone in a house where nobody was home. They had robbed the Keg River Cabins the night before. The police had been called to the area because of the break-in and were still in the area when this suspicious telephone activity took place. They were able to apprehend the thieves in this home.

The promised radio-telephone system was a complete and very expensive failure locally, functioning less than 50% of the time. The microwave system from Peace River to Hay River, North West Territories, was inaugurated with great fanfare on April 2, 1962, to connect with the Canadian National network in the North West Territories. This made it possible for Edmonton to communicate with Alaska, but north from Hotchkiss to Hay River there was only the radio-telephone.

It was March 1967 before the buried cable telephone party line service proposed by Alberta Government Telephones came to Keg River and Paddle Prairie. The system installation was completed by November 1968. The party lines were converted to private lines in 1990.

MAIL SERVICE

Before the Dominion Government Telegraph Line was cut through, the mail used to come down the Peace River by boat once a month in the summer and by dog teams, or teams and sleighs, in the winter. There were usually three mails through the winter but it depended on the time of freeze-up and break-up. By 1932 air mail started. There were no airports; planes were on pontoons in the summer and skis in winter. Meteorological stations were put in at the Keg River telegraph office and in Fort Vermilion, and they telegraphed the weather reports at 5 A.M. each day.

Mail plane.

Once there was sufficient snow in winter the planes landed on the prairie at Keg River, close to the telegraph office (which was also the post office). The arrival of the plane was always a great event, and everyone turned out to greet it.

The mail for Carcajou was then taken from Keg River, either by dog team or team and sleigh. In 1935 when Octave Ducharme was taking the mail to Carcajou, the temperature went down to 70° below zero, and he froze his heel down to the bone. It was June before it was finally healed. In the summer when the planes were on pontoons, they landed at Carcajou on the Peace River and Harry Bowe brought Keg River's mail from there with team and wagon.

TRACTOR TRAIN ROUTE

Gold was discovered in the North West Territories at Yellowknife in 1935, and this started a real gold rush. It was very difficult to get supplies down there, as the nearest point on the railway was at Grimshaw, about 400 miles from Great Slave Lake, and there was no road north of Notikewin.

Bert Neeland thought he could haul freight with caterpillar tractors pulling sleighs, if he could cut out a trail. The trail along the telegraph line couldn't be used for hauling heavy loads as there were too many steep hills. Bert thought that by keeping further east they could avoid the worst hills, and could cut out a road that would be passable after it was frozen.

Tractor train stopped at Keg River while on its way to Yellowknife with Dave McDonald's dog team in front.

Burt Neeland and cat outfit freighting to Yellowknife.

He hired 20 men to travel with him, cutting road as they went. This was in the depths of the Depression, so there was no difficulty in finding men, particularly as they wanted to stay in the gold fields when they reached Yellowknife. They managed to get through the winter of 1936-37, even though it was a winter in which the snow came early and the muskegs didn't freeze underneath. They continued freighting each winter but had some hair-raising trips across Great Slave Lake because of the cracks that developed in the ice at different times. Other big Cats managed to get through, hauling the heavy machinery for the gold mines and the Snare River power plant.

The Provincial Government decided that a proper winter tractor train route should be cut through, and thought it would be a good job for some of the unemployed men in Calgary , who had been existing on meals at soup kitchens. The men were in poor physical condition, were poorly clothed and didn't have winter footwear or mitts. The authorities decided to build cabooses at Keg River, so the men had to walk from Notikewin to Keg River.

Cabooses built for McKenzie Highway Survey Crew.

Keg River road, near site of present day water treatment plant, 1951.

The temperature went down to 40° below zero and all the food that had been provided – bread, bologna, and canned pork and beans – was frozen solid, and couldn't be thawed at camp fires. Many of the men had frozen noses, ears, fingers and toes by the time they reached Keg River.

A surveyor was appointed to go ahead of the men to scout a suitable road, but this was difficult because the snow was so deep that the horses were pushing snow with the neck-yokes. They spent a miserable winter trying to cut through the swampy country that hadn't frozen under the snow. The road passed about nine miles east of the Keg River village, where the MacKenzie Highway goes now. Keg River farmers thought it was going to give them a passable highway to Grimshaw in the summer, but the first vehicle that tried it took over 12 hours to get there and was almost shaken to pieces!

WATER TRAVEL

The first steamer to ply the Peace River was built by the Roman Catholic Mission in 1902. This mission was situated close to the mouth of the Smokey River. The boat, unnamed as far as we know, travelled from Hudson's Hope to the Vermilion Chutes, a distance of 575 miles, until 1909. It was built mainly for mission work but was also used for general freight and passenger purposes.

Unloading freight at Carcajou, 1930.

In 1906 the Hudson's Bay Company built and named a boat for the river. The steamer, *Athabasca, replaced the Peace River in 1915.*

The D. A. Thomas was built in 1918 by the D. A. Thomas Company and they contracted to haul the Hudson's Bay Company freight. This boat was a wood-burning paddle-wheel steamer. This boat was larger and more cost-efficient, so the contract

Wood for the steamers on the Peace.

Power boat and scows stuck on a sand bar in the Peace River.

was considerably less than the Bay could haul their own goods for. However, it was soon found the *D. A. Thomas'* operating season was considerably shorter than expected, due mainly to the low water in the fall.

D.A. Thomas on the Peace, Photo Courtesy of Peace River Centennial Museum.

The settlers were beginning to move into this country as homestead land was taken up. They often built barges, scows and rafts to get their belongings moved in. The natives had used the river to travel on for many years. They used birch bark canoes or dugouts made from whole logs hollowed out.

By 1930 the *Wolverine* was put into service but this boat, too, was unsatisfactory due to the large

O'Sullivan and Stigsen passenger and freight boat going north on the Peace.

amount of fuel it used. The *Wolverine* was built and operated by O'Sullivan and Stigsen. After several trips it was converted from paddle wheel to propeller and with a name change to the *Beaver*, it became the most efficient and successful boat. They kept up a reliable service every two weeks from Peace River to Fort Vermilion until 1951, when river freighting was taken over by truck on the new MacKenzie Highway.

THE CANOL PROJECT

In 1942 the war in the Pacific was going very badly for the United States. The Japanese were not only taking the South Pacific almost as far as Australia, but they had also attacked and taken the western most island of the Aleutians. Oil and gas were urgently needed if the United States was going to defend Alaska.

The nearest oilfields were in California. Back

in 1922 oil had been discovered at Norman Wells on the MacKenzie River in the North West Territories, just south of the Arctic Circle, but it had only been used locally. This oil was more that 500 miles from Alaska and a pipeline would have to cross the MacKenzie Mountains. Not only that, all the heavy supplies would have to be taken down the tractor train route in northern Alberta, from the nearest railway at Grimshaw to Great Slave Lake, and then down the MacKenzie River by barge, another 500 miles.

The American survey party trying to scout a possible route for a pipeline through the MacKenzie Mountains became badly bogged down when they followed the route they had seen from a plane, and had to abandon it. The Indians of the Fort Norman district told them that they knew of a better route, and in October 1942 they took the surveyor with five dog teams and showed him the way that was finally used for the pipeline.

Meanwhile the American army was busy transforming our tractor train trail into a wonderful winter road. Luckily for them this was a winter when there was extreme cold before there was any snow, so they were able to cross swamps and creeks on the ice. Most of the troops were from the southern States and had never endured severe cold before. They couldn't imagine why anyone would want to come and live in a place like Keg River!

The United States army erected a 20-bed hospital at Paddle Prairie alongside their big trucking camp. This was to cope with any accidents that might occur on the highway, but there wasn't a doctor available to staff it, so they sent in a New York dentist! He was able to keep up his skills doing free dental work on the Metis Settlement.

Hundreds of trucks started hauling tons of supplies, equipment, and pipe to Mills Lake, where the MacKenzie River leaves Great Slave Lake.

Everything was unloaded there to be freighted on scows down the river after the ice broke up in June. On their return trip south they hauled the uranium ore from Great Bear Lake that went to make the first atom bombs.

Keg River people were delighted to have such a good winter road to Grimshaw, but at first the Americans were not going to let us use it. They couldn't believe that farmers could be raising grain and hogs so far north. Some of them had heard of the Edmonton Eskimos and expected to find Eskimos here.

Horses and sleigh used for freighting.

Trappers at the trading post.

Freighting in a snowstorm.

D. McMullen, Hudson Bay Manager from Fort Vermilion with a homemade snowmobile.

Keg River road repaired with corduroy, 1951.

A washout on the Keg River road, 1951.

"Yellowhound Bus Lines" from Jackson's to MacKenzie Highway.

Agriculture
by the History Book Committee

Agriculture has taken many forms in the Keg River, Paddle Prairie and Carcajou districts over the years. Keg River and Paddle Prairie are on land that used to be natural prairie, which provided the feed for the first animals brought in. The native Indians in the area also made hay from the grass to provide for their animals through the winter. This abundant supply of grass for animals was one of the attributes of the area that drew people.

The Carcajou settlement is located on a flat along the Peace River. The proximity to the river, the first transportation route into the area, and the rich soil of the flat were major attractions of Carcajou. The long days in the summer also provide excellent growing conditions for the crops of this district.

A short frost-free growing period of about 90 days has made it necessary for farmers in the area to continually seek crops and other products that can thrive under the conditions presented here.

Many animals and pieces of equipment were moved into the district on the steamers that worked on the Peace River, or brought on homemade scows on which entire families and all their belongings floated to their new life in our district.

To apply for a homestead lease, a person needed to be 18 years old, agree to live on the property a certain number of months each year, clear and break a specified number of acres and put those into cultivation in subsequent years.

Cat clearing land on Marius Vos homestead.

Homesteading on the Bud Bouma place!

48

TOWNSHIP 101   RANGE 19   MERIDIAN 5

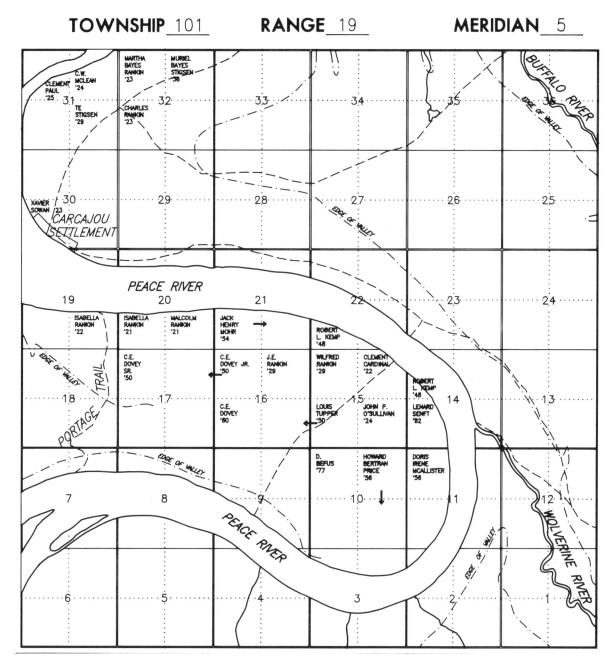

The homesteader was to pay a portion of earnings from the crop each year. Full title to the land was granted if the leaseholder kept the lease agreement for 20 years and paid off any loans against the property.

Many homesteaders needed to work off the homestead for at least the winter months to keep their families fed and have the money for the clearing and breaking required.

Agriculture has taken many forms in our area. Most people grow big vegetable gardens which are generally very successful. Some people also have greenhouses in which to grow those vegetables which freeze easily, such as tomatoes and peppers.

Pete Friesen pulling the binder with his caterpillar.

49

Crops of the district have ranged from flax to brome grass to canola and wheat. Potatoes and peas have also been grown commercially. Farmers and ranchers have also raised different types of animals, from sheep to purebred Aberdeen Angus cows, and foxes. Some farmers only grow grain, while others are into mixed farming for the protection that diversity offers.

Tractor and wagons hauling pigs to the boat on the Peace, 1948.

O'Sullivan and Stigsen freight and passenger boat loading grain by shute at the original La Crete Landing.

Some agricultural highlights of our history:

1882   Reverend Gough Brick plants wheat at Dunvegan.

1883   The summer has a frost every three weeks – not much prospect for growing anything.

1885   The Bricks plant a variety of grains on two and one half acres at Shaftesbury.

1886   The Lawrence brothers begin farming at Ft Vermilion, growing the Ladoga variety of wheat. It makes excellent flour and the price is $1.50 per bushel.

1896   Clement Paul brings farm machinery to Keg River over the pack trail from Carcajou – a six-foot mower and several other items.

1897   Wheat is grown in large quantities in the Fort Vermilion area. Estimates are that 35,000 bushels were made into flour and shipped all over the north as far as the Arctic – especially for Hudson's Bay Posts.

1908   The Dominion Experimental Station in Fort Vermilion begins testing grain varieties on a rented acreage of fertile river flat. In 1935 they will move to a permanent site.

1916-19 Land in Carcajou and Keg River is surveyed.

1920   The settlers at Keg River are making hay on New Year's Day! The weather is unusually warm and there is no snow. The snow came early before the hay was harvested, but then it melted.

1924   Farm implement prices jump by 10%. A seven foot binder costs $269, a seed drill $252, a cultivator $121 and a 12-inch gang plow $155. Labor costs are blamed for the increase.

1925   Wheat shipped to Toronto Canadian National Exhibition from Dunvegan grown by Reverend Gough Brick wins first prize.

1929   Land for homesteads is opened up in Keg River. A number of homesteaders move into the Keg River district via Peace River and overland by the Carcajou trail.

1930   People pass by Notikewin every day on their way to settle in Keg River. The telegraph line is a great help in keeping people from getting lost.

Stacking Hay with hay stacker made by Lonnie Root, 1930.

1932   Keg River needs a road connection to the Notikewin area. The provincial and federal governments are urged to help in seeing that the road is built quickly because Keg River is situated on "highly desirable agricultural land".

1934   The year of the devastating floods at Carcajou and Fort Vermilion. The ice jams below Carcajou and the water floods the Carcajou flat, the Rankin flat, and the Armstrong flat causing no human deaths but much hardship on the few settlers. In the same season, the Keg River district farmers suffer heavily from June frosts and what is not destroyed by frosts is further destroyed by grasshoppers despite a strenuous program of bait spreading.

1941   Excellent crops are reported. Large flax fields are 14 inches high. Heavy yields of barley, oats and wheat are also recorded.

1946   The *Peace River Record Gazette* carries the announcement that the Grimshaw – Great Slave Lake highway is to be built the following year. "The Grimshaw – Great Slave Lake highway is being built jointly by the federal and provincial governments. The Keg River district with its open prairies and brush land has been famous for many years, but due to its isolation has not often been visited by travellers. Here vegetables of all varieties can be grown and grain crops give high yields."

1951   Rabies in wild animals bring the dreaded disease into the district and many farm animals get sick and die or have to be done away with, which is a severe blow to local farmers. Animals suffering from rabies exhibit strange behavior, foam at the mouth and die. There is no cure. The disease is spread from one animal to the next by bites or foam entering the breaks in the skin. Mice spread rabies rapidly even by biting people in their beds. The vaccine available for human use is a dangerous drug that has to be administered very soon after the initial infection. The treatment consists of 14 shots in the stomach, one each day. It is a very painful procedure.

1953   The Frank Jackson family of Keg River is one of five provincial farm families to receive the Master Farm Family Award.

1955   Clearing costs $4.50 an acre and breaking can cost another $4.50 per acre. The Alberta legislature passes a bill granting financial assistance of up to $1000 to homesteaders with leases.

1963   The Great Slave Railroad passes through Keg River.

1964   An elevator opens in Keg River as United Grain Growers is impressed with the agricultural potential of the north Peace district.

1965   The district's Member of the Alberta Legislature, Mr. Montgomery, recommends that "more land should be opened up for homesteading. There should be no charge for the land but a portion of the money spent on development should be recovered before the title is issued. That this will cost money is obvious but what better way can Alberta make use of its resources than investing them in the development of its land resources. And the sooner the better."

1975   The Northern Alberta Rapeseed Producers Cooperative has grown to 2500 members. The Sexsmith plant for processing canola is being built by German investors. One of the directors is Ted Krause of Keg River.

16 foot Brush Piler built by Mike Papirny, 1976.

Rootpicker built by Mike Papirny, 1977.

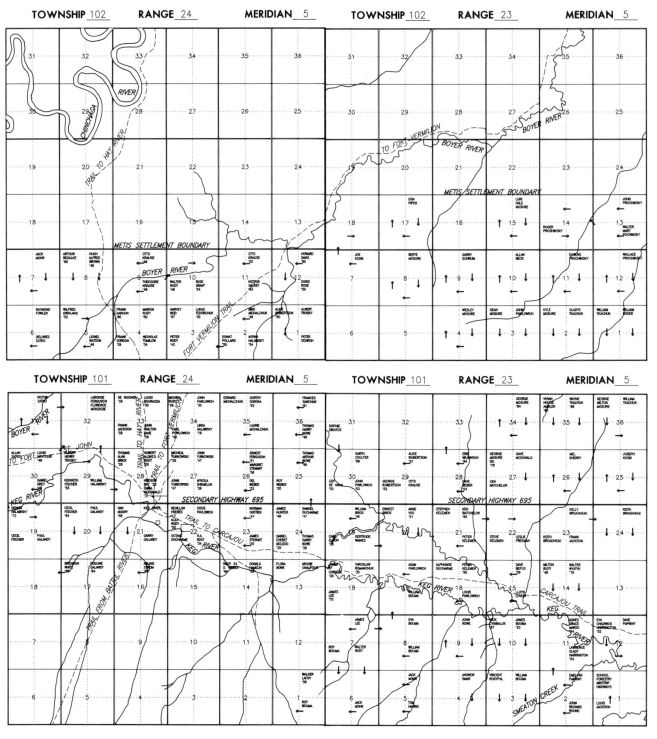

TOWNSHIP 101   **RANGE** 24   **MERIDIAN** 5   **TOWNSHIP** 101   **RANGE** 23   **MERIDIAN** 5

Keg
River
Farmland

TOWNSHIP 100   **RANGE** 23   **MERIDIAN** 5

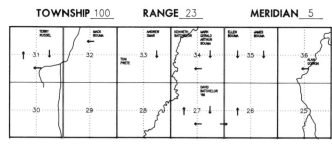

1980's   There is a new land rush in the Carcajou area at Scully Creek. The land is surveyed and opened up for a draw at a set price. Roads built earlier give access. Power and telephones are available.

1990's   Grain prices have fallen to new lows. Fuel prices continue to rise, along with freight rates. Diversification is necessary. "Zero till" is the new farming technique.

The Homesteaders
by Ellen Bouma

They came in faith
And filed a claim
Those brave young pioneers
Some thought insane
Who cut and cleared
And plowed the land
They built their homes
Where rivers ran
Their food was garden
Their meat ran wild
And often mothers did chores
When heavy with child
While their men were away
Working in mills to earn extra pay

Only the moon
Saw their plight
And heard newborns cry
In mid of night
And wolves howl in chorus
Where school marms came
From far off places
Children learned to count
And tie their laces
In one room schools
Where little red lard pails
Lined the wall
Stood like toy soldiers
Waiting their call

Where only their ghostly shell remain
Still stand with time
Through wind and rain
A broken oak table
Some tarnished brass
An old man's cane
And a metal rasp
Lie covered in mold
Where only the deer and coyote
Still tread the narrow wagon trails
Over barb wire fence
And broken rails

Their fields now turned to gold
Where only the dandelions grow

Picking Roots
by Margaret Befus

They plowed it up,
The virgin soil.
No more it's poplar brush.

But now the roots!
We pick the roots
By hand with ceaseless toil.

From morn 'till dark,
We pile them on
The wobbly old hayrack.

Mosquitoes, too, are there to help.
For every root, a bite.
The piles of roots – the piles of bites.

Grey tractor used to pull the rack
Is sick of picking roots.
Sometimes it starts – sometimes it won't.

The sun beats down as on we work.
A small sip from the water jar
Is warm and tastes of moss.

Next year we plant this;
A crop of golden wheat,
Will make it seem worthwhile.

But when we combine the wheat,
We find amid the wheat
More roots – we missed some roots.

Ah well, we'll pick again
And next year's crop
Will have no roots – just weeds.

Alberta's First Environmentalists: The Farmers
by Donna Elizabeth Kuhl (nee Pawlowich)

In these past few years, a major emphasis has been placed on educating people about being environmentally friendly, doing things like recycling, building compost heaps and minimizing waste in landfills. Young people can now train to be environmental engineers, and millions of dollars are being spent annually to help save our planet.

The amusing part is that the three "R's" of recycling: reduce, reuse and recycle, may seem to be a trend in the 90's, but for almost any farmer in Alberta, these practices are not new; as a matter of fact, they are and have always been a farmer's way of life.

When I look back at how we were raised, I realize how my parents were way ahead of their time in many ways. Perhaps the motivation might not have been concern for the future of the ozone layer as much as it was concern for making ends meet; nevertheless, my parents are two of the most environmentally friendly people I know.

One of the experts' major concerns seems to be the rapid filling up of landfills with all kinds of things from diapers and plastics to newspapers and yard wastes. Mom and Dad had no problem with these types of garbage.

First of all, disposable diapers were a luxury that either were not yet invented or were beyond the farmer's meagre budget. Instead, one of the duties of the farmer's wife was to make a day of the week "washday", which usually included a myriad of dirty diapers. The job was no great inconvenience, just a part of life on the farm. When one baby would grow out of diapers, the collection would be passed on to the next expecting mother in the family or the neighborhood.

Plastics were also not a major problem. There was a "bread bag" drawer in our house where all the bags were stored for reuse after they were carefully washed and dried, reused inside out and right side out again until the words would be worn right off, and thrown out only if they would not hold anything any more. On occasion, when the cow dried up, those margarine tubs Mom had to buy were great for freezing or storing or saving leftovers, and were also used until well after the labels wore off.

We never worried about styrofoam meat trays or egg cartons because we wrapped our own meat in butcher paper and used and reused egg cartons to eternity, for they never seemed to wear out. And the occasional store-bought styrofoam would make its way to school to use for crafts in elementary art classes, or become trays for Mom's icing roses.

When it came to paper, Mom had a great use for it all. After the *Western Producer* had been examined from cover to cover, she and I would use them to wash windows. Although our hands were black at the end of the chore, the windows would sparkle!

We would put our muddy boots on any spare newspaper, we would save any bond paper for notes, rough work, or for little people to "create" on the backs.

One lunch bag had to last us a week, once we "matured" out of our lunchpails, and we were in trouble if we forgot to bring our bags home from school. Eventually the paper made it to the burn barrel, and Dad would use the resulting ashes for the chickens, the garden or the ice in the winter.

When it came to yard waste, we never had any. Any lawn clippings went to the chickens, any weeds or plants from the garden went to the cows or the pigs, or into a pile where they would deteriorate, nowadays called a "compost heap". Household scraps were the same. Although the veterinarians no longer recommend it, all the table scraps went to the dogs or cats or into a slop pail for the pigs.

Any housewares that Mom and Dad no longer needed or replaced were never thrown away–they were given to us to help us get a start on our own, or stored in a shed to be taken to auction where, as they say, "one man's junk is another man's treasure"! Mom always used the glass jars for her canning. The bottles were never, never trashed. We kids industriously washed and saved them to return for money to be used on holidays or at the fair, often combing the local ditches on our bicycles to increase our bounty.

Energy consumption has also become a major concern for people in the past few decades, but Mom and Dad had us trained early. We went to town only once a week and did all our business at once instead of running in every day, which certainly helped save on gas. We did not leave a light on if we were no longer in the room, and our thermostat never got above 70°F, and was always turned down to 65 at night. Instead, if we were cold, we put on a sweater or an extra blanket, for it is hard to expect any house to maintain shirt-sleeve weather in the dead of winter.

On the topic of heat, one of my favorite memories is of that old wood stove. Although it was replaced when I was about nine for the modern convenience of the electric stove, that old stove not only took the chill out of the house and used up the dead trees that Dad would cut down in the yard -it kept the family together as a group. There were many nights that we would sit there with our feet on the oven door, or be sprawled under or behind it and have Mom read to all of us, or discuss the day's affairs or do our homework. It took a long time to get used to not having that extra warmth, especially in the mornings -almost like the house had lost some of its personality.

Water consumption is currently a major issue, another area that Mom and Dad had under control. Rather than depending on the hot water heater, Mom would often have a pot of water heating on the stove, for it was going anyway.

We never had a brick in our toilet tank to

displace the amount of water used in every flush, but we were conservative about flushing every time we used the facilities. If we were outside, we were encouraged to use the "little shack out back".

Also, when we were really little, nobody was concerned about bathing in someone else's water, so we bathed cleanest to dirtiest! As we got older, we used water for individual baths but did so sparingly.

Even my dad's farming practices, which may have seemed to be behind the times at one point, showed his common sense and mistrust of anything other than the natural. When many farmers were piling on the chemicals and fertilizers, Dad would rotate his crops, or summer fallow. He would have us out in the field picking wild oats or sow thistle instead of using what we now know were very harmful sprays. After all, some joke that one of the reasons a farmer had lots of kids was to help around the farm!

We had a great time doing what seemed to be tedious chores because we did them as a family. Mom always made these tasks into an excuse for a picnic, or we had a swim in the river afterwards as a reward for a job well done.

As for enriching the garden, Mom and Dad had both a safe and an economical way of fertilizing. Dad would take the old stoneboat and load it up with manure from the pile the boys had made from cleaning out the barn. He would then dump it on the garden and work it in with the tractor.

Later, that task became even easier; he would sweep a landleveller through the manure pile and pull it onto the proposed garden plot and the fruits of our labours would flourish. Even now, Mom and Dad plant their garden where the barnyard used to be, and they have one of the most beautiful and bountiful harvests you will ever see!

When they were developing their farm, Mom and Dad also took advantage of a government program that was set up to help the environment. They applied for and received various types of trees to build shelterbelts for the yard. They carefully planted the caraganas, the poplars, the blue and white spruce trees, and lovingly took care of these little seedlings and saplings until they became strong enough to make it on their own. Nowadays, these trees tower majestically in the yard as monuments of the hard work that my parents did all those years ago.

However, people will say, "That was then, and this is now," and many will not compromise the conveniences and luxuries that our throw-away society has cultivated. But everybody must realize that just because there is more money at our disposal, our earth is not for our indiscriminate disposal. We must change, and yes, in many ways, go back to the old days.

Maybe when society needs some environmental advisors, they should look right under their noses for some of the greatest role models they can find, Alberta's first environmentalists, the farmers. And, thanks, Mom and Dad, for being such great role models for me!

Medicine
by Dr. Mary Jackson

I arrived in 1929 from England and lived in Battle River on the Notikewin River, halfway between Notikewin and North Star. (Manning did not exist until 1946.) The provincial government had contracted me to provide medical care for the people who lived in the area and those who continued to pour into the district.

Prior to my arrival, people of the district were either treated by those with the most expertise, treated by the Indian medicine man, transported to Fort Vermilion, Berwyn or Peace River, or simply died. Often the patients died anyway.

In 1921 a large number of people of the Keg River area died in a smallpox epidemic. None of those born and raised in the area had been vaccinated. Frank Jackson, an independent fur trader, and Harry Bowe, a rancher who had moved into the district a few years earlier, had been vaccinated as babies in England. There was not much they could do to help but they travelled from house to house, helping where possible. In some cases whole families died in the epidemic.

Trappers travelled very long distances in the 1930's before there were any registered traplines. Injuries or illnesses like pneumonia and appendicitis quickly became life-threatening.

The only doctors in the whole north Peace River country in 1930 were Dr. Sutherland in Peace River, Dr. Matas in Berwyn, Dr. Hamman in Fort Vermilion and myself.

In 1931 I married Frank Jackson of Keg River and moved there, where I continued to practice medicine until 1974 when I retired. In Battle River I had had a government contract but now my patients paid me when and if they could and with what they could.

The Dominion Government telegraph line from Peace River to Fort Vermilion was completed in 1932, but there were no telephones. In 1932 when Archie Fife's lower jaw was shot off in a shotgun accident, he was in Rainbow Lake. It took three days to get him to Keg River, and we had to wait a further two days before Wop May was able to pick him up in his plane to fly him to Edmonton. It was April 1st and the snow was getting very soft. Wop had to taxi up and down the prairie to make a runway firm enough for him to be able to take off. Archie died in hospital.

Jean Marie (Peeweeno) Cardinal was a teenager who came from Sucker Creek and was out in the bush trapping alone when he developed pneumonia. He was very lucky that another trapper found him and brought him in. There were no antibiotics in those days, sulpha drugs and penicillin had not been developed and many people with pneumonia died. But Peeweeno survived well and had another narrow escape when he was hunting moose down towards the Peace River.

He was crossing through some heavy windfall and broke through, and his gun swung round and shot him up the back of his arm. He had a 35-mile walk to get help in Keg River. He lived in the area until his death at 84 in 1993.

Sapwastice, the Indian medicine man, lived in Keg River for years. He made special medicines from wild plants and roots. Some of the medicines provided relief and cures. I wish I could have obtained the recipe for these medicines because in some cases their positive effects were dramatic and undeniable. Fractured bones did extremely well even though they were not set or seen by doctors. The old native ladies also knew of these special plants and potions. It is a great pity the knowledge was not handed down.

The Indian medicines had no effect on tuberculosis, another disease which sometimes claimed whole families. In 1931 there were no drugs for treating TB and hospitals would not accept Indian or Metis patients. In 1935 the Aberhart Hospital was built in Edmonton and it began to admit native patients. Doctors in this era treated tuberculosis in the lungs with surgical removal of the affected area. Peeweeno had this type of treatment and he was able to return home to a normal life.

By 1950 drugs such as streptomycin and isoniazid had been developed and the death rate from TB dropped dramatically.

Midwives looked after women in childbirth in their own homes. Elsie Sowan was a midwife in the Carcajou area in 1910. Charlotte Hamelin and several others were midwives in the Keg River area. Elizabeth Ducharme was also called upon at Chinchaga.

The Revillon Freres trading post was sold to the Hudson's Bay Company when the company stopped operating in western Canada. The HBC had no use for another set of buildings so my husband bought them. The store and warehouse were moved to our farm. The house became the Eileen Elgar Outpost Hospital. Mrs. Elgar, a wealthy English lady, provided $1000 to equip the building with four beds, a cook stove, a heater, an operating table, a gas lantern, a kitchen table, chairs, and utensils.

Whole families came and camped in the yard while the sick member of the family was looked after in the hospital. The family did the cooking, hauled water from the river in buckets and cut the wood. Women expecting babies could come ahead of time and stay.

The hospital made my job slightly easier as I no longer had to travel to all of my patients for the initial and follow-up visits. At least some of them could come to me. The hospital was not used after 1952 when access to the "outside" hospitals became easier with the construction of the new MacKenzie Highway.

Registered nurses were sent into the district from the Peace River Health Unit in 1954. They did immunizations, checked on the school children and looked in on the new babies. BCG (Bacillus Calmette Guerin) vaccinations were started at this time and all the school children were vaccinated in an attempt to halt the spread of TB.

In 1948 a mobile X-ray survey was completed on 302 residents of Paddle Prairie and Keg River. Pulmonary TB was diagnosed in eight cases and only one of these was active.

After this survey the Tuberculosis Association provided me with an X-ray machine and a power plant to run it, enabling me to do follow up X-rays on people returning from the sanatorium and those with whom they came in contact.

When a sub-unit of the Peace River Health Unit was established in Manning, nurses came from there. Mrs. Martha Strom travelled the MacKenzie Highway many times through dust, mud, snow, and construction. She usually stayed overnight with us.

When we moved from the village to our farm in 1948, my husband built me an office and waiting area in the basement of our home. I saw the introduction of the health care system and dealt with the accompanying paperwork by myself. I hired someone to help keep the house running and clean, but I operated my medical practice on my own. I spent many hours reading medical journals in an attempt to keep up with the changing world of medicine. The isolation of the Keg River area made it difficult for me to communicate with my colleagues in a way I would have liked to.

In the 1930's many of my patients were penniless due to the Depression and therefore could not afford to pay for my services and the drugs I did have available for them. I was grateful to my family and friends who sent me money from time to time. I was able to use this money to supply drugs to my patients.

I served as coroner in Keg River and at least as far as I know, was the only female coroner in all of Alberta. I got paid by the government for the coroner's inquests that I did.

As coroner I had to investigate the death of Hume Stewart in September 1936. We were experiencing a snowstorm when Mr. Stewart failed to show up to take someone to Carcajou. When a friend went to check on him, they saw that he was lying dead in his home. I was called. Mr. Stewart had shot himself inside of his locked home.

His death was a shock in a community where he was well-liked. He had been making home brew and had a 50-gallon crock on the go. The whole house stunk because of that brew. Hume had come to Keg River and received land under the Soldier's Settlement Act after serving in the First World War.

I saw one very bad case of scurvy in my years of practice. A Mennonite lady in Carcajou in 1934 had all the classic symptoms. It takes six months of poor diet to develop scurvy, but without a garden that year and with the difficulties of bringing in fresh fruit and vegetables, I could understand the development of this ailment. Vitamin C was not being synthesized yet, so I provided her with canned tomatoes, turnips, and potatoes from my garden. She recovered quickly.

I saw at least four cases of carbon monoxide poisoning over the years. It can be difficult to diagnose because the patient has a good color although he is unconscious.

The Hudson's Bay had trouble with a pump down the well and one man went down to fix it. When he lost consciousness due to the CO, another went after him. Luckily the second was able to bring the first out without losing consciousness himself. The first man's heart stopped after he arrived at my place. I had to perform artificial respiration; the man survived.

Jack and Gladys Round had a faulty propane refrigerator fill their home with odorless carbon monoxide. Gladys collapsed and died and Jack attempted to leave but collapsed by the door. He was close enough to the door that he was getting some fresh air through the crack between the door and the floor. He was unconscious but alive when a neighbor found him.

I was completely frustrated when three children from the same family were brought in to see me for the same sort of accidental poisoning over a period of a couple of years. Many families stored coal oil (kerosene) in bottles beside their stoves and used it to help them light a fire in the stove each morning. This family used a beer bottle to store the oil and they left it on the floor beside the stove.

It was when their toddlers, who had watched the adults drinking beer from bottles, imitated them with the bottle containing coal oil, that they were brought to me with poisoning. The babies survived. I threatened the mom that I would see her put in jail if one more of her children were poisoned.

There were a great many burns, particularly in small children, because of the red-hot airtight heaters which were the only source of heat in many of the homes. There were no furnaces or propane heaters; we all depended on firewood and used a tremendous amount of it. Axe wounds were common, even in people who had been splitting wood all their lives. Several people chopped fingers or toes so they were just hanging by pieces of skin. Glady Harrington chopped his thumb off completely. Larone Ferguson split his foot right through.

Mary Ann Wanuch felled a spruce tree and it landed on her head, cutting her temporal muscle away from her skull. The gash was full of spruce bark. I cleaned the wound with a saline solution on the kitchen table. Helen Wanuch gave her an anaesthetic while I sewed her up. She returned to Paddle with instructions, and a thermometer to take her temperature twice a day. The first time she reported, her temperature was 107°! I found out that she had sterilized the thermometer with boiling water before putting it in her mouth!

I thought I was doing the people of the district a service when I got some cod liver oil from the Red Cross, but the local trappers quickly found that the foxes loved the faint smell of the oil and they started using it to bait their traps!

I saw the development of many drugs over the years. In 1936 sulphanilamide was the first sulpha drug I used. I had a shinbone infection from a fall over a log and was running a fever, so I used the sulphanilamide on myself. It worked almost immediately – it was like a miracle.

Penicillin came out during the war when it was given only to the troops. It was expensive at first. I got my first supply of the drug from my friend, Dr. Emma Johnstone, as a gift. It came as a yellow powder and needed to be mixed with sterilized water. It only had a 48-hour shelf life after it was mixed.

We had a rabies epidemic here in 1952 and I had to make the difficult choice of whether or not to use the rabies vaccine on my new son-in-law. I did and he survived.

As I had been warned in England before coming to Alberta, I was called on to serve as a dentist as well as a doctor. I pulled a lot of teeth as there were no other alternatives available. It seems a shame now that all those teeth were lost. Before I was around, Frank had pulled some teeth, too. He had been given a great set of forceps by some people who were going north for the gold rush in 1898.

From 1930 to 1974 I looked after all types of ailments including axe wounds, burns, broken bones, gunshot wounds, and car accident injuries. I also delivered many babies. For the most part I enjoyed my work. My work days (and nights) were certainly filled with variety and no two days were the same!

The Outpost Hospital
by Dr. Mary Jackson

When I was in England in April, 1937, on a sabbatical financed by the Fellowship of the Maple Leaf, Canon Andrews sent me to Bournemouth to visit Eileen Elgar. She was an enthusiastic supporter, who had sent some money to Keg River to help me supply my patients with badly needed drugs.

She was totally deaf as a result of an attack of scarlet fever when she was a teenager, so she could talk but I had to write down everything I wanted to tell her. She was quite appalled to know how far from me some of my patients lived. In England it seemed unbelievable that people could be as far as 50 miles from the nearest doctor.

I told her I was hoping to get an empty house that had been Revillons Trading Post, and equip it with a heater, a bed, a table, and chairs. Patients coming from Carcajou, Rainbow Lake or Paddle Prairie could then stay there and be within a quarter of a mile from my house. There was water in the river, and firewood nearby, and they or a family member would have to provide and cook their own food.

Eileen Elgar immediately said she would donate enough money to furnish the place. She would donate it to the Fellowship of the Maple Leaf, who would send it to Bishop Sovereign in Peace River. Her gift was enough to buy a cook stove, a heater, three beds, a table and chairs. The Fellowship of the Maple Leaf also provided a simple operating table and a couple of gas lanterns, and other Anglicans in Toronto sent some bedding and baby clothes.

It was a very primitive outpost hospital, but extremely useful. It was ready for use in September, 1937.

Eilene Elgar Outpost Hospital which was originally the Revillons Freres Post, Keg River, 1937.

The first serious case arrived soon afterwards, brought in from Paddle Prairie in a bad September snowstorm. I was thankful not to have to ride to the Paddle, and very thankful not to have to treat the patient in my kitchen! I had done some surgery on my kitchen table before we had the outpost.

In 1937 the United Church built a Mission Hospital close to the Notikewin river to serve the Battle River district, which by that time had more than 3000 people. Dr. Doidge was sent in by the United Church from Ontario.

This was now our nearest hospital, instead of Peace River. In the winter, when the muskegs were frozen, it was possible to get from Keg River to Battle River via the trail along the telegraph line. Frank Jackson's teams hauled freight that way, but it was a 75-mile journey that often took two days.

When Dr. Doidge and Rev. Inglis drove to Keg River (to remove tuberculous tonsils from three Keg River children) it took them two days even though they had no load. They said they had never

George and Alice Robertson and new baby in front of Keg River Hospital ready to return to the trapline.

been so cold. So although it was possible to get emergencies out to Battle River Hospital, sometimes it was still quite a problem. One patient with an acute appendix went out driving his own dog team!

Dr. Doidge arriving by cutter from Notikewin, 1937.

The MacKenzie Highway had been built as far as Keg River by 1949. It was a rather narrow, gravelled road, but passable most of the time, at least for trucks, so maternity cases and emer-gencies could get to the hospital in Battle River. The outpost hospital in Keg River was closed down in 1950. It had served its purpose very well. There are several people alive who probably would not have survived without it.

Keg River Cabins (1946 – 1994)
by Anne Vos

Mr. and Mrs. Glady Harrington had the idea of a stopping place on the MacKenzie Highway as a job to which they could move when they retired from the Government Telegraph Office at Keg River Post. They obtained the land in 1945 but were not quite sure where the survey posts were.

Eva Harrington, owner of original Keg River Cabins.

The main building was built with logs for the lower portion and the second floor was a frame construction. The store and cafe were downstairs, while the rooms for rent were upstairs as well as Mrs. Harrington's living quarters. After the building was completed it was found to be on the wrong piece of land! That problem was solved by getting title to the land on which the building was located.

Eva Harrington and friends on the first Keg River bridge on the MacKenzie Highway.

The original plan was to build individual cabins. Fred Martineau and Louis Houle were hired to start building these log cabins. When completed they were single-room cabins equipped with bunk beds, airtight heater, and washstand. If you were lucky, you were provided with a pail of water and an armful of wood. If not, you had to get your own. The bathroom was the "little brown shack out back".

Ma Harrington, as she was known, managed with a couple of helpers because Glady would soon be retiring from the telegraph office and he would come and help her. Louis Jackson was chief cook and bottle washer for several years. Some of the helpers were Susie Parenteau and Shirley Martineau.

Glady was unable to retire and join Mrs. Harrington at the Cabins because the government was unable to find another telegraph operator. Finally Harry Bowe moved to the Post and looked after the office. Glady did not spend long in retirement. The new separate cafe was built in 1952.

"Skinner" Tardiff, wife Dorothy and daughter Peggy from Fort Vermilion bought the business from the Harringtons. While the Tardiff family operated the service station and cabins, Mr. and Mrs Victor Rudy ran the cafe.

In 1960 Charlie and Muriel Isaac became the operators after purchasing the Cabins from the Tardiffs. The first flood was in 1962. The original store building burnt down in the fall of 1962. The business was busy during the railroad construction in the early 1960's and the Rainbow oil boom a few years later. During that time the business was open 24 hours a day.

In 1964 Irene Schroh took over the operation of the cafe, while Charlie Isaac continued to run the rest of the Cabins.

John and Jessie Buhler and daughters Velma, Linda and Dianne bought the business in 1965. They operated the cafe, cabins, fuel pumps, store, and garage where they did minor repairs and fixed tires. The new rooms with running water were a great addition in 1968. The post office was moved from the Keg River Post to the Cabins at that time.

Ted and Elnora Petersen and family returned to Keg River in 1969 and purchased the Cabins. Previously they had managed the United Grain Growers Elevator. Ted cleared away the old log cabins and brought in a trailer kitchen that they added to the store and garage. The family was able to look after everything in one building.

Bob Riczu and his wife Mardena bought the

Mardena and Bob Riczu with daughters.

Cabins from the Petersens in 1976. In 1977 Bob was hit by a devastating spring flood of the Keg River. The yard became a lake and the buildings and their contents were heavily damaged. Bob was the owner until 1986. In 1980-81 part of the Cabins operation was rented to Terry and Benita Price and was run as TerBen Esso.

Mark and Sondra Viau bought Keg River Cabins in 1986. They are the current operators of this, the only commercial establishment in Keg River.

Post Offices
taken from Post Offices of Alberta (1887-1987) by Neil Hughes

KEG RIVER POST OFFICE
Present location SE-12-101-23-W5.
Opened July 23, 1932
Postmasters:
L. G. Harrington
Mrs. Emma McDonald
T. Harry Bowe
J. R. (Bob) Jackson
N. G. Simpson
W. Osborne
T. Petersen
J. R. Riczu
Mark and Sondra Viau
Doreen Brick
Betty Hasenack

PADDLE PRAIRIE POST OFFICE
(19-103-21-W5)
Opened June 1, 1946
Postmasters:
Mrs. A. Martineau
Mrs. P. Johnston

Charlie with team that he hauled mail from Paddle Prairie to Carcajou, 1955.

Mail plane.

J. Cahill
F. E. Farwell
Mrs. V. Chalifoux
W. R. Wood
E. J. Tomlinson
F. Wilkie
F. E. Lackwood
G. W. McCullough
Mrs. C. E. Parenteau
Mrs. E. Olson
Mrs. E. J. Martineau
Mrs. B. Ghostkeeper
Barbara Auger
Greta Ghostkeeper
Lisa Webber
Joan Wanuch

CARCAJOU POST OFFICE
(30-101-19-W5)
Opened December 1, 1923
Postmasters:
C. Rankin

M. M. Rankin
M. H. Stigsen
S. Sivertsen

Carcajou Point Memories
by Muriel Stigsen

Supposedly one of the oldest settlements along the mighty Peace River, Carcajou Point had a trading post that opened in the early 1800's. It was the first settlement along the river to have a post office.

My dad was an adventurous person who came to the Point in 1920. He "saw the place and liked it". It became our home. My dad enjoyed gold-seeking, so we had moved from place to place prior to this.

My mother, Mrs. Martha M. Rankin, became involved in persistent letter writing, had a petition signed by all that could, and finally was granted the post office for Carcajou in 1927.

The Rankin farm and Carcajou Post Office in the 1930's.

In those days the mail was carried by boat in the summer, mostly on the Hudson's Bay *Weenusk*. It made the trip every two weeks with Doug Catenhead at the wheel.

In the winter it was a different story. Louis Bourassa was the mail courier and there were no pleasure trips. He travelled overland and on the river ice with teams of horses and bob sleighs. Northbound, he hauled sacks of mail, horse feed and other necessities. Southbound, bales of fur were added to the outgoing mail.

Once, Louis and his helpers had a close call as the river started breaking up behind them. They made a mad rush for shore and scrambled up the bank somehow. Then they had to slash their way overland to Carcajou, where they could resume their trip to Fort Vermilion on the ice.

Carcajou portage trail.

Depending on the freeze-up date, Louis tried to make a trip once a month. Generally there was one trip just before Christmas. In doing this he became our Santa. The last trip was late in March.

The postmistress was always on duty – day and night. Time was never considered. Whenever anyone happened by, he or she stopped for mail, had a visit and caught up on the news about neighbors.

The trappers and travellers came from up and down the river as far as 30 or 40 miles in any direction. Some of these were Jack Costello, Al Boyd and later, Hans Leu, the photographer. He thought the portage was a great advantage.

Hal Boyd and his dog that performed tricks which included smoking a pipe.

CARCAJOU PORTAGE
Just a pioneer trail
With an historic memory of the past,
It provides an interesting tale
For those who pass-
Trapper, trader, white man and Indian alike
Armstrong's later it saved many a mile
Although quite a pull or hike.
Our mail courier Louis Bourassa
Regarded it quite a trial.

The people coming from Keg River for mail had the worry of trying to find a way to cross the river. They usually chose row-boat or canoe. In later years a rifle shot would bring Ted over to get them with his boat. A few of the Keg River people who got their mail here were Hutchings, Jackson, Wilson, Root, Lane, Bowe and Trosky.

In the late 1930's and 1940's, mail was delivered to Mrs. Rankin's post office in Carcajou and into Keg River by airplane, which also carried passengers. One pilot, Stan Warren, was killed due to poor visibility caused by forest fires at Fort Vermilion. The last planes were Norsemen.

In the mid-40's the planes stopped flying and mail was once again brought to Carcajou by boat in the summer. Harry Bowe then had the contract to haul the mail on to the residents of Keg River. This lasted until the end of boating in 1952. By that time the old MacKenzie Highway, referred to as the "Cow Path", took over all traffic, making another change in mail service.

C. G. Rankin had the contract for several years. He hired different people to take and bring the mail from the closest point on the highway at Paddle Prairie. Charlie Christian with his horse and flat sleigh was one of the last haulers.

In 1958-59 Mr. Rankin was stricken by illness and left Carcajou for medical care. It was my husband Ted Stigsen who took over the mail-hauling contract.

Just two years later I took over the post office from my mother. This ended her 33 years as postmistress. Things went well for us since we had both been involved previously. I had been assistant post mistress for some time.

Quite a change occurred in 1963-64 when a road was built so the government could haul gravel out to the MacKenzie Highway. Thousands of loads have been hauled out to the stockpile for paving and gravelling local roads. This development finally gave Carcajou access to the MacKenzie Highway.

We handled the mail ourselves until 1982, when I retired after 22 years on the job. The post office has been handed on to another family member. Our daughter, Sandra, and our son-in-law, Dennis Sivertsen, have had the mail contract for the past 11 years. It is picked up at Keg River and brought to Carcajou on Fridays.

Well into a lifetime, just a few loyal patrons are left – those who don't mind weekly mail. Marie Christian, who passed away in February, 1992, started getting her mail in Carcajou in 1927. Vincent Armstrong and myself are also original patrons.

Trappers who lived here and there along the river at that time have been replaced several times down through the years. Most have died, like the memorable couple, John and Olive Okerholm. They were as different in nature as two could be. He liked entertaining with his accordion. She liked being entertained by a house full of kids. They left for the coast in 1935.

The Okerholms returned 10 years later and lived for a time in an abandoned trapper's cabin up river from Carcajou. He later built a house right in the settlement. They loved the old Peace.

In the 1960's they had to move to where they could get medical care. They chose Westerose. Several years later they passed away.

Great Slave Railway
by Anne Vos

The Great Slave Railway or GSLR was promised in Peace River in 1957 by then Prime Minister John Diefenbaker. As early as 1954 Consolidated Mining and Smelting had established that sizable deposits of lead-zinc ore existed at Pine Point. It was decided that railway would be the method of transportation used to get this ore to market. Many forestry products and grain could also be transported via the railway.

For two years a Royal Commission studied the proposed routes. Two of the routes considered were an eastern one via Waterways and a more westerly one via Peace River and Grimshaw. The distance and cost of construction on the two routes were believed to be comparable.

Gerald Baldwin, who served as the Conservative Member of Parliament for more than 20 years, was convinced there would be more benefits to Alberta if the railway travelled through the more settled area of the province. With Ged's strong voice lobbying for the route through Peace River and Grimshaw, this was the route that was finally chosen. Once the route was selected, the residents of Keg River knew that they too would see the benefits of the new railway.

Gerald Baldwin is better known for his crusade to enact legislation to allow Canadian citizens more access to government files. The Freedom of Information Act is now law, but it was his action in regard to the railway that has had the most impact on the residents of Keg River. Ged was praised in the *Peace River Record Gazette* for his work in seeing that a railway was built. "If it hadn't been for his prodding and hard work the railway may never have become a reality in our area".

The line was to begin at Roma (between Grimshaw and Peace River) and travel through Manning, Keg River, High Level into the North West Territories and end at Hay River on the Great Slave Lake. A 53-mile line was to leave the main line and run to Pine Point. The 377 miles were to be the longest piece of railway construction in North America for many years. It was also the most northerly with Hay River being at latitude 61°.

Initial surveys began in January 1961 and by the end of 1962 most of the land agreements were concluded. Groundbreaking occurred at Roma in February 1962. The construction was expected to take until 1966 and cost $86 million but the railway was ready for use in October 1964 at an actual cost of $75 million!

The extreme conditions of cold under which the men worked made breakdowns the norm. For much of the time the men were isolated in their

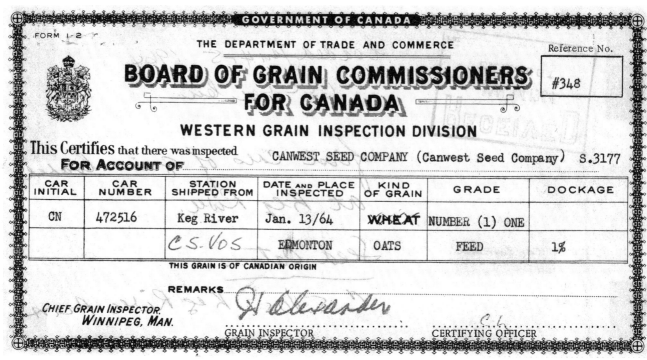

FORM I-2

THE DEPARTMENT OF TRADE AND COMMERCE

BOARD OF GRAIN COMMISSIONERS FOR CANADA

WESTERN GRAIN INSPECTION DIVISION

Reference No.

#348

This Certifies that there was inspected

FOR ACCOUNT OF CANWEST SEED COMPANY (Canwest Seed Company) S.3177

CAR INITIAL	CAR NUMBER	STATION SHIPPED FROM	DATE and PLACE INSPECTED	KIND OF GRAIN	GRADE	DOCKAGE
CN	472516	Keg River	Jan. 13/64	WHEAT	NUMBER (1) ONE	
		C.S. VOS	EDMONTON	OATS	FEED	1%

THIS GRAIN IS OF CANADIAN ORIGIN

REMARKS

CHIEF GRAIN INSPECTOR.
WINNIPEG, MAN.

GRAIN INSPECTOR   CERTIFYING OFFICER

Inspection Certificate of first railroad car of grain to leave Keg River, 1964.

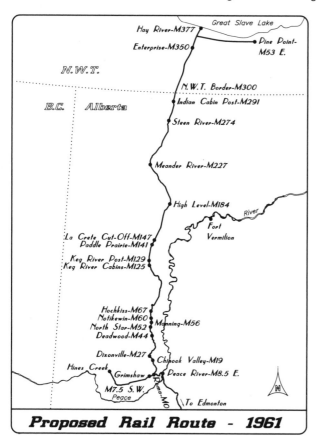

Proposed Rail Route - 1961

Proposed and final rail route.

work camps, but from time to time they were greeted by local folks welcoming them and offering them food and hot coffee.

The people of Keg River were no exception.

They held a fundraising raffle for the community hall based on the time and date the track would be laid across the Keg River road!

The railway led to the building of the United Grain Growers elevator at Keg River. The direct benefits of the elevator to local farmers have been immense. Some farmers now even ship their grain themselves by ordering railcars through Canadian National (CN) and filling the cars themselves on the siding at Keg River.

When the pipeline was built later in the 1960's, many carloads of pipe were shipped to Keg River on the rails. Power line poles were also delivered to our area in this manner.

United Grain Growers Elevator in Keg River
by Johnny Vos

The Great Slave Lake Railway (known as the Pine Point Line) was built in the years from 1962 to 1964. The railroad was primarily for minerals and forestry products but United Grain Growers (U.G.G.) saw the opportunity to better serve their customers and applied for a site at Keg River in July 1964.

There was no siding at Keg River and one would be necessary for railcars to be moved off the main railway and loaded at Keg River. Canadian National Railways was not optimistic about building a siding in 1964, stating that the grounds were in poor condition and impassable when wet.

However U.G.G. started building, with construction of the 64000-bushel elevator complete by December 8. Living quarters for the elevator operator were built adjoining the office and a large feed and farm supply shed was added the next year.

Prior to this time, Grimshaw was the nearest point to market grain grown in Keg River. It was one of the largest grain handling sites in Western Canada in the 1950's. Delivering grain to Grimshaw meant a 120-mile haul over roads that were often in very poor shape, a trip that took about five hours one way.

With the new elevator the trip was reduced to between three and 20 miles for Keg River farmers. The elevator also serves as a delivery point for Carcajou, Paddle Prairie, Buffalo Head Prairie, and La Crete farmers.

The Keg River elevator became the most northerly elevator in the U.G.G. system. It is located at NW-23-101-23-W5. The elevator was also one of the first to use a steel leg. The elevator opened on December 15, 1964, when Ted Petersen became the first operator.

UGG elevator just after it was completed, 1964.

Official opening ceremonies were held in April 1965 and were attended by the United Grain Growers President, Mr. Runciman. W. G. Winslow, the Western Division Manager, and D. J. Burch, the Elevator Superintendent, also joined the 300 local people who turned up for the celebration. Alex Hamelin cut the ribbon and Len de Haan delivered the first load of grain. Following the ribbon-cutting ceremonies at the elevator, a supper was served by the ladies club at the community hall. Mr. Runciman spoke at the supper, which was followed by a dance.

When the elevator was opened, the goal was to ship 100 000 bushels of grain per year. Now over two million bushels have been shipped!

The first United Grain Growers Local was organized at a meeting on April 20, 1971. Some members had previously taken part in the Manning Local. I was elected secretary of the local and have remained in this position since. Others elected to the first local board were:

Steve Kelemen, Jr. – chairman
Garth Coulter
Pete I. Friesen
Paul Galandy
Otto Krause
Mike Michalchuk
Adam Pawlowich
Steve Pawlowich
Walter Prochinsky
Peter J. Schroh
Wim Vos
Victor Zatko

Steve Kelemen was the first delegate to represent the Keg River local at the annual meeting. Steve Kelemen was the chairman from 1971 to 1974, followed by Garth Coulter (1974-76) and Pete I. Friesen (1976-93).

The elevator managers at Keg River: Ted R. Petersen from December 15, 1964, to January 9, 1969 Norman R. Lowe from January 9, 1969, to January 15, 1972 Bruce Meashaw from June 15, 1972, to April 10,1973 Les Freeman from April 10, 1973, to present.

Oil, Gas and Pipelines
by Anne Vos

On September 29, 1965, the *Peace River Record Gazette* reported: ''Rainbow Oil Activity Continues to Flourish''

''The Banff-Aquitane Socony group has chalked up quite a score to date this year. Six oil wells in four separate pools, four dry holes and six wells are presently drilling. All this in a 15-mile radius. The newest well was brought in half a mile north of the discovery wells which launched development in Keg River reef for Imperial Oil.''

The Imperial Oil road from Keg River Village to the Rainbow oil patch was used for a couple of years during the winter months. The effect of all this oil business travelling through our tiny community was immense. Local farm people were

Tanks on the road by the Post headed to Rainbow Lake, 1960's.

Tank heading for Rainbow Lake, 1960's.

able to get jobs through the winter. Adam Pawlowich drove fuel truck. Paul Galandy was camp caretaker. Garry Galandy worked on the pipeline where he lost a thumb attaching a pipeline anchor. The Zatko family operated the "gate" on the ESSO road.

Looking south from the elevator, notice pipe for the Rainbow Pipeline and Vos warehouse in the distance.

Several businesses moved into the district. Ace Explosives, owned and operated by Bert Allen, supplied the seismograph companies. Dirk Vos Transport operated a warehouse at the railroad siding and hauled many truckloads of drilling supplies to the rigs. Henry Dillman of Manning set up a bulk fuel station to supply the oil patch. Garth Coulter was one of the operators at the station.

During the winter of 1965-66 there were 70 or more drilling rigs working in the region.

Dillman's camp and Esso bulk fuel station which was located north of the UGG elevator.

Oil drilling rig on Adam Pawlowich's.

GAS

The Keg River-Paddle Prairie area is covering a large store of natural gas. There are a number of compressor stations working nearby. We are on the southeast corner of a gas field that extends northwest almost to Rainbow Lake. At Keg River the wells are about 1200 feet deep and most of them produce sweet gas.

Gas exploration at Keg River.

This area is served by the North Peace Gas Co-op of Fairview. They buy gas and have a pipeline distribution system to the farm homes, grain driers, and any other requirements. This industry also provides jobs to area residents.

The *Oilweek Magazine Archives*, 1991 Leslie Roland "An Extraordinary Exercise in Engineering Expertise" "Laying pipeline across sub-zero muskeg of northwestern Alberta is no picnic on the prairies. In 1966 Rainbow Pipe Line Company Ltd. (now equally owned by Mobil Canada, Shell and Imperial Oil) was created to design and build a pipeline to stretch from Rainbow Lake to the Nipisi oilfield near Slave Lake.

By the time the line was built in March 1966 the Company had broken nearly the entire Canadian supply of ditcher teeth on the rock-hard soil. But Rainbow grit its own teeth and laid the pipe foot by foot, setting a record for speed and equipment volume that hasn't been matched on other remote lines in 25 years." The lack of a communication system was frustrating to many of the workers who came to our remote area of Alberta. One described the situation, "The telephone service was terrible. They can put a man on the moon but you couldn't make a phone call out of that area."

Transportation through the bush was also difficult. There were no roads when they started! The hastily developed "roads" could only be travelled when the ground was frozen or with swamp-buggies when soft.

Gerry Dawson was the first Mobil employee sent into the area. He recalls, "The second winter up there was unbelievably cold. A welding truck was sitting on the line with its cables out. One of the welders went out to wind up the cables and they actually disintegrated in his hands."

The enormous quantity of pipe used in building this section of the line came in on the railroad to the Keg River siding and was hauled by truck from there.

Fifteen miles south of the Keg River at the Kemp River, there is a large pumping station on the Rainbow pipeline. It is operated entirely by the Supervisory Control and Data Acquisition System. During the 25 years of service, 1.4 billion barrels of oil have been pumped through this system.

Bannister Construction was a subcontractor on this pipeline job, putting a large, 300-man camp at Keg River Post during the winter of 1966.

The community held dances and showed movies. Attendance was no longer a problem, as many of those in camp were happy to have some entertainment. Some of the dances got out of hand with fights erupting, but fund raising in Keg River had never been so profitable. Nor had the dances been so interesting as when the ratio of men to women increased to about 10 to one!

Seismograph testing with Jackson's house in background, 1942.

Keg River Forest Rangers
by Anne Vos

Forest rangers and game guardians were one and the same in the 1920's. The first guardian here was Rene Gicquel. He was a World War I veteran. In 1918 when he was discharged, he married Celestine Lisotte Bourgault of Fort Vermilion. She had three married sisters in Keg River: Mrs. Flora Bowe, Mrs. Rose Beaulieu and Mrs. Philomene Elson.

Packed and ready to go fight forest fires. Thomas Stoney, Pete Rudy, Dan Gray and pack dogs.

Eusebe (Babe) Bourassa was the next warden. He arrived in the early 1930's and stayed for at least one winter. It was an extremely cold winter. New Year's Day it was -60°F. Babe was at a party and had to go home by dog team. When he arrived at his home he was sleeping so soundly he never went into the house. Unfortunately, one foot was out of the cariole and it froze very badly. He was on crutches the rest of the winter, but in time the foot healed completely.

Fred Hartley came to his job as warden in 1937. He was originally from England. Fred was in our area until 1940, when he enlisted in the Canadian Air Force. While here he married Mary Rudy and their first daughter Marilyn was born here.

Aerial photo of Keg River Forestry Station.

The following is a list of the forest rangers and game wardens that followed Fred Hartley.

"Frank" L. LaFoy	1946 – 1951
"Jack" W. Grant	1951 – 1953
S. "Eddie" Beebe	1952 – 1954
B. H. "Johnny" Johnston	1955 – 1961
Horst Rohde	1964
J. H. Moll	1964
Ken South	1964 – 1966
Gordon Bisgrove	1964 – 1967
Ray Kover	1965 – 1967
Peter Nortcliffe	1968
Wayne Rutter	1968
Frank Vandriel	1972
Brian Carnell	1972 – 1973
R. T. Stewart	1973
R. A. "Terry" Van Nest	1973 – 1975
G. F. Crowder	1973 – 1976
Ross Graham	1975 – 1979
Rob Thorburn	1976 – 1980
Kevin Freehill	1980 – 1981

In 1981 the Keg River Forest Ranger Station was closed. The operations were run out of Manning following the closure.

Keg River Forestry Lookout Tower, 1993.

Hawk Hills Tower which is located twenty miles south of Keg River cabins was built in 1961 and electrical power was installed in 1991. Keg Tower, located twenty-five miles southwest of the cabins, is accessible by helicopter only and was built in 1959. A local lookout tower was constructed in 1955 on the Naylor Hills south of

1974 Native Fire Crew Competition, Keg River.

Keg River Native Firefighting Crew, 1974. L-R, Thomas Stoney, Arthur Chalifoux, Coosta Hamlin, Dan House, Archie Chalifoux, Freddy House, Clifford Ghostkeeper with Manny Ducharme in front.

Competitor Crest.

land now owned by David Batchelor. It was 80 feet high and was removed in 1976.

Local Government
by Anne Vos

Prior to 1940 the usual method of communicating our problems to the "powers that be" was a letter expressing our concerns or a petition signed by community members. The mail was reliable but it could take a month for an answer to be received.

If the problem was urgent there was the telegraph office and we could have the operator send a message to Peace River by Morse code!

Territorial units were amalgamated as improvement districts in 1945, 12 units became Improvement District (I.D.) #146. The Administrator would come to the district twice a year and consult with local people regarding problems and where roads were required. Mr. Harry Goy was our administrator for a number of years. Meetings were held on the hood of the administrator's pickup and were usually over in half an hour!

In 1968 I.D. #146 and 147 were joined to form I.D. 23. Several representatives were appointed from Keg River. Johnny Vos and Vic Zatko served as advisory councillors in 1971 on a seven-man board with meetings held in High Level. Again in 1974 the advisory council was appointed. This was changed in 1977 to locally elected councillors serving three-year terms.

The boundaries were altered again in 1977 to allow for two new divisions or wards and two more representatives. Johnny Vos continued as chairman until 1981 when the boundaries were changed one more time and Keg River was moved into I.D. 22. The meetings were then held in Manning or Peace River. Two of the others who served on the I.D. advisory board were Harold Dutchuk and Ted Petersen.

We were represented on the council of I.D. 22 by J. Vos until the 1983 election. Louis Pawlowich was elected from Keg River on a seven-man board. He attended for two years. Henry Vos was elected in 1986 followed by Alan Godkin in 1989. Alan is currently serving his second term and is the chairman of the board.

Keg River Library.

Daishowa – Marubeni Pulpmill, Peace River.

CHAPTER IV
COMMUNITY LIFE

Spring Song
by John M. Okerholm

Now spring has arrived, and new life is about,
In the valleys and dells all around
Now rills and creeks have all broken out,
From the winter which had them all bound.

This is the time I love so to roam,
When the bushes and trees come to life.
The squirrel is building his summer home,
And the robin is courting a wife.

I set out this morning to enjoy a stroll,
Among evergreen: Spruce and Pine,
And here in the dell, right behind the knoll,
I found flowers of the loveliest kind.

Sky-blue crocus, they stood all around,
A Heavenly Host, indeed.
There were scores and scores, all over the
    ground,
Like children at a Jubilee.

They would nod and sway in the morning
    breeze,
Like dancers on a beautiful green.
They all wore robes, against a late spring
    freeze,
Of the loveliest fur I have seen.

Their sky-blue faces they all turned to me,
And showed me their beautiful pearls,
Which the dew had brought, and they wore
    with glee,
Like a tiara on the loveliest curls.

And there they stood in their lovely array,
As proud as a well-robed Queen.
No doubt they were as happy as a bride on
    her way
To her wedding on some bowery green.

Beautiful blossom, you brought joy to me,
And I will remember your dance to the end.
And when I grow old, you will come back to
    me,
And dance in my memory again.

School at Carcajou
by Margaret Befus

Mrs. Martha Rankin taught her daughter Muriel at home prior to any school being built in Carcajou. Probably others did the same.

The first school was built at Carcajou Point in 1934 and is still standing today. It was not ready for use until after New Year's 1935. The teachers boarded with Mrs. Rankin.

Carcajou Point School sketched by Vi Hopkins.

The teachers at the Carcajou Point School were:

1935   Agnes Thompson
1935-36 Betty Pope
1936-37 Marie Siren
1937-38 Charlie Allen
1938-60 Closed
1960-66 Edna Kiselczuk
1966-68 Margaret Befus

During the period from 1938 to 1960 when no school was open in Carcajou, the Tupper family among others were educated with the help of correspondence lessons. 1955 Correspondence School records show Dianna, Patsy, and Noviena were all doing Grade nine by correspondence.

Students of Carcajou Point School.

In 1960 Mrs. Kiselczuk bought Slim Kemp's farm with the intention of setting up a school for local children. She had made a trip in during the summer, travelling by team and wagon. There was only a poor wagon trail to this isolated community. In August she returned with all of her supplies. Clarence Ferguson was hired to haul her belongings in with a team of horses. Dennis Sivertson was along to help her move. He walked ahead of the horses.

The school was in her yard and the students had to walk there. The Christian, Tupper and Stone children were the first pupils.

The following year, Fort Vermilion School Division built a school for the district on SE-16-101-19-W5. The school was equipped with a wood stove, but no power.

Carcajou School – Mrs. Kiselczuk and children.

Mrs. Kiselczuk stayed on as the teacher. Now she, too, had to travel to the school. The new school was two miles from her place. She walked, travelled on snowshoes or skied to the school. Finally she bought a Fordson tractor and drove it to school.

During the five years she taught at Carcajou, seldom was she unable to be at school, even though she was often in poor health. She had a very painful problem with her legs and feet. Her deep religious beliefs and a desire to help the children kept her going. A number of people helped her with her farm, including the Stone family, Matt Raey, Mr. Zurovec and Len Clare.

I began teaching in Carcajou in 1966, by which time Northland School Division was in charge.

Those sending their children were Charlie, Archie, George and Joe Christian, the Tuppers, the Stigsens, and my husband and I.

This was one of the best-equipped schools I had ever seen. There were supplies for ten years including a battery-powered record player and piles of records.

In 1967 we had a road connecting Carcajou with the MacKenzie Highway and I took the students on a field trip to Peace River. Northland supplied the bus, which was driven by Clarence Houle. We had to raise money for food and rooms. The kids did all sorts of things to raise the money. Some even picked roots! We took our sleeping bags and had two motel rooms.

We enjoyed the trips we made to Keg River for the track meets. We didn't have many participants compared to the Paddle Prairie and Keg River schools but we had fun anyway.

In the late fall of 1968, the Carcajou school was no more. All 23 students and myself were moved to Dr. Mary Jackson school in Keg River. Later the school building itself was moved. The building was used as a classroom at Keg River for a short time, then it was moved to Garden River.

Since 1968 the school bus drivers have been Donald Stigsen, Bill Brick, Claude Estelle, Wilf Dupuis, Larry Michalchuk, Garth Coulter, Leonard Senft, Ted and Nora Petersen, Skinny Christian, Leona Christian, Berta Mosure and Doris Christian. They have taken varying numbers of children to school.

Carcajou School – Sunday School.

Keg River Schools
by Mary Lou Ng

(Much of the information in this article was obtained from documents in the Alberta Archives.)

In 1927 the struggle for a school in the Keg River district began with a letter dated March 1st from Frank Jackson to the Minister of Education. Mr. Jackson estimated that there were 30 children of school age in the district. He offered to "build the school with the exception of the cost of the floor and windows, providing a sod roof was sufficient to meet the laws regarding schools".

In further information that was provided to the Department of Education later in 1927, it was estimated that 38 children of school age lived in the district. According to the requirements of the department, the children were divided into the following categories: 2 whites, 24 metis, and 12 treaty Indians.

The matter was referred to the Inspector of Schools for the area, Bill Yule of Grande Prairie. He made a trip to Fort Vermilion and spoke with two Hudson Bay employees on the boat who informed him that it was impossible to get into Keg River. So without being able to visit the area and speak to the residents, he made the following recommendation: "I am very doubtful if an attempt to establish and operate a school in this settlement could be successful." He did not support this point of view with a reason.

In a letter dated September 15, 1927, the deputy minister then responded to Mr. Jackson advising him of the doubt of operating a school. "... The Department feels that until we are supplied with more definite information as to how it is proposed to finance the operation of a school in that locality, it would be very unwise to sanction the formation of such a district."

During this time, the Department of Education would support school districts with a very basic allowance of $1.10 per day for each day that the school was open, and the district was responsible for the remainder of the needs of the school. No grants were available for the building of schools. This was done through local property taxes and volunteer work of the people of the community.

For districts that had been in operation for more than two years the per-day grant decreased to 90 cents! The grants were payable at the end of the school term. An equalization grant was also available for 160 days in the year and was dependent on the valuation of the land in the school district.

On July 12, 1930, a meeting was held for the

KEG RIVER TRADING CO.,

Keg River
Per Peace River Crossing
Mar 18th '27.

The Minister of Education
Edmonton.
Alta.

Dear Sir

I am writing to you in regards
to an proposed school that we need here in
the settlement of Keg River. Last summer I
wrote to a Archdeacon White. trying to
get his support so as to get the Indian Department
to help in the maintenance of the school.
us their will be treaty Indian's children going to the
school. But I hear he has taken sick,
& enrolled home to England. And not hearing
from him, so do not know what was done.
However, I am trying to get a school, regardless
of Mr White. their are very few homesteaders
now in this locality. thei are mostly trappers
living in a compact settlement.

2.

Their are about thirty children that should
be going to school here.
What my idea was, is to incorporate this as
a village. their are the Hudson Bay Co. Junction
Stores Trading Co. & Myself also a Trader
& about twelve families living in this settlement
They are all willing to assist in paying for
the up keep of the school. That is the families.
I do not know about the Companys
If we could do this we could levy a scool tax
so they would have to all pay
And Tax them on assessment Plan.
The Companys are making their living out of the
residents so why not help to educate them.
For my part I will more than do my share.
I have two boys that I have sent to Sheridan
Lawrence School this winter at Vermillion
Naturally I would prefer to have them at home
Still we want for a start is a six month school
during the winter months.
I my self will build the school. excepting the cost
of the windows. floor & door.
Providing a sod roof is sufficent to meet with

3.

the laws regarding schools
I think it is perfectly good enough for a start.
kindly let me hear your opinion on this.
subject. at your earliest convenience
As we would like to get this under way by next winter
if possible.

Your Obedient Servant.

Frank Jackson.

P.S. On reading through this letter, I find I should
have stated, in building the school it would be done.
without any cost to any one. but myself.

Petition for school, 1927. Document courtesy of Alberta Provincial Archives, No. 84.37/3850a.

KEG RIVER TRADING CO.

FUR TRADERS AND DEALERS IN FINE FURS

KEG RIVER, July 12th 1930.
VIA PEACE RIVER
ALBERTA

The Department of Eduication,
Eduication,

Dear Sir,

On attached sheet you will find the minets of the first
school meeting held at Keg River.

The comittie that was appointed requests the Department to
send all regulations pertaining to the opening of a school ,also
the Alberta School Act.

The following is a list of the children and there age.

Mike Ternowski	age six years.
Toney Ternowski	age ten years.
Mary M., Rudy	Age ten years.
Fred Rudy	age seven years.
Walter Rudy	age six years.
John Yurkowskie	age fourteen years.
Annie Yurkowskie	age fourteen years.
Earl Elson	age six years.
Luie Jackson	age twelve years.
Arthur Jackson	eleven years.
Ethelyne Root	age fourteen years.
Elma root	age twelve years.
Fredrick Desheram	age fourteen years.
Samul Desheram	age ten years.
Jamery Desheram	age ten years.
John Desheram	age eight years.
Vina Ferguson	age nine years.

(17)

Trusting that this will be satisfactory,and that you
answer us as soon as possible.

Yours uery truely

Chairman   Mike Rudy

Sec   D.E. MacLeod

Trust   J. W. Stewart

Letter for school, 1927. Document courtesy of Alberta Provincial Archives, No. 83.37/3850a.

purpose of discussing the possibility of getting a school. The land owners that were present were:

Mr. A Brick	Mr. Lane
Mike Yurkowski	Mike Rudy
H. A. Trosky	John Elson
Hume Stewart	Nick Tomilou
Fred Deursice	D. E. MacLeod
H. Bowe	D. M. Rudy

At this meeting this list of students of school age was drawn up. (Their age is given in brackets.)

Mike Ternowski (6)	Mary M. Rudy (10)
Toney Ternowski (10)	Fred Rudy (7)
Earl Elson (6)	Walter Rudy (6)
Louis Jackson (12)	John Yurkowski (14)
Arthur Jackson (11)	Annie Yurkowski (14)
Ethelyne Root (14)	Frederick Ducharme (14)
Alma Root (12)	Samuel Ducharme (10)
Vina Ferguson (9)	Jean Marie Ducharme (10)
John Ducharme (8)	

In March 1931, the Department of Education approved the boundaries applied for and asked that another public meeting be held. It was, but the result was a setback for those who wanted a school in Keg River. A disappointed Mr. Jackson wrote to the deputy minister, "It was voted by the majority of voters that we let the matter ride for the time being, as the people were too poor to maintain a school. Now what can a person do, where you have all the foreign element voting against a school, so they do not have to pay taxes."

In 1932, a school inspector was able to visit the Keg River area. George L. Wilson reported the following: "I believe that this settlement could support a short-term school but it appears that the people do not wish to take any action at the present time and I did not urge that they should."

He also reported that the total assessed value of all the lands within a four-mile radius of the central point of the settlement (SW-28-101-24-W5) was approximately $13 000 and the number of quarters filed was 35.

Dr. Jackson became directly involved in the struggle to establish a school in Keg River in April 1937 with a telephone call to Fred McNally, the Deputy Minister of Education. And finally things began to happen! On August 5, 1937, the Keg River School District #4784 was established by order of the Minister of Education, Mr. William Aberhart.

By August 30, Miss Winifred Lawrence had made her way from England to take charge of the students. They first met in the hospital building. Miss Lawrence welcomed students of any age provided they really wanted to learn! There were 23 students in the first class. My mom was one of the youngest at the age of five.

The students in that first class sat on the floor, learned to spell long word lists and practised their arithmetic on small slates that Miss Lawrence had brought with her from England. Mom still hates the noise of chalk on slate!

The first Keg River school 1937-1951.

The school was completed through volunteer community effort. The windows were added as soon as they arrived and the shingles were being installed by Nick Tomilou and Harry Bowe as the students began to study in their new school! George Hrytciuk built desks that were sturdy and each had room for two students! The teacher's desk is still in use today at the community hall, 56 years after it was made. The total cost to the Department of Education for the first school was $150 for the shingles and windows!

During the first year of operation of the school, Miss Winifred Lawrence with her 2nd class teaching certificate taught for $4.00 a day and taught for 197 days. The school was closed from April 25 to 29 because of an epidemic of influenza. Most of the time during her employment at the school she was not paid regularly, as the school board waited for receipt of government grants and taxes from local property owners.

The names of the students who attended during the first year of the school's operation, their ages, grades and the number of days they attended are given in the table below.

Name Attended	Age	Grade(s)	Days
John Ducharme	14	3	18
Malcolm Ducharme	13	3/4	196
Alphonse Ducharme	11	3/4	193
Lloyd Elson	12	3/4	179
Bill Rudy	10	3/4	182
Mike Rudy	12	3/4	182.5
Clifford Minault	11	1/3	164

Russell Minault	9	1/3	183
Frank Chalifoux	13	1/2	147
Donald Chalifoux	7	1	183.5
Billy Yurkowski	8	1/3	194.5
Tommy Ducharme	9	1	192
Jim Hamelin	10	1	154
Donald Hamelin	8	1	133
Louisa Ferguson	6	1	191
Anne Jackson	6	1	187.5
Emma Noskey	6	1	181
Clarence Ferguson	7	1	187.5
Eddy Halabisky	6	1	193
Dan Trosky	7	1	180
Marie Cardinal	6	1	129.5
Fred Rudy	14	1/5	150
Lloyd Wanuch	7	1	158
Arthur Bowe	7	1	38*
Emma Cardinal	9	1	83.5*
Archie Christian	8	1	53.5*
Dorothy Dumont	13	3	61*

* started during the January to June term.

The school had an average attendance of 88.3% from September to December and 89.2% for January to June.

During the years Miss Lawrence was at Keg River, she also operated a night school. In 1937 the school was attended by six students for 43 nights. The students were charged 50 cents per night!

No problems were reported regarding the collection of taxes until 1940. Then the school board appointed R.C.Catherwood as bailiff for the school district. He was asked to begin collecting the taxes from those in arrears on March 1, 1940.

Students with teacher Pat O'Connor in front of Keg River School, 1942.

Mr. Yaroslow Romanchuk must have been targeted on the first day because it was March 1, 1940, when he telegraphed the Alberta Attorney General with a plea. Mr. Catherwood had seized two cows from Romanchuk's farm for nonpayment of taxes. He said he didn't have the money to pay his taxes because he had not had the opportunity to work. Later on May 20, he wrote the school department saying, "Harry Bowe and Frank Jackson have something against me". He also alleged that the school board was not properly accounting for the money they were collecting in taxes.

With difficulties continuing in the operation of the school, 20 Keg River residents asked the

School Gathering. Back Row, L-R: Anne Jackson, ?, Billy Yurkowski, ?, Dan Trosky, ?, Mrs. Eva Harrington. Middle, L-R: ?, Mrs. Trosky, Mary Pawlowich, Sophie Michalchuk, Pat Hague, Eddie Halabisky, ?, Arthur Bowe, ?. Front, L-R: Trosky boy, Alma Ferguson, Noskeye girl, Marie Trosky, Myrna Halabisky, Emma Noskeye, Martha Fedorchuk, John Jackson, Daisy Fedorchuk, John Hague, Mervin Rudy. Man seated – unknown.

Inspector of Schools that their district be incorporated into the Peace River District. During the discussions that followed, the estimates for operating the school ranged from $1200 to $2000 per year. The Peace River District protested the idea of adding the Keg River school to their district and the plan did not proceed.

A new school with a built-on teacherage was built in Keg River in 1950 at a cost of $6500. It was opened on November 24, 1950. Miss Paul was teaching at Keg River then and her students celebrated the opening by writing "thank you" letters or drawing sketches of the new school and sending them to the Minister of Education.

The Catholics of the district tried to hire Catholic teachers for the school, but were not always successful.

In 1955 the school board authorized Father

The grade 8 class of 1954, winners of the third consecutive silver cup for their essay in the Alberta Tuberculosis essay contest. Back, L-R: Dr. Jackson, Arthur Chalifoux, Roderick Ferguson, Henry Ducharme, Miss. Paul, Superintendent Hooper. Front, L-R: Helen Michalchuk, Allene Brick, Violet Ferguson, Pat Ross.

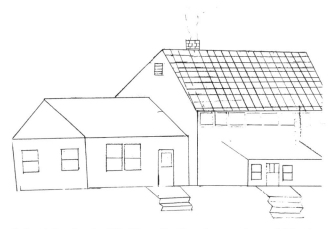

School drawing by Rita Hamelin. Drawing courtesy of Alberta Provincial Archives, No. 84.37/3850d.

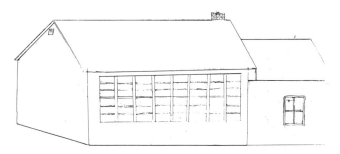

School drawing by Roderick Ferguson. Drawing courtesy of Alberta Provincial Archives, No. 84.37/3850d.

Letter to Dr. Swift thanking him for the new school. Document courtesy of Alberta Provincial Archives, No. 84.37/3850d.

Michalchuk children going to school with horse and sleigh, 1952.

Miss. Paul's class of 1954, Keg River School.

Jean to visit the school to teach Catechism every Friday from 3 to 3:30 pm, but they failed to inform Miss Mallinger of their decision. On Father Jean's first visit to the school she refused to let him enter!

Many families in the district lived far enough from the school at the post that their children could not regularly attend school. Some of these children took correspondence lessons at home. Records show that Gordon Reid took grade one by correspondence in 1955.

In the 1950's other schools were started for the education of the children of the sawmill employees, and one along the highway near the cabins for children living in that area. The Naylor Hills, Kemp Creek and Tall Timbers schools were operated with funding from the provincial government, providing they had certified teachers. The Kemp Creek School operated at the sawmill owned by the Boucher family. One of the teachers there was René Garant. Mrs. Robertson, Mrs. Louise Schultz and Mrs. Ressler taught in the Naylor Hills school. Mrs. Jean Polasek and Mrs. Shultz also taught in the Tall Timbers school.

In December 1956 the school districts of Keg River, Naylor Hills and Blackbirds Creek and Carcajou were transferred to Fort Vermilion School District #52 and Dr. Jackson became a

Mildred Mallinger's class of 1955, Keg River School.

Tall Timbers School at Bryan's Mill, 1961. Notice the homemade furniture.

Shirley and Irene returning home from school. A round trip of 13 miles, 1958.

Pat Ross's class standing to leave the room, 1960.

trustee representing our area. More change came on July 1, 1963, when Keg River was transferred to Northland School Division #61 by order of the Minister of Education.

Dr. Chalmers of Northland School Division picked the Naylor Hills site as the geographical centre of the district and decided that the centralized school would be located there. He was not well liked locally and has been referred to as the "big-wig who pulled the wool over our eyes"!

In 1964 Dr. Mary Jackson School was opened at the site chosen by Dr. Chalmers and where it is still located. There were three volunteer trustees during that year: Walter Prochinsky, Bob Peel and Johnny Vos.

School was cancelled for January 9 and 10 while materials were moved into the new school. The four-classroom school with a principal's office, staffroom and library was built at a cost of $177 652.

Starting in the 1964 – 1965 school year, junior high students were bused from Paddle Prairie to Keg River. Portables were added as the school population headed to the all-time high of 151 in the 1969-1970 school year.

Ged Baldwin, the long time Member of Parliament for the Peace River country, made a habit of visiting schools in his constituency. He wanted the young people to learn how their country was governed and to know what was going on in Ottawa. One year when he visited the junior high class at the Keg River School, he talked about his work and asked for questions. The questions were few except for those from Raymond "Baby" Houle who kept Mr. Baldwin busy with many questions about the whys-and-the-wherefores. Before Ged left, he urged Baby to become a lawyer or a member of parliament. Sadly, Baby died before any such dreams became a reality.

A permanent addition to the school was made in 1975. It cost $258,293 and included a gym. A few years later the school population dropped as junior high students from Paddle Prairie were no longer bused to Dr. Mary Jackson school. (A table showing the school population is included at the end of this article.)

September, 1986 brought grades 10, 11 and 12 to Keg River for the first time. Prior to this, all students who wished to graduate from grade 12 had to travel to at least Manning or High Level. Students were given assistance for room and board because these distances did mean that they would have to stay away during the week and return on weekends, if then. Students did attend schools in

Grade 8, 1967 – Back, L-R: Phillip Schwindt, Wallace Prochinsky, Tommy Ghostkeeper, Noreen House, Pat Vos, Mr. Fish. Front, L-R: Sarah Omoth, Betsy Parenteau, Jeanette Chalifoux, Irene Batchelor, Florence Gouchier, Winnie Labocan, Benita Omoth.

Junior High trip to Edmonton, accompanying adults, Mr. and Mrs. Chorney, Katherine Larivire, Mrs. Mary Roth, 1973.

Grades 7 & 8, 1965-66 – Back, L-R: Verna Ducharme, Michael Pawlowich, David Batchelor, Michael Rosypal, Gordon Reid, Mac Bouma, Carl Pawlowich, Bobby Bouma, Debbie Trosky. 3rd Row, L-R: Benita Omoth, Edwin Ducharme, Patsy Reid, Roy Dupuis, Lawrence Cardinal, Irene Batchelor, Stanley House, Billy Trosky, Fred House, Terry Trosky, Pat Vos. 2nd Row: –, Elizabeth Pawlowich, Fern Rudy, Joanne Galandy, Gerthie Ferguson, Sarah Omoth, Linda Galandy, Noreen House, Barbara Bouma. Front, L-R: Phillip Schwindt, Cyril Hamelin, Wallace Prochinsky, Hugh Jackson.

Grades 3 & 4. Back, L-R: Declan Cartier, Dennis Bowe, Brad Papirny, Douglas Sowan, Don Hamelin, David Vos, Louis Pawlowich, William Pawlowich, Teddy Peterson. Middle, L-R:, Lorna Bowe, Sheila Weber, Lily Yurkowsky, Mary-Jane House, Susan Ferguson, Johnny Pawlowich, Ron Ducharme, Pete Sowan, Susan Peel, Kevin Coulter, Yvonne Sowan, Grant Tkatchuk, Mrs. Elizabeth Cartier. Front, L-R: Marylou Vos, Karen Cardinal, Grace Prochinsky, Dianne Buhler, Irma Ducharme, Sandra Galandy, Alice Batchelor, Brenda Rudy, Ruth Estelle.

Grades 1 & 2 – Dr. Mary Jackson School, 1977.

Peace River, Fairview, Grande Prairie and even Edmonton and beyond. It often meant a difficult transition before graduation could be achieved.

Al Van Oers was the principal in 1986 when high school grades were first offered in Keg River. The students did some of the courses in a regular classroom, while others were taken through Distance Education (correspondence). Some of these students withdrew before the end of the school year, their withdrawal is shown with the month in brackets after their name.

Grade 10	Grade 11
Corey Beck	Rick Basarab (October)
Carol Evans	Tina Lotoski (November)
Cindy Chalifoux (March)	Angel Mosure
Priscilla Christian (April)	Kymo Van Oers
Rex Parenteau	
Shirley Parenteau (September)	
Fran Villeneuve (February)	

Mrs. Marlene Belton's grades 1-3 class visiting Dr. Jackson, 1985.

In the 1991-1992 school year, the operating budget for Dr. Mary Jackson School was $815,728.56. There were 54 students registered. This works out to $15,106.08 per student. For comparison the Alberta average that school year was $5700 per student.

The next table shows the school population from 1937 to 1991. The second lists the names of the teachers and the dates that they taught in Keg River.

Year	School Population
Sept. – June 1938	27
Sept. – June 1939	25
Sept. – June 1940	28
Sept. – June 1941	– (no school – no teacher)
Sept. – June 1942	28
Sept. – June 1943	31
Nov. – Dec. 1943	36
March 1 – July 14 1944	36
Sept. – April 1945	– (no school – no teacher)
May 14 – Aug. 24 1945	34
Sept. – June 1946	41
Sept. – Dec. 1946	– (no school – no teacher)
Jan. – June 1947	36
Oct. 1947 – August 1948	31
Sept. 1948 – Sept. 1949	34

(All other school years ran from September through June.)

June, 1950 41	June, 1951 39
June, 1952 41	June, 1953 42
June, 1954 39	June, 1955 35
June, 1956 42	June, 1957 56
June, 1958 48	June, 1959 55
June, 1960 52	June, 1961 75
June, 1962 81	June, 1963 79
June, 1964 93	June, 1965 109
June, 1966 101	June, 1967 125
June, 1968 137	June, 1969 149
June, 1970 151	June, 1971 118
June, 1972 119	June, 1973 115
June, 1974 102	June, 1975 111
June, 1976 107	June, 1977 55
June, 1978 72	June, 1979 64
June, 1980 72	June, 1981 64
June, 1982 67	June, 1983 56
June, 1984 53	June, 1985 47
June, 1986 55	June, 1987 58
June, 1988 57	June, 1989 54
June, 1990 70	June, 1991 54

Teachers and dates they taught in Keg River:

Teacher	Dates of Service
Winifred Lawrence	September 1937 – June 1940
Patrick O'Connor	September 1941 – June 1943
Rachel Weatherup	Nov.–Dec. 1943; March 1 – July 14 1944
Nancy Nylosolyshyn	May – Dec. 1945; Jan. – June 1947
Christine Van der Mark	May – June 1946; July – Aug. 1948
Donald Duff	July 2 – Aug. 5 1946
June Jackson	Oct. 1947 – June 1948; Sept. 1948 – April 1949

Henry Thomassen	May 3 – September 9, 1949
Theodora May Paul	Nov 1 1949 – June 1955
Mildred Mallinger*	Sept. 1955 – June 1957
Margaret Befus	Sept. 1955 – June 1959;
	Sept. 1968 – June 1980
Ethel Robertson	Sept. 1956 – June 1957
Joseph E. L'Heureux*	Sept. 1957 – June 1960
V. Storcer	Feb. 1 – June 30 1958
Emma Mcdonald	Jan 6 – Jan 31 1958
Patricia Ross	Sept. 1959 – June 1962
Leonard F. Clare*	Sept. 1960 – June 1962
Joseph Leclerc*	Sept. 1959 – November 1964
Allene Brick	Sept. 1959 – June 1960
Stella Backstrom	Sept. 1 – Dec. 31 1962
Gwen Ressler	Sept. 17 1962 – April 30 1963
Muriel Isaac	Jan. 6 – May 2 1963
Jeannette Raby	May 3 – June 30 1963
Maureen Patterson	May 1 – June 30 1963
Marvin W. Tkachuk*	Sept. 1963 – June 1964
Victoria Unwin	Sept. – December 1963
Raymond Hall	Jan. – June 1964
Ernest Marr*	Sept. 1963 – June 1968
Nyna Marr	Sept. 1963 – June 1967
Elizabeth Cartier	Sept. 1964 – June 1969
Louise Schultz	Nov. 1964 – June 1965
Allen J. Brown	Sept. 1965 – June 1966
Iva Grubb	Sept. 1965 – June 1967
Orville Shonrock	Sept. 1966 – June 1967
Robert Henderson	Sept. – December 1966
Brian Fish	Jan. – June 1967
John R. Cooper	Sept. 1967 – June 1968
Susan Cooper	Sept. 1967 – June 1968
Elsie Heppner	Sept. 1967 – June 1969
Sheila Douglass	Sept. 1967 – June 1971
Lloyd Chorney*	Sept. 1968 – June 1974
Donna Chorney	Sept. 1968 – June 1974
Ian Rabjohns	Sept. 1969 – April 8 1971
Jessica (Jill) Rabjohns	Sept. 1969 – April 8 1971
Wayne Berlinguette	April 26 – June 30 1971
Patricia Berlinguette	April 26 – June 30 1971
Bevin Wray	Sept. 1971 – June 1974
Janie Wray	Sept. 1971 – June 1973
Attila Greschner	Sept. 1973 – June 1974
Thomas J. Malloy*	Sept. 1974 – June 1977
Beverly Malloy	Sept. 1974 – June 1975;
	Sept. 1976 – June 1977
Dale Bashaw	Sept. 1974 – June 1975
James Aird	Sept. 1974 – June 1975
Rhonda Griffiths	Sept. 1974 – June 1984
Doreen Cardinal(Batchelor)	Sept. 1975 – June 1980;
	Sept. 1986 – present
Denise Woolard	Sept. 1975 – June 1976
Keith Fraser	Sept. 1975 – June 1976
Walter Mast	Sept. 1975 – June 1976
Constance Read*	Sept. 1975 – June 1980
Daryl Hurtak	Sept. 1977 – June 1978
Tom Hasenack	Sept. 1978 – June 1980
Neil D. Conlan	Sept. 1979 – June 1980
Carol Fox	Sept. 1979 – June 1980
Karen Nash (Hohner)	Sept. 1980 – June 1982
Gaylord Rundle*	Sept. 1980 – June 1981
Barbara Forbes	Sept. 1980 – June 1982
Alfred Magee*	Sept. 1981 – June 1982
Bob C. Dickson	Sept. 1982 – June 1983
Marlene Belton	Sept. 1982 – June 1985
Sarah Price	Sept. 1982 – June 1986;
	Sept, 1989 – June 1993

Al Van Oers*	Sept. 1983 – June 1993
T. Humeniuk	Sept. 1985 – June 1986
Faye Van Oers	Sept. 1986 – present
Eugene Hennessy	Sept. 1986 – June 1986
Ron Bonertz	Sept. 1986 – June 1986
Angelika Meyer	Sept. 1986 – June 1988
Barbara June Code*	Sept. 1986 – June 1990
Lucinda Summers	Sept. 1987 – June 1988
Marianne Szabo	Sept. 1988 – June 1989
Wagner Saende	Sept. 1988 – June 1989
K. J. Jagisio	Sept. 1988 – June 1989
Ron Thornhill	Sept. 1989 – June 1990
Michelle Senetza	Sept. 1989 – June 1990
Bill Carr	Sept. 1990 – June 1991
Greg Kostiuk	Sept. 1990 – June 1991
Thomas Nagel	Sept. 1990 – present
Perry Fehr	Sept. 1991 – present
Dallas Rossman	Sept. 1991 – present
Kim McLean	Sept. 1993 – present
Mrs. P. Fehr	Sept. 1993 – March 1994
Lynn Barchuk	April 1994 – present

* These people were principals in a two-or-more-teacher school during all or part of their teaching time at Keg River.

Teachers, Mrs. Befus, Mrs. Griffiths, Mr. Neil Conlin, Mrs. Read.

Teachers of 1982. Carol Fox, Sarah Price, Rhonda Griffiths, Janice Freeman (Secretary), Doreen Batchelor, Margaret Befus, Mr. Dixon (Principal).

The first school bus was provided for the district in 1961 and was driven by Mr. Floyd Schwindt. Other bus drivers were:

Mr. Bill Brick
Mr. Pete Hodgsen
Mr. Wilf Dupuis
Mrs. Margaret Coulter

Mr. Stan Slemming
Mr. Norman Lowe
Mr. Garth Coulter
Mr. Ted Petersen

Mrs. Nora Petersen
Mrs. Berta Mosure
Mrs. Gladys Rudy
Mrs. Randy Christian
Mr. Dan House
Mr. Leonard Senft
Mr. Claude Estelle
Mr. Octave Parenteau

Miss Doris Christian
Mr. Stan Rudy
Mrs. Susan Russell
Mr. Laurie Michalchuk
Mr. Jimmy Lee
Mr. Donald Stigsen
Mr. Charlie Christian, Jr.
Mr. Jim Omoth

Grades 5 & 6, 1975. Mr. Fraser. Back, L-R: Glen Vos, Greg Pawlowich, Fabian Stigsen, Darcy and Dean Weber, John Clarke, Davy Christian, Curtis Stigsen, Chester Omoth. Front: Brenda Freeman, Lorna Christian, Barbara Christian, Joan Prochinsky, Lorna Hamelin, Wendy Wilkins, Valerie Ferguson, Chris Roth.

Grades 1 & 2, 1975. Mrs. Befus. Back, L-R: Frank Zatko, Richard Hamelin, Dale Vos, Clifford Chalifoux, Dion Stigsen, David Freeman, Tim Petersen. Front: Gail Pawlowich, Delores Loonskin, Kirsten Wollard, Alice Pawlowich, Susan Brick, Debbie Vos, Corrine Christian, Shawn Halabisky.

Grade 3, 1982-83, Teacher, Sarah Price.

Grade 9 graduating class of 1983. Teacher, Mrs. Rhonda Griffiths, Maxine Holtz, Susan Brick, Gail Pawlowich, David Freeman.

Rhonda Griffith's 1983 Junior High class.

Original Keg River School, 1937.

Kindergarten (E.C.S.) Class of 82-83. Doreen Batchelor, Teacher. Colin Bouma, Jamie Mosure, Daryl Chalifoux, Tracy House, Bernadette Price, Kyla Mosure.

Kindergarten (E.C.S.) Graduating Class of 1989. Mr. Keith Spencer, Doreen Batchelor, Teacher. L-R: Shauna Christian, Cody Russell, Dustin House, Kim Halabisky, Shawna Riva.

Grades 1 & 2, 1980.

Keg River School with built-on teacherage. The school was built in 1950.

Dr. Mary Jackson School, Keg River, built in 1963.

A KEG RIVER FRIDAY AFTERNOON
by Donna Chorney

The truck arrives, a parent at the wheel. The troops stand ready at their assigned stations.

SQUAWK! SQUAWK! SQUAWK! ... ... CHOP!

FLAP..FLAP..FLAP...

Noise...Movement...Seeming Confusion... Chaos!

Out by the ball diamond chopping is done. Plenty of room to maneuver – to avoid the splatter...

Closer to the building, steaming hot water awaiting its victims.

Pull them out...Pull them ALL out..Let none remain!

Crackle..Crackle..The acrid smell of burning feathers!

Now the knife slits – not too wide or too deep.

Small hands enter the warm sticky cave drawing forth wonders for all to see...

Quickly now or we'll finish too late!

Washing...Splitting...Cutting...Washing..Hygiene is important.

Cream, potatoes, carrots and onions – all donated by parents – IGA's rice – Alberta Power's heat.

Finally the fruits of our labour are set before us steaming hot – smelling like heaven. We have all earned our supper – done our share – all like the Little Red Hen.

Today we call it collaboration and/or hands on manipulation. Twenty years ago, we didn't have the fancy names. We just knew that we could have fun working and learning together. (Note: At this time Dr. Mary Jackson School in Keg River had about 70 students in grades one to nine in five classrooms. Whole school activities were a regular occurrence ..... Next instalment ..... Noon hour hockey even at – 30°F.)

Christmas Roll-Call
by Emma MacDonald (written in December, 1956)

Every year about this time it is my job to go through the village to count the pre-school children in order to prepare little gifts to be given out at the Christmas concert. It's a lot of fun! First I hear a dog bark to announce my coming. Then I knock at the door. I hear little feet scampering across the floor; then I hear a faint "Come in!" from the mother.

Usually the first thing they do is to get a chair and ask me to sit down. Right away I tell them what I have come for (for even though they all know me by my first name, they are still shy with me). I get out my pencil and paper and start asking the names and ages of their little ones. It's interesting and I love it. Each year the last one is a year older and in most cases there is another baby to take its place. I'm always curious to know what they have named the wee newcomer.

On I go from cabin to cabin. This year I started about 3 P.M. and as I neared every cabin I could hear radios blaring away – the western hour is on CKYL, "The Voice of 12 Foot Davis".

Another interesting thing is that every year there are different families. The natives have not changed – they are still here today and gone tomorrow. Very few of them stay put for long.

The little ones are from age six and down. Although most of them understand English, I usually talk Cree to them to make them feel more at home. Their little faces shine like stars when I ask them if they are looking for Santa. Although there is no Cree word for Santa, they know him all right!

This year we did not raise as much money as usual. Money is scarce in the community right now. We thought we might cut out gifts for the wee babies, but after my visits I have made up my mind that no little one will be forgotten.

Christmas Concert Memories
by Anne Vos

Ever since a school opened in Keg River, Christmas concerts have made our Decembers brighter. Community members crowd into the building. The hall (the new and the old) were used before the school had a gym. The original school building was used even before there was a hall. Often the buildings are packed to capacity.

The students have sung, acted and entertained in many different productions over the years. Many school and after-school hours are put into preparation for the big night. Props and costumes are made and lines are rehearsed.

The community donates time, energy and musical instruments to make the event a success. Over the years different groups have been responsible for fund-raising to provide Christmas treats for the children.

On the evening of the big event the little ones perform first, then the older students. In between productions, the trek of Santa from the North Pole to the event is followed for those in attendance. When Santa does come, he brings a small bag of goodies for each child.

Some of the productions that we remember are:

1940   The highlight of the concert was when Frank Jackson who had helped prepare the children for a play about black boys, came out from behind the curtain to announce the next play. He had no idea why the audience burst into laughter. He had as much black (burnt cork) on as the kids!

1941   Pat Hague, Eddie Halabisky, and Steve and Mary Pawlowich did the Cossack dance, sitting on their heels and kicking with alternate legs. Mary and Steve had on the proper embroidered Polish blouses.

1942   The small boys were to provide us with a boxing match for fun. However they forgot and got into a real fight that Eva Harrington had to stop! "Pack Up Your Troubles in the Old Kit Bag" was the number one song and when everyone joined in, the whole building was vibrating.

1967   Mrs. Befus and the grade ones performed a shadow play which is done behind a white sheet and only shadows can be seen. It was very funny. The class was going to the Christmas concert, but the tires on the car kept going flat. The loss of air pressure in the tires was accompanied by very authentic sound effects! Each tire was then pumped with a bicycle hand pump. The play had the audience laughing!

1970   "The Shoemaker and the Elves" was the star performance of the year.

One year the junior high class performed a shadow play set in a hospital surgery. The patient lay on the table as the surgeon and his assistants transplanted many of his major organs. A saw replaced the scalpel, and a string of sausage links was pulled from the patient. Some limbs were removed and the necessary sawing was accompanied by the appropriate sounds!

Christmas Concert, 1987.

Christmas Concert, Shawna Riva, Kim Halabisky, Shauna Christian, Cody Russell, Dustin House, 1988.

Christmas Concert, Dana Russell, Tamara Griesbrect, Krissy Oster, James Hasenack, 1990.

Paddle Prairie Christmas Concert, note the log heater, 1971.

Another year "The Shooting of Dan McGrew" was re-enacted for our entertainment.

Whether the plays were well-known or original works, they provided enjoyment for us and learning opportunities for the students. They continue to provide each of us with fond memories.

H. M. S. Pinafore
by Janice Freeman

The musical H.M.S. Pinafore was presented by the students and staff of Doctor Mary Jackson School in 1979. All singing lessons and directing were done by Connie Read, the principal at that time. The actors ranged from ECS to grade six. Props, backdrops and stage paraphernalia were the responsibility of the grade seven to nine students. Overseeing was left to the teachers and staff.

Able seaman costumes were made by Margaret Befus and myself with help from many others who were willing to donate time and ideas. Other costumes were made and donated from wherever possible and alterations were made as required. Teacher Rhonda Griffiths became an instant make up artist, along with Gladys Rudy and any other help that could be acquired. Teacher Neil Conlan became a man of various theatrical trades and master of none, I'm sure, as well as painting and carpentry supervisor.

Without Connie Read's musical ability and persistence, none of this would have been possible. She was not only the director but responsible for all the piano playing, if a child could not sing their part on the note required, she played at a note level that they could sing.

It turned out to be a great success and was held for two evenings. It was just too bad that with all the time and work put into it, it could not have travelled to other schools, but with the number of children and the ages involved (age four to 15) it was not possible. The two nights the production played in Keg River, the gymnasium was full and viewers came from High Level to Manning and everywhere in between. The show was thoroughly enjoyed by all and received only good reviews!

The H.M.S. Pinafore was done from the book by W. S. Gilbert and music written by Arthur Sullivan. The synopsis of the story follows.

Sometime before the opening of Act I, Ralph has fallen in love with Josephine, the daughter of Captain Corcoran, commander of the H.M.S. Pinafore. Buttercup, a peddler woman, has fallen in love with the Captain. Social class and pride keep both the Captain and his daughter from returning this affection, although both would like to do so. The Captain has pledged his daughter in marriage to Sir Joseph Porter, the First Lord of the Admiralty, who is in a social class even higher than the Corcorans.

At the opening of Act I, the sailors are busy preparing the ship for Sir Joseph's visit. Ralph and Josephine each sing a sad song bemoaning the fact that they both love in vain. Buttercup hints that she is hiding a secret, and Dick Deadeye grumbles that there is only trouble in store.

Sir Joseph arrives, attended by his sisters, cousins and aunts. He explains how he became Lord of the Admiralty and examines the crew, assuring them they are any man's equal, excepting his own.

Josephine finds Sir Joseph unbearable, Ralph confesses his love to Josephine. When she rejects him, he threatens suicide. She then confesses her love for him and they agree to elope. The act ends with great rejoicing.

Act II finds the Captain in despair that his daughter is not happy with Sir Joseph, Buttercup tries to cheer him, saying there is a change in store. Sir Joseph appears and says he wishes to call off the marriage since Josephine does not take kindly to him. The Captain suggests that his daughter may feel inferior to Sir Joseph and urges him to tell Josephine that difference in social rank should not be a barrier to marriage.

Sir Joseph does this, not knowing that he is really convincing Josephine that it is acceptable for her to marry Ralph. Sir Joseph thinks she has accepted him and they are all happy again.

Dick Deadeye informs the Captain of the planned elopement and the Captain angrily halts the couple's getaway. Sir Joseph hears the disturbance, learns what has happened, sends the Captain to his cabin in disgrace and orders Ralph put in irons.

Buttercup must now come up with her secret. She tells that many years ago she was a nurse and had in her charge two babies – one a commoner and one of noble birth. Her secret is that she made the dreadful error of exchanging the babies, so that when they grew up, the nobleman became a sailor – Ralph – and the commoner became the Captain of the H.M.S. Pinafore. Sir Joseph orders the two men to assume their real identities, which prevents him from marrying Josephine (the daughter of a commoner), but permits her to marry Ralph and her father to marry Buttercup. Sir Joseph is left with his cousin Hebe. There is general rejoicing.

The Cast of Characters
Captain Corcoran .... Tim Petersen
Buttercup .... Maxine Holtz
Sir Joseph .... Shawn Halabisky
Josephine .... Gail Pawlowich
Ralph .... David Freeman
Dick Deadeye .... Sheldon Hamelin
Cousin Hebe .... Susan Brick
Boatswain's Mate .... Clifford Chalifoux
Ladies of the Chorus
Sir Joseph's sisters,
  cousins, aunts .... Girls ECS through Grade Six
Gentlemen of the Chorus
Sailors aboard H.M.S.
  Pinafore .... Guys ECS through Grade Six

Scene from H.M.S. Pinafore.

Scenes from H.M.S. Pinafore.

Future Schools: A 1976 Prophecy!
by an unknown student of Dr. Mary Jackson School

In the future you will walk through automatic doors. Glancing at your watch you see that you are right on time. It is 12 noon. You get into a bumper car and go to your classroom, stopping at the pop fountain.

You then go through revolving doors and park beside your desk. At the push of a button, your books and pencil appear.

Looking around, you see that the teacher is sitting in a large reclining chair. Behind the teacher is a small room in which he or she goes if students get in a brawl.

There are no bare walls. Each is covered with a chalk board or a bulletin board. In the corner opposite the teacher's desk is a large fireplace that covers three-fourths of the back wall. There is wall-to-wall carpet in every room, which keeps a dozen janitors busy. There is one teacher for every 10 students and the superintendent has a body guard!

At 3:30 you will get on a bus which is equipped with a cafe, a record player and seats along the walls.

This school is designed to help take care of unemployment!

Keg River Play School
by Susan Russell

Our play school operated from 1985 to 1988 and the organizing members were myself, Jennifer Taylor, Donna Halabisky, Vicky Zatko, Jo-ann Wilkins, and Linda Halabisky.

The mothers would pick up the children and drive them to the school or the hall twice a week (weather and time permitting). There crafts and games awaited the children. We bought supplies by selling concessions at various events. Then we put together the Keg River cookbook and sold 500 copies. It was a great success and a good cook-book. Large swings were put up at the hall and picnic tables were bought.

In My World
by Brenda Lynne Freeman

(Written when Brenda was completing grade nine at Dr. Mary Jackson School and was 14 years old.)
In my world I dream
Of a lake and a stream;
So fresh is the air;
And the spring so fair.

In my world I dream
Of silence, that it is waiting
Ready of what will happen,
And what goes on.

In my world I dream
Of wild animals,
Of friends, of enemies,
Of how nice and how cruel.

In my world I dream
That love is everywhere.
Not war, but peace
In my world.

In my world I dream
And when I dream,
It is for me.
In my world.

My Hill – My Secret
by Chester Omoth
(Written when he was 14 years old and in Dr. Mary Jackson School)

Come with me
To the top of my hill
Where nature is playing
This very day.

Come with me
And see the animals and insects.
Play with the darkness soon coming
To dwell on my hill.

Come with me
And hear the bee's buzzing
And the bird's singing making
Their own sweet symphony.

Come with me
And feel the pine needles
And the moving grass as the
Wind touches your face.

Come with me
To the top of my hill where
Nature and its wonders
Make me feel alive.

Summer's Evening
by Wendy Wilkins
(Written when she was 14 years old and in Dr. Mary Jackson School)

Serene summer's
evening
Green and gold

glowing
Reflection of the fading
scarlet
sunset.

Glistening diamonds
flowing
Sparkling river of
brilliance
Reaching for fading
receding
horizon.

Rambling hills of
green
Dipped in pools of
shadow
Saluting the last fading
rays
of day.

Summer's sunset
recedes
Sparkling waters
die
The day is fading
going
gone.

WE THANK THEE
by Margaret R. Pawlowich

For mother – love and father – care,
For brothers strong and sisters fair,
For love at home and here each day,
For guidance lest we go astray,
Father in Heaven, we thank Thee.

For this new morning with its light,
For rest and shelter of the night,
For health and food, for love and friends,
For everything His goodness sends,
Father in Heaven, we thank Thee.

For flowers that bloom about our feet,
For tender grass, so fresh, so sweet,
For song of bird and hum of bee,
For all things fair we hear or see,
Father in Heaven, we thank Thee.

For blue of stream and blue of sky,
For pleasant shade of branches high,
For fragrant air and cooling breeze,
For beauty of the blooming trees,
Father in Heaven, we thank Thee.

Anglican Church
by Mary Jackson

There have never been very many Anglicans at Keg River, but in the 1930's and 40's Bishop Sovereign managed to come here from Peace River about once a year to hold a service. The first time he came down the Peace River on the *Weenusk*, and then had the rough journey by wagon from Carcajou to Keg River, and back again in time to catch the boat on its way upstream. His next trip was over the rough trail that preceded the MacKenzie Highway, which was a very rough trail indeed, but he was always interested in new homestead settlements and their problems.

Three babies christened. Dennis Halabisky held by Annie Rudy, Donnie Morrison held by Emma McDonald and Donnie Jackson held by his mother June. Others are L-R: John Jackson, Myrna, Jim, Elsie, Norma and Eddie Halabisky, Anne Jackson.

Bishop Sovereign suggested that the "Sunday School by Post" ladies, Miss Hassell and Miss Sayles, should visit Keg River and they did. The two ladies spent the summer travelling from settlement to settlement in a van holding Sunday School and Vacation Bible School Camps for the children of the district. They also visited the Anglican families of the area.

Photo of van that was identical to the Sunday School Van that used to travel to homestead settlements.

Bishop Sovereign also visited Canon Andrews in London when he went to England, and told him of our need for an outpost hospital, and a school, so that when I went to England in 1937, Canon Andrews was already interested in the idea of an outpost. I personally received a great deal of support from Bishop Sovereign and I also received support for the hospital and supplying medicine to my patients through the Fellowship of the Maple Leaf, which was supported by Anglicans in England.

Today Anglican ministers usually visit the district once or twice a year and when a minister comes to our area, services are held in private homes, the school or in the Catholic Church.

St. Michaels Catholic Church, 1992.

St. Michael's Roman Catholic Church and Cemetery at Carcajou Point
by Laura Christian

Roman Catholic Church records show that Father Joussard first visited the Carcajou area in May, 1904. Later, Father Joussard retired and Father Habay became the missionary to the distant posts. They had both lived in Fort Vermilion. Father Habay visited the Carcajou and Keg River areas twice a year between 1904 and 1911. In May, 1911, Father Habay and Brother Michael Mathis constructed a chapel at Carcajou Point.

The Catholic Church had 10 lots at the southeast end of the settlement, according to the survey done by Pierce and Buchanan in 1916. An Indian graveyard existed at Carcajou Point for many years, but with the changes in the river, many of those graves may have been washed away. Although no graveyard was ever registered at Carcajou, the Roman Catholic Church records show the following people buried there between 1904 and 1942. The cemetery was not used after 1942, and while people of other faiths were buried

Carcajou Cemetery, closed since 1934.

in the Carcajou cemetery, we do not have their names.

NAMES	AGE	DATE OF DEATH	BLESSING OF BURIAL (priest visited)
Emile Hamelin (son of Charlie)	?	1904	May, 1904
Marguerite Hamelin	?	Jan 1, 1906	Jan 5, 1906
Elizabeth Horseman	?	Nov 11, 1906	Jan 6, 1907
Albert Horseman	60	Sept 3, 1907	Jan 1, 1908
Norbert Wanuch	50	Sept, 1907	Jan, 1908
Adeline Horseman	2	Spring, 1908	Jan, 1909
Marie Wanuch	75	Sept, 1910	May, 1911
Charles Hamelin (spouse of Jeanette)	60	Feb, 1910	May, 1911
Patrice Francois (son of Adelaide Cardinal)	4	1910	May, 1911
Helen Wanuch (daughter of Louis Wanuch)	3	Jan, 1911	May, 1911

Name	Age		Date
Marie Eve Hamelin (daughter of Oliver Hamelin)	?	?	May, 1911
Cyprien Sowan (son of Xavier and Adelaide)	?	?	May, 1912
Julien Sowan (spouse of Mabel Horseman)	30	Winter, 1913	Sept 19, 1913
Alfred Sowan (son of Julien)	9	Winter, 1913	Sept 19, 1913
Elisa Sowan (daughter of Julien)	4	Winter, 1913	Sept 19, 1913
David Hamelin (son of Charles and Jeanette)	?	July, 1913	Sept 19, 1913
Joseph Sowan	?	Sept, 1913	March 8, 1914
Marie Sowan (wife of Joseph)	?	Sept, 1913	March 8, 1914
Jeanne Gauthier (nee Kutchie)	?	Feb 26, 1914	March 8, 1914
Marie Hamelin (daughter of Jeanette)	16	April 21, 1914	May 10, 1914
Michael Sowan	14	March 14, 1915	March 14, 1915
Elsie Sowan (Marie Rose Elizabeth)	4	June 1919	
Arlisio Adelaide Armstrong (daughter of James and Adelaide Leduc)			born: March 3, 1916 date of death: ?
Cecile Armstrong (daughter of James and Adelaide)	15 days	?	Aug, 1920
Adelaide Sowan (wife of Clement Cardinal)	?	March, 1930	Sept, 1930
Eliza Couterielle (spouse of Augustine)	?	Jan, 1930	Sept, 1930
Marie D. Dionne	9 months	1930	Sept, 1930
Jimmy Wanuch (son of Edward)	5	July, 1931	July, 1931
Adelaide Cardinal (daughter of Clement and spouse of Paul Couterielle)	?	Aug, 1931	Aug, 1931
Moise Chalifoux (spouse of Rosalie Sowan)	?	May, 1931	
Jeanette Sowan (spouse of Benjamin)	84	Sept, 1931	Jan 4, 1932
Xavier Sowan (spouse of Adelaide Hamelin)	57	Jan, 1934	
Tommy Wanuch (son of Edward and M. A. Beauchamp)	14 months	July, 1934	Aug, 1934
Richard Cardinal (son of Alfred and Julienne)	25	March, 1936	Aug, 1936
Xavier Sowan (spouse of Angeline Wanuch)	83	Summer, 1936	Nov, 1942
Winnifred Armstrong (daughter of James and Adelaide)	13	June, 1942	Nov, 1942

St. Jude's Catholic Church in Keg River
by St. Jude's Altar Society

1904 The first recorded visit of a priest to Keg River. Father Joussard celebrates the marriage of Clement Paul and Eliza Chalifoux.

1905 Father Habay visits Keg River for the first time. In following years he visits Keg River and Carcajou twice a year.

1906 Father Habay visits Keg River, Carcajou and Cypress Point, which was supposed to be 40 miles from Carcajou, but we have been unable to find the location. Each year the priest continues his twice-a-year visits. Part of the trip in the summertime is made on the Peace River. From there he either walks or travels by horse and wagon. He usually performs marriages and baptisms and blesses the graves of those who have died since his last visit.

1911 The winter trip this year is impossible due to the extreme cold. Records show the temperature is below -40°F most of January.

1912 There are no records for the next 22 years although it is believed that Father Habay's successors continue to visit the district twice a year.

1934 Father Quémeneur's visits lasting two weeks from February 27 to March 14. He is determined to build a church in the district. Father Habay visits in September and celebrates Mass at the Chalifoux home in Hay River (Chinchaga). In October the church construction begins. The church is to be 20 feet by 30 feet and have a 14-foot by 14-foot sanctuary. Miss H. Ferland gives $503.00 to build a church dedicated to Saint Jude Thaddeus, patron saint of lost causes. The church is situated on a two-acre plot on NE-21-101-24-W5.

1935 Father Habay, assisted by J. Ducharme and Ben Charles, continues to work on the church.

At the Catholic Church, L-R: Louise Chalifoux, Emma Noskey, Maria Nooskey, Helen Ferguson, Mrs. Richards, Madeline and Frank Ferguson, 1940.

1936 The church is completed with a bell tower surmounted by a cross, some 30 feet high. Inauguration of the church is held in February.

Clara Bottle and Joe Feguson wedding at Keg River Church.

1948 Father Quémeneur begins construction on the presbytery (church house).

1951 Father Boucher comes for a visit.

1954 Father John, with the help of Dave McDonald, Ernie Brick and others, put the church on a cement foundation and stuccoes it.

1965 Father Joseph Habay dies at 90 years. As a missionary in the Peace River District and Grouard Mission for 62 years, he was responsible for construction of the first chapel at Hay River and the construction of the churches at Keg River and Eleske.

Christening of a number of babies at the Catholic Church, 1941.

The first communion held at the Keg River Catholic Church. Back, L-R: Father Quemeneur, Larone & Donald Ferguson, ?, ?, Bishop Routhier, Esther McLeod, Lena Noskey. Front, L-R: Rita Hamelin, Sophie Michalchuk, Violet Ferguson, Alma Ferguson, Rita Sinclair.

Putting a foundation under the Catholic Church.

St. Judes Catholic Church and Keg River Community Hall.

His life was dedicated to serving the people of Northern Alberta.

1975 Renovations in the church take place. It is painted and a porch is added.

1994 Sixty years of weddings, baptisms and funerals in the church building!

Keg River Cemetery
by Anne Vos

On land donated by Lonnie Root a new cemetery was opened in Keg River in 1933. It was located on two acres of NE-28-101-24-W5 and replaced the older cemetery, which was right along the river. With some of the changes in the path of the Keg River, the older cemetery was being washed away. Some of the grave sites and their crosses and houses still exist today. The location of the old cemetery site is SE-28-101-24-W5.

The names of those buried in the old site are not available but what follows is a list of all those who have been buried in the new cemetery, along with the month of burial.

NAME	MONTH/YEAR
Michael Rudy	01/33
Pierre William Chalifoux	01/33
Henry Ferguson	01/33
Eileen Christian	01/34
Emilieu Chalifoux	04/34
Fred Miles Cardinal	11/34
Annie Hamelin	02/35
Eleanor Minault	02/36
Mary Louisa Chalifoux	04/36
James Hume Stewart	09/36
Moise Richard	09/36
Frederick Anderson	09/36
Clifford Hunter	10/36
Clement Cardinal	10/36
Thomas Alan Brick	04/38
Jean Baptist Wanuch	05/38
Susan Weiler	10/38
James Armstrong	03/40
Isadore Capotblanc	03/40
Rosalie Chalifoux	05/40
Samuel Noskey	06/40
Alma Joyce (Gladue) Yurkowski	12/40
Marie Stoney	01/42
Barbara Pawlowich Sr.	06/42
Elizabeth Agnes Chalifoux	09/43
Willie Hamelin	04/43
Flora Bowe	11/43
Thomas Chalifoux	05/44
Adele Richard	10/44
Mary Shemeluik	11/44
Henriette Capotblanc	01/45
Phillipine Elisha Tupper	07/46
Clemence Sinclair	07/47
Richard John Leslie Ross	01/48
Infant Rudy	05/50
Olivier Hamelin	10/51
Mary Eleanor Sinclair	05/53
Infant Pawlowich	08/55

Carl Pawlowich Sr.	??/55
Alfred Malcolm Chalifoux	05/57
Floyd Garry Christian	09/57
Margery Reid	08/59
Maria Noskey	01/60
Alex Gauchie	10/60
Michael Yurkowski	11/60
Joan Befus	11/58
Infant Grace Trosky McKenzie	05/61
John Christian	12/61
Chester Rudy	??/62
Gladys Almseda Lewis	06/62
Emma Ferguson	10/62
Thomas Ducharme	11/62
Infant Bowe	04/63
Infant Nellie Trosky McKenzie	05/63
Charlie Noskey	08/63
Nick Tomilou	03/66
Lorna Jean Cardinal	04/66
Marie Noskey	05/66
Dell Weber	07/66
Henry Cardinal	06/67
Joseph John Cardinal	06/67
Eli Cardinal	06/67
Louis Hrytciuk	09/67
Milton Rudy	03/68
Julia Yurkowski	05/69
Emma McDonald	08/69
Elmer Omoth	08/70
Mervin Rudy	12/70
George Hrytciuk	01/71
Charlotte Hamelin	01/72
Jean Baptiste Sowan	??/??
Elmer Ducharme	??/??
Annie Rudy	12/72
Benjamin Tupper	01/73
Evelyn Parenteau	02/73
Douglas Rudy	03/73
Malcolm Ducharme	11/74
Frank Chalifoux	05/74
Dallas Christian	03/75
Alex Hamelin	11/75
Isobel Chalifoux	??/??
Helen Ferguson	09/76
Peter Rudy	10/77
Dave Weber	12/77
Roderick (Mannie) Ducharme	06/78
Ambrose Hamelin	08/78
Emma Weber	09/78
Kate Bowe	10/78
Emma Ducharme	04/79
Mike Michalchuk	07/79
Frank Jackson	09/79
Larone Ferguson	12/79
Frankie Ferguson	05/80
Harry Bowe	10/80
Dwayne House	11/80
Sammy Ducharme	06/81
Jean Galandy	07/81
John Pawlowich	04/82
Howard R. (Red) Davis	02/82
Edward Hamelin	11/82
Carl Pawlowich Jr.	06/82
Mellissa Mosure	08/82
Frank Ferguson	12/83
Vern House	06/85
Vance Hamelin	01/85

Jim Hamelin	02/86
Paul Galandy	10/86
Anna Ferguson	07/87
Val Hamelin	12/87
Robert Cardinal	12/87
Darrell Chalifoux	01/88
Chris Lacasse	04/89
Ed Halabisky	08/89
Irene Hamelin	09/89
Ernest Ducharme	07/90
Marion Rudy	08/90
May Sapp	10/90
Malcolm Christian	04/91
Louise Chalifoux	04/91
Marie Christian	02/92
Archie Chalifoux	03/92
John Ducharme	11/92
Jean Marie (Peeweeno) Cardinal	06/93
Priscilla Ferguson	12/93

Grave at the old cementery.

Moise Chalifoux, died aged 84 on May 4, 1901. Grave is located in old cemetery.

Paddle Prairie Church
by Father J. Marsan, O.M.I.

The church in Paddle Prairie was built in 1949 by Brother Aime Allie, O.M.I., with the help of

Amedee Bellrose. Construction started on June 4, 1949, and was completed on March 12, 1950.

Twenty years earlier on January 1, 1929, Father Jean Louis Marie Quémeneur, O.M.I., celebrated the Holy Eucharist for the first time in Paddle in a family home.

Father Henri Routhier, O.M.I., Oblate Vicar of Missions before he was appointed coadjutor to Bishop Ubald Langlois, had suggested the name of Christ the King Mission for Paddle Prairie on February 23, 1945.

Already in 1944 on November 19th, a donation of $500 had been received from the Church Extension Society of Canada (Toronto) for the construction of the future church.

On August 28, 1950, the same Catholic Extension Society sent out two donations one of $500 and a second of $263. The total cost of building the church was approximately $6000. The church is 100 feet by 40 feet and it is approximately 70 feet to the top of the steeple.

Paddle Prairie Catholic Church.

During construction the weight of the roof trusses and steeple caused the walls to bulge. This problem was remedied by installing threaded steel rods and tightening them to straighten the walls.

Father Joseph Jean, O.M.I., was appointed missionary of Paddle Prairie, Keg River and Carcajou Point in July 1949.

The Paddle Prairie Church was blessed on September 18, 1950, by His Excellency, Bishop Henri Routhier, under the name of Christ the King Mission.

Father Merriman.   Father John.

Paddle Prairie Cemetery
by Rita Nooskey and Susie Parenteau

The cemetery in Paddle Prairie is located at NW-18-103-21-W5. The following is a list of those known to be buried in the cemetery and the year in which they were buried.

Julia Ross (Delorme) (Parenteau) 1949
Garnet Supernault 1949
Maria Parenteau (Lariviere) 1950
Josephine Poitras 1953
Louis Lariviere 1957
Samuel Peter Parenteau 1958
Josephine (Desjarlais) Johnston 1960
Paul Wanuch 1960
Mary (Johnston) Cardinal 1961
Liza Cardinal 1963
Larry Freeman 1963
Alex Auger 1963
Joseph Ackerman 1966
James Paul Lariviere 1966
Charles Gordon Wanuch 1967
Mary Louise Ghostkeeper 1967
George Auger 1969
Delphine (Chalifoux) Parenteau 1970
Baby Strong 1971
Richard Allen Beaulieu 1971
Flora Anderson Parenteau 1971
Margaret Ghostkeeper 1972
John Gabriel Gaucher 1973
Robert Armstrong 1973
Karen Parenteau 1973
Joyce (Cardinal) Parenteau 1973
Owen Parenteau 1973
Ed Parenteau Jr. 1973
James Cardinal 1973
Nora (Armstrong) Laboucane 1975
Margaret (Chalifoux) Strong 1975
Gordon Hansel Chalifoux 1976
Louis Armstrong 1976
Mary Ann Wanuch 1977
Fabian Stigsen 1977
Kelly Ducharme 1977
Sarah (Smith) Martineau 1977
Adeline (Cardinal) Armstrong 1979
George Gaucher 1980
Robin Lizotte 1981
Doyle Lizotte 1981

In 1987 two bodies were found in Notikewin Park. The identities of the men were not known. They were buried in the Paddle Prairie cemetery as John Does.

Survival at Keg River in the Dirty Thirties
by Mary Jackson

The Great Depression started abruptly with the stock market crash in October 1929. It was felt even back in the Peace River country. Prices of grain, cattle, and fur went down rapidly, and there were no jobs and no money. In those days there were no family allowance cheques, no unemployment insurance, and no welfare.

When Frank Jackson and I were married in 1931 it had become obvious that we couldn't afford the trip to England. My early memories of Keg River are of the struggles to learn to cook, bake bread and care for a garden. I had grown up in cities in England and didn't know anything of farming.

Frank and I were better off than many of the homesteaders, because Frank had a good house and was raising cattle and hogs as well as running a fur-trading post. Still with fur prices falling all the time, even the fur-trading was not a very profitable business.

Louise Jackson (Frank's first wife, who died following the birth of their third son) had been a wonderful farm wife, and had put up hundreds of sealers of meat, fruit, vegetables, pickles, jams, and jellies, and there was enough left to keep us going until I had learned to do the same.

We grew a huge garden, and as well as all the usual vegetables we tried to grow everything from peanuts and popcorn to watermelon and mushrooms.

There were no refrigerators or deep freezers, so it was necessary to can beef and moosemeat in sealers. Without pressure cookers, that took three hours of steady boiling, and if done in wash boilers on wood-burning cook stoves, it was an enormous chore. Frank had a big cooker for cooking pig feed, so he had a wooden rack to fit into it, enabling us to do 30 quarts at a time. It was still a big chore! Peas and corn had to be done the same way, in sealers that were boiled for three hours.

When pigs were butchered we had to salt the hams and bacon, and render the lard. We put the lard into pails and kept them down on the ice in the icehouse. We made any surplus fat and drippings into laundry soap to use with lye and gasoline to get grease out of dirty overalls.

Hens hadn't been bred to lay all year the way they do these days, and of course we had no lights in the hen house to keep them laying in the fall. The selling of day-old chicks by commercial brooders didn't start until about 1938.

Before that we had to set hens that were clucking, and pray they wouldn't quit their nests before the chicks hatched, and pray that there would be no blizzard or bad weather just when they were hatching. The surplus eggs that would be needed all winter had to be preserved in big stone crocks in a slimy liquid called waterglass. Old hens that had finished laying were killed and canned in quart sealers.

Picking wild fruits, strawberries, saskatoons, raspberries, and blueberries was another major chore, but one we enjoyed very much since we usually made the picking an excuse for picnics, and at least the sealers only needed boiling for half an hour. We made lots of jams and jellies with wild fruit, too.

One year we ran short of sealers (even though

we had about 700) and there was such a good crop of wild fruit that we made bottles into jam jars by tying gasoline-soaked string around them, and then lighting it. With any luck this would crack the bottle along the string line, leaving a nice jam pot.

The sugar for all this canning and jamming came in the freight by boat down the Peace River to Carcajou, where our teams picked it up and hauled it to Keg River. It came in 100-pound cotton sacks. But one time our teams hadn't reached the Peace before the boat arrived, and our freight was just unloaded and stacked on the river bank. The cotton, gunny sacks of sugar soaked up the dampness all night, and when it reached Keg River Post 36 hours later, the contents were a horrible-looking damp brown mess.

We couldn't afford to lose all that sugar. so we dissolved it in water, and let the mud settle out of it a bit, then strained the liquid through cotton batting, and finally boiled the syrup down and stored it in sealers. The process took days and the kitchen got very sticky, but the syrup was O.K. for canning fruit or, with some Mapleline, it made quite a usable syrup for hot cakes. We salvaged more than half of the 100 pounds I think.

Another procedure that made for a very sticky kitchen was extracting honey. We had a few beehives started in 1937 and used a hand-powered extractor.

Frank always milked one or two cows, and the cream was saved for churning into butter every Saturday. While sitting churning, I used to read the British Medical Journal, so I quite enjoyed it. The surplus butter was put into pails and stored down on the ice in the icehouse. As long as it had been thoroughly worked, it would keep for months.

We even had our own whole-wheat flour, because there was a little bolt missing in the hammer-mill where flour leaked out when Frank was milling wheat for pig feed. I tied a little cotton sugar sack over the hole to catch the flour. We used some of the chop as porridge. It was very good, but had to be started in the double boiler overnight if it was to be cooked by breakfast time!

We made our own vinegar in a 10-gallon crock behind the stove. It was started by dissolving sugar in the water, then floating rounds of toast, heavily laden with yeast, on the top – which of course made the kitchen smell as though we were making home-brew, illegal in those days. After a few days one added the "vinegar mother", a peculiar, flat, greyish-colored, slimy, thick circle that floated on top of the brew, and gradually transformed the water into quite good vinegar. The process took months.

The vinegar mother was very precious and had to be transferred to a new brew once the vinegar was full strength. We once had a disaster with ours. Louis stood on the edge of the crock to reach something behind the stove, and his mocassined foot went into our vinegar and right through the vinegar mother!

Life was a continual struggle – some new problem would arise to challenge our ability to cope. Frank used to have to repair all his farm machinery himself. One day he found that he had run out of babbitt for running a new bearing when one wore out. This was a real disaster until he thought of using ointment tubes. I carefully squeezed out the ointment into little jars from all the tubes I had, and then cleaned the tubes very thoroughly, but there wasn't quite enough until we emptied the toothpaste tubes too. The tubes were melted down to form a liquid which was poured around the shaft to form a functioning bearing.

Looking back at all our struggles, I can't help wondering how on earth we ever had time for all the things we did. Of course Louis and Arthur were big enough to be a tremendous help, and they knew how to do all the things that I didn't, from churning butter to butchering hens. I provided them with an enormous amount of amusement as I did stupid things in the learning process. But we survived!

A Couple Weds in the 1940's

Taken from a newspaper clipping found in the Root family papers. Unfortunately, the names of the newspaper or the man and woman are not known.

It is well-known that weddings involve a lot of bother, but few weddings have been quite so determinedly approached as was that of a bride and groom living in the Keg River district of northern Alberta. The couple decided to go to the town of Peace River, 160 miles away, to be married in St. James Cathedral.

From Keg River to the nearest highway, a distance of 60 miles, they rode horses. There are no houses on this trail and the young people spent two nights under the stars in below-zero weather, wrapped in sleeping bags. At Notikewin the groom helped to shovel a load of grain in return for a ride on a truck that carried them to Grimshaw. They completed the journey from Grimshaw to Peace River on a beer truck. We are happy to report that the officiating clergyman, the Rev. F. E. Smith, declined to accept a fee for performing the ceremony.

Growing Up in Keg River
by the Vos children

The six of us were born to Anne and Johnny Vos between 1953 and 1961. In many ways our childhood was similar to that of children anywhere in rural Canada in the 50's and 60's. In other ways it was profoundly different. Keg River was a small farming community and our experiences growing up were very much affected by how our parents made their living.

For at least a decade money was scarce as our parents worked to get the farm established. We were expected to do our part in making the farm successful, no matter what our age, so we always had plenty of chores to do. As we matured, our responsibilities increased. In contrast to many children growing up today, we were never bored. Farm chores, house chores, school work and extracurricular activities like hockey, 4-H, Brownies and Girl Guides, made for an active bunch of kids and an even busier mom and dad.

For organizational purposes the three oldest children – Patricia, Henry, and David – were called "the big kids". Mary Lou, Penny and Neil were "the little kids". These designations didn't just describe our size. They also determined our bedtimes, chores, and who had to listen to whom when Mom and Dad were away.

We were lucky to have our maternal grandparents living in the same community. We saw them daily and have wonderful memories of happy times playing tag on their lawn or exploring the treasures in the old farm buildings. Granddad was a great gardener and always grew the nicest crop of greenhouse tomatoes. Grandma showed immense tolerance with us, even as we bumped down her steep staircase on the seats of our pants while she tried to see patients in her basement office.

Our dad's parents lived in Holland. Mom and Dad visited them every two or three winters and they came to see us a couple of times. They didn't speak English and we didn't speak Dutch, but we managed to communicate and have a good visit anyway.

Despite Keg River's small population we all had many friends who enriched our childhood. The Coulter, Batchelor and Weber families lived within easy walking or riding distance from our farm. We spent hours exploring, playing, fighting,

riding bikes and horses and just being a merry group of bandits. Aside from Kevin Coulter's broken leg we didn't get into much mischief. (We were snowmobiling at our house when Kevin was struck by a snowmobile and instead of taking him seriously when he said his leg was badly hurt, we laughed thinking he was trying to trick us. We found out later that Kevin's leg had been broken.) Before the two Jackson families left Keg River in the early 60's we had lots of cousins to play with, too.

Grades one through nine were taught at the Keg River school. The small size of the school did not adversely affect our education. For the most part we had excellent teachers and remember many of them for the fine example they set. We remember others for their not-so-fine example and learned from them also!

In order to complete high school we had to leave Keg River at age 14 or 15 and board away from home for three years. In the early 70's, the agricultural college in Fairview offered room and board to high school students, so our parents chose Fairview High School as the place we would complete grades 10 through 12. When it was our turn, we would make the 160-mile drive Sunday night or early Monday morning, then spend Monday through Friday in Fairview at the college dorm. When the college no longer offered room and board to high school students, we lived with Fairview families who opened their homes and hearts to us.

Boarding with families was a learning experience equal to the actual academic work. We were able to integrate successfully (we think) into families with lifestyles very unlike the one we knew, and learn a great deal about cooperation and tolerance in the process.

Neil got part of his high school education in Manning, where he was already well established on the local hockey team. He completed Grade 11 and 12 in Grande Prairie.

The academic transition between our small 90-student Keg River School and a larger high school was usually not difficult, but the adjustment to being away from home and "growing up quickly" was always more arduous. The lesson in responsibility that our parents taught us from a very young age was put to the test during our teenage years away from home. Like most kids living away from home for the first time, we missed Mom's great cooking the most.

With our parents' encouragement and support,

each of us completed high school and continued to some form of postsecondary education.

The weather was an important feature in our lives. From early in the spring until late in the fall, our day-to-day activities were decided by the sun, wind, and rain. The only season when the weather didn't matter was winter. It was predictably cold but, as we remember, always fun.

We didn't hide from the cold indoors. We tobogganed off the roothouse until we got caught, then moved to the other side where Mom couldn't see us. We spent hours shovelling snow off the dugout, playing hockey, or just skating. In the 70's we got a ski-doo (snowmobile) and winter wasn't the same again. We tested Dad's patience when he dug us out of the tenth snowbank of the day, but he never let on.

A midwinter chinook was always a joyful break from the intense and seemingly endless cold. The mercury could hold steady at -40 for days, then within a matter of hours the temperature would rise to well above freezing. The good news would usually be relayed to us by our grandparents on the old party line. They lived five miles west and two miles north of us and could hear the wind in their spruce trees minutes before it arrived at our house. We eagerly shed our heavy winter layers and used the strong westerly winds to propel us down icy roads on our toboggans.

The northern lights and full moon are other displays of nature that bring back childhood memories. The northern lights brightened the intense darkness of our unlit farmyard and seemed magical as they danced and crackled on the coldest nights of winter. The full moon cast eerie shadows behind us as we raced to the roothouse for spuds for supper, insuring a hasty trip and a breathless return.

Spring and fall were filled with work in the garden and the fields, but still we found time to play. We had a creek running through the yard, which provided many hours of amusement when it overflowed its banks. We built a raft and as we poled around the barnyard we pretended we were Tom Sawyer and Huck Finn floating down the Mississippi! When the roads dried up we hopped on our bicycles and met our friends halfway, then we would spend hours exploring the ditches for frogs and other critters. We also had time to play baseball and attend rodeos in Keg River, Paddle Prairie and Lac Cardinal.

The boys put their mechanical skills to the test early on by building a motorized go-cart from an old lawn mower engine and other salvaged "junk".

We would race around the yard and up and down the road to the farm. We had a few problems with the steering, and of course there were no brakes, so it's a good thing that there was the odd tree to slow us down.

Summers in Keg River are beautiful. By afternoon the temperature usually rises into the 70's and often into the 80's. Days are long, with the sun rising early and setting late, providing lots of daylight hours to get the work done, then play. Our summers were dominated by hilling potatoes, fighting off biting insects, and trips to the river.

If Sunday dawned bright and sunny and promised to be hot we would gather swimsuits and towels, pack the grub box with picnic essentials and begin our journey to the river.

The Chinchaga runs to the northwest of Keg River. After a dry spell it becomes a shallow river with large sandbars and can be easily walked across. In the summer the water warms up to a comfortable temperature for swimming, or so we thought when we were kids. The current is swift and we would spend the afternoon floating downstream and struggling back up repeatedly. When our lips finally turned blue and our skinny knees knocked together we would warm ourselves by playing in the sand and searching for clams along the water's edge. If we were really cold there was always a campfire burning and lots of food to restore our energy.

Navigating the dirt road to the Chinchaga was the most challenging part of a Sunday outing. One thunderstorm could leave the road impassable and more than once we ended up stuck deep in the mud, miles from home. With plenty of able bodies and a lot of ingenuity we always made it home, sometimes quite a bit later than planned. Only the milk cow really seemed to mind.

Driving to the Peace River at Carcajou often created the same difficulty – we had to forge our way over the 40 miles of "road", much of it through muskeg that stayed wet no matter how dry the conditions elsewhere. We think this is one reason we would take several friends along with us. We enjoyed their company but their help in pushing, pulling and devising ways out of mud holes was also extremely valuable!

In the days before the Carcajou road was upgraded, we often took the grain truck on our all-day expeditions to the Peace. This made it easier to get through the mud holes, but meant we rode in the back of the truck. "Bad hair days" were the norm after a trip to the river. If you've ever ridden in the back of a truck for a couple of hours at 30 miles an hour on a dirt road you will understand what we mean!

In the early 70's Dad and the boys built a boat. We left it at the Peace all summer and enjoyed many informative trips up and down the river. We saw bear, beaver, and moose swimming across the river and eating along the shore. We also observed many ducks, geese and other birds that lived along the water, often with their young paddling madly behind.

We sometimes travelled upstream to the Wolverine River. It flows into the Peace across from present-day Carcajou. The fishing was remarkably good in the Wolverine in early June. It became something of a family tradition to go fishing on Farmer's Day, the second Friday in June that marked the end of spring seeding. It was a reward for enduring the madness of that season.

On extremely hot days Mom would drive us down to the South Keg (Kemp) in the late afternoon and we played in the river as a way of cooling off. The river is only two to three feet deep and although it looks brown, the water is quite clean.

When we look back at these trips and know how scarce good water was on the farm we think it may have been a sly way for giving us all a bath! Well water in some areas of Keg River was unavailable. In other areas it was unusable.

On our parents' farm, rain water was collected in a concrete cistern in the basement. During shortages Dad hauled it by truck from the South Keg and later from our uncle's well in Carcajou. In the winter we filled the cistern with snow and enjoyed the softest water anywhere. We would all bathe on Sunday night, youngest to oldest (in order of bedtimes). We would often joke that it was cleanest to dirtiest because we used the same water for all the baths. We had the convenience of running water after 1965, but the water shortage never seemed to abate.

Another way of saving water was to use the outdoor two-hole toilet. This was extremely cold in the winter, so after we had running water and a septic system we used it only in the summer.

We were almost self-sufficient in terms of food. Mom grew a very large garden and still does today. It was a challenge to keep enough food in the house with six growing kids, especially with the nearest grocery store 60 dusty miles away.

Preserving the year's harvest was a big undertaking each fall. Some vegetables were frozen or canned. Carrots, potatoes, cabbages, celery and onions were stored in the rootcellar so successfully the surplus would be fed to the pigs the following summer when the garden started producing the new crop.

The garden yielded plenty of rhubarb and our grandparents had several good crabapple trees but we also picked many wild berries to make up for the lack of other locally grown fruits. The Keg River area has the perfect climate for berries, with many varieties growing within a 30-mile radius from the farm. They aren't always in easily accessible places, but that never stops our mother. A true berry picker, Mom is undaunted by bears, bees, bugs and bush in her search for the perfect patch. Even several whining children trailing along never fazed her. We picked chokecherries from the back of the truck, blueberries on our knees with our noses two inches from the ground, and black currants with our feet in swamp, all the while alert for crashing and snorting that signalled the approach of a bear.

Raspberries grew in old brush piles along the road, but those same piles were also favoured by yellow jackets and hornets. A couple of times all of our work ended up scattered in the underbrush when we inadvertently stepped in a yellow-jacket nest. In the haste to get out of harm's way the berry pail went flying in one direction and the poor screeching victim in the other. Sometimes it seemed that mom was more worried about the spilled berries!

High-bush cranberries and chokecherries made wonderful jelly for toast; black currants were made into jam. Low-bush cranberries became sauce for the Christmas turkey. Blueberries and saskatoons were delicious in pies, eaten fresh with cream, or were canned and enjoyed in the middle of the long dark winter. Wild strawberries were tedious to pick, but the resulting shortcake made them worth the time.

Each year Mom raised about a hundred chickens, a few turkeys and some ducks. The chickens were butchered and frozen in July. About two dozen were kept to supply eggs until the following summer. Beef and pork were raised on the farm and were part of our diet. Dad also hunted moose each year. Wild ducks and geese migrated through Keg River in the fall and they would sometimes become our supper as well. We ate the occasional rabbit when they were plentiful, although Mom had to tell us they were chicken to make them more palatable. She didn't fool us.

For a few years we kept honeybees. They were certainly educational for all of us – we learned that it was a lot of work to keep up with them. Over the years we harvested and sold tons of honey, but it was a hot sticky job, and eventually Mom and Dad decided it was a business best left to people who had teenagers at home.

We learned a great deal about community spirit from our parents. They are very community-minded and supported many organizations as we were growing up. They helped organize fund-raisers for building, and maintaining the library, community hall, and skating rink. They seemed to be the first to arrive at functions and the last to leave, making sure that all the necessary jobs got done.

Our parents never locked the door. Most people in the community didn't. They thought that if someone needed to get in, they should be able to. A large barking dog also gave them plenty of warning if someone needed assistance in the night.

Keg River is halfway between Manning and High Level. In the "early" days, services were few and far between and not always reliable. Travellers who ran into difficulties had to rely on the goodwill of the next person who happened along. We remember an incident one spring when Dad came home about suppertime with a couple of men. (It was not that unusual for Dad to arrive at mealtime with unexpected guests. Mom always welcomed the visitors and quickly came up with something delicious to eat from her fully stocked pantry.) This particular evening one of the men was covered from head to toe in mud. We were told in no uncertain terms that we were not to ask any questions. The man was shown to the bathroom, he bathed, then joined us for supper.

We found out later that Dad had found them and their little convertible stuck deep in the mud between Keg River and High Level. The one unfortunate soul had an epileptic seizure while trying to get the car back on solid ground. Dad pulled the car out of the mud, loaded it in the back of the truck and convinced the men that they would be welcome to spend the night with us. He drove them on to Manning the next morning where we assume they were able to have their car cleaned and made roadworthy. We never heard from them again.

Another memory that we all recall vividly is the day that Ben Hayes arrived at our house. It was the first day we had ever seen a black man. Before that we knew of black people only from picture books and *National Geographic.*

Our Dad had been sick and had asked Employment Canada to find someone to help on the farm. Ben arrived before we were notified that he was on his way, and just before the school bus brought us home from school. He was standing on the doorstep as we got off the bus and we stared, speechless, as did all the kids on the bus.

Thankfully Ben survived that first day with us and stayed to work on the farm for several years. We still marvel at his strength, endurance, and patience. He often took time to play hide-and-seek or baseball with us in the evening, despite working hard all day. He became our friend in the time he spent with us and his assistance on the farm will always be remembered. He is now retired and living in Calgary.

Keg River was a unique place to grow up. Many people consider it isolated, but we do not. Our childhood experiences were certainly different from those of our town and city relatives, but we did not suffer because of it; instead, we believe that our lives were enriched by it. Our parents and grandparents played a key role in making our memories all positive ones.

At this writing in the spring of 1994, Patricia and Garry live outside of Drayton Valley with their two sons. Henry and AnneMarie and their two daughters farm at Fairview. David and Joyce farm at Keg River. Mary Lou and Bobby live in Edmonton. Penny and Tom and their two children are currently in Montana, and Neil and Mir and their kids live in Manning. As scattered as we are, we all enjoy going "home" to Keg River because in many ways our hearts are still there.

Keg River Community Halls
by Anne Vos

The social life of any community revolves around those people who see a need and create opportunities to get together, whether it be a bridge game or a native tea dance. Over the years recreational and social life in Keg River has taken many forms. Mrs. Eva Harrington and friends loved bridge games in the 1930's and 40's. Whist, crib and poker were also popular card games with tournaments being held in the community.

Native tea dances with the accompanying beat of drums were held outside in the summer and often carried on long into the night. In the winter the parties were held indoors in the largest house available. Since Larone Ferguson had one of the biggest houses in the village during the 1940's, dances were often held there. The music was provided by Charlie Noskey, Dan Grey, Fred Noskey, and many others on guitars or violins.

The 1940's and World War II brought the Red Cross Club.

Nick Tomilou, a bachelor farmer, generously offered his home for dances, wedding suppers and ''Keg'' parties! The school house also became a popular spot, especially when Christmas concerts were given. In 1950 when the new school was built the old school became the first community hall.

The United Farmers formed sub-local 235 here in 1957 and began the process of procuring land for a recreation area. Some of the farmers on the board were Louis Hrytciuk, Ted Krause, Emma McDonald, Frank Jackson, and Harry Bowe; Dr. Jackson, was secretary of the local. After more than a year of letter writing, sixteen acres were approved for a recreation lease. This land is next to the Catholic church.

Building a new hall was a top priority. Since this would be a public building, blueprints had to be completed, then approved by the government. Frank Jackson drew up the plans that were approved.

Meanwhile the community worked raising money with card parties, bingos, box socials and selling memberships to everyone in the district. As the railway was being built at the time, one other unique fund raiser was designed. Tickets were sold on guessing the exact hour that the railroad would cross the Post road; $500.00 was realized on this event alone!

Finally, with a bank loan backed by local farmers, the building began. Volunteers spent their spare time in the summers of 1959 and 1960 completing the hall.

In the new building, movies were shown once a week and proved to be very popular. (Regular bus service to and from Edmonton allowed us to bring in the movies.) Christmas concerts were held in the hall in the 60's and 70's as the school population soared to a high of 150 students in 1970. There wasn't room at the school because the addition which included the gymnasium was not built until later. Many of these Christmas concerts were occasions when the hall was filled to capacity with standing room only.

This hall was decorated with a number of murals done on plywood by Frank Jackson. In 1966 Leonard Hunter gave the hall a set of moose antlers measuring 61 1/2 inches across, the largest ever seen in this area. The antlers were hung above the kitchen windows at the back of the hall. The ladies of the district eventually purchased a set of melmac dishes to use in all the catering they did. There was no indoor plumbing and the water was carried from the river.

The hall served us well for over 16 years. It was destroyed by fire in March, 1978.

It was a terrible loss to the community, leaving no place large enough to gather for social events or even funerals. There was limited insurance money -a total of $18,000.

The community pulled together and plans got under way for rebuilding. Two years and many meetings later, we were ready to start again.

A newly elected board began the task of raising money and deciding on a design and location. The board consisted of: Margaret Coulter, president; Linda Pawlowich, vice president; Anne Vos, secretary-treasurer; and directors: Garth Coulter, Steve Pawlowich, Johnny Vos, Annie Michalchuk, Len de Haan, and Louis Holtz.

A Culture and Recreation representative in Peace River arranged a tour of 12 Peace River country halls and community centers where we learned first-hand many good ideas. We also heard some things we should not do! Grovedale, south of Grande Prairie had a hall we liked and at a price we could afford.

Marius Vos did the architectural blueprints for us -a considerable donation. With the help of a bank loan and donations from people of the district, work began on the building in the summer of 1980.

Summer students working on new hall foundation. L-R: Jan Befus, Penny Vos, Lorna Hamelin and Tracy Coulter wheeling the wheelbarrow, 1979.

Hall mural painted by Frank Jackson.

Through the Student Summer Employment Program six students were hired that summer: Tracey Coulter, Beth Befus, Lorna Hamelin, Kenny Tupper, Penny Vos and Allan Zatko. The Prochinsky brothers brought their bulldozer to remove the dirt for the partial basement and crawl space under the building. Jaeger Concrete poured the cement for the cistern and basement. All labour and equipment was donated or volunteered, except for Jeager Concrete and Dale's Plumbing from Manning.

Patricia Vos found a sawmill at Rocky Mountain House that would cut tongue-and-grooved V-joint pine. Garth Coulter and Johnny Vos each hauled a truckload of this pine to Keg River. Arch ribs had been ordered from Edmonton. The students were supervised by the directors and work progressed rapidly with the base floor done by the time school started in the fall. Coulters had donated a granary to store supplies and the library building was used for headquarters.

Unloading arch ribs for hall, Garth Coulter, Johnny Vos, Tracy Coulter, truck driver and Evelyn Malina, 1979.

Raising the arch ribs for hall.

Harvest was quick and dry, so construction was able to continue. A late fall and many people volunteering enabled us to enclose the building before the snow fell. The last spike on the top was driven by Len de Haan and Louis Holtz.

Installing the siding.

Len deHaan and Louis Holtz.

Margaret and Garth Coulter with Rose Pawlowich closing in the west end.

The first event held in the new building was an auction sale of donated items, conducted by Ken Bachelor. The $1000 profit was a great help towards the furnaces. (And heat was needed as winter was here!)

During November and December work continued with power, plumbing, cupboards and partitions installed. Plans were made by the Ladies' Club for a New Year's Party, just six months after work began! January brought us Katimivik, two groups of six, young exchange students from Quebec. They helped with various projects in the district, some at the school and others finishing the work at the hall. They all stayed at Dr. Jackson's and were fed in other homes and at the hall.

The Queen crocheted by Donna and Linda Halabisky.

You and your family are cordially invited
to come and participate in our
Homecoming 1980 Celebration

Official Opening
Keg River Community Hall

Keg River

July 1, 1980

New hall at Keg River.

Ribbon cutting. Peeweno, Muriel Stigsen and Bill Halabisky, July 1, 1980.

A Keg River Homecoming and the hall's grand opening were held July 1st, 1980. Jean Marie Cardinal, Bill Halabisky and Muriel Stigsen participated in the ribbon-cutting ceremony. They were chosen because of their many years of residence in the Keg River area. Dr. Jackson gave the address and Gene Dextrase brought greetings from the Northern Economic Development Council. The Ladies Club served a bountiful supper for the large crowd. Music and song were provided by Harry Rusk and his band, originally from Kahntai River.

This hall continues to serve as a gathering place for the community and the recently added pavement in the parking lot is a great improvement.

The Library
by Anne Vos

The Keg River library began when a federal Centennial grant of $1670 was received for recreation and culture in 1967. A building was built by Frank Jackson and Harry Bowe, both in their seventies and Floyd Schwindt, using this money. Initially this building also housed the dressing room for the hockey rink, but later was converted entirely to library use.

Sheila Douglass, Anne Vos and the Jacksons began searching for books, accepting donations and getting any help available. The Keg River Library was officially registered as an organization in 1968.

The building was hooked up to electrical power and heated with an oil heater that was very temperamental. We thought the heating problems were solved when we switched to a small propane heater but found it was another problem. The door-handle lock would get ice in it and we couldn't unlock the door.

One day Leslie Carnell was working in the library with her three little boys and the door-handle froze. She was unable to get out! She finally managed to get a window open and she climbed out that way. She was able to open the door from the outside using gasoline alcohol from her car. It seemed that burning propane in the library was causing condensation in the door-handle!

Books by the box and suitcase arrived; and we received a large donation from the Hudson's Bay Library. The next problem was keeping up with cataloguing and finding shelf space. When the first half of the building was full, it was decided by the board to take over the recreation part of the building, too, since the skating rink had been moved to the school.

With all this new space, we used the library for meetings, wedding and baby showers, and bake sales. The library membership continued to grow but with only a few volunteers, it was hard to keep regular hours. Len de Haan kept building shelves and we kept on filling them!

It was a great benefit when the community hall, which is located next to the library, put in natural gas and hooked up the library as well. The telephone arrived at the same time.

Soon we found that the shelves were again full and no more space existed for building more. In 1980 we planned an addition to the building, also adding a wheelchair ramp. We might not be good carpenters, but the job once again got done!

Janice Freeman and Linda Halabisky set up library hours. The library is open one afternoon a week and Tuesday evenings. Sarah Price also helps at the library during some of the hours it is open.

In the last few years we have added a number of talking books on cassette, Disney movies, craft and other VHS video tapes. There are approximately 11,000 books available for loan, including some very old ones on every topic from Art to Zebras.

Keg River Ladies Club

by Linda Halabisky

The Keg River Ladies Club had its origins in the 1940's, when Mrs Eva Harrington began a sewing circle for any local girls that wanted to learn to sew.

A year or so later the group expanded and changed purpose. The Red Cross was appealing for help in supplying hand-knit helmet liners, socks, mittens, gloves, and scarves or turtle-neck dickies to Canadian soldiers. Anyone who knew how to knit was asked to join the Red Cross knitting club. Emma McDonald got the ladies in the village to participate, too. Depending on the weather, the ladies got together weekly, when they had completed an item or had to pick up more wool. The Red Cross shipped in several large boxes of wool in colors that conformed with Army requirements. The ladies were told that they should knit according to wool color and of course according to their abilities. Boys and girls as young as 10 years old joined the ladies of the district to produce many needed items.

The adults also started sponsoring card parties and dances to make money for the Red Cross. This money was used to send special kits to the men overseas.

After the war, the group continued to help the Red Cross, but the focus gradually became needy families of our district. In 1951-52 there was a push for the ladies to join the Women's Institute but since we were such a small group the majority decide to stay local and keep any money raised here. There were a number of projects. The ladies staffed the concession booths at the annual Sports Days and they became the best fund-raiser of the summer months. The ladies looked after supplying bags of treats that Santa gave to the children at the annual Christmas concerts. Card parties and dances were still held to fund-raise.

The only building large enough to hold sizable gatherings was the school, so we kept to smaller groups. When the school moved to the new building in 1952, the old building was used as a community hall. The group of ladies were still around but were inactive except for looking after Christmas treats. In 1957 Alice Robertson and a few others thought they should get busy and do more for the community. Then plans to build a new hall began to interest everyone. There was plenty to do in the way of fund-raising.

The Ladies club purchased a set of Melmac dishes, 12 dozen place settings and silverware. Once the dishes were in place in the new hall the ladies had a new task, washing all those dishes after each event. It was quite a job, especially when there was no running water in the hall!

Graduation suppers were special, and so was the Brick's 50th anniversary, candle-lit supper! There were wedding suppers and farewells. The hall was being used by Adult Upgrading when it burnt down in March, 1978, which was a great loss to the ladies club and the district.

When Miss Paul was here in the 1950's, she taught more than 40 students each year in nine different grades. She also encouraged community involvement in the school. The ladies club began providing prizes for various school endeavors, such as a fountain pen for the boy and the girl with the best handwriting. (This award is still given today and is called the Penmanship Award.) A small prize for the neatest school work was also given to a girl and a boy. When the students took public speaking, the ladies provided an engraved trophy for the best speaker in each grade. Now the ladies sponsor kids to attend Alcohol and Drug Abuse Commission programs.

The ladies club meetings have provided a place to meet newcomers and enjoy the companionship of neighbors while either working or having fun.

Dine and Dances are the usual method of raising money. The good food is a drawing card. Funds are always necessary for many things from Christmas treats to buying equipment for the hall. A television set, Ninetendo and VCR are the latest purchases.

There have been funny incidents as well from the unbaked potatoes to mopping up the basement in our New Years finery. We have provided entertainment by acting out a skit, at Muriel and Ted Stigsen's anniversary party!

The ladies have certainly helped with the social life of the community.

Ladies' Club members Muriel Stigsen and Mary Boyce.

Naylor Hills Ladies Society
by Margaret Befus

The Naylor Hills Ladies' Society was formed in the 1950's to raise money for Christmas treats for the Naylor Hills school children and many other projects.

Every winter there were house fires in homestead shacks. The stove pipes from the wood stove went out through the roof or sometimes the wall and often caused fires. A family would be lucky to get out, let alone save their worldly goods. Our group made quilts and helped out in these cases.

Under the supervision of Mrs. Round, this organization was formed, registered and operated. Even though most of us were busy raising families, gardening and picking berries, we made time to make quilts, plan card parties and put on bingos. To get to meetings we came with our little children. There were often more children than members!

Some of the members of the Naylor Hills Ladies Society were: Mrs. Jack Round, Mrs. Louis Jackson, Mrs. Bud Bouma, Mrs. Jim Bouma, Mrs. George Price, Mrs. Dave Befus, Mrs. Mary Rudy and Mrs. June Papirny.

Mrs. Round's untimely death was the reason our organization stopped functioning. We honor her memory as she was a real community-minded citizen.

Sports Days 1941
From the *Peace River Record Gazette July 26, 1941*

Keg River's two-day Sports Days were enjoyed by many people, who came from miles around for the annual event. Best of all was the old-time hospitality and community spirit shown everywhere. The community put on the best sports program we have seen in many years. In the organizing committee were Ernie Brick, Hilare Minault, Frank Ferguson and treasurer Louis Jackson. They had $150 to finance the whole thing.

Mrs. Glady Harrington and other ladies furnished the food. It was sold and the profits turned over to the Red Cross.

The rivalry in the sports events was keen with everyone anxious to take part, showing the old fighting spirit.

Below are the winners and the amount of their prize money.

EVENT	WINNER	PRIZE MONEY
Horse Race	Harvey Daunchia	$5
Pony Race	Joe Auger	$3
Ladies' Horse Race	Betty Chalifoux	$3
Free-for-all Horse Race	M. Noskey	$3
Mile Horse Race	Bob Biswanger	$10
Novelty Horse Race	M. Noskey	$2
Bucking Contest	Ed Strong	$10
100-Yard Dash	Jean Cardinal	$1.50
Men's Half Mile	Celesta Bottle	$4
Girls' (under 16) Dash	Katherine Ghostkeeper	$1
Boys' (under 16) Dash	Billy Yurkowski	$1
Men's High Jump	Celesta Bottle	$1
Thread-the-Needle Race	Celesta Bottle Katherine Ghostkeeper	$1
Women's Race	Tillie Pawlowich	$1.50
Wheelbarrow Race	George Sinclair Sam Johnston	$1
Old Man's Race	Fred Ducharme	$1
Girls' (under 10) Dash	Pat Hague	$.50

Boys' (under 10) Dash	Eddie Halabisky	$.50
Long Jump	Jean Cardinal	$1
Putting the Shot	Sam Johnston	$1
Hop-Step-Jump	Jean Cardinal	$1
3-Legged Race	B. Dourchie	$1
	Jim House	
Moccasin Race	Ambrose Noskey	$.75

With the 1941 Sports Days a thing of the past, Glady Harrington, Albert Trosky, Frank Jackson, Harry Bowe, Ernie Brick, Doug Stevens, Dave McDonald, Hilare Minault, Louis Jackson and our old friend big Nick Tomilou are talking about the 1942 Sports Days.

They plan to hold a two-day frontier sports event the like of which is not seen in the Peace country. There are lots of good riders and bucking and race horses in the district. They will certainly put on a show equal to anything ever seen in the country.

(By 1942 our country was involved in a war, so the next Sports Days held in Keg River were not held until 1946.)

Another horse race. Picture taken from grandstand.

The home stretch. Notice Teepees in the background.

Peanut scramble.

Sports Days June 21-22, 1946
From the *Peace River Record Gazette*

Spirited horses and gala trimmings combined to make the Keg River sports carnival a festive scene. With the aid of good weather and an enthusiastic crowd, Keg River enjoyed a carnival that did justice to the hard-working committee of Frank Ferguson, Larone Ferguson and Nick Tomilou.

Teams, trucks, cars and saddle horses brought in visitors from the outlying district as well as

Hobbled race.

Paddle Prairie, North Star and Fort Vermilion. Unfortunately, due to an error with the date, some folks from Notikewin arrived on June 24th!

Feelings were running high when truckloads of children turned up ready to do battle with contestants from Keg River on the baseball field. Susie Parenteau captained the Paddle Prairie school team, putting up an excellent fight. However, the Keg Riverites under Mervin Rudy were really into winning. The final score of the final game was 40 to 11.

Reminiscent of the pioneer days when the mail got through at all costs was the Pony Express race. Hard-riding mailmen spurred their horses to the halfway mark, hurriedly dismounted, then sprang into the saddle of fresh horses that awaited them. Dan House carried off the prize in this race. Johnny Cardinal was a close second.

Judges Nick Tomilou, Frank and Larone Ferguson, sitting on the grandstand high above the crowd, had a hectic time keeping track of the many events. Typical of the time and forethought spent in preparation was the speed with which drivers of teams, trucks and cars got together to form a safety wall to protect the crowd when the popular bucking contest took place. Thanks to this wall, there were no real accidents and no one was hurt.

Ambrose Parenteau must have taken some real punishment when his blue roan gelding went to town in the bucking contest. At one moment his foot was in his horse's mouth! However, it was Jim Hunter's red roan that carried off the prize.

The slow horse race was another popular event. The horses were anxious to show their stuff while the riders tried, often in vain, to hold them back. Little Edward Strong put on an amusing show by whipping his horse all the way around the track and still coming in last! He carried off the prize all right but he was the only rider whose horse was going rhythmically up and down while the others were doing their best to slow down their horses. John Cardinal's dapple grey came first.

The half-mile horse race was run in three heats. Joe Laboucan's favorite black gelding, Nigger, was the final winner. Anne Jackson's mare, Brownie, was a close second.

In the half-mile pony race Raymond Houle's strawberry roan captured the main prize in the third heat, while Tommy Ducharme's Black Star was runner-up.

Sports Day – Bronc Riding.

Sports day – Horse Race.

Sports Day – Bronc Riding.

The open-air dance pavilion, illuminated by glowing bonfires, was the centre attraction for both evenings. George Sinclair, Sam Johnston, Frank Chalifoux, Charlie Noskey and John St. Germain spelled each other in a united effort to keep pace with a crowd eager for square dances, circle two-steps and waltzes. Even the children showed real community spirit by inaugurating a clean-up campaign for the joint purpose of cleaning up the sports grounds and keeping the bonfires glowing.

When the carnival crowd finally played out congratulations were exchanged amid firm resolutions to do even better next year. Watch out, Paddle Prairie!

The main event winners were:

EVENT	FIRST PLACE	SECOND PLACE
Half-mile Horse Race	Joe Laboucan	Anne Jackson
Half-mile Pony Race	Raymond Houle	Tommy Ducharme
100 Yard Dash	Albert Wanuch	Tommy Ducharme
Girls' 75 Yard Race	Anne Jackson	Ivy Ghostkeeper
Boys' 75 Yard Race	Lawrence Lariviere	Mervin Rudy
Men's Hop-Step-Jump	Dan House	Roger Wanuch
Men's 3 Legged Race	Edgar Poitras	Tommy Ducharme
	Albert Wanuch	John Cardinal
Girls' 3 Legged Race	Katherine Ghostkeeper	Mary Pawlowich
	Mabel Martineau	Susie Parenteau
Running High Jump	Sonny Bellrose	Dan House
Standing Long Jump	Celesta Chalifoux	Sammy Auger
Men's Sack Race	Donald Hamelin	Malcom Ducharme
Slow Horse Race	Lawrence Lariviere	Cliff McGillivray
Slow Horse Race	John Cardinal	Edward Strong
Thread-the-Needle Race	Ambrose Parenteau	Tommy Ducharme
	Ivy Ghostkeeper	Mabel Martineau
Girls' Egg Race	Mary Pawlowich	Ester McLeod
Figure-8 Race	John Cardinal	Octave Parenteau
Wheelbarrow Race	Tommy Ducharme	Sammy Auger
	Alphonse Cardinal	Edgar Poitras
Moccasin Race	John Cardinal	Alphonse Cardinal
Half-mile Foot Race	Dan House	Albert Wanuch
Free-for-all Horse Race	Albert Wanuch	Sonny Trosky
Fat Man's Race	Dan Supernault	Archie Chalifoux
Married Women's Race	Alvina Supernault	Tillie Beaulieu
Novelty Horse Race	Fredrick Hamelin	Donald Chalifoux
Girls' Pony Race	Anne Jackson	Ivy Ghostkeeper
Married Women's Egg Race	Dr. Mary Jackson	Annie Michalchuk

Special races were run for the small fry, and as usual everyone came in first and each child was awarded a prize.

(Editor's note: These sports days were held directly across the road from the Hudson's Bay store on land generously donated by Johnny Yurkowski. There was just enough clear land to make the half-mile circle race track.)

Sports Days 1947
From the *Peace River Record Gazette*

Another successful sports day was held in Keg River on June 27th. Good weather and a varied program planned by Jim Hunter, Nick Tomilou and Larone Ferguson kept the crowd happy. Visitors arrived from miles around. Two refreshment booths were a boon, providing special treats of ice cream and cake.

Sports Day – Food booth and open air dance floor in background.

There was fun for everyone. The children each won a prize, whether they were fast or slow. Ball teams from the Paddle Prairie and Keg River schools put on a good show. Victory went to Keg River with Anne Jackson as the captain over the Paddle team with captain Harvey Tronjeau. The score was 31-12!

The men's ball game was won by Paddle Prairie.

The results of the major contests were as follows:

EVENT	FIRST PLACE	SECOND PLACE
Stone Throwing	Alphonse Cardinal	Jim Hamelin
Hop-Step-Jump	Jim Supernault	Jim Hamelin
Standing Long Jump	Jim Hamelin	Dan House
Men's 3-Legged Race	Dan House	Leo Parenteau
	Russell Minault	Jim Supernault
Running High Jump	Dan House	Jim Hamelin
Pony Race	Mitchell Christian	Joe Christian
Ladies' Egg Race	Annie Michalchuk	
Boys' 50 Yard Dash	Leonard Hunter	Donald Trosky
	Third – Jimmy Richards	
Girls' 50 Yard Dash	Mary Pawlowich	Anne Jackson
	Third – Ester McLeod	
Boys' Race	Jimmy Richards	Norman Hunter
Girls' Race	Katherine Ghostkeeper	
Thread-the-Needle	Alvina and Sylvester	Supernault
Boys' 3 Legged Race	Jimmy Richards	Norman Hunter
	Lorne Minault	George Trosky
Girls' 3 Legged Race	Mary Pawlowich	Ester McLeod
	Anne Jackson	Alma Ferguson
Married Women's Race	Alvina Supernault	
Men's Sack Race	Tommy Ducharme	Sammy Ducharme
	Third – Dan House	
Boys' Moccasin Race	Jimmy Richards	Wilfred Ferguson
	Third – Donald Ferguson	
Girls' Moccasin Race	Alvina Supernault	Stella Wanuch
Wheelbarrow Race	Tommy and Sammy Ducharme	
Novelty Race	Frederick Hamelin	Albert Wanuch
Potato Horse Race	Sonny Bellrose	
Free-for-all Horse Race	Eddy Halabisky	Sammy Ducharme
	Third – Norman Hunter	
Men's Moccasin Race	Tommy Ducharme	Jim Cardinal
	Third 8 Sammy Auger	
Men's Half-mile Race	Jim House	Albert Wanuch
Bucking Horses	1st-Jim Hunter on Celesta Bottle's roan	
	2nd – Tom Parenteau on Gene Cardinal's grey	
	3rd – Alphonse Stoney on Pawlowich's black	
	4th – Sammy Supernault on Rudy's bay	
Horse Race	1st – Len Hunter (on A. Jackson's Brownie)	
	2nd – Jack House (on Albert Wanuch's Wiggles)	
Slow Horse Race	1st – Keith Onstien (on Ray Ross's Silver)	
	2nd – Norman Hunter (on John Jackson's Dan)	

In the evening an enjoyable dance was held at the home of Nick Tomilou with music provided by Charlie Noskey, Babe Beaulieu and Dan Grey.

High jump.

Posture Race – balancing a plate on their heads.

Bronco Busting.

Three legged race.

Keg River Fall Stampede 1956
From the *Peace River Record Gazette*

The Keg River fall stampede was held on the Ken Batchelor homestead on September 3rd, 1956. The day arrived with snow-laden skies and in the morning many thought that it might snow.

However, the skies cleared in the afternoon. Dave Befus turned out some of the most difficult stock in northern Alberta, resulting in few qualifying rides. The results in the events follow:

Saddle Bronc Riding	1st – Len Hunter, Keg River 2nd – George Heninger, Chestermere Lake 3rd – Walter Gaucher, Paddle Prairie
Bareback	1st – Art Jones, Balzac 2nd – Walter Gaucher, Paddle Prairie 3rd – Gordon Cole, Chestermere Lake 4th – Tommy Ducharme, Keg River
Wild Horse Race	Only 2 outfits made it out of 11 starts. Tie for 1st – George Heninger, Pat Gaucher
Wild Cow Milking	1st – George Heninger, Chestermere Lake 2nd – Earl Hunter, Keg River 3rd – Dan Hadke, Sundre
Boys' Steer Riding	1st – Edward Michalchuk, Keg River 2nd – Jim Trosky, Keg River 3rd – Everett Michalchuk, Keg River
Best-Dressed Cowboy	Lorne Minault, Keg River
Top Horse	Gentle Boy brought in by Len Hunter
Greased Pig Race	Lorne Minault *This race turned out differently than planned. The boys put on a stampede trying to catch the pig but it was just too slippery! George Heninger saved the day by turning loose a trained skunk. It took a lot more nerve but much less skill to catch the skunk!
Men's Bull Riding	1st – Earl Hunter, Keg River 2nd – Jim Hunter, Keg River 3rd – George Cole, Chestermere Lake 4th – Art Jones, Balzac *This was an added unadvertised feature because the directors did not know if enough good bulls would be entered.

A tip of the hat to the Batchelors for a great show!

Other Stampedes
From information in the *Peace River Record Gazette*

Keg River, Paddle Prairie and Carcajou residents have put on their own stampedes and have participated in the Stampedes of other communities.

In the July 1973 Fort Vermilion, stampede a number of area residents did very well. The results of some of the events follow.

All-round Cowboy	Budson Davison, Manning
Bareback Champion	Ron Minualt, Rocky Lane
Saddle Bronc	Ernest Beaulieu, High Level
Bull Riding Champion	Garry Houle, Paddle Prairie
Men's Steer Riding Champion	Louis Houle, Paddle Prairie
Calf Riding Champion	Earl Hunter, Manning
Wild Cow Milking	Len Hunter, Grimshaw
Wild Cow Race	Allan Martineau, Paddle Prairie
Little Britches (under 16):	
All-round Champion	Louis Houle, Paddle Prairie
Bareback Champion	John Juneau, Rocky Lane
Steer Riding Champion	Terry Houle, Paddle Prairie
Best Bucking Horse	Tall Cree owned by Bob Lambert, Fort Vermilion

Tied for first:
Arlene Bellrose, Paddle Prairie
Lauralyn Houle, Paddle Prairie

In 1973 Alice Batchelor of Keg River and Arlene Bellrose of Paddle Prairie were among the girls competing for North Peace Stampede Queen. They were judged on personality, appearance and riding ability. Alice Batchelor was named Queen!

In 1975 Sandra Stigsen from Carcajou was one of the contestants for Queen of the North Peace Stampede.

Annette Stigsen of Carcajou was a contestant for the title of North Peace Rodeo Queen.

Great Train Wreck of 1968
by Anne Vos

The Keg River train wreck on the Great Slave Lake Railroad happened in the spring of 1968.

Two miles south of the Keg River elevator, across the Keg River a southbound train crashed in the middle of the night. No one saw the accident or heard the tremendous noise it must have made.

A wheel bearing seized, causing an ore car to jump off the track. Thirty-eight other cars of various sizes left the track, spilling lead zinc ore in all directions. The wheels were sheared off some of the cars as they piled up.

The first great train wreck.

What happens when car meets train in the dark of night. Luckily there were no injuries to the occupants but the car turned into a convertible, 1985.

Later when we visited the site, the wreckage was difficult to believe. The value of the spilt ore was more than one million dollars and the destroyed railway cars were of almost equal value. The repair crews arrived quickly and a detour rail line was in place in several days.

Second Train Wreck
by Johnny Vos

On January 6, 1994, a truck owned by Grad Transport, La Crete, and loaded to the limit with poplar logs, was heading for the Daishowa Marubeni Pulpmill in Peace River. It was hit by a southbound Canadian National locomotive pulling a train loaded with lumber at the uncontrolled crossing on the Keg River Post road. The lead locomotive of the train collided with the truck at about the middle of the log load. BANG!!!

There were no major injuries. The lead locomotive and the truck ended up in the ditch, facing in the direction the truck had been travelling with the logs scattered around. Three more locomotives and two railcars loaded with lumber were also derailed. It was lucky that the lead locomotive did not flip over the truck.

Train Wreck of Jan 6th, 1994.

The engineer and crew of two ducked in the cab of the locomotive when they saw what was about to happen. When the noise died down, the train crew looked out to find the truck driver standing on the highway. His only injury was a scratch on his head. No one from the train crew was injured.

Some of the logs were on top of the second locomotive. At least two sets of wheels were knocked out from under the locomotives.

When log truck meets train, Jan 6th, 1994.

Equipment had to brought in from Edmonton to lay new sections of track and get everything back on track.

The accident happened about 9:30 that Thursday morning. All the railcars were able to continue south on Sunday morning, being pulled by other engines. Late Sunday the lead locomotive was hoisted and winched out of the ditch. Monday morning it was placed on its wheels on the track, to be towed with the other three to Edmonton and possibly to Winnipeg to be repaired. The truck was a complete writeoff.

The weekend of the cleanup was the coldest of the winter, with the temperature hovering between -40° and -45°C. If boys want to play with trains, they would be better off to do it in the living room!

Brownies and Guides
by Mary Lou Ng

The 1st Keg River Brownie Pack was formed in October, 1967, under the guidance of Mrs. Marr and Mrs. Cartier. The meetings were held at the school during lunch hour on Fridays.

One of the first things I remember us doing was dividing into small groups and having to decide on a name for each group. We were given a number of choices and a description of the qualities that each name represented. Pixies and Fairies were among the choices. My group lobbied quite strongly for the name we wanted because other groups wanted the same name. But in the end we got the name we so desperately wanted – we were to be called the Fairies! Little did I know that my brother David and his friends would tease us for years about being Fairies!

Mrs. Marr worked along with fellow teachers Mrs. Cartier and Mrs. Befus in providing us with many fun-filled hours of learning and fellowship in Brownies. We learned about the Brownie organization including the motto, the promise and the salute. Braiding practice, sewing buttons, cleaning shoes and setting tables were among the activities that kept us busy. Home safety, making lunches and using a compass are learnings we continue to use today. Mrs. Dave Weber and Mrs. W. Laboucan were two moms who came in to help with our activities.

We had a girl guide group (1st Keg River Company) in Keg River for two years. It was a busy time! Miss Margaret Bolton started the group during 1969, the year she taught at Keg River. My mom, Anne Vos, and Gladys Rudy were among the other volunteers who helped out with the guide programs. Our regular meetings were held during the lunch hour at the school. My small group was called the Lily-of-the-Valley Patrol.

Keg River Girl Guides raising their flag on top of the gravel pile.

Girl Guide Flag.

Many parents and other community members were involved as we worked towards badges. I earned sixteen in those two years. But I found it funny that even though one of the badges was for sewing, a couple of my badges are pinned to my sash!

Mrs. Lowe tested me for my cooking badge. One of the things I had to do was to make a white sauce. I had practised making it at home, but the margarine and flour still got very close to scorching while I was finding and measuring the milk to add to the mixture! I think she passed me because I don't remember having to go back and experiment with more of her food! I still think of Mrs. Lowe every time I make white sauce!

We did many other things besides working on badges. I remember the hiking trips. We would set off from the school, hike south to the Carcajou road, then to the Kemp River and along the river. We learned to recognize different plants and trees as well as animal tracks. We made campfires and listened to the animal noises. We also made friends. Closer bonds were formed by being together in these experiences.

Margaret Bolton (now Lyall) says now that she didn't really care for tenting. That explains why we ended up back in the school yard when it was time to pitch the tent for the evening. She would sleep in her house and we would sleep in the tent that was yards from her front door! In the morning she would join us as we built a little fire and cooked pancakes on an overturned five pound coffee can over the fire.

Miss Bolton also arranged for us to travel to Edmonton at spring break in 1970. We raised money for our trip to Edmonton by holding a walkathon. We asked for sponsors, then walked the nine miles (14 kilometres) from the MacKenzie

Highway to the Keg River Post. The Brownies also participated. I don't remember how much money we raised, but I do remember the sore feet!

Girl Guide Walk-a-thon on the Keg River road, 1969.

The following is a list of the others that went to Edmonton: Sandra Galandy, Bonnie Ridsdale, Valerie Parenteau, Lorna Bowe, Brenda Rudy, Esther Johnson, Alice Batchelor, Sharon Tupper and Linda Parenteau.

Susie Fischer drove us to Edmonton in her van. We were to stay at the home of Miss Bolton's parents in the city, so when we thought we were at the correct address we all piled out and rushed up to the door, only to find we had the right house address but on the wrong street! We did finally find the right house.

While in the city, we visited the University of Alberta campus and saw the city from the top of the Henry Marshall Tory building. We toured the

Girl Guides on a trip to Edmonton. Back, L-R: Valerie Parenteau, Margaret Bolton (Captain), Esther Parenteau, Alice Batchelor, Sandra Galandy. Front, L-R: Bonnie Ridsdale, Brenda Rudy, Marylou Vos, Lorna Bowe, Linda Parenteau, Anne Tupper.

Alberta legislature and a fire station. The whole trip was an eye-opening experience for us as many had never been that far from home before.

During the summer of 1971 some of us attended camp for a week. It was held at Lac Cardinal and organized by other Peace Country Guide companies. We had to take turns cooking meals, cleaning up after meals, cleaning bathrooms and providing campfire entertainment. I remember being involved in acting out the song "*Waltzing Matilda*"! We also had daily competitions based on the cleanliness of our tents! Miss Bolton joined us at that camp even though she had been away from Keg River since the previous summer. We met some wonderful people and formed some close friendships.

Being in Brownies and Guides provided exposure to so many activities and opportunities I would not have otherwise had, growing up in the small community of Keg River. I'm grateful to the teachers and parents who invested many hours of themselves in providing us with these life-enriching adventures.

Brenda Freeman in her Brownie uniform.

Sheila Weber and Harriet Befus in Brownies.

Brownies – Pearl and Edna Chalifoux, Wendy Wilkins, Vicki Zatko.

Brownie Camp at Twin Lakes.

The Hockey Rink and Moosenose Hockey League
by Anne Vos

Centennial year, 1967, brought us a federal grant of $1670 to be matched and used for improving culture and recreation in our

116

community. Floyd Schwindt, Frank Jackson and Harry Bowe built a small building on the corner of the recreation lease at the Post.

The building was divided in half, part being used for a library and the rest as a dressing and storage room for the skating rink. The outdoor rink was built just below the hill to the west.

There were a lot of problems with this location of the rink, such as getting water to make the ice, inaccessibility, lighting and vandalism.

The new principal, Mr. Lloyd Chorney suggested to the recreation board that the rink be moved to the school so that it could be better utilized. This sounded like a very good idea since it would be much more accessible and could be used by the students for healthy outdoor exercise. The rink was moved to the school yard. The Improvement District had six yard lights installed around the new location and provided a heated shack for changing and keeping warm.

Many parents volunteered countless hours to construct the rink and flood it from Smeaton Creek. Tons of snow were shovelled off the ice surface during just the first winter! Wim Vos donated a snow blower the next winter. Garth Coulter built a hot flood machine. A great effort was put forth to buy, beg or borrow enough skates as well as the essential hockey sticks. Many nights a vigourous game of hockey or broomball could be found in progress on the outdoor ice surface.

Moosenose Hockey League game – Stampeders vs. Huskies.

The school students and staff also enjoyed the use of the rink. Mr. Chorney organized a league that included all the students from grade one to nine and the staff. Play took place in the noon hour in the Moosenose Hockey League. The students voted for the captains of the teams and they in turn chose their teams. Each student and staff member was placed into a category based on their ability and the captains needed to select from each category. One year the team captains were:

Team	Captain
Bears	Cory Anstee
Crusaders	Ray Wanuch
Mohawks	Ronnie Wanuch
Regals	Terry Houle
Tornados	Penny Vos

Bears – Captain Cary Anstee.

Tornados – Captain Penny Vos.

Regals – Captain Terry Houle.

Mohawks – Captain Ronnie Wanuch.

Crusaders – Captain Ray Wanuch.

Keg River Mites hockey team, 1972. Back, L-R: Neil Vos, Tracy Coulter, Wayne Sowan, Kelly Coulter, Ronald Cardinal, Eugene Galandy, Kenny Tupper, Fabian Stigsen, Mr. Lloyd Chorney. Front, L-R: Dean Weber, Darcy Weber, Allan Zatko, Lawrence Wilkins, Marcel Dupuis, Orville Sowan, Davey Christian.

In 1972 a Pee Wee team was formed to take on the Manning Pee Wees as part of the winter carnival. The team members were:

Ronald Cardinal	Orville Sowan
Kelly Coulter	Kenny Tupper
Tracy Coulter	Neil Vos
Davey Christian	Lawrence Wilkins
Marcel Duprius	Dean Weber
Eugene Galandy	Darcy Weber
Fabian Stigsen	Allan Zatko
Peter Sowan	Coach Lloyd Chorney

Our team had to have some type of uniform, as they usually played in ordinary clothes. The only thing available in Keg River on short notice – overnight, were fifteen yellow cotton T-shirts of various sizes. Armed with felt pens, the mothers put "Keg River" and the numbers on each very quickly. Then the game was played and Keg River won! We even got a trophy!

With the rink so close to the school, physical education class was never more exciting and the class wasn't skipped no matter how cold it was!

My children remember skating on the rink when it was so cold their skates would squeak instead of glide on the ice (about -40°)! There are many fond memories of the hockey teams and games against the Dads and Moms, and each other. The rink was certainly worth the time and effort put into it.

For All Those Born before 1945
Alberta Farm and Ranch, North Hills News, Calgary

(reprinted with permission) We are survivors! Consider the changes we have witnessed. We were born before television, penicillin, polio shots, frozen foods, Xerox, plastic, contact lenses, frisbees and the PILL. We were born before radar, credit cards, split atoms, laser beams and ballpoint pens. Before pantyhose, dishwashers, clothes dryers, electric blankets, air conditioners, drip-dry clothes ... and before man walked on the moon.

We got married first and then we lived together. How quaint can you be? In our time, closets were for clothes, not for "coming out of". Bunnies were small rabbits and rabbits were not Volkswagens. Designer Jeans were scheming girls named Jean and having a meaningful relationship meant getting along with our cousins.

We thought fast food was what you ate during Lent, and Outer Space was the back of the Outdoor Theatre. We were before house husbands, gay rights, computer dating, dual careers and commuter marriages. We were before day-care centres, group therapy and sun tan parlors. We never heard of FM radio, tape decks, VCR's, electronic typewriters, artificial hearts, word processors, yogurt and guys wearing earrings. For us, time sharing meant togetherness ... not computers or condominiums. A chip meant a piece of wood. Hardware meant hammers and nails, and software wasn't even a word.

Back then, "Made in Japan" meant junk and the term "making out" referred to how you did on your exams. Pizza, McDonalds and instant coffees were unheard of. We hit the scene when there were five and 10 cent stores, where you bought things for five and ten cents. The dairy sold ice cream cones for a nickel or a dime. For one nickel you could ride a street car, make a phone call, buy Orange Crush or enough stamps to mail one letter and two postcards. You could buy a new Chevy coupe for $600 ... but who could afford one? A pity, too, because gas was 11 cents a gallon!

In our day, GRASS was mowed, COKE was a cold drink and POT was something you cooked in. ROCK MUSIC was a grandma's lullaby and AIDS were helpers in the Principal's office. We were certainly not before the difference between the sexes was discovered, but we were definitely before unisex and "operations". We made do with what we had and we were the last generation that was naive enough to think you needed a husband to have a baby.

No wonder our kids don't understand us!!!

Interesting Events
by Anne Vos

At the start of World War II in 1939 Russia was an ally of Nazi Germany, and between them they attacked and divided Poland. By June of 1941 Germany had turned against Russia and had attacked them. Churchill said, "Any state who fights against the Nazis will have our aid", so it was decided that fighter planes would be sent from North America via Canada to Siberia and on to Russia, since it was impossible to go across Europe.

In March, 1942 a number of small, very fast fighter planes were headed for Siberia when one of them went down at Keg River after it ran out of fuel. The pilot had been looking for another plane from the group that had gone astray. The plane went down west of the cemetery and the pilot survived. He was amazed that he couldn't make a telephone call out of our area, but he was able to get more fuel and soon continued his journey.

Kenny Jackson and U.S. Airforce fighter plane, 1940's.

Three earthquakes have gently rocked the community. 1. December 18, 1984: What a strange feeling! The swag lamps swayed from the ceiling. We could not have explained it except for the media reporting that a quake of about six on the Richter scale was centred in the Northwest Territories near Yellowknife. 2. October 20, 1986: We had visitors who were staying in their camper in the yard. Thinking she had been the victim of a prankster, Mrs. Aabak shouted, "Stop jacking around with this camper!" We all laughed when we found it was Mother Nature that had caused her camper to move! 3. January 9, 1993: It was more gentle than the others and most of us didn't notice that the earth was moving under us.

On July 27, 1993, a huge balloon laden with expensive research equipment struck a power line near Prochinskys' and burned. Fortunately, the company conducting the research for the North American Space Agency had detached their equipment from the balloon prior to it striking the line. This accident caused a major power outage north of Keg River. It took over eight hours to restore power to High Level.

National Scientific Balloon Study Parachute and payload vehicle dropped into L. de Haan's field, 1994.

ROLL OF HONOUR

In Memory of You
by Ellen Bouma

Through the cabin's rotted base
Entwined the red willows grow
Hiding the window's face
Where once an oil lamp did glow
Of one man's dream
To find the hidden wealth;
A tattered rawhide poke
Still lies upon the shelf;
A rocky mound marks this man;
The cross splintered and grey
Now lies face down on the ground
With no words to say
In memory of you.

Veterans

The following men and women from our area served our country in the First and Second World Wars and the Vietnam and Korean Wars:

First World War
Ernie Brick
Fred Brick
Rene Gicquel
Glady Harrington
Dick Hutchings
Louis Hrytciuk
Charlie Noskey
Hume Stewart
Nick Tomilou

Second World War
Ken Batchelor
Howard Randall (Red) Davis
Alphonse Ducharme
Jean Marie Ducharme
John Ducharme
  (killed in action)
Samuel Ducharme
Tommy Harris
Fred Hartley

Bertha Houle
Betsy Houle
Jerome House
Louis Jackson
Harold Larivee
Walter Lariviere
Almer Omoth
George Price
Howard Price

Raymer Ross
Walter Rudy
Charles (Bud) Seward
Johnny Yurkowski

Korean War
Charles (Bud) Seward

Vietnam War
Charles (Bud) Seward

In June 1930 the H.B. Co. launched the M.B. Buffalo Lake which was used until 1937. Because of its costly operation it lay idle for a few years then it was stripped and used as a barge.

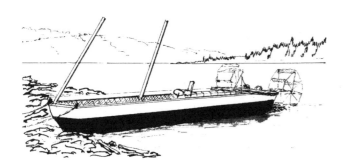

In 1930 Mike Raychyba built a barge with twin paddles. Later he made it into a push barge (i.e. covered barge) with one paddle wheel, sleeping quarters and a cook house. He lashed feed barrels at the side and pushed a barge of freight. He provided transportation to Ft. Vermilion for eight years with his "Russian Navy".

In 1904-1905 the H.B. Co. built the S.S. Peace River at their post at Ft. Vermilion. The machinery for it was rafted from Peace River Crossing (later Peace River).

CHAPTER V
FAMILY HISTORIES

The Family
author unknown

The family is like a book -
The children are the leaves,
The parents are the covers
That protecting beauty gives.

At first the pages of the book
Are bland and purely fair,
But time soon writeth memories
And painteth pictures there.

Love is the little golden clasp
That bindeth up the trust;
Oh, break it not, lest all the leaves
Should scatter and be lost.

Connie and Elmer Anderson

by Connie Anderson (nee Houle)

I was born on June 17, 1945, in the Peace River Hospital, one day after my mother's 48th birthday. I was the second child to be born in a hospital and the youngest of 14 children born to Louis and Emilie Houle. I always thought that they used all the leftover names as I am Georgiana Isabel Constance, alas better known as Connie.

I came to the Paddle Prairie Colony by boat, down river from Peace River to the Paddle landing, which was about 12 miles due east of our home. Transportation was of course by horse and wagon, which was quite a journey. I remember going to the river twice in all the time we lived in Paddle.

As a baby I was breast-fed as were most babies in those days. Our neighbors, George and Mary Gaucher, had a new baby also. His name was Norman. Unfortunately Mary had milk fever and she was unable to nurse Norman. My mother had lots of milk so she took over nursing Norman. This was the kind of thing people did to help one another in those days.

Norman and I grew up being the brunt of a joke due to this. I grew up to be a healthy, plump child and Norman on the other hand was a skinny, slight child. So we often heard the story of how I got the cream and Norman got the skim milk (which was probably true).

As a child I was happy and carefree and knew nothing else but the security of life on the Colony. Our life centered around home, the church, the store and later the school and recreation hall. Our home was loving and caring. I grew up knowing I was loved. In fact I was spoiled!

We didn't have a lot but we always had enough to eat and clothes, blankets, and such. My mother and father took care of what we had. We always had a big garden as well as canned berries. Meat was mostly moose but we also had pork, beef and chicken. We also ate goose, duck and squirrel. We always had a cow for milk and chickens for eggs.

I remember the egg shells in a pan on top the cook stove. They were dried and crushed and given back to the chickens to peck at. Collecting eggs was not something I could do as the roosters always seemed to find me. I would run to the house crying at the top of my lungs with the rooster in hot pursuit. They always seemed to be watching for me. My only gratification was in knowing that Dad would soon take the axe to them and we would have roast chicken for Sunday dinner.

I was raised as a Catholic – no one worked on Sundays. We always went to church wearing our church clothes and always wore a hat or scarf. After church someone would usually come to our house for dinner. My mother was a great cook and she loved to have people over.

Midnight Mass was a grand event. We would bundle up and walk or we went by horse and sleigh which had a caboose on with a wood heater to keep us warm.

I recall one Christmas Mass in particular, I was not of school age yet and was supposed to have a nap so that I could stay awake for Mass. Well, I didn't sleep that afternoon, so guess who fell asleep? My dad never said a word. He just took me outside and washed my face with snow and brought me back inside. I don't remember saying anything either. I can imagine that everyone must have had a hard time keeping a straight face.

In those days you did not talk in church at all. Women sat on one side and the men on the other. There was a balcony at the back where the choir sat. I loved the services. They were in Latin and so were some of the songs. Other songs were in Cree. One had a hard time not turning around to look at the choir. The church is the only familiar building that is a reminder of the old days.

When I was growing up on the Colony the members of my family that were living at home were the twins, Thelma and Velma, with Clarence and Jeannette. Ray and Max (Flavin) were away working but came home often.

We never had a car or truck. In fact Dad never owned an automobile. We had a Cockshutt tractor as well as horses, which were used to do the fieldwork such as plowing, disking, seeding and running the threshing machine.

I remember that during harvest time we would take lunch out to the men. Lunch consisted of tea in two quart sealers and round bannocks wrapped in towels. It was fun to jump in the straw stacks except for the mice. I didn't do any work as I was too young. The twins worked, as well as Clarence and, I guess, Ray and Max when they were home. I remember the twins making chop for the pigs. It was a dusty job.

Water was a problem. We had a well but it was salt water and we weren't allowed to drink it. In the winter we used snow water and Dad put up ice for the summer in the ice house. It was a square frame of logs about five feet high, filled with sawdust. The ice was layered alternately with the sawdust.

We still needed to haul water. We did this with barrels on a stoneboat pulled by either the tractor or horses. The barrels were covered with cloth and tied. Boards were floated on top of the barrels to keep the water from splashing out. Of course you had to go slow to keep the dust out also. We went to Lariviere's creek for the water. It was a real event. Dad had two speeds on the tractor – slow and slower. When anyone else drove it, "they blew the carbon out", as we would say.

My mother baked bread once a week, I believe. This was done in a tub made of shiny metal which might have been aluminum as it was not galvanized steel like the washtub or boiler. It was half the size of a regular washtub. Mom's arms must have been very strong to work that dough. She made delicious bread and buns. If we were out of bread on baking day she would fry bread dough in lard in the frying pan. "Squaw bannock", it was called, and it was good with syrup on it! Mom also made the best bannock! We made hot chocolate from cocoa and snow ice cream from cream, snow, and vanilla for flavoring. YUM!!

Some of the games we played as kids were hopscotch, "house" and mud pies. I can remember making mud pie cookies and mud sandwiches using leaves as bread. We would draw hopscotch in the dirt and would use pieces of glass for tossing. We would play house in the woodpile. We made rooms and totally destroyed the neat piles of wood.

Dad would cut hay at the hay meadow and he had a small cupboard where he kept his tools and a very sharp axe. We had been told to not touch it.

Velma and Thelma were looking after us as I recall when someone came to visit and they chased me outside. I was probably being a pest. I then went into the cupboard and unwrapped the rag from the axe. I bent over to chop a piece of grass but chopped my big toe instead.

I was afraid to say anything so I covered the blood on my toe with dirt and went back into the house. The twins heard me crying and took me to the nurse who was stationed in the colony. I remember her cleaning it and using iodine, which hurt. The twins got in trouble. I don't recall them getting a licking – I don't know if anyone ever got a licking. Needless to say, Dad babied me and I never got into trouble. I really took advantage of this!

He even cut two willows from the bluff west of the house and made me crutches to walk with. We went to the Eliske Pilgrimage that year in the back of Ambrose Parenteau's truck. I remember being carried around and still have a scar from that injury. We always had a nurse's station in Paddle

and the nurse at that time was Mrs. Bresingham. The clinic was like another world to me. Everything was so sanitary. They had real wood chairs and a metal stool – we had benches in our house.

Dad was a good carpenter. I remember him building granaries. It was fun to go out and play with the scrap wood. In our house we had a long table with a bench on either side and a small bench on each end, an icebox, one cupboard with dishes on top and a large flour bin that held 100 pounds of flour. A washstand and slop pails where the waste water and scraps went were also found by the cupboard. I remember Mom was always glad to put them outside come spring.

In the summer we had mosquitoes. A smudge would be made in a pail and carried throughout the house before we went to bed. I don't know which was worse for us, the smoke or the mosquitoes!

We had kerosene lamps with two mantles. One lamp was hung from the ceiling. The bedroom lamp was glass and had a wick. The globe had to be washed every day as it would get smoked up. We used the lantern for the barn and outhouse. Mom and Dad were always cautious with the kerosene and it was not wasted. We used a "bitch light" (a twisted rag in tallow) when we wanted to get something from another room.

We had a large heater in the front room which heated the whole house. If I got cold during the night I would call Dad and he would come and cover me up. In the morning he got both stoves going, then woke us up. We would huddle around the heater to dress. White bloomers, long brown stockings with a garter belt and thick undershirts were the bottom layer of clothing.

We wore wrap-around moccasins with over boots that closed with a clip-type snap, or we had felt boots. We were so bundled up when we went out we could hardly move, but we needed it because it was so cold. We made igloos in the snow and we would cut the snow into large blocks where it had drifted against the fence lines.

We walked straight north from our house across the prairie, the airstrip, and the pasture to school. It was about a mile, but it always seemed further. I look at it today and it seems to have gotten shorter than I remembered! We just had a packed path and when it blizzarded you could not see the path. If you missed it you would be in snow up to your waist. My savior was my dog named "Sparky". He was black and white, just a mutt, but he would go ahead and break trail. Ray also reminded me that Dad would mark the trail with spruce branches.

When I started school it opened up a whole new world to me. Mrs. Jean Johnson was my first teacher. The school was just like the one in "Little House on the Prairie". I remember laying my scarf on the floor and folding it in a perfect triangle shape. My readers were the Dick and Jane series. I could not pronounce my "f's" and "th's" so I would say "Dick's fauder" instead of "father". I still have my grade one report card. It is like a greeting card, hand written in beautiful penmanship on onionskin paper.

We carried our lunch to school in a lard pail. They came in different sizes: two-, three-and five-pound pails with handles. (Today they are collector's items.) We started the school day with "The Lord's Prayer" then our cod-liver oil tablet. Yukk! I also remember learning nursery rhymes, especially the one about "Georgy Porgy" and we would tease Georgie Beaulieu.

The school had no janitors, so Myrtle Ghostkeeper and I stayed to clean the brushes and the boards and to sweep the floor. The cloak room and the book room were at one end of the school with an eight-foot wall but no ceiling. There was a glass french door lying over top. Myrtle and I climbed up the bookshelves and would walk around the top of the wall. One day we broke one of the panes in the door.

The next day I was literally sick and stayed home in fear of what would happen to me. I don't really know what I thought they would do! I returned to school with heavy feet and a lowered head. I did not raise my head from the desk and didn't rise for the prayer. Lessons started and the teacher never said a word to me, not one word. I guess she knew I had punished myself enough. I never walked the wall again.

My memories of one Christmas concert are also vivid. It was when Myrtle Ghostkeeper (now Brown) and I acted out the song "Little Brown Jug". The jug was a brown glass Perfex jug with a handle!

The hall was used for showing movies such as Hopalong Cassidy and Roy Rogers films and really good old westerns. One summer Teddy and Alice Martineau opened a restaurant. They served pie and pop. Orange crush in a brown bottle comes to mind. What a thrill that was!

The Colony pasture was across from our land. During the war it was used as an airport. The tie down pads are still there. It was also a pasture for breeding the cows. The Colony had a bull which was put in there. The pasture seemed to me to be about a mile by one-half mile in size. It was probably smaller than that. Anyway like the rooster, the bull liked to chase me. I learned to run pretty fast across that pasture, it seemed no matter how far away that bull was, he would see me. I wonder if it had anything to do with my red sweater.

In the spring on the prairie, there was water everywhere. You had to zigzag to avoid the puddles. During Lent we would always give up something. I can remember it was the year I gave up candy that Wagon Wheels came out. As soon as Lent was over I bought one for five cents and they were much bigger then than they are now.

One fall I went with Mom, Dad and Ray to Peace River with a load of grain. On the way home we stopped at Ernie Shannon's in Manning. That was where I first met Gladys. I had never seen a red-haired person before. Ray and Gladys married and lived in a caboose in our yard during their first year of marriage. It was so cold the water froze in the basin overnight. Bunnie (Laverne) was born on January 4th; she was a healthy baby and never got sick despite the bitter cold.

After we left Manning I remember Dad yodelling. I thought it was funny as he was saying, "old lady, ol ooold lady". I guess he was drunk, as Mom was upset with him. I never saw a lot of drinking as a child. I never saw my Mother drink and Dad drank on only two occasions that I can remember. This made a big difference to our lives. Max and Ray would drink when they were home and other people came over – they would pass out. This was so scary as I thought they had died. If my mother had not been there for me I don't know what I would have done.

Too many children today know no other world. I work with native students in the school system today and see how they have been affected by alcohol and drugs. We need to support these students so they can see success in their future.

We left the Colony in 1953 due to Dad's poor health. We went to Grande Prairie where the twins graduated from business school and were working. My sister Agnes also lived there; she was married to Phil Lessoway. This move was a real culture shock for me. The only thing that kept me going was a supportive family and the caring sisters at St. Joseph's School.

The upbringing I had on the Colony was a strong base which I look back on with pride. We learned the values that are important in forming our characteristics. I had good role models.

I live in Quesnel, British Columbia, now. My husband Elmer and I are still working. We have three children in their 20's and one four-year-old grandson Mathew from our oldest daughter Jody. Our son Marty and daughter Deanna both went to High Level to work. With them living there, and Jeannette, Clarence and Ray all living in the area, we keep coming back every summer. There have been a lot of changes on the Colony, some good and some not so good.

A lot of successful people have branched out to work in other areas of the country. My dad was not educated in school, but he was very wise in life. I will close with a statement which Dad told me that carried me on my way many times. "ALWAYS REMEMBER THAT YOU ARE NO BETTER THAN ANYONE BUT YOU ARE JUST AS GOOD."

James and Adeline Armstrong
by Vincent Armstrong as told to Margaret Befus

Jim Armstrong was born in Ireland. He was a sailor on tall ships and travelled around Cape Horn three times under sail.

He came to the Peace River country with a survey crew in 1915. Others in the crew were Dick Naylor, Carl Norquist and Colonel Hubble. They worked on cutting two baselines, the 26th and either the 25th or the 27th. Jim also worked under Glady Harrington in putting the telephone line from Keg River to Carcajou. Jim was a big strong man and often carried equipment when the horses would get bogged down in the muskeg.

Jim married Adeline Couterielle of Carcajou. Eleven children were born to them: two girls who died in infancy, Winnie (deceased), Florence, Norah (deceased), Lorna, Vincent, Willie, Jim, Louis (deceased) and Bobbie (deceased).

The Armstrongs lived upriver from Carcajou Point until a school was built. Jim wanted his children to go to school, so they moved to Carcajou Point. Vincent, born in 1919, was too old for school by the time they moved, but most of the rest attended the school.

One winter Jim froze his feet badly on the trapline. He was not able to get to Dr. Jackson until early spring when he rode to Keg River on horseback. His feet still were very painful, but the doctor could see that they were slowly healing. She said, "Jim, it will be a while before you can walk without pain, but I don't think you will lose your toes." Jim's only reply was, "My neighbors will be so disappointed."

Armstrong brothers in Carcajou.

Vincent was away from Carcajou for nine years. During that time he and some of his brothers trapped in the Whitesands area near Wood Buffalo National Park. They returned in 1956 to help their mother look after cattle on what is now known as the Armstrong Flat. Vincent and Willie have made their home there ever since.

Dick McGrane planted a patch of brome grass on this flat in the 20's. Brome is very prolific and it spread. It was once combined by Charles Dovey and in 1976 by Dave Befus. Both found that getting machinery into the flat ate up all the profits of harvesting and selling the seed.

A truckload of Brome, Dave combined at Armstrongs.

Pat Ambler plowed up part of the flat in the sixties and planted it to canola. When he harvested it, it was left in a pile. During the winter, Ted Stigsen went over with a truck and grain auger, loaded it, hauled it on the ice to Carcajou and then over the Carcajou trail to an elevator.

(Editors Note: The following story from the *Edmonton Journal* was written in 1990 by their staff writer, Erin Ellis, and reflects the concerns of Vincent Armstrong regarding pollution in the Peace River.)

People have already stopped eating fish from the Peace River because they fear it's contaminated, says a man who lives near the river.

"The damage is done," said Vincent Armstrong, 71, from his life-long home on the edge of the Peace River, about 500 kilometres northwest of Edmonton.

"There used to be lots of fish in the river and lately, now, hardly anything," said Armstrong in a telephone interview from Carcajou.

People living on the Paddle Prairie Metis Settlement bordering the Peace River were warned last summer to eat only one fish meal a week, said Armstrong. Local residents also used to get their water from the river, but now they wouldn't wash their floor with the Peace, he said.

"Nobody uses it any more down here in Carcajou."

David Schindler, an aquatic scientist who served on the Alberta-Pacific pulp mill review panel, said people living on the Peace River can be justifiably afraid of the pollution making its way from a pulp mill at Grande Prairie.

The Wapiti River - where Procter and Gamble operate a bleach kraft pulp mill - flows into the Smoky River, which then joins the Peace River.

Schindler said studies indicate sediment can travel 500 kilometres downstream, and fish, such as the mountain whitefish, can migrate hundreds of kilometres. Carcajou is 300 kilometres north of Grande Prairie.

"My guess is that the sediment is still on its way to native people down below," said Schindler.

Procter and Gamble has been under fire after records revealed it discharged a higher than standard amount of solid wastes into the Wapiti River 36 times in 1988 and 1989. The wastes are suspected of containing trace amounts of toxic dioxins and furans.

"I would think the one place you could put these things that you're sure they're going to go some place harmful is to put them in the river," said Schindler.

Rose and Ken Batchelor and Family
by Ken Batchelor

I was born on October 7, 1925, in Prince Albert, Saskatchewan, and was one of five children born to Catherine and Alfred Batchelor. I was the only boy and my older sister died from appendicitis at age five. I started school at Carrigana in 1932. We left there in 1937 and went to Vancouver Island, where we had a dairy farm. We delivered milk for 12 and one-half cents per quart or eight quarts for one dollar!

In 1939 the war broke out in Europe and the government was building a fort at Albert Head on Vancouver Island and we had no more pasture for our cows.

We moved from there to Alix, Alberta, in 1940 to a run-down farm where we milked cows and shipped cream. My dad had been an officer in the Canadian Army in the First World War. The army asked him if he would consider joining again at the same rank of captain.

Dad accepted in the fall of 1940 and I was asked to look after the farm for the family.

In 1941 with the help of my two younger sisters and my mother, we ran the farm. My older sister had already joined the army (Canadian Women's Army Corps). I did all the field work, the crops and haying with horses. There were no combines then, or power, or any modern conveniences. In February 1943, I joined the army and took my basic training at Red Deer in the Royal Canadian Army Service Corps. I got 30 days spring leave to put the crop in and 10 days in the fall to cut the crop. A neighbor threshed it for us. I was low category physical and they took me off the embarkation train on the way overseas.

I was sent back to Calgary and Red Deer and spent the rest of the time as an instructor. In the spring of 1944 I got 30 days spring leave to put in the crop and that was when I met Rose Radke.

Rose was born to Ephraim and Bertha Radke, at Bench, Saskatchewan, in 1924. She is one of 12 children. Their family farmed and moved around a lot renting land. They moved to Alberta in 1933, where they farmed in Duchess, Gadsby and later in Erskine. There were always lots of kids

Armstrong's original cabin on the Peace – sketched by Vi Hopkins.

to help with the milking of 18 to 20 cows and separating the cream, which was sold.

Their family had just moved into the Alix area from Gadsby and rented the farm next to ours when we met. We corresponded for the next six months and in September 1944 I was discharged. We got married on April 22, 1945.

We started farming on our own on some rented land. Rose's dad had about 40 head of horses and that is where we got our horse power.

The war had ended and tractors were starting to be manufactured again. Horses weren't worth anything. There were no packing plants and everyone was waiting for tractors and had horses to sell.

On July 13, 1946, our first son was born at Lacombe. We lost him when he was three years old. This broke our hearts but life must go on. We worked for farmers and ranchers for the next few years and on August 27, 1951, our oldest daughter Shirley was born in Olds. On April 28, 1953, Irene was born in Calgary.

We could see that working out down there we would never own a farm, so I came to the Peace River Country to look for a homestead. I ran into a couple of other fellows who were also looking for land. In the Peace River land office we were told that Keg River was opening land for homesteads. I filed on N-22-101-23-W5 on June 1, 1953, and went back to Calgary and on the fourth day of July we had our leases.

On December 28, 1954, David was born in Calgary. In the spring of 1955, I came to Keg River and got 40 acres cut and piled by Karl Marx for $10.50 an acre. I built a 12' by 16' shack and broke the 40 acres. Dave Befus was homesteading just south of us, so Dave and I went back to Calgary together.

On May 28, 1956, we landed at Keg River and moved into that 12' by 16' shack with three kids. We had brought 12 chickens, a rooster and two dogs with us. It was a struggle but that summer we built a 16-foot by 24-foot house and I'll never forget Rose exclaiming, "It's a mansion!"

From then on we had something of our own and started getting a few head of stock. I started working on oil rigs in the winter and Rose and the kids looked after the animals.

When Shirley had to start school, there was a one-room school where Dr. Mary Jackson School is now, and she rode horseback six miles each way. She didn't miss many days. The next year Irene started school and they had moved Naylor Hills School to the Keg River Post, so the girls rode the

same horse the six miles to that school. The next year Louis Jackson started hauling the kids in his van.

In the winter of 1958 I was cutting and hauling logs from 23 miles west of Vic Zatko's place to our home, when on February 11th I stopped at the Hudson's Bay, Dr. Jackson met me and said that I had a new baby at home. I said the baby wasn't due until May, but the doctor assured me that she had already arrived!

Walter Chalifoux took my horses and looked after them. I got Glady Harrington to wire Manning to see if they had an empty incubator. They did. I got Mr. Ross from the Hudson's Bay to drive my wife and baby to Manning. In those days the road wasn't always plowed but George Robertson had gone through with his Cat and bunkhouses and said the road was good. We got to the hospital and I hadn't seen the baby yet but had held her all the way on a hot water bottle.

What a surprise I had when I saw her! She weighed only two pounds and she went down to one and a half before she started to gain.

Margaret Befus had a baby on April 1st, and on April 10th we brought both babies home. Our daughter Alice then weighed five pounds.

Alice never had any formula, just cow's milk. She had one spoon of pablum and spat that all out! She ate cream of wheat, vegetables, meat and eggs. She never even had a cold until she started school!

The years went by and we got two more quarters of land. Then in 1974 we bought Vince

The Batchelor family. Alice, David, Irene, Shirley with Ken and Rose seated.

129

Royspal's estate and sold our homestead to Keith Broadhead.

We have a good farm here now and it is all paid for. Farming has been good to us. We still have a nice little herd of cattle, some horses, pigs and chickens. Some are descendants of the first 12 we brought to Keg River in 1956.

Shirley married Stanley Parenteau; they have one boy, Rex, and one girl, Amie.

Irene married Marlo Travers and they have one daughter, Tammy. They divorced and Irene married Stan Bzowy. They have one boy, Tyler.

David married Paula Halkewich and they divorced. David married Doreen Cardinal. They have two boys, Lenny and Clinton.

Alice married Wayne Tkachuk and they have two girls, Fershell and Latoya.

We now have three great-grandchildren.

Batchelor grandchildren. Back, L-R: Tammy, Tyler, Rex, Amie, Lenny. Front: Latoya, Clinton, Fershell.

Allan and Diana Marian Beck
by Diana Beck

Allan and I and our children moved to Keg River in July, 1978. Allan is originally from Edmonton, Alberta. I was formerly a Prochinsky and had lived at Keg River for two years from July 1963 to August 1965.

In 1971 we had a section of homestead land in Keg River. By 1976 Allan had bought a big truck and was logging around the High Level area. In 1978 we moved to Keg River because we had to put in our residency according to government regulations for keeping the homestead land. We wanted to be there to get more improvements done on the land.

Our homestead was situated seven miles north of Keg River Cabins and then two miles west. The road to our place off the MacKenzie Highway was just built the year we moved up. It was pretty soft when it rained, which seemed to be all the time! It seemed like we never saw any sunshine that summer.

We moved into a two-bedroom camp trailer until we had the house that we bought from Jake Guenther moved down from High Level. The house didn't get moved until November; we also didn't have electricity until November of that year. We bought a small power plant from Dave Papirny until the electricity was put in. It's a good thing there are many daylight hours here in the North.

It was a real experience for the kids coming from Edmonton, where everything was available at the touch of a switch. There was no television to watch, no indoor toilets, etc., and the mosquitoes were unbelievable. They sounded like bees when you went outside in the evening. Talking about bees, that summer was just horrendous for wasps. In the city you hardly ever saw things like that, so it took some getting used to. Even though I originally grew up on the farm, the 12 years in the city made me forget a lot of things.

Did you ever see a woman try to outrun a bee? I'm sure the kids wondered about their mother running around frantically outside when there was a bee nearby. Ask Benita (Omoth) Price about how far I can jump when I happen to sit on a wasp and how fast I can dodge and run from a wasp. It has taken a few years but that fear is no longer there.

For a city boy, Allan found the experiences of homestead life were also very varied. One that is sure to stick in his mind happened one night when both the outside dogs were in the back porch. They kept giving out little barks and wanting to go outside. Allan told them, "You wanted in, you stay in." Finally after about a half-hour of this I said "You might as well boot them out or no one will get any sleep tonight." Allan grumbled at the dogs and complained as he went to let them out. When he opened the back porch door, there was a black bear looking at him. The bear had been eating the dog food sitting just outside the back door!

We had two children when we moved to Keg River – Corey and Dayna. Corey was in grade two and Dayna was in pre-school. Both Corey and Dayna completed their schooling at Keg River and went on to college. Corey obtained his diploma in Agricultural Sciences, and Dayna, her certificate in Office Administration. Corey presently works in Hines Creek, Alberta, and Dayna in Fairview.

Allan and I still live in Keg River, where we grain farm and are slowing diversifying into livestock. We both have off-farm jobs: Allan is a custodian at the Dr. Mary Jackson School and I do bookkeeping services for different companies and organizations.

Dave and Margaret Befus and Family
by Tom Befus

Dad (Dave Befus) met Mom (Margaret Mortimer) in 1952 when Mom worked at Temple Lodge in Lake Louise. Dad and two friends, Wilbur Olsen and Roland Burney, had chased 19 wild horses from Sundre to Lake Louise to sell to Ray Le Gace, an outfitter there.

Ray was shorthanded, so he offered Dad a job for the summer. That winter Dad worked in Banff and Mom taught school in Lake Louise. The next summer found them working back at the lodge and pony stand.

When the summer season of 1954 was over, they were married in Bowden. They then moved to a rented farm north of Sundre. The owner wanted to sell the land for $300 a quarter but mom and dad could not afford it.

They heard of homestead land available at Keg River, so Dad, Ken Batchelor, Ted Befus and Dan Radke came up in the winter to have a look. They each put their names in for a quarter, but Ken and Dad were the only ones that came back to prove up (complete the homestead lease requirements) the land. Dad's plan was to make the improvements and sell the land so he could buy the farm he had rented in Sundre.

Dad built a homestead shack and a slab barn, then went to break the land with a John Deere D. He also did some catskinning for Carl Marx. He raised pigs as well because it was more profitable to feed the grain he was growing to them than to haul it to the nearest elevator in Grimshaw.

Following local practice Dad did some horse trading. He acquired horses named Queenie, Tarzan and Rocket. Oliver Travers owned Rocket and gave her to Dad in payment of a $300 debt. Dad then sold her to Charles Dovey for $300, as he needed the $300 more than he needed another horse!

From 1955 to 1959 Mom had a teaching job at the Keg River Post, so she stayed in the teacherage during the week and returned to the homestead on the weekends. During that time Mom also boarded with Bill and Elsie Halabisky.

The old wagon road from Carcajou to the Post went through Dad and Mom's homestead yard, so they met the people from Carcajou as they travelled to Sports Days and dances at the Keg River Post.

One time Dad and Daniel Sowan chased Dad's nine cows to Carcajou from Keg. They got as far as Keg Crossing by nightfall so they chased the cows across the river and stayed in an old cabin there. It was early summer and there were a lot of snakes around, so Daniel wouldn't sleep in the cabin. He spent the night on his horse! During the night the cows tried to go back but Snuffy, our German Shepherd, held them east of the river.

Dad started driving Ted Stigsen's truck to Peace River to pick up supplies for Ted's store and barrels of gas for the farm at Carcajou. At this time there was only a wagon trail to Carcajou so the Stigsens, Tuppers, and Charles Dovey left their vehicles at Tompkins Landing and travelled the river from there to Carcajou.

One fall day in 1962 they met Ted at Tompkins Landing with a truckload of supplies for him. Ted asked if Dad could help him thresh his crop. We (myself, my brother, two sisters and Mom) were all with Dad and the only luggage Mom had with us was a diaper bag. Nevertheless, we went back upriver with the barge loaded and three boats pushing it to the Carcajou townsite. There we moved into Okerholm's cabin. Later in the fall when it rained, Dad went with Lou Tupper and Howard Price to Tompkins Landing, then to Manning. On the way back, Dad picked up more clothes for Mom and for us.

When Dad and the other men returned to Tompkins Landing, the wind was up and the water was too rough, so they went back to the homestead at Keg and stayed the night. They ate fried baloney as it was the only food they had.

When harvest was over we moved to Calgary, where Dad found work in building construction. The summer was spent back at Keg River, then in the fall we moved to the Okerholm's cabin again. Dad bought a half-section from Charles Dovey on the west side of the Peace at Carcajou. Later, Dad bought lumber from Ted's mill and built a house on that land. We lived there for 10 years. Mom taught school at Carcajou and then at Keg River while Dad raised cattle and grain.

In 1970 Dad bought a house from Jim Basco at Notikewin. Ray McKenzie moved it up the MacKenzie Highway and east onto the Carcajou road, where it was found too wide to go over the little green bridge. A trail was cut down to the river to let it cross the South Keg River. By some quirk of fate, someone shot the transformer at the corner of the Keg River Post Road that same day. Boy, did we hear about it, but the grey house with the blue roof did not knock down any power lines!

On April 21, 1974, an ice jam blocked the Peace River, causing water to back into the Carcajou flat. Mom and the kids were at school in Keg River that day. Dad was eating lunch when Ted Stigsen phoned from across the river, warning him of the rising water.

Dad took Rocket and, with the help of Sandra Stigsen and Jack Christian, chased his cows to higher ground. After getting the cows out, he and Jack went back to rescue the ponies, but by then the water was too deep for Rocket, so they took a boat.

The ponies were huddled on the half-floating bale stack. Dad and Jack were able to drive the ponies off and they swam towards the hills. Halfway there, one of the new colts played out and was foundering. An older mare, Belle, saw this and circled back. She positioned herself in front of the colt so it could rest its chin on her rump. They then swam off after the rest of the ponies toward the hills. The colt that Belle saved wasn't even her own!

By that evening the water was up three inches in the second story of the grey house. Eventually our house was flooded to the eaves and the water stayed until a ditch was blasted out to drain the flat. Dad stayed with Charles Dovey in Carcajou while our house was flooded and we stayed with Mom in a teacherage at Dr. Mary Jackson School in Keg River.

We certainly appreciated all the help given by neighbors near and far. Even our Member of the Alberta Legislature advised us to squat on some high land rather than wait for the red tape to run its course.

Later that summer Dad bought NW-10-101-19-W5. We were able to pour a basement quickly. By the end of the summer we got a modular house and built a barn and shed. So we moved from having the lowest home in Carcajou to the highest. The Paddle Prairie Metis Colony allowed us to pasture our cattle on their community pasture for the summer.

Perhaps this next tale should be called Three Men in a Boat. We had a Shetland stallion, Bill, who got across the Peace River on the ice. Come spring, he was causing havoc among the Stigsen horses. Ted came across the Peace in his boat to get Dad and together they caught the rebel pony.

The next step was more difficult – to take him by boat to his home on the other side of the river.

Ted looked after the motor, and this was no mean feat as one minute the motor was deep in the water and the next it was completely out of the water. The high-strung little pony danced from side to side and bow to stern with Dad in tow.

They finally reached the west side of the river and Dad let the pony out of the boat on to the bank, expecting him to go home. In less time than it takes me to write about it, the pony plunged into the water and swam back to Carcajou Point and those enticing mares of the Stigsens!

For years most people at Carcajou had a power plant pounding away, but in 1986 we got power! The cost of power from the line is half what it cost to run a power plant, but we grumble about the cost of electricity just the same!

Our family includes: Mom and Dad, who still reside on the hill in Carcajou; Joan, who was only lent to us for two years; Harriet, who was born on the day John Diefenbaker was voted in as Canada's first western Prime Minister; myself; Tom, who came home from hospital in a Cadillac; Wendel, whom Mrs. Reimer delivered without the help of a doctor, as he was out for lunch; Beth, the only one of our children not born in the

Befus family at Jans wedding, Dave, Beth, Jan, Harriet, Tom, Wendel, Margaret, 1985.

Beth Befus and Glen Seigle wedding, with niece and nephew, Serena and Drew as attendants.

Manning Hospital (She was born in the Calgary General Hospital. At one time that made her decide that she must be adopted!); and Jan, who was born on Friday the 13th, but it doesn't seem to interfere with her luck with bees and horses.

Our family is scattered but all have a piece of Carcajou in their hearts. Carcajou has changed – whether it is for the better is not for me to say – but Mom misses the days when you couldn't walk down one of Carcajou's many trails without meeting youngsters on horseback.

Margaret Anne Bolton
by Margaret Lyall (nee Bolton)

I arrived in Keg River to teach school at Dr. Mary Jackson School in the Northland School Division in August 1969. I had heard about teaching in remote areas and thought this might be interesting.

You never forget your first class, so Keg River has always stayed fresh in my mind, even though I taught there only one year. Fresh from the University of Alberta, I knew very little about teaching and learned a lot from my students.

Miss Bolton and Brownies, Beatrice Armstrong and Hazel Christian, 1969.

That autumn at a Ladies' Club meeting, I heard someone mention Brownies, so I piped up and said that I would be happy to help with Girl Guides. I was considerably startled when I was given the job of starting a brand-new Girl Guide company, with myself as the captain! I was very glad indeed to have Anne Vos as the lieutenant – especially since she had a car and I didn't! My old dog Scamp enjoyed all the girls' outdoor activities!

The highlight of our Girl Guide year was a trip to Edmonton during spring break. We stayed at my parents' house, visited a fire hall, the University of Alberta, the legislature, the museum and a swimming pool.

When the school year was over, I left to travel around the world. On a boat from India to Malaysia, I shared a room with three Girl Guide leaders from Germany, which led to my visiting Guide leaders in Malaysia, Thailand, Australia and Fiji. None of that would have happened if it hadn't been for my experience in Keg River.

When I came back to Alberta in June, I returned once more to Keg River to go to camp with the girls who were in Guides. We went to a camp near Lac Cardinal.

The children I remember are grown up now, with children of their own, but in my memory they will always be 10 or 11 years old.

I married Charles Lyall in 1973. We have a son, James. James and I live in Leduc where I have been a teacher-librarian for the last 17 years.

Isobel and Harry Borbridge
by Harry Borbridge

I first joined the Hudson's Bay Company after completing high school in Winnipeg. My first post was Fort Vermilion, I arrived there in July, 1933, when I was just 18.

The flood in the spring of 1934 was the first major disaster I faced. The awesome power of water compounded with huge blocks of ice was unbelievable. The mud and mess when we moved back to the buildings was something to see.

Edward Lambert Jr. and I had to travel from Fort Vermilion to Upper Hay River Post (now called Meander River). High Level was just one big bog in the trail those days.

The temperature was minus 70° Fahrenheit. We had four horses pulling 3500 pounds of freight with two of the mares heavy in foal. Had it not been for Eddie, I would certainly not be here today. I was all set to lie down for the big sleep, but Eddie knew the danger signs and made me keep going.

I was suffering from hypothermia. It is very easy to freeze to death at 70 below!

I spent a year and a half at Fort Vermilion. Not only did I clerk in the Hudson's Bay store but I also tended the horses, cleaned the barn and milked the cow, to say nothing of the continual hauling of wood. I assisted in establishing a post at the fifth meridian, north of Little Red River, and I spent two years at Upper Hay.

Harry Borbridge and his 1927 Chev.

I arrived in Keg River in 1936. The first project there was sprucing up the Post! The log buildings had to be remudded. I personally had that honor! Next, they had to be whitewashed and the roofs were redone with red shingle stain.

These buildings are all gone now except for the store, which was moved to the new Post site. It is still used for storage, even though it is 96 years old.

Harry and Isobel Borbridge, Keg River, 1938.

It was while I was in Keg River that I met Isobel. Isobel Moulton was visiting Keg River from California. She was a niece of Frank Jackson. We were married in 1939. We worked at many northern Posts. Our first son Tim was born in Fort Ware. Our second son Glady arrived later.

I worked for many years with the company back home in Winnipeg before retiring after 47 years with the company. Isobel and I continue to enjoy life here in Winnipeg.

Ellen and Jim Bouma
by Ellen Bouma

I was born in Flin Flon, Manitoba, and Jim in Parkside, Saskatchewan. We met when he was working in the mine in 1949. We were married in 1951.

When Jim's mom and dad took land in Keg River, we decided we would, too. We applied for the E-10-101-23-W5. The first winter we lived at Clarence Williamson's sawmill. Jim got a job in the bush cutting logs, and his mom and dad got the jobs as cook and bull cook (a cook's helper). In the summer we moved back to the farm of Jim's dad. The log house they lived in was very small, so we helped build another one in which we lived temporarily. They later used it as a barn.

In 1952 when rabies broke out, our dog must have eaten some of the poison that was set out, so we had to put him down. One day a fox came into the yard and just stood there looking at me. I didn't know if it was sick or not, so Eva, Jim's mom, got the gun and Bud, Jim's dad, shot it. We burnt it in a brush pile just in case it had rabies.

One other time Eva and my little girl were sitting out in the shade, when suddenly a moose came tearing down the baseline road. When it got to our turn-off, it kept right on running towards us, so we both made a beeline for the door. It was almost in the yard when it stumbled and fell. It tried to get up once more but couldn't. The blood was spurting from its neck, then it died. Bud was disking in the field and Eva went and got him. He dragged the moose carcass out to the back field across the creek. The coyotes soon cleaned it up.

In the time that followed, Jim worked for Ken Fischer, skidding logs. Once he worked up in the North West Territories driving a Cat pulling a lowboy hauling men and equipment across the Kakisa River. The river was very swift and wide and had a really hard gravel bottom. The water wasn't that deep, coming just up to the top of the track, but a lot of the guys became confused by the swift moving water and nearly wound up going over the rapids. One man did, but he was lucky – the grader he was driving got hung up in the rocks. The fellow was later seen and rescued.

Jim also worked for Camille Boucher. It was his Cat we used to build the road to our homestead, and Jim also did some cutting and piling. It was in 1958 when we finally moved to our farm. Two fellows from the mill helped Jim to build the house. The Keg River was just down the hill behind our house, so we hauled water on a stone boat.

We later built a barn and bought some chickens, and a horse called Pablo. In the morning if you looked out the window, you could see hundreds of prairie chickens feeding in the field. The ground was a grey mass of them. They later died out, infected with tapeworm.

Debbie and Bobby.

Lynn, Barbara, and Mack.

We had five children, two boys and three girls. They had to walk two miles across country to school. Granny gave them a bell to ring in case they saw a bear. We later bought them a horse called Buck, and Granny bought them a cart and harness but the horse seemed to have a one-track mind, and that was to get back to the barn and eat. At first, leading him was the only way you could get him to move, so I spent more time pulling him than he spent pulling the children!

Coming home was a completely different story – I could hardly hold him back. He knew how to move in the direction of food, ears back, tail straight out, running like the wind, and in no time at all we were home! I didn't always know if we would be alive, but we were fast! We finally decided to sell him back to the original owner.

When fall came it sometimes rained for days on end. The kids would be mud from head to toe if they walked to and from school. Taking them on the tractor was even worse. The mud from the wheels would fly, often landing on them – they were a sorry sight! We were unable to get the road gravelled. Jim later got a D-4 Cat and we were able to do a lot of work with it. Mike Papirny built a cutter, and Jim cleared some more bush. Jim also built a road for Ted Stigsen down the hill where they live now in Carcajou.

We lived on our homestead for five years. Farming was never easy. When the rain started, it seemed like it would never stop. The last year we were there we had the best crop ever, but were unable to get it harvested.

In 1962 we moved to N-35-100-23-W5, George Price's place at that time. We were there for seven years. In that time we cleared off the whole half except for about 35 acres that were already done. We had the power put in, and we pulled our house down with Jim's dad's D-7 Cat. Later we dug two wells. The kids were picked up by the school bus on the road.

Jim and Ellen Bouma, 1958.

In 1979 we sold the land to my youngest daughter and son-in-law. We moved to Buck Creek, Alberta. We bought a trailer and a new truck and spent that year doing a lot of fishing and driving around the country. In 1980 Jim died of a massive heart attack. Later I returned to Keg River so I could be near my kids.

Steve and Lynn Skrlac, my oldest daughter and her husband, raise cattle in Buick, British Columbia, with their two children, Allan and April.

Mack and Shirley Bouma are living in Peace River. They have two children, Shauna and Shannon. Mack's two older children, Kevin and Nadeen, are living in Whitecourt.

Roy and Barbara Merrifield live in Whitecourt, Alberta. Barbara has one son, Stacy Nadeau, of Fairview, Alberta.

Bobby and Correen Bouma live in Rainbow Lake with their two children, Clayton and Christine. Bobby's three eldest children – Robbie, Colin, and Cheri – all live in Calgary.

Debbie Godkin (our youngest child) moved back to Keg River from Edmonton, with her husband Alan Godkin, of Milo, Alberta, in 1979.

Neil Godkin, Alan's cousin, also bought a quarter from us.

William and Eva Bouma
by Debbie Godkin (nee Bouma)

My grandfather, William (Bud) Bouma, was born on June 24, 1898, in Springfield, North Dakota. Grandmother, Eva Harris, was born on September 3, 1903, in Day Mills, Ontario. Both families moved to Prince Albert, Saskatchewan, where Bud and Eva later met and were married on May 31, 1922.

After they married, they moved to Parkside, Saskatchewan, where they raised two boys, Roy and James (my father). Sometime later they moved to Sled Lake, Saskatchewan, where Bud operated a sawmill. From there they moved to a small farm in Shelbrook, Saskatchewan.

In 1949, after their two sons had left home and married, they sold their farm in Shelbrook. With all their possessions packed into a caboose mounted on the back of their old Ford truck, they headed for Keg River. After looking the area over, they applied to homestead on E-3-101-23-W5.

Granny, as she was affectionately known, said they never broke one dish on the trip up. They unloaded the caboose by jacking it up and lowering it onto posts that Bud had pounded into the ground, and then they drove the truck out from

Bud Bouma and wife Eva just arrived at homestead with their "mobile home".

under it. It was spring when they came, and they managed to cut logs and build a house before winter.

They spent the first few winters working at various sawmills in the area. Granny cooked for the crew and Bud was bull cook (a cook's helper that makes the fires and hauls the water.). The money they saved working out in the winter helped them buy machinery. Bud bought a D-7 Cat and he cut and piled for many of the people in the area over the years.

They built their house on the Smeaton Creek. Granny chose a garden spot on the opposite side of the creek. The only way to reach it was to walk (or crawl as some of us did) across a narrow log. Granny was the only one I knew who could walk across the log with ease. There was no convincing her to find a more accessible location for her garden, as it grew with such vigor in the creek bottom.

Over the years my grandparents had an assortment of animals, including pigs, goats, a milk cow and chickens. Back then there were so many hawks, that a fence had to be built over the chicken pen to keep the hawks from a free dinner.

Every fall Bud would get a moose and Granny would can it and put the jars in the cellar (beneath the kitchen floor) with the rest of her preserves. They relied on a good garden and a moose to get them through the winter.

After Bud had the homestead broke and had grown a number of crops on it, he sold it and took another homestead in section 8-101-23-W5. I called it the frog farm as it was so wet. When it rained, the road got so muddy they couldn't get in or out for over a week at a time, but a little wet land never deterred Bud. He had a passion for clearing land,

and not farming! Granny always joked that someday he'd die on that old Cat.

In 1974 after Bud had cleared and broke the land on the new section, he sold it and moved to E-34-100-23-W5 and started all over again, with the help of his grandson, Mack. Granny was happy not to have to fight the muddy roads any more.

In May 1974 Granny's mother, Harriet Mable Harries, came to live with them. It was easy to see where Granny got her youthful appearance and vitality from, as Harriet insisted on helping with the dishes and other household chores. She enjoyed her daily walks with Granny and the hours they spent reminiscing about the past. She was looking forward to celebrating her 100th birthday here in Keg with her family, but that wasn't to be. She was here for less than a year when she became ill. She died in the Manning hospital on October 22, 1974, at the age of 99.

In 1979 Grandpa and Granny sold the land to the Prochinskys, but continued to live on a few acres they rented back. My husband Alan and I had just moved to Keg River that fall and Alan bought Bud's old D-7 Cat along with some other machinery.

Eva and Bud's Fiftieth Wedding Anniversary.

Bud and Eva resided in Keg River until Bud became ill and entered a nursing home. Eva stayed in Keg for a few more years, then moved to Heritage Towers in Peace River so she could be near Bud.

In 1988 Granny learned she had cancer and passed away in the Peace River hospital on December 16, 1988, at the age of 85. A year later Bud passed away in the Peace River Auxiliary hospital on November 12, 1990, at the age of 92. Eva's Christian faith helped her endure many family trials and hardships common to the homesteader's life. She remained spry and active and kept her positive outlook on life right to the end. In spite of those hardships neither of them ever regretted the time they spent in Keg River.

Roy Bouma, my father's older brother, came to Keg River in the early 60's. He applied for the SE-1-101-24-W5. He lived in Keg River for 10 years, then moved to Red Deer, Alberta. Roy has three daughters: the oldest, Diane Legault, lives in London, Ontario; Laurie Thomson lives in Toronto; and the youngest lives in Red Deer. Roy passed away on January 8th, 1990, in Red Deer.

Louis Bourassa
by Anne Vos

Louis Bourassa was born in 1888. He homesteaded in Keg River on NE-33-101-23-W5.

Louis hauled mail from Peace River to Fort Vermilion, 300 miles a trip. He travelled overland through the bush from prairie to prairie, sometimes by horses, other times by dog team. When ice conditions permitted, he travelled on the river. Summers, the mail was hauled by boat. In recognition of his endeavors, Louis became a member of the Order of the British Empire in 1935.

Louis was married to Maria St. Germaine and they had six children. The family lived in Fort Vermilion.

Louis was a veteran traveller of Northern Alberta. He envisioned travel by water down the Chinchaga connecting to the Hay and MacKenzie Rivers with a portage at Alexander and Lady Evelyn Falls.

The *Peace River Record Gazette* on January 21, 1936, told of Louis Bourassa completing one of the most hazardous trips in the history of the northern mail service.

The Fort Vermilion mail courier arrived in Peace River late Wednesday afternoon, just as arrangements were being made to send out a police patrol to find him and his load. He was more than three weeks overdue.

Mr. Bourassa, who was accompanied on the trip by Father Habay of Fort Vermilion, unloaded the mail at the local post office and went immediately to his home to welcome the arrival of his youngest daughter, born three weeks earlier.

Mr. Bourassa in his quiet way, in answer to enquiries, told of his trip down the river on the ice which, unknown to him, was rapidly breaking up a few miles behind him until he was 20 miles from Carcajou Point. Along this portion of the river, the banks are rather steep and high. He camped by night at the river's edge, either on the gravel or the ice as the occasion demanded.

On his last night on the ice, 20 miles south of Carcajou Point, he had made camp and was about to go to sleep when the roar of the flood and breaking ice alarmed him. Realizing what was coming, he commenced a hurried removal of his horses and sleighs to the top, then proceeded to carry his load of mail and supplies up the steep bank.

Despite his best efforts, a number of the parcel bags got wet and some were lost. The river rose very rapidly in a few minutes. Quickly the ice was sweeping past with a huge noise. Louis spent the entire night getting out of the mess.

The next huge problem was how to travel from where he was to Carcajou Point. There were no roads, not even a trail. The only possible solution was to cut his own trail and so he did – for 100 miles! Louis never thought he was being heroic. There was a job to do and he did it. The mail was entrusted to him and he overcame the hardships thrown his way to get it to its destination.

Sadly, Louis died on his homestead in Keg River of a heart attack when he was only 55. His body was taken on the *Stigsen O'Sullivan* boat to Peace River, where he was buried.

Art and Emily Bowe Family
by Doreen Bowe

Art and Emily (my husband Dennis' parents) were both born in Keg River. Harry and Flora Bowe's only child was Thomas Arthur born on February 25, 1931. Emily was born to Antoine and Lucy Chalifoux. Art and Emily married in Keg River, took up homesteading and began their family there. They have seven children: Lorna, Gloria, Dennis, Larry, Ann, Rhonda and Darrel.

The children started school in Keg River while Art struggled with his homestead (NE-25-101-24-W5). They worked the homestead from 1949 to 1970.

Art and Emily now live in Dawson Creek, British Columbia, close to their daughter Lorna and her family of three daughters and one son. Their daughter Gloria also lives nearby with her daughter. Dennis and I live in Taylor, British Columbia, with a son and a daughter and we will soon have a grandchild.

Larry is married and also lives in Taylor with a son and a daughter. Ann and her husband have one daughter. Rhonda lives in an apartment in Taylor. Darrel, the youngest, lives with us.

We manage to get together as a whole family at Christmas and to celebrate birthdays. We also make trips back to visit in our hometown of Keg River.

Arthur Bowe family. Back, L-R: Dennis, Gloria, Lorna, Ann, Larry. Front, L-R: Emily, Arthur, Rhonda, Darrel.

Marriage of Dennis Bowe and Doreen Alexander.

Thomas Henry (Harry) Bowe
by Anne Vos

Harry Bowe was born in 1890 in a small village in Staffordshire, England. He came to Keg River in 1918, bringing cattle and haying equipment down the Peace River to Carcajou on a scow that he built for himself. He took his cattle out to the Chinchaga, built a log house there, and did some trapping, too. But it was hard to put up enough hay to see his cattle through the very long, very cold winters, particularly when the hordes of flies and mosquitoes kept them thin in the summer. So he gave up ranching.

There was a big outbreak of smallpox in northern Alberta in 1923, and Harry Bowe and Frank Jackson went round doing their best for those who were sick, since both of them had been vaccinated in England during infancy, they were immune, but about 40 of the local people died, many of them children.

Harry married Flora Lizotte on January 3, 1930, and their only child, Arthur, was born on February 25, 1931. By this time Harry had built a house on a homestead in Keg River.

Flora, Harry and young Arthur in front of their home in Keg River.

Keg River's mail came to Carcajou on the boat called the *D.A. Thomas* once a month through the summer, and Harry Bowe got the contract to haul it from Carcajou to Keg River.

This was a trip of about 40 miles over rough wagon trail that could be very arduous after heavy rain. It involved fording the Keg River, going overland to the Peace River, crossing it in a canoe, picking up the mail from the post office at Rankin's and returning the same way. He received $15 a round trip, which sometimes took four or five days. Sometimes he had to wait for the boat; its arrival time was erratic because the Peace River was usually in flood in June, and sometimes very low in the fall.

For Harry it was an honor to carry the Royal Mail, and if he couldn't make it with the horses, he walked, carrying the first class mail on his back.

In May, 1939, there was a heavy snowfall when the first boat came down the Peace. Harry then carried a couple of packages of bees in a sack on his back, because he was sure they wouldn't have survived if there was any delay.

His wife Flora was accidentally killed in November, 1943, when she was thrown from the wagon after the horses were startled and ran away.

Steve Kelemen Sr. traded a steam engine to Harry for his homestead. The steamer was used to saw lumber for a number of years. It was fired by wood and burned an enormous amount.

Through the years Harry served the Keg River community in many ways. After Glady Harrington retired Harry took over the radio-telephone, the meteorological station and the post office. He was secretary-treasurer of the first Community Hall Association. He was also a Justice of the Peace.

His mechanical skills were well-known throughout the area, and he was never happier than when he was dismantling and rebuilding some old tractor. One cold winter he was outside washing some parts in gasoline when his hands started to freeze and he ran indoors to warm them over the stove. The gasoline caught fire and set fire to clothes that were hanging over the stove to dry. Luckily his whole house didn't burn down, but his hands were badly burned.

One of his favorite pastimes was telling stories about his life, some true and others that were very TALL! One of the highlights of his days was when the Sunday School By Post van arrived. Miss Hassell and Miss Sayles were Anglican church ladies who drove to remote areas in the summer to provide religious instruction and inspiration to Anglican families. Their van was equipped to take them over very rough roads, and gave them a place to live when necessary. Harry was happy to provide them with tea and all the news of the district.

Harry always planted a very large garden from which he was able to give a lot of vegetables away.

Harry at 90, with grandsons, Dennis and Larry.

He grew broad beans, from which he made soup. This soup and rolled oat porridge were two mainstays of his diet.

Harry married again when he was 80. Kate was a chronic invalid who died of a heart attack after a few years of marriage. In his last years, Harry started to re-read all of the Dickens novels. Harry died on October 10, 1980, at the age of 90.

Most of all he is remembered for his generosity.

Arthur Bowe married Emily Chalifoux and they have six children. They now live in Dawson Creek.

Carl and Evelyn Brakstad
by Margaret Befus

The Brakstads came north to Manning, where Carl was head carpenter in the building of the new hospital. They homesteaded on S-27-101-23-W5 across the Keg River road from Ken Batchelor. Carl broke only a few acres with a Case tractor and a breaking plow and then built a house. He helped build the Roots' house. Carl was not a farmer and they only stayed a few years.

I remember him best for his Bel-Air Chevrolet. He owned it when nice cars were few and far between. Their house was sold to Otto Krause and it was moved to Otto's land, north of the Keg River post.

Later, Ken Batchelor bought the land and it was there where he built corrals and held a rodeo each Labor Day for several years. It is now part of the Broadhead farm.

Karl and Evelyn Brakstead, 1956.

Brewer Family
by Margaret Befus

Frank Brewer, his wife, and son Everett arrived in the Carcajou area in the 1920's with a large herd of cattle. They came down on the river boat and settled on the north end of the McGrane flat. They didn't live in Carcajou for very long.

Frank was known for his temper. When their bull insisted on getting out of the pasture, he slowed it down with a 30-30 rifle!

The family brought along a hired-girl. Due to a great shortage of young eligible women, she was soon married to John Okerholm.

Thomas Allen Brick
by the Women's Institute of Peace River and the Keg River History Book Committee

T. A. Brick is known as the oldest pioneer farmer of the Peace River country. Credit is due him for bringing to the attention of the world the grain-growing possibilities of this vast empire of the north. Rev. J. Gough Brick came to the Anglican mission at Dunvegan in 1882.

Allen came west in 1884. He carried dispatches for Generals Middleton and Steele during the Riel Rebellion. At this time there was little settlement west of Brandon and Winnipeg.

Allen joined a survey party and spent the summer on the Athabasca and Peace Rivers, joining his father in October at the Dunvegan Mission.

The grain grown that summer was excellent quality. Allen took a load to Grouard by ox team, taking two bags on to Edmonton by dog team. The grain reached Dr. Saunders, who sent the wheat in 1893 to the Chicago Exhibition where it won championship honors.

Mr. Brick was quoted in the Toronto Star in 1925 as follows: "My father and I went into farming to demonstrate the possibility of growing wheat and other grains so far north. We had some hardships, but we proved that No. 1 Hard Spring is a sure crop in the Peace River district."

Following the formation of the province of Alberta in 1905, the first election was held in November 1905. In the Peace River country the results of that election were discounted because of irregularities in the voting. Another vote was held the following year to elect a Member of the Legislature for the Peace River district. Mr. Brick was harvesting grain when a group of his neighbors came to the field with a suggestion: "Allie, we want a member of the legislature in Edmonton and you're the man."

It was a simple election campaign. A meeting was called on the river bank, he addressed the few settlers present, mostly native, and the nomination papers were completed. On election day, February 15, 1906, Brick was elected over Jim Cornwall to represent the constituency that then comprised one-third of the total land area of Alberta. It extended from south of Grande Prairie to the northern border of the province. The number of voters on election day was eight!

Mr. Allie Brick's farm at Shaftesbury on the Peace River, 1907. Photo Courtesy of Provincial Archives, Victoria, B.C.

The trip to Edmonton had to be made by horses and sleigh. Since he intended to combine business with politics, he had quite a number of freight teams as well. The whole procession was followed all the way to the capital by two tame moose! They were in the habit of cavorting about the barnyard with the horses. So Mr. Brick's progress down Jasper Avenue in Edmonton was something of a sensation!

When the settlers began to pour into this district about 1910, Mr. Brick took a keen interest in the establishment of schools and other public services. He directed the building of the first telephone line from Peace River post upriver to Shaftesbury. A line that saw regular service waited until the government telephone service was established many years later.

Well-read, witty, charitable to a fault, always ready with a kind word and a helping hand, Allie Brick was known for many years as an outstanding figure of the Peace. His name is not only linked with the development of the Peace River Country, he also made much of that history himself. In doing so he demonstrated the measures of a great man in that he gave more to the country than he took for himself.

Allie married a Metis lady, Nancy Grey, the

H.A. George, Sheridan Lawrence, Thomas Allen Brick.

daughter of a Hudson's Bay employee at Red River. They had two sons, Ernest and Fred, and a daughter, Emma, who became Mrs. Dave McDonald of Keg River.

Nancy died during a visit to the dentist. Allie, heartbroken, decided to leave his home on the bank of the Peace River and move north with Emma. They both took out homesteads in Keg River. He recorded in his diary on April 30, 1926, "Today we are seeing Keg River for the first time."

Allie travelled north to Zama Lake where he traded furs for Revillon Freres for several winters but his post showed a loss each year. In other winters Allie and Emma travelled to Rainbow Lake where they operated a trading post for Frank Jackson of Keg River Trading Company. During the summer Allie and Frank travelled with team and wagon to build a small cabin that would be used as the trading post. They followed the

Emma and her father, Allie Brick.

Chinchaga River part of the way, then they had to widen the pack trail in order to get the wagons through.

The land Emma and her dad homesteaded was mainly prairie which was producing grass for pasturing animals or for making hay without cultivation. After they got some cows, they stayed in Keg River year round.

Allie's son Ernie moved to Keg River with his family in 1940 where they lived for many years. After a lengthy illness Allie passed away at home in 1938. He is buried in the Keg River cemetery. Emma married Dave McDonald and also lived in Keg River until her death.

Elsie and Eddy Halabisky with Allie Brick.

Ernie and Susan Brick and Family
as told by Sue Brick to the *Herald Tribune* in Grande Prairie on the occasion of her 92nd birthday

I've lived in so many places, I can't even begin to tell. I had my 10th birthday on the train, arriving in Edmonton Halloween night. My family (the Ratigans) moved west from Canterbury, New Brunswick, where I was born.

Dad homesteaded in Innisfree, then took a notion to come to the Peace Country. One of my brothers got land at Grimshaw and the family joined him.

I met my future husband there but didn't marry at that time. A friend and I lived in Los Angeles for a couple of years. We had a wonderful time there, visiting San Francisco and San Diego. We lived in the shadow of the Hollywood Hills back when movies had no sound.

My father didn't like it when we got there – all the cars and people. We all returned to Alberta later – stopping at Banff, Rocky Mountain House, Calgary, and Edmonton.

I wed Ernest Brick in Edmonton in December of 1927. Our children were born in different places.

Bill was born in Edmonton, Larry in Tofield, and our daughter Allene in Keg River.

Ernie was the second son of the well-known Thomas Allen Brick of the Peace River Country. Ernie was born on the Brick ranch at Shaftesbury on the west side of the Peace River. His early years were spent helping his father on the farm.

During the First World War Ernie and his brother Fred were overseas in England. When Ernie returned, he worked on farms around Mildou, Saskatchewan.

Ernie got into the cement and stucco business in the 1930's while the family lived in Fort Nelson. When the family moved back to Keg River, Ernie and Dave McDonald replaced the foundation under the Catholic church with cement and then Ernie stuccoed the church. He also stuccoed the houses of Johnny Vos and Adam Pawlowich.

Ernie did carpentry work around the Keg River district and also went along on the annual telegraph line repair trip.

We moved to Keg River in 1941 and I found myself expecting another baby at the age of 47. There I met the legendary pioneer doctor Mary Jackson, who was destined to become a very close friend. Dr. Jackson gave 48 years of her life to the north. She put a finish to tuberculosis there.

The first time I went to Keg River, I took a boat from Peace River to Carcajou. They called it a boat, but it had no sides so it was more like a barge. I was met in Carcajou by my brother-in-law and Dr. Jackson with her English Blitz children. The doctor fostered the children, sent here to escape the wartime bombing raids in London.

My first ride over the road to Keg River was one I'll never forget if I live to be 1000! We'd just miss one tree stump, then hit another. I was black and blue and I was pregnant and didn't know it. I don't know how my daughter Allene ever survived!

It was beautiful country up there, but so lonely looking. Dr. Jackson said she loved it and so would I, but I didn't believe her then. I wanted to leave immediately, but I couldn't face that tortuous road again!

I did grow to love the North. Keg River is lovely. It's the people, I guess.

I once dreamed of being a nurse and although I was never able to realize it as a profession, I helped Dr. Jackson deliver babies and nursed my father through his final six years.

Dad had single-handedly raised and cared for

our family of five boys and two girls as my mother died when I was just three.

I am very fortunate, I've had a good life. I've never had an operation in 92 years, never smoked or drank, but I worked plenty hard. I'm not going to give up yet. I never overdo things today, I plan ahead and take it easy. I do my own housework in my own apartment.

I still like to travel, and last Easter I went to Manitoba to visit family, but for now I've had enough travelling.

I'm a great reader and I have lots of company. I go to church every Sunday and join in things for seniors the Catholic Women's League puts on.

I manage to keep pretty busy. When I get bored I go to Allene's and help out on their farm (near Wembley) or I visit the boys. I'm able to get around good. I come from a long-lived family, Dad was 86 and my eldest brother Tom, 87.

I still write letters if I want to, but the phone is handy, too. Occasionally I play the piano today after having been the organist and singer for services at both Keg River's Catholic and Anglican churches for 25 years!

We raised three children: Bill lives in Keg River, Laurie in Calgary and Allene in Grande Prairie. We moved to Grande Prairie to our apartment in 1971 and Ernie passed away in 1982. (Editor's Note: Susan Brick died in 1991 at the age of 97. Ernie and Sue have eight grandchildren and 11 great-grandchildren.)

William and Doreen Brick and Family
by William Brick

I came to Keg River in 1940 with my mother, father and brother Larry. We boarded a boat in Peace River. The boat belonged to O'Sullivan and Stigsen. We really enjoyed the trip down the river. One night it got foggy and the boat had to tie up on shore. Dad, Larry and I slept on deck with the freight but Mother stayed in the cabin.

Two children from England, Pat and John Hague, were on the boat with us. They were coming to stay with Dr. and Frank Jackson until the war in Europe was over.

We arrived at Tompkins Landing and were met by Dr. Jackson, Dave McDonald, Louis Jackson and Johnny Arnault. Johnny had an old two-ton truck. Mother rode in front with Johnny and Louis and the rest of us rode in the back. It was a very rough ride on an old wagon trail. After a few miles my mother wanted to know when we would get to the road. The driver just looked at her!

On one corner we hit a dead tree with the truck box and part of the tree broke off and struck me on the knee. I sure remember that! We finally arrived at the Keg River Prairie.

Years later Mother and Dad were coming home with Dave McDonald's truck. It broke down crossing the Keg River where the cabins are now. Dad told Mom he would walk to the post at Keg River for help and they would come back for her. She said, "You are not leaving me here! I'll walk too!" It was quite a muddy, wet hike (10 miles), but they made it to Dave McDonald's.

We were still living in Nelson, British Columbia, in 1938 when my grandfather, Allie Brick, who was living in Keg River, passed away.

In the 40's in Keg River we listened to the BBC on the radio, where we could hear war news every day direct from London.

Larry and I attended the old log school. Pat O'Connor was the teacher. He was quite handy

Ernie and Sue Brick on their 50th Wedding Anniversary.

Sue Brick on her 92nd birthday, 1988.

with the "cane"! The school house was also used for dances.

We remember one "Box Social" when the community was trying to raise money for the Red Cross. It was a very cold night and the big log heater was stoked up. My friend and I thought it would be fun to plug the chimney, so we climbed on the roof and dropped a sack and a block of wood down the chimney! Soon the hall was empty with everyone outside coughing and choking. Someone had seen us, so we were caught. It wasn't much fun after all!

I went out to Battle River to stay at Uncle Fred's to finish school. I also worked for him for a while. Later I got a job with the Alberta Bridge Department. While working there, Dad and I applied for homesteads at Keg River. Mother and Dad were living in Manning so my sister Allene could go to school. We lived between two places for awhile.

I drove Cat and brush cutter trying to improve the homestead. It wasn't all work though; there were the "Keg" parties held on Saturday night during the summer. Everyone would throw in a dollar and this would buy the next keg. The ladies would bring some lunch and with local music, a good time was had by all.

I met my wife Doreen in Calgary. We were married in Peace River in 1968. We celebrated our 25th anniversary in 1993 with family and many friends.

Laurie and Kathy Brick, Pete and Allene Hodgsen, Doreen and Bill Brick on their 25th anniversary, 1993.

I worked for Alberta Transportation as a grader operator from 1971 until retirement in 1990. Doreen still works full-time at the Keg River Cabins.

I have two stepdaughters – Sherry-Lee and Wendy – and a stepson, Lawrence. We have one

daughter, Susan. All of these children now have children of their own. Sherry-Lee has a son and a daughter and lives in Edmonton. Wendy also lives in Edmonton with her two daughters. Lawrence and his wife Joanne have three daughters and live in Lac La Ronge, Saskatchewan. Susan, her husband Rick MacDougall and my grandson Jay live on the farm with us here in Keg River.

Susan and Rick MacDougall.

Jack and Edna Bryan
by Jack Bryan

In 1962-63 I went to work for Ken Mitchell in a sawmill at Keg River. I worked the following winter, then Glen McDonald and I purchased the mill. I was there for three more winters.

Cookhouse at Bryan's Mill, 1961.

During those three years we had a private school named "Tall Timbers", which the Department of Education funded with the stipulation that we hire a qualified teacher. There were men working in the mill whose wives were qualified teachers.

My sister Jean Polasek taught the first winter. The youngsters were Heather and Faye McDonald, Theresa Sontay, Leanna and Cary Polasek and Carmen Bryan. Theresa Sontay's parents were cooking at the mill. The following two winters Louise Schulz taught.

At the end of the year I sold my share of the mill to Glen McDonald. He operated one more year. I believe Mrs. Schulz then taught at Naylor Hills School and the children from the mill were bussed down there. I went back and worked three more winters for North West Lumber at Keg River. We then went to Bassett Lake. Garth Coulter was the manager and he and I operated two mills up there for two years. I operated one winter by myself. During those years a lot of local men from Keg River, Carcajou and Paddle Prairie worked for us.

About 1970 I was Colony Manager for Paddle Prairie Metis Colony for one and one half years.

There were many interesting events I recall from our stay in that area. We enjoyed singing as I think most of the Colony did, so we went Christmas carolling around the Colony. The carollers were John and Jill Davidson, Roseann Chirpanik, three teachers, Trig and Wilma Kjenner who operated the Government store, and myself. We all enjoyed the house parties and so many were very talented as musicians and entertainers.

During our stay we got the skating rink going again and between Father Companeau and ourselves we were instrumental in getting a lot of secondhand skates for the kids.

The home economist from Peace River had sewing classes which brought out a lot of people who sewed well.

One of the amusing things was when one of the teachers built himself a garage out of poles and black plastic. After he drove his truck in, he couldn't open the door so he had to kick a hole in a wall to get out. Another time some of the local boys decided to take over from Dr. Jackson and remove a small growth from the ear of one of the settlers. Needless to say, they had to go down to Dr. Jackson, who finished the job!

At another party, one of several that we had in the rumpus room at the Government store, we were all amazed at how Mr. Peter Lambert could dance the Red River Jig for so long. Thinking he would be stiff the next morning we looked out and saw him riding bareback on a horse along his road in high gear!

Roger Wanuch went trapping and his horse was attacked by a wolf and the horse had quite a hole in its hip. Alan Martineau took it home and doctored it.

I also remember roaming around the village at night and walking on those wooden sidewalks. The boards would squeak loudly from the frost.

It seems I was always in sawmills after I left as Colony manager. I went back to Bassett Lake for another winter. I then ran the Co-op Mill at Paddle Prairie for awhile.

Summing it up, we enjoyed our time at Keg River and Paddle Prairie and we felt honored when the people of Paddle Prairie invited us back to their homecoming.

Jack and Edna Bryan, our 50th Wedding Anniversary, 1989.

The Jean Marie Cardinal Family
by Doreen Batchelor (nee Cardinal)

Dad, Jean Marie Cardinal (better known as Peeweeno), was born in Slave Lake on February 24, 1910. He was in a mission school in Fort Vermilion and came to Carcajou with a priest from Fort Vermilion when he was 16 years old. He then stayed with his uncle Antoine Couterielle in Paddle Prairie, where he then met his wife, Mary Jane (Jean) Christian. Mom was a daughter of John and Marie Christian. She was born at Chinchaga on December 13, 1919. Mom and Dad were married in Fort Vermilion in 1937.

They lived in Carcajou for a while and Dad hauled mail to Keg River by dog team for one winter. He made his living by trapping and later on as a guide to American hunters. Mom supplemented the income by tanning hides, which she made into moccasins, jackets, mittens and mukluks. Her craftwork is known throughout the north country.

Mom and Dad moved to Keg River to Frank Jackson's farm, where Dad helped with the chores

Jean Marie Cardinal (Peeweeno) with daughter Eileen, Charlie and Joe Christian.

for about one winter. They then moved to Paddle Prairie. In those days Dad would get Dr. Jackson by dogteam if someone got sick. Dad was diagnosed with tuberculosis and went to the Charles Camsell hospital in Edmonton, where he spent four and one half years.

When Dad returned, Mom and he moved back to Carcajou. There was no school in Carcajou at this time, so Raymond, David, John and Eileen had to go to a boarding school in Grouard. Later Mom and Dad moved back to Keg River Post, where there was a school which the younger children were able to attend.

When Dr. Mary Jackson School was built in the early 60's, Mom and Dad moved onto Slim Kemp's old place near the Keg River Cabins. When daughter Karen and Boxer Christian moved onto the Paddle Prairie Metis Settlement, Mom and Dad moved to a home beside them where Mom still lives.

Mom and Dad had 10 children. Two daughters passed away: Lorna died in 1966 from meningitis; Joyce and her two sons, James and Owen, died in a fire in 1973. Mom and Dad raised four grandchildren – Ricky, Dorothy McFeeters, Randy Cardinal and Lawrence Cardinal. Randy has always called his grandparents "Mom and Dad" as they always were parents to him. Dad would call Randy "my baby". Lawrence Jr. is the son of Lawrence Sr. and Sharon McLean.

Mom and Dad's children are, from oldest to youngest:
1. Marlene Andrews had two children, Gordon Gaucher and Dorothy McFetters. Gordon lives in Paddle Prairie. Dorothy (raised by Mom and Dad) married Dennis McFeeters from Cold Lake and now lives in Grande Centre. They have three children.
2. Raymond married Rita Hamelin in a double wedding ceremony with their daughter Lila and Robert Kilkenny on December 11, 1992. Raymond and Rita live in Keg River and have seven children.
   a. Lila and Robert Kilkenny live in Peace River and have four children – Carmen, Tracy, Amanda and Robert.
   b. Ricky (raised by Mom and Dad) – lives with Rachelle Juneau in High Level and they have two children, Quinton and Brandon. Ricky also has three other children: Melissa, Kimberly and Ricky Jr.
   c. Ronald lives with Pam Sapp. They have six children Candy, Kelly, Mae (passed away in 1991), Saphrin, Jennifer and Veronica.
   d. Robert (passed away on December 15, 1987)
   e. Richard lives with Sapolee (Chippy). They have seven children: Elizabeth, Jerome (J.R.), Shane, Lance, Kelly, Terrance, and Kenneth.
   f. Rhonda lives in Keg River with her four children, Tommy, Jonathon, Jason and Desiree.
   g. Rusty also lives in Keg River.
3. David married Stella Smith from Fort Vermilion. Stella passed away on January 28, 1989. They had six children.
   a. Troy married Sharon, has two daughters and lives in Peace River.
   b. Sarah lives in Montreal and has two sons and one daughter.
   c. Tyson lives in Montreal with his sister Sarah.
   d. Stacy also lives in Montreal with Sarah.
   e. David Jr. works at the Peace River Correctional Centre as a guard.
   f. Kirby lives in Peace River and works for Michalchuk Construction in the Zama area.
David now lives with Patsy Wanuch in Manning. They are raising a grandchild, John.
4. John lives with Donna Jacklin in Keg River.
5. Eileen married Robert Smith from Fort Vermilion. Eileen works as a nursing assistant at the Fort Vermilion Hospital. They have five children:
   a. Loretta married Brent Johns and lives in Rainbow Lake. They have twins, Amanda and Garret, and two more daughters, Stacy and Jessica.
   b. Roberta married Berry Johns and lives in Fort Vermilion with their two sons and one daughter.
   c. Jollie married Ken Latender and lives in High Prairie. They have two daughters and one son.

d. and e. Leslie and William (B.J.) live at home and attend high school in Fort Vermilion.

6. Joyce was married to Ed Parenteau and passed away in a house fire with her two sons, James and Owen, in 1973. Her oldest son Randy was raised by Mom and Dad. Randy married Carol Paul and lives in Keg River.

7. Lawrence lives with Rosanne Lizotte in High Level. Lawrence has nine children:

   a. Roxanne has two daughters and one son and lives in Fort Vermilion.

   b. Lawrence Jr. (raised by Mom and Dad) lives in Keg River and sometimes with his father in High Level.

   c. Kurt has two children and lives in Fort Vermilion.

   d. Jason has one child and lives in Fort Vermilion.

   e, f, g, h. Larry, Danielle, Michelle and Chantelle live in Sexsmith with their mother Debbie.

   i. Kiera, the baby, lives with Lawrence and Rosanne.

8. Doreen (myself) married David Batchelor of Keg River where we farm. We have two sons, Lenny and Clinton. I remember when I moved out here to the farm, Mom and Dad thought it was too far from anywhere as David would be working most of the winter and I'd be home alone with the kids. Now I don't think of it as being that far. I worked as Early Childhood instructor at the Dr. Mary Jackson School for 21 years. I am still employed there and David goes out on the road during the winter as he now owns and operates his own trucks. Lenny works in Zama.

Clinton, Doreen, Lenny and David Batchelor.

9. Lorna passed away in 1966 at the age of 11.

10. Karen lives with Donald (Boxer) Christian in Keg River and has two daughters:

   a. Dawn presently working at Paddle Prairie school.

   b. Shelley presently lives in Keg River. Karen is currently learning how to bead moccasins and is doing a great job at it.

Mom and Dad got involved in the school through the Native Language Program, in which they shared their knowledge of the Cree culture and language through storytelling, dancing, singing and playing the drums. Dad loved to play the drum and sing in his native tongue. They met many people through their travels.

Later on in life, Mom and Dad got much enjoyment playing cards. Dad was a great card player. Sometimes they forgot how the game was to be played but as there was just the two of them, they would agree on their own rules.

Altogether Mom and Dad have had 39 grandchildren and 53 great-grandchildren!

We sadly miss our father, grandfather, and great-grandfather, who passed away on June 25, 1993, at the age of 84. Mom, who is now 74 (1994), still lives in Keg River and does most of her own work.

Peeweeno (Jean Marie) and Mary Jane.

John and Donna Cardinal
by Donna Cardinal

John Clifford Cardinal was born in Keg River on October 8, 1943, the fourth child of Jean Marie and Mary Jane Cardinal. He lived in Keg River and trapped with his father and worked for local farmers until 1978.

In 1980 we met in Grande Prairie. We have three children: Janine, Shawn and Gary. For a period of time we lived in Grimshaw where John was employed by Estabrook Construction. Since then we have resided in Peace River (two years), Bezanson (two years) and Grande Prairie (six years) and Fort St. John, British Columbia. We have recently returned to Keg River where we plan to live in the Paddle Prairie Metis Settlement. Our children are now grown and we have two grandchildren Lance (three) and Cody (six).

Randy and Carol Cardinal
by Carol Cardinal

Randy, son of Joyce Cardinal, and myself, daughter of Lindy and Connie Paul of Fort Vermilion, met while working in a northern Alberta logging camp in 1989. We began a long distance courtship between Keg River and Fort Vermilion in 1990 and by the winter of 1991 became officially engaged. After a short engagement Randy and I were married on September 28, 1991, in Peace River. In 1993 we made Keg River our permanent home and live not far from where Randy's grandfather, Jean Marie, raised his children.

Randy and Carol Cardinal.

Brian and Leslie Carnell
by Brian Carnell

My wife Leslie, myself and our son Neil moved to Keg River in the spring of 1970. Jeffrey came in the same year and Darren was born in 1972. We lived at the ranger station until 1974. Wayne Rutter (Reine and Dena) were also living at the ranger station.

Some of the other Alberta Forestry Service people before me were: Peter Nortcliffe, Gordon Bisgrove, Horst Rhode, Johnny Johnston, and Kenny South, although not necessarily in that order.

I spent most of my time in Keg River doing fire permits, fighting fires, and in the winter inspecting seismic operations to see that the clean-up was being done. I have a lot of fond memories of good friends in Keg River. Jim Hamelin was a good man, a good father, and a good foreman. He taught me most of what I needed to do for my job. Steve Kelemen was a good friend. He taught me what I needed to know about farming and trapping. I enjoyed winter afternoons drinking tea with Frank Jackson and learning about the early days in Keg River. Looking back at the time I spent in Keg River I have a flood of memories, including Squeaky Larivee disappearing and the speculation about that!

I remember helping Louie Armstrong leave Carcajou on the 2nd of January, 1973, with a team of 13 dogs. It was quite a struggle controlling the dogs while the final items were tied on the toboggan. When everything was ready there was a horrific confusion of curses, shouts, barks, yelps and then the explosion of man, dog, and rigging heading up the Peace in the clear cold January air. I drove up the hill to the break and watched the team go out of sight. I could still hear him talking to the dogs and he was three miles away. That was a sight I will never forget.

I remember having tea with Howard Price one spring morning. He related to me with a grin and a chuckle how a bear had come into his yard during the night with the idea of having a nice fat pig for a late night dinner. Howard's dog had barked and woke him up. With rifle in hand he went out to investigate. Moments later the bear was dead and in the pen with the pigs. Howard had a real laugh commenting on the irony of the pigs having bear for dinner instead of the bear snacking on the pigs.

I remember when the Tuppers were burned out and came to live with us for a few weeks until they found accommodations near the post. Those youngsters had never lived in a house with flush toilets and running water. They nearly ran the well dry experimenting with that new gadget. They were good hearted and uncomplicated folks.

Louis Tupper showed me how to catch pickerel in the Wolverine River with frogs for bait on a treble hook, six feet of green fish line and a willow pole. There are more fishing gadgets around now, but it seems like when I really want to catch a fish, I try and think how Louis would have done it.

It was on the Naylor Hills tower road that I saw the first ground hog that I had ever seen. I was curious about what the heck kind of critter that was, so I got out of the pickup. The crew laughed so hard they nearly fell out. I think Donald Ferguson and Raymond Cardinal were among that bunch who had a good laugh at my expense.

It was in Keg River that I learned about the 10th of October wind. In 1973 after summer had turned to autumn and the harvest was over, Lloyd Schroh was doing his fall work and cleaning up a field north of Garth Coulter's. There were a bunch of root piles and Lloyd got a fire permit to burn them. The piles barely got burning before a warm wind came up. Quickly the fire jumped from the roots into the bush.

That wind blew for three days and three nights without letting up. Three days and three nights I worked on that fire. I have noticed since that nine years out of 10, we get a warm wind that blows day and night for at least three days in the first two weeks of October. Some things a fellow learns easily, some things he has to learn hard. That was one I learned hard.

Our family left Keg River in the spring of 1974. We had arrived on the gravel and left on the pavement. If you did not experience that dusty piece of road you probably can't even imagine it. You could be driving along in the evening at five miles per hour not able to see past the hood ornament looking forward, but able to see the Naylor Hills to the west. It was a strange feeling.

During the time I lived in Keg River I felt in tune with the community, felt as though the work I did was important, and made some good friends. It happens only a few times in a lifetime, and I'm glad I had the experience of living in Keg River.

Elizabeth and Gordon Cartier

by Elizabeth Cartier

It was a big decision to move from Fort St. John, B.C., to Keg River, Alberta. My husband, Gordon, was in the heavy equipment construction business in Fort St. John and the business just wasn't there any more. Gordon wanted to take out a homestead in Keg River and work his equipment at the same time, doing land clearing and whatever else he could do. I wasn't going to move unless I could get a job teaching. I wrote Northland School Division and was hired on at Dr. Mary Jackson School. This was in 1964.

Come July we packed up all our belongings, rented out our house in Fort St. John and headed out for Keg River. All five kids were bawling. They didn't want to leave their home and friends. Needless to say I was rather weepy myself.

What a trip we had! The truck kept breaking down, we were caught in a rainstorm and the roads were something else. We arrived in the middle of the night at a dark and desolate place. However when morning arrived, the sun was shining and things didn't look so bleak. Even the children were happier, running around and exploring things. I was impressed with the beautiful new school.

Summer went by very quickly while we were settling in and discovering the local habitat, picking berries, making jam and fighting off mosquitoes. My, they were big and left big welts on us! The countryside was beautiful. Gordon did land clearing on the homestead and also some custom work for the local people.

September was very exciting, getting back to school, meeting the children, the parents, and of course the other teachers. The school population was about half Metis and half whites, I loved every minute of my teaching career in Keg River. The children were so eager to learn.

We remained in Keg River five years; I joined the local ladies club, thus becoming more aware of what was happening in the community. We attended most of the functions in the Keg River Hall, such as the dances, suppers and grade nine graduations. We sure had some delicious suppers.

One time there was a special supper honoring Dr. Mary Percy and Frank Jackson. Dr. Mary was a wonderful doctor and person. Many were the times we had to take our daughter Donna, who had asthma, to the doctor in the middle of the night for a shot. Dr. Mary never complained about being awakened. She deserved to be honored!

While in Keg River I organized a Brownie Pack. Since most of the children came to school on the bus, we decided to have the meetings during lunch hour. Edmonton Guide Association supplied us with uniforms, which the girls proudly wore.

Gordon in the meantime got a contract clearing and burning brush for the power line right-of-way to Rainbow Lake. This was a very strenuous job and took its toll. Gordon ended up with T.B. and spent six months in the sanatorium in Edmonton. He came back completely cured.

We had our trials and tribulations as you do anywhere. One year while we were at the teachers' convention in Edmonton, the teacherage burned down. We lost everything. It's a terrible feeling realizing you haven't got a pot to cook in or a blanket to cover up with.

Thanks to Sears we were able to charge up the necessities. Northland moved some trailers in and we managed for the balance of the year. During the summer holidays new trailers were moved in and we were quite comfortable except for the propane problems. The temperature could drop very drastically in the winter, causing the propane to freeze. Consequently we had no heat and weren't able to cook. I remember one time Lorraine made coffee in the electric frying pan. The men who were thawing out the propane sure appreciated that coffee.

Once our children reached high school, they went out to boarding school in Grouard. Dr. Jackson School tried grade ten one year but it was too limited so it wasn't successful.

Lorraine, our oldest daughter and Willie Janke had two children, Desiree and Michael, while in Keg River. They lived on the homestead. Willie passed out cigars and even Ernie Marr, the principal, who never smoked, was puffing on a cigar in the hallway of the school. This was a special day and event.

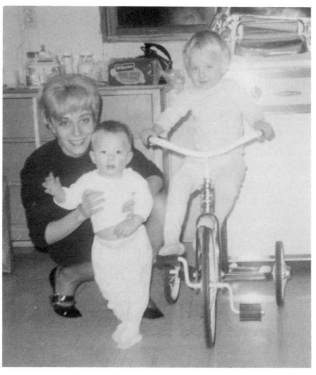

Lorraine Janke and her children Desiree and Mike at the homestead in Keg River.

We spent five years in Keg River and I qualified for a sabbatical leave which I took. Farmers we were not, but I wouldn't trade those five years for anything. They were rich and rewarding and I'm sure we grew a few inches.

Twenty-seven years have gone by and our family has all grown up. Lorraine and Willie Janke are living in Cranbrook, B.C. Their three children

are Desiree, Mike and Tammy. Desiree is married and has three children, a daughter and a set of twins, a girl and a boy. Mike is in the Armed Forces. After spending four years in Germany he is now stationed in Comox, B.C. He will train as a pilot. Tammy is a dental assistant in Vancouver.

Declan Cartier's birthday.

Cheryl married Dwayne Ensign and has two children, Leigh-Ann and Murray. They live in Donalda, Alberta.

Annette married Marvin Tews and has three children, Daylien, Dayna and Dale. They live in Edmonton.

Albert is living in Edmonton and Declan is in Donalda. Donna married Jerome Lowe and has three children, Alon, Candice and Jordan. They also live in Donalda.

As for Gordon and me, we are retired and live in Donalda. We do a bit of travelling. The summer of 1992 we travelled the Alaska Highway. We took in some of the festivities, celebrating the 50th anniversary of the Alaska Highway.

(Editor's Note: Gordon passed away in the spring of 1993.)

Archie and Louise Chalifoux
as told by Arthur Chalifoux

The Chalifoux families have lived in the Keg River and Chinchaga country for many years, back into the 1800's for certain. A number of relatives are buried in the old cemetery. One cross there marks the grave of Arthur's great-grandfather, who was buried in 1920 at the age of 81 years.

Alphonse and Elizabeth were the parents of Henry, Archie, Tommy Donald, Frank, Clemence, and Harriet. The family lived at various locations along the Keg River. Hume Stewart traded a quarter of land located west of Trosky's, with Alphonse at one time.

Louise was born at Fort Resolution, North West Territories, and spent her early years there. She and Archie were married at Fort Vermilion in 1932. Archie learned trapping from his father. He also worked at many other jobs, including several on survey crews.

Louise Chalifoux with baby in moss bag.

Archie and Louise had a family of eight, four of whom are alive today. Two sons and two daughters passed away when they were quite young. Louise was six when she died of a ruptured appendix. Walter, Arthur, Edwin and Jeanette live in Keg River and High Level.

Mrs. Clemence Sinclair and baby in front of Dr. Jackson's house.

During the period from 1940-45, the price of beaver pelts was good but there was a quota of 10 per trapper. They brought $60 each. Archie was able to buy a team of horses, a set of harness and a wagon with the money he got from beaver pelts.

Alphonse Chalifoux with large wolf pelts.

The family lived on their homestead (NW-13-101-24-W5), which created a four-mile walk each way to school for Arthur and Edwin. When Jeanette was old enough to go to school, the family moved to a small cabin at the Keg River Post. Later the homestead was sold to Adam Pawlowich. The family then moved to the Metis Settlement area north of Keg River (SW-15-102-24-W5) where Arthur, Walter, Edwin and their families still live.

The Chartrand Family
by Barbara Chartrand

My husband Peter Chartrand was born in Meadow Lake, Saskatchewan, on September 25th, 1941. I was born in Edmonton on May 12th, 1945. We were married in Red Deer on May 27th, 1961.

We have two sons: Larry was born May 20th, 1963, and Todd was born on September 27th, 1967. Todd has two children now. Melissa was born on April 28th, 1986, and Louis arrived on September 27th, 1987.

On April 28, 1986, my husband and I arrived

to live on the Armstrong Road in the Carcajou area. We walked into the bush to the river bank, and as it was a rainy, cold day, we put up our tent under a spruce tree as fast as we could.

We had only a chain saw, but in two weeks we had a trail in and a small cabin built. It was a good thing we had hurried as our tent blew apart the next day.

We had to work hard, but we had a lot of fun, too. Sometimes a bear would drop in for breakfast, but our dog Basset soon had it chased out of the yard.

After two years we lost our first home to a fire. In February 1992, we lost our second home to a fire also.

We moved into the garage after the fire and then got a trailer for the rest of the winter.

Peter and our son Todd built us a lovely, third home in the summer of 1992. After six years it was great to have running water, electric lights and heat with the turn of a knob or a flip of a switch.

In 1988 Todd and his wife Wendy moved in next to us. They returned to the city in 1991 for a year. Todd, Melissa and Louis came back home in 1993.

Our son Larry lives in Edmonton. He is a professor of law and is the director of the Indigenous Law Program at the University of Alberta.

The day we arrived in Carcajou, I felt like this was home and that it always would be. The people and the land of Carcajou are both special and unique!

Lloyd and Donna Chorney and Family
by Donna Chorney

In the spring of 1968, my husband Lloyd got word from Northland School Division that he had been appointed the new principal at Dr. Mary Jackson School in Keg River and I was informed that I also had been granted a teaching position at the same school. We were very excited about the prospect of taking our young family of one-year-old twin daughters, Karen and Karlene, to a brand new community.

Keen to see the site of our new future home, we travelled to Keg River in early June and spent some time looking at the school and at the trailer in which we would be living. The Marrs were great hosts and we left even more excited about the move than when we came.

August arrived and we settled into our new home. It didn't take long for us to discover that we had moved to a friendly community with concerned citizens. We hadn't been there more than a day when Anne Vos arrived to make sure we had everything we needed.

Shortly after that, we were invited to the home of Sheila Douglass, also a teacher at the school, and it was there that we met Dr. Mary Percy Jackson. What a dynamic lady! I'm not sure what else we discussed, but I do remember a conversation about the new decision made by Northland to close the Carcajou school and bus the students and their teacher, Mrs. Befus, to Keg River. The doctor was concerned about the length of the bus ride especially during the cold winter months.

One concern we had as parents was finding a baby-sitter willing to travel to our home each day since the school was 12 miles from the Keg River community. Our problems were easily solved when a student we had taught at Grouard told us about her mother who lived only a couple of miles away from the school. Thus we were able to hire someone whom we all still remember with fondness, Ellen Bouma. Not only did she care for the physical needs of our children, but she also used her artistic talents to provide wonderful activities to fill their days.

Besides this, she was also willing to ride our Arctic Cat to school on winter days. We felt truly blessed to have found such a brave person to care for our girls and our son, Brett, who arrived in October of 1970. Later on, when Mrs. Bouma was no longer available, we were indeed fortunate to have Margaret Coulter help us out by caring for Brett while the rest of us were at school. Brett speaks fondly of his time spent at Margaret and Gar's farm.

SCHOOL!!! When I think about our six years at Dr. Mary Jackson School, I can recall so many memories that it is difficult to decide what to write about. Perhaps the best way is to just list the memories as they come.

I remember:
- children from three communities (Carcajou, Keg River and Paddle Prairie) learning to work together and play together, sometimes the hard way;
- buses arriving each morning and unloading their occupants;
- nine grades in five rooms;
- home economics classes on Thursday afternoon in the classroom and in our trailer. Margaret Coulter and Anne Vos brought their sewing machines to the school and volunteered their help every week.
- spring teas and fashion shows in the hall.

This was the time for students to display their cooking and sewing abilities.

- Dr. Jackson presenting information on child care. School was more than learning to read and write. It was also about learning life skills.

- gathering wild cranberries in the bushes by the school to use in home economics class and getting stung by wasps;

- listening to new Christmas songs over and over while Lloyd decided which ones would work well for the Christmas concert that year;

- rehearsing for Christmas concerts never believing that the productions or the songs would be ready on time. Of course, they always turned out fine and everyone felt so proud.

- having a community skating rink right outside the school. The parents and students were always so willing to make sure the rink was flooded and kept clear of snow so that everyone could enjoy skating.

- dividing everyone into teams for the hockey games played at noon and sometimes in a tournament on Friday afternoon. I was happy to be put on the Good list, because I was certainly not good enough on my skates to qualify for the Better or Best list. I don't remember if the team I played for ever won, and I think that is the best part of the whole thing. It didn't matter who won. It only mattered that everyone had fun playing together.

- students upset when we wouldn't allow them to skate when the temperature fell below minus 30 degrees Fahrenheit;

- softball and broomball games;

- track meets, sometimes even in the rain;

- a birthday cake from my French class;

- the beginnings of a school library;

- watching the Canada-Russia hockey game which was won by Canada with Paul Henderson's goal;

- travelling to Edmonton by school bus and visiting the Alberta legislature, Al Oeming's game farm, a fire hall, etc. The girls slept in a gymnasium at the YWCA and the boys slept in the basement of a church.

- taking a team of hockey players to a tournament in High Level where they did very well. It was very quiet at school for the next couple of days, because everyone was hoarse from cheering so hard.

- graduation banquets in May followed by dances;

- students who left Keg River to attend high school in Fairview, or Edmonton or Camrose.

Halloween – Chorney twins at Rutters, 1969.

Some went on to post-secondary institutions as well.

These are only some of the many fond memories of teaching in Keg River. I also have many memories of living in the community. I remember all the good friends we made while being included in the activities of the community. I remember visiting Dr. Jackson, both as a friend and as a patient. Keg River may have been small, but it had one of the best doctors around. I remember walking in the fresh air, playing with our children in the wide open spaces. I remember skidooing at midnight on Christmas Eve when a chinook came through. I remember family wiener roasts on Friday evening or fishing trips on the weekend. I remember our station wagon becoming an ambulance on a couple of occasions. I remember clouds of mosquitoes on a spring evening. I remember the long June days and December nights.

There are so many memories, I can't list them all, but I can record the lasting impression I have of Keg River as a wonderful place to live, to raise a family and to teach. I will never forget our six years as members of this small, but friendly community. We speak so fondly about it that our daughter, Charese, who was born a month after we left Keg River, is sorry that she never had a chance to live there too.

Today Lloyd is the principal of Hillside

Junior/Senior High School in Valleyview and I am an English teacher there.

Karen has a Bachelor of Science in Biology and Chemistry and is finishing an honors degree in Slavic Languages. She is presently serving as an interpreter for Komi Arctic Oil in Russia.

Karlene has a Bachelor of Education from the University of Alberta with a major in English. She is teaching grade nine at S. Bruce Smith Junior High School in Edmonton.

Brett has one year left in a bachelor's degree in Petroleum Engineering at the University of Alberta.

Charese is finishing her second year of a Bachelor of Arts in English at the University of Alberta.

Donna and Lloyd Chorney with daughters Karen, Karlene, Charese and son Brett.

John and Marie Christian
by Margaret Befus

John was born in Rumania but the date is not known. Marie Coutoreille was born at Little Prairie about 1888.

Joe ran away from home at the age of 12 and stowed away on a ship to the United States. While there he had cause to see a doctor. John spoke no English and the doctor wished to know his name. Some believe that John thought the doctor wished to know his religion and said "Christian", being of Greek Catholic faith. Some believe that John's surname was Christian, but written in the language, it looked much different.

Thus to all in North America, he was John Christian. He did not read or write and it was not until John met Steve Kelemen Sr., who was also from Rumania, that he tried to get word about his whereabouts to his family in Rumania. Steve wrote the letters for him, and perhaps received news from his far-off family. No one other than Steve ever knew his true family name.

He met Marie Couterielle and her daughter Lucy about 1918. A daughter, Annie, was born to them before they moved to Keg River. Here John took out a homestead where Skipper Villeneuve now lives. There was no Metis colony at that time and the area was considered part of the Keg River community. The following children were born to John and Marie while they resided there: Mary Jane (Cardinal), Charlie, Joe, George, Archie, Eileen (died in infancy), Annie (Sowan) and Malcolm.

When Paddle Prairie Metis Settlement was drawn up, John was forced to move off this land even though he had a native wife. The colony paid him a small amount for his land, as he had improved his homestead. Some of his neighbors who also had to move were Jim Hunter, Scotty Watson, Harry Wilson, Lonnie Root, Reg and Les Bendle, the Fitzsimmons, and the Colemans. Some received cash for their land, some were given other land, while still others who had not received their patent were simply told to move.

John and Marie moved to Carcajou where some of their now grown-up children live. Over the years John became blind. He lived for 17 years with Charlie and Laura. John Christian died in 1961 of a stroke and is buried at Keg River. Marie, known to many as Grandma Christian, lived for nearly a century – some say more – before leaving more than one hundred descendants in 1992. She is also buried in the Keg River cemetery.

(Editor's Note: The following tribute was written by Priscilla Ferguson (Christian) for her

Marie Christian and daughter-in-law, Laura and great-granddaughters, Tara and Rhonda Stewart.

grandmother at her death in 1992 at the age of 100. Priscilla joined her grandmother, when she died on December 26, 1993 at the age of 44 after a courageous battle with cancer. She left her husband Leo and loving family of four sons and one daughter.)

Mrs. Christian, Mary Jane Cardinal, Doreen Batchelor and Karen Cardinal.

Going Home

Mother, grandmother, great-grandmother, great-great-grandmother, we saw you getting tired and knew your strength would not return; so with many regrets and sorrows we'll let you go. You faced your pain with courage, your spirit did not bend.

We realize you are happy going home to your son but the ones you leave behind would walk the path to heaven just to bring you home again.

Mother, grandmother, great-grandmother, great-great-grandmother, if only our tears could build a stairway to heaven and a golden lane to heaven with all the love we have for you, we would see the sparkles in the heavens as we did so many times in you. So we'll let you go home just knowing you are with God.

Charlie and Laura Christian and Family
by Laura Christian

Charlie and I have lived in Carcajou for 49 years. Seventeen of those were spent on the east side of the Peace River.

We always grew a garden and canned the vegetables. I canned moosemeat and berries, too. The children have always loved picking berries but were scared of bears.

We used to carry water from the river in pails. One day we went for water and a big brown bear was drinking out of the river. I told the children not to be afraid because the only time bears are

dangerous is when they have cubs or if they are injured.

One day there was a small bear up a tree by the graveyard. My daughter Pat saw it and ran to get the .22 rifle to shoot the bear, then she found she had no shells. After Uncle Malcolm came and shot it, he teased Pat saying she would not kill much without shells!

Grandma Marie Christian taught the children many things when they used to go to the bush with her. She showed them how to make birch syrup in the spring. They cut the birch tree and attached the pail to catch the sap as it dripped out. Then the sap was boiled down and it was very good on pancakes. We make it every spring.

Charlie used to haul mail for Carcajou from Paddle Prairie every two weeks. It didn't matter what the weather was like. Rain or snow, he had to go. One year just before Christmas, Charlie had to walk in deep water and leave the horse at Slim Kemp's. Donald Stigsen and the children used to watch for him because they did not want to miss the Christmas parcels! He was their Santa Claus complete with reindeer!

Charlie travelled with a single horse and sleigh to haul the mail. One time Raymond Cardinal went with him. The mail truck was late and they had to stay over in Paddle a couple of days. By the time they got back to the Peace River it was full of ice, so they had to stay at Kemp's for the night. The next afternoon it was frozen hard enough for them to cross on foot, pulling the sleigh. We were glad to see them get home safely. Then in a few hours the river was moving again, Charlie had to help Ted Stigsen move the boat up higher on the bank.

We always used to watch for the boats in the summer. When they stopped in Carcajou we would go and see who was travelling.

We lost our home and everything we had in a fire on October 6, 1951. Our baby boy was five months old, Charlie was working for Ted Stigsen out on the farm and I was alone with the kids. I had a hard time getting my father-in-law out of the house because he was blind. My daughters Pauline and Patricia kept him and the baby away from the house. Priscilla was in the bedroom looking for the tomatoes Muriel Stigsen had given us. She couldn't understand when I rushed her outside just in time. Joe Christian saved one blanket! Then we had to put out the fire in the grass around the yard.

We were lucky to have such good neighbors. They helped us a lot. Ted and Muriel Stigsen gave us bedding, dishes, pots, and pans and even lent us a bunkhouse. Mrs. Martha Rankin and Charlie, and Mel and Sadie Price helped us, too. We will never forget what they did for us.

Charlie Christian children with Grandma Christian. Boxer, Skinny, Priscilla, Walter, Neil, Doris, Grandma, Russell.

When Pauline was six years old, Muriel Stigsen taught her using correspondence lessons for two winters. Pauline enjoyed going to Muriel's. We finally got a school on the west side of the river. The children would then go and stay at Mr. Kemp's place from Sunday night to Friday night. Ted Stigsen would take eight of them over by boat on Sunday: Pauline, Patricia, Jack, Priscilla, Donald, Charlie Jr., Walter and Ronald. Next term we moved to this side of the river. Neil, Doris and Russell went to school later.

Charlie, Laura and family. Boxer, Jack, Skinny, Neil, Henry, Walter, Pat, Priscilla, Doris, Barbara, Russell.

The teacher, Mrs. Kiselczuk, was very nice and stayed for a long time. When she left, Mrs. Margaret Befus taught for a long time, too. Then our school was closed and the school bus took the children to the Keg River school.

I worked for Mrs. Befus doing washing and baking. Charlie and Joe hauled oat bundles for Dave Befus. I had spare time, so I went outside to help. Charlie showed me how to drive the tractor, somehow I didn't run over anybody and we hauled bundles all day. I never got to drive tractor again!

I worked as a teacher's aide for five years. I rode on the bus with the children and teacher. There were lots of children at Dr. Mary Jackson School from Paddle Prairie, Carcajou, Twin Lakes and Keg River.

Charlie worked spring and fall for Charles Dovey and Wim Vos. They kept him pretty busy. When Howard Price was alive he used to come and play cards a lot. He was a real friend.

We moved to our new place in 1978 and lived in a trailer for a few years. Then we got a new house where we have been living for six years. We have a wonderful view here about 400 feet above the Peace River. It sure is nice to have electricity and running water and not have to go and get wood any more! We have 24 grandchildren and 15 great-grandchildren.

Joe Christian and Family
by Loretta Beaulieu

Joe Christian, my dad, was born in the Twin Lakes area in 1925. From there his parents, John Christian and Marie Couterielle, moved to the Keg River area. Dad had four brothers and three sisters: Charlie, Archie, George, Malcolm (deceased 1991), Lucy Chalifoux, Annie Sowan, and Jean Cardinal. For a number of years they lived at Paddle Prairie, where they had a farm. John Christian had to leave Paddle Prairie when the government started the Metis Colony at Paddle as he had no Indian blood. John and his wife then moved to Carcajou.

When their parents moved, Dad and his brothers stayed in Paddle Prairie and kept the farm going for a while, but gradually drifted their separate ways to find work.

Dad met Mom (Mary Noskey) when he was 34 and she was 16. Mom was born and raised at Keg River, along with three sisters – Emma Ducharme, Ellen Ducharme, Flora Noskey – and one half-brother, Alphonse. Her parents were Maria Stoney and Charlie Noskey. Her dad fought in World War I.

After Mom and Dad married, they moved to Carcajou. Joe made a living by working for farmers in the summer and trapping in the winter. He was known as one of the best and fastest stookers around. Mom and Dad had 10 children. Most of us attended school in Carcajou during the years we lived there. The rest went to school at Dr. Mary Jackson School in Keg River. Mrs. Margaret Befus taught our Mom and each of us at one time or other!

Mom and Dad stayed in Carcajou for about 10 years. In those years they lost two homes to fire. Dad still lives in Keg River and Mom lives in Dixonville. Dad still traps. His favorite pastimes are visiting his neighbors and playing cards with them. Most of my brothers and sisters still live in the area around Keg River.

Loary lives at Keg River with his wife Tammy and their four children. He is a heavy equipment operator. I married Ken Beaulieu in 1992 and have two children. Ken is a self-employed mechanic in High Level. Lorene is attending Fairview College and hopes to complete grade 12 in a couple of months. Lorna married Gary Cardinal in 1983. They have three children and live in Grande Prairie.

Davy is still single and lives at home. He traps and hunts and was a guide for American moose hunters. He also works as a tree-faller for Randy Christian and is known as one of the best. Alvin lived in Grande Prairie for many years but he recently moved back with his son to our area, where he is now working. Johnny and his wife Lynette live in Grande Prairie with their four children.

Bruce lives in Paddle Prairie with his wife Sharmon and one daughter. He works for the settlement. Corrine married Robert Bouma in 1992. They have two children. Both Corrine and Robert work at Rainbow Lake. Priscilla lives at Paddle Prairie with her two daughters and is now attending Fairview College.

Harry and Vitaline Clarke
by Margaret Befus

Harry Clarke was born in 1892 at Fort Vermilion, the first son of Gus and Liza Clarke (Lizotte). Liza was born at Fort Smith to Pauline and Joe "Dollar" LaFleur.

In 1916 Harry was sent to Keg River to work for the Hudson's Bay Company. In 1917 he brought his bride from Fort Vermilion to live at Keg River for a year. They lost their two oldest daughters in infancy. The third daughter, Laura, was born in 1920 at Fort Vermilion. Later, Beatrice (Lizotte), Jessie (Gardiner), Jeanette (St. Arnault) and Warren were also born in Fort Vermilion. The family moved back to Keg River where Theresa (Smith) was born.

Working for the Hudson's Bay Company kept this family on the move. Keg River, Fort Vermilion, Upper Hay (Meander River), and Little Red River were all home at one time or another. When Theresa was eight years old, John (now married to Pat Broadhead) was delivered by Dr. Hamman, at Fort Vermilion. He told the children that the baby had come on the boat. Theresa's response was "Let's put the baby back on the boat and send it back!"

Harry Clarke and George Lambert took care of the Hudson's Bay horses as well as horses of their own. Harry was quite fond of horses and had several very good ones in his time.

When working in the winter at Keg River, Harry, who had a very fast dog team, would take any sick person by dog team to the nearest doctor, Dr. Hamman in Fort Vermilion.

The children attended St. Henry Mission School at Fort Vermilion while their parents were at different Hudson's Bay posts. Each fall the children looked forward to the time the priest would come to take them to school. They learned many other useful things besides what was taught in their classes and they were well fed at the residential school.

One Sunday evening the sisters decided to teach the girls to dance. The priest came to see what all the noise was about. He sat, listened and watched for a while before saying, "Carry on, they are learning something that they will use."

One summer when the family was returning

Vitaline and Harry Clarke, 1980.

157

from Keg River to Fort Vermilion by team and wagon, they ran into a prairie fire in the area that is now Paddle Prairie. Harry put a tarp over the children in the wagon so they could not see the fire and be afraid and to protect them. They drove safely through.

Harry Clarke died in 1971 in Lower Hay at the age of 79. Vitaline Clarke died in Hay River in 1984 at the age of 92.

Benjamin DeCoteau (pronounced Dakota)
by Margaret Befus

Ben was born to Pierre DeCoteau and Mary (Wuttunee) on May 22nd, 1881, in Battleford, Saskatchewan, and was baptized at St. Vital's Roman Catholic Church. His given name was Henri Benjamin. He was the second of six children. His father died when he was ten years old. They then moved to the Red Pheasant Indian Reserve where his grandfather Wuttunee was the chief. Ben's last name was often spelt Dakota, just as it was pronounced.

Ben came to the Peace River country in the 1930's and taught school at Prairie Point, near Fort Vermilion, and at the Anglican Mission School. Rumor has it that he left Fort Vermilion with a broken heart. He moved to Carcajou, where he settled three miles up the Little Buffalo River.

Ben did not have a registered trapline, for he could not afford to buy one, but he poached a few beaver for a living until he was old enough to receive the old age pension. He became quite a hermit, happy with his own company and his books.

In the fall of 1962, Ted Stigsen took a boatload of supplies downriver for Ben and left them at the mouth of the Little Buffalo, as was his usual practice. Several days later, someone travelling the river told Ted that Ben's supplies were still there.

Ted went down the Peace and up the Little Buffalo to Ben's cabin to find that Ben had died in his sleep. Later, Ted took the body to Fort Vermilion to be buried in the Anglican cemetery there, as had been Ben's wish.

Although Ben passed away, his legacy lives on. Ben was trying to develop a potato specifically for our short growing season. He had developed one that produced well here, but it did not keep well.

Ben's brother Alex was a well-known long-distance runner, and also the first native motorcycle policeman for the city of Edmonton. He ran in the Commonwealth Games, but was killed in action in World War I. They still have an annual run in the city of Edmonton to honor Alex DeCoteau.

Len de Haan
by Len de Haan

I arrived in Canada from Holland in 1948, then spent a year on a dairy farm in Ontario. In 1949 I moved west to work in southern Alberta. I filed on a homestead in Keg River in 1952. It was SW-30-101-23-W5. It was just 160 acres of trees! There was no house, no power, no water – nothing but trees. I began by building a small cabin and digging a 25-foot well for water.

Johnny Vos and Len deHaan ready to homestead, 1950.

Karl Marx had a brush cutter and was working in the district. He did my first clearing and piling. I had more clearing work done by Mike Papirny. Later the rest was cleared by Ken Fischer's outfit.

Whenever there was a job in the winter months I went out to work for a telephone company. When the oil rigs were closer, I worked for them.

I bought more land, the quarter west of my present land, from Sammy Ducharme and began to clear it. I also began raising pigs, farrow to finish. I hauled them to Grimshaw, where they were then shipped to Edmonton. When Bob Peel sold out, I bought another quarter west of the others. In 1973 I went into straight grain farming and I bought another quarter in a homestead sale.

The one thing I remember most about those early years was the roads. Some were awful and others were worse! The Keg River road from The Post out to the highway was partly corduroyed. (To corduroy was to place tree trunks crosswise in the mud to form a roadbed across a swamp.) The muskeg by Dave Weber's place burned all through one winter. The MacKenzie Highway was a very long, narrow, dusty gravel road or a very long, narrow, slippery one! Its paving was welcomed by all of us.

When the recreation board was formed, I was elected to several terms and spent many volunteer hours at the skating rink, building the hall and working on the library.

Here in Keg River many of us have had close encounters with wild animals. I am no exception. One night I was reading at the table. Hearing a noise, I looked up to see a large, black bear looking at me through the window. It was not more than three feet away! There was another time when I had cured and smoked ham and bacon. I had left them in the cool porch, but when I came home I found a bear had broken into the porch and stolen them!

I have retired from farming and have rented out my land. I continue to live in Keg River, where I enjoy television received through my satellite dish and reading. In the summer I still grow a garden and tomatoes in my greenhouse.

Sheila Douglass
by Sheila Douglass

"Come Teach in the Land of the Moose," the advertisement in an English paper said. I applied. It was 1967 and I didn't know where the "Land of the Moose" was, but Northland School Division #61 offered housing, half as many students in a class, and twice as much salary as I was getting in England. Maybe the tail piece of the ad, "No Weaklings Need Apply", appealed to my vanity.

I spent a weekend travelling to an interview which consisted of "What questions have you got to ask me, Miss Douglass?" and before I could get over the astonishment at not being questioned about my abilities, etc., I was asked to sign here, please! That should have told me something!

When I heard I was going to Dr. Mary Jackson School in Keg River, I looked for it without success in my atlas. I finally found Keg River marked on a map of Canada in a very small atlas belonging

to a friend. I guess Keg River was on that map because of its Hudson's Bay Company associations, but I came to discover that Keg River was more than just another "Bay Post".

I came to Keg River on the bus. We travelled overnight and it was a harrowing experience because I had with me in a flight kennel, my prize-winning, pedigree pet pug. She travelled in the luggage compartment of the bus. Every time we stopped during the night, others went to the cafe for a hot coffee and I took my dog for a walk. She towed me up and down the parked cars looking for "her" car.

At Peace River I was told that it was against regulations for a dog to travel in the luggage compartment. Neither the dog nor I were happy about it but what else was I to do? Fortunately they allowed her to complete her journey to Keg River.

In 1967 there were still 12 miles of gravel between Peace River and Manning and no pavement north of Manning. The sun was brassy, the air was stifling, and the road very dusty. As we climbed out of the valley of the Third Battle, I looked back to see, for the first but not the last time, a windy cloud of dust still hanging in the air.

The bush seemed to go on forever before the big sign at the end of a school, proclaiming it to be 'Dr. Mary Jackson School', came in sight. The bus pulled up at Keg River Cabins, which was then a set of rough-looking log cabins with a utilitarian building serving as the cafe, gas station and bus depot.

Thankfully we got out of the bus and stood there with our luggage like weary refugees. John and Susan Cooper were also bound for Dr. Mary Jackson School. John organized a ride for us and our luggage up to the school and we were soon standing outside our new homes.

Emigrating to another country was an adventurous thing for me to do, and knowing there was accommodation at the end of the journey was a comfort. I was allocated a small house. I went inside. It smelled dry and dusty, different from the constant Cornish damp I was used to. The mosquito netting was damaged, so when I opened the windows the mosquitoes came in. There were no curtains on the windows, and no relief from the bright sun on my tired eyes, nor from the stifling heat.

I stowed the groceries I had brought, in the large fridge, put my dog's blanket on one of the chairs where she soon settled down, and I went through to the bedroom. I sat on the bed – tired, disoriented and wondering what I had done. I just had to have a sleep, so I lay down on the bed, which at once collapsed under me!

After I'd tried to sort out my bed, I started to unpack. I took my dog for a walk and fed her. Then I sat down on one of the chairs and an enormous black rodent ran out from under the gas furnace. Pug Peggotty, who had a well-developed sense of self-preservation, ignored it!

My preconceived idea of Canadian scenery was of rocky mountains, lakes, waterfalls and sparkling, fast-flowing rivers. Keg River was different. There were some hills away in the distance, which were pleasant, but not very prominent, and the river was muddy, brown and sluggish. The farms seemed huge and raw, unlike the cosy Cornish farmsteads.

When the fall sun was weakening and the leaves were glowing orange and yellow, Anne Vos took her children, Miss Hepner and me to visit the Naylor Hills Forestry Tower. The rungs of the ladder up to the top of the tower were one foot apart, so it required effort to climb up if you weren't too fit, but what a wonderful view from the top! On the ground the developed farmland had seemed extensive and the MacKenzie Highway significant. Viewed from the top of the forestry tower the country was seen in perspective.

The patches of brown soil where the farmers had cleared away the "bush", black poplar, spruce, some birch and tamarack, seemed paltry. You could see the occasional minute house and the railway line drawn across the landscape with a tiny toy train creeping along it. The highway forging north was almost concealed by the bush. Stretching to the 360° horizon, the rest of the scenery was bush. It was like a beautiful enormous carpet – flaming green, yellow and orange with a few brown holes in it. It made a deep impression on me.

Another evening that fall Anne and Johnny Vos came around after school to pick up their children and me. A freight train had derailed on the line not far from the school and we went to inspect the result. The train had been carrying ore from Pine Point and there were wrecked cars and piles of ore tumbled over the line.

A gang of Portuguese workers were building a new line around the crash so that rail service which carried ore from Pine Point and grain from elevators could be resumed as soon as possible. The only casualty seemed to be a nest of baby robins. The mother robin had built her nest in a tractor which had been brought north to work on the line. As she was left behind, the babies died without her attention.

The hunting season was soon upon us, and a young English teacher ordered a gun out of one of the mail order catalogues. One Friday evening it arrived. He immediately stood outside his house and started to take potshots at things, including a disused biffy in the middle of the school field. He stopped when I reminded him that children sometimes played there.

When he needed a hole drilled beside his porch door so he could rig up a door bell, but didn't have a drill, he decided to shoot a hole through the door! My house was opposite his, so I wasn't very happy.

Food shopping was a problem. When some local people came around with large fresh vegetables for sale, this was like a treasure. I don't remember that Keg River Cabins had many groceries for sale in those days. If they did, I guess they were relatively expensive. Someone went to pick up mail at the Bay twice a week and groceries could be bought there.

I found that Woodward's, the big department store in Edmonton, would deliver a box of groceries by Grimshaw Trucking, so I made an order. There was gravel on the highway, but so far, no gravel in the school yard. When it rained heavily and you walked across the yard from the house to the school, three or four pounds of thick gluey mud on each boot would impede each step. I ordered groceries from Woodward's about twice between my arrival and Christmas, when I bought a car. Both times the truck got stuck in the school yard, which as it had been raining was a morass of gumbo. I was surprised at how good-tempered the drivers were about it!

Nyna Marr was going to Manning by car on Saturday and offered to take Miss Hepner and me so that we could go shopping. It rained heavily all week and the gravelled road was muddy and full of potholes, so I was quite surprised when the trip was not called off. I said so on the way and I remembered and heeded Nyna's words, "Sheila, if we stayed home because of the weather in this country, we'd never go anywhere!" So after I acquired a car I too went wherever, whatever the weather.

I met the rest of the staff and got to know my students. In Cornwall I'd had 40 young children between the ages of four and seven, but I'd had a very well-equipped classroom, with lots of practical things to do and plenty of good books. At Keg River I had fewer children, an American

Reading Scheme which seemed highly unsuitable for northern children, scribblers, New Math books, pencils, crayons, chalk and some library books. I spent some of my own money supplementing these supplies to make life a bit more interesting for the students.

I didn't know who Dr. Mary Jackson was, and asked the children. I guess they thought I was stupid, or they were just shy, because even though Dr. Mary Jackson's grandson was in my class, I didn't find out who she was until later.

The teachers were invited to join other members of the community at the home of the Pattersons to celebrate their wedding anniversary and her birthday. The house was a large log cabin and quite spacious inside. I was surprised and amused to find all the women congregated around the big table, and elsewhere in the room the men gathered to talk and drink. There was much food and lots of talk. A young couple came in closely joined; they had to drag themselves apart so that the young man could join the men and the girl join the women. This was strange to me.

It was here I met the Jacksons, and Dr. Jackson's English accent made me feel at home immediately. We were invited to supper. Meeting the Jacksons and visiting in their home was a special privilege.

In those days before the MacKenzie Highway was paved, it was a delightful surprise after travelling over the tiresome gravel highway and through endless bush to arrive at the Jacksons' home. Beautiful wrought-iron gates, a substantial house surrounded by lawns, flowerbeds and strutting peacocks seemed like a mirage. Inside, the house was furnished with many books, plants, handsome hand-made furniture and interesting artifacts.

I think the first shock to my system was Halloween. In the United Kingdom they celebrate Halloween in Scotland to a degree, but not in England. In Scotland guisers go around to the houses, and are expected to sing or entertain in some way before they are given any money or goodies.

I was uncomfortable with the North American custom, which seemed to me like plain begging. I was grateful to be warned by another teacher to lay in a pile of candies, but no one would tell me how many I might need. In the 90's the American commercial Halloween, like many other American customs, is gradually creeping into the British way of life.

There were many amusing incidents, although daubing my pickup truck with eggs wasn't one of them. A couple of teenagers came to the house. I could recognise one boy but not his companion, who refused to speak and wore a nylon stocking over the head. I found out later that the boy had no one to go "trick or treating" with, so his mother had dressed up to accompany him. I thought that was very sporting of her.

I began to settle down to life in Keg River. I managed to adjust myself to receiving mail only twice a week and having no corner shops. I liked the children in my class, and although I found the education system very frustrating and altogether foreign to my training, I managed to compromise and satisfy the bureaucracy.

The first winter was very cold at times and the fuel lines in the propane tanks used to freeze occasionally. Several times I saw Elizabeth Cartier stepping out while it was still dark, with a fur coat over her nightie and a pan of water in her hand to thaw the line, so that she could make coffee and warm up the trailer.

After the first Christmas break when I drove from Edmonton to Keg River in clear sunny weather, I was surprised to find the temperature in Keg River was -60°F and the school furnaces were all frozen up. Maintenance men had been working on them all day. There was also a foot of snow in the front of my house, which had to be cleared to allow me to park near enough to the house to plug my car block heater into the extension cord.

We had several chinooks that winter, which were another new experience for me. People from "outside" don't believe it when you tell them that Keg River experiences chinooks, but it's true.

One evening after admiring the lovely sunset with its peculiar arched cloud, I sat at my table in the house marking books, and at seven P.M. I noticed on the thermometer outside my window that the outside temperature was -40°F. An hour later I happened to look at it again and it was 40°F above! The snow was beginning to melt on the roof and the warm wind was blowing strongly.

One evening after a chinook, when my car was standing in melted snow, it started to freeze rapidly. I thought the car would get frozen in and I would never get it out, so I found some boards and jacked the car onto them.

This strained my back and tired me out, so I changed into my night clothes including a shocking pink dressing gown and matching pink mules. I put some steak in a pan on the stove to fry, and started to run a bath, then I put something out in the porch and accidentally locked myself out of the house.

I ran through the puddles to Elizabeth's trailer to see if she had a spare key for my place. She had visitors who were strangers to me, so I tried to act nonchalantly, as if I always went visiting in my pink dressing gown, with frozen pink toes peeping out of pink mules. Bradley Papirny found the key and ran over to my house to turn off the stove and the taps, while I sat down to drink the inevitable cup of coffee!

I never favored tea, and drank coffee from a young age. In England I drank fairly weak instant coffee with milk. In Keg River I learned to love strong, black, brewed coffee. Wherever I went in Keg River, the coffee percolator would be on the stove, and a cup of delicious strong black coffee would be offered. I drank it constantly until, after a few years of overdosing on Keg River caffeine, I was forced to give it up.

I was impressed with the local people who had cleared their farms out of the bush, and with their children who had picked roots with their hands. They didn't waste much and were so self-sufficient.

I grumbled to one of my Canadian friends about the inconvenience of the gravel road, and she said, "Sheila, when we got a gravel road, we thought we had it made!" There seemed nothing to say to that, so I learned not to grumble, and in fact I was quite sorry really that life wasn't harder, so that I too could boast of being a pioneer!

Soon after I arrived I bought a vacuum cleaner. It had a retractable cord, and one day I pulled it out too far. The dealer was 140 miles away in Peace River, so I decided that I would try and fix it myself. I got out a screwdriver and undid a few screws. Suddenly a large metal spring and a million and one ball bearings burst out all over the floor!

I was too embarrassed to collect all the pieces and take it to the dealer, so I said to myself, "Well, you want to be a pioneer, so get on and fix it." I don't know how I got that spring and all those ball bearings back so that it worked, but I was sure proud of myself when I did.

Another time I thought I deserved a pioneer's badge had to do with the piano in the school. It had actually been loaned to the school, but I wasn't told this until later. It needed tuning and there was no one to do it. One of the notes was way out of tune with the rest.

The next time I went to Edmonton I bought a tuning hammer, which wasn't cheap. I had been warned that I would probably break the string, but

I went ahead and tried to tune the note anyway. I almost succeeded but the string broke. I sent to Edmonton, got another string, installed it myself and tuned it. I was very proud of myself.

One Christmas Lloyd Chorney decided that we needed the piano in the community hall for the Christmas concert, so although it was -30°F six large boys and I took the piano to the hall in my pickup truck. Three husky lads rode in the cab, and three supported the piano. When the lads outside got cold, which didn't take very long, they knocked on the window, I stopped, and they changed over.

During one change our progress was observed and reported on, resulting in the owner of the piano claiming it and taking it home from the hall after the concert. I tried to learn to play the guitar!

Everyone seemed to be clearing land and burning up the young trees that had been cut down. It seemed to me such a terrible waste to burn all this wood. Surely it could have been used to heat the houses. Some people had wood stoves, but many had gas (propane) heating.

I had an old propane furnace in my house which was always giving trouble. Its favorite trick was to come on with a great explosion in the middle of the night, blowing out the side of the stove, and causing me to leap out of bed with shock. When the ducks came back in the spring, one somehow fell down the stove pipe, and when the stove came on there was a terrible scuffle until I hastily switched it off and had the duck rescued.

I enjoyed seeing the beautiful northern lights, and hearing wolves and coyotes hollering on moonlit winter nights, but the sounds I will never

Sheila Douglass, Dr. Mary Jackson and Mary Lou Ng.

forget are the sounds of break-up. The sound of the snow melting and the water running, the emergence of the noisy frogs, and the song of the birds returning to the north are permanently imprinted on my memory.

I was wakened by a flicker who thought it a good idea to excavate a hole in the side of my house at five one morning. It was so lovely to hear birds again that it was soon forgiven. The lengthening of the days and the warmth of the sun were such a blessing after the long dark winter nights. After that, time raced by to Sports Day, grade nine graduation, goodbye parties and the end of the school year.

Charles Elmer Dovey
by Patsy Lindberg

Charles Elmer Dovey was born in Calgary to Charles Sr. and Hepsey Dovey. He had one older sister, Eugenie (my mother). His mom favored the Baptist and Quaker faith. He claimed no particular allegiance to any church or faith.

Times were hard – his dad worked wherever he could, which often meant moving. While he was young, they moved to a little country home near Vulcan, 75 miles south of Calgary.

He and mom attended the Dairy school for about two years. They had a close friend with whom they spent a lot of time – Charlie Campbell.

They liked to mold dishes from a special clay found in the area. If the clay had any sand in it, the dishes would melt when they were put in the oven. They soon knew which clay worked best.

On November 11, 1933, the family left Vulcan and headed north, arriving in Keg River in November 1937.

Charles moved with his parents into Carcajou in the fall of 1945. Charles broke a lot of the horses to ride or pull a load. He said that the best horses were the ones that never bucked or fought a bridle. He made friends with his animals and gently introduced them to the bridle, bit, and harness. His favorite saddle horse was a gentle light brown horse named Ace.

One day Charles bought a new rifle. He told my dad, Lou Tupper, how well he could shoot with it. To demonstrate, he fired at the box of a grain truck nearby. Two shots got all four tires! Dad laughed and teased him for days afterward. Charles was very annoyed and embarrassed. Fixing the tires was no joke either!

Charles often cleaned his guns in his bedroom to keep the mess away from his mom's working area. One day he was cleaning a rifle he thought was empty. It fired just as his mom entered the room. The bullet grazed her leg and blew a big hole in his dresser. It was a shocking experience for both of them. His mom told everyone what had happened and cautioned all on the folly of ever thinking that a gun was safe.

One spring a little gold and white dog followed Charles home. It had the appearance and agility of a fox. Charles called him Jinx. Trouble seemed to follow that dog everywhere. Jinx constantly trailed around after Charles, always trying to help until it disappeared about a month after it had appeared. Charles liked the little dog even though he got into so much trouble.

After losing his home to a fire, Charles lived in a little trailer. He then sold his land to Wim Vos and moved the trailer to another location, where he added a rickety little porch to it.

He raised cattle, sheep and a few hogs. Coyotes got a few of his newborn calves and a bear tried to take a few pigs. One milk cow had a taste for crankcase oil! Many times she was so sick that we thought she would die.

One day she got bogged down in quick-sand on the riverbank. That day Wilbur Crowder brought the Christian kids and my family to the river to go swimming. We informed Charles of his cow's problem. He came with his tractor and pulled her out. She was weak and tired but strong enough to stand on her own.

Charles sold his livestock and bought a few goats. They mowed his grass and kept him company, often sleeping in his porch. The trailer

Charles stretching beaver on spring hunt.

163

itself was small and narrow and had a very low ceiling. You could sit on the bed and cook supper or wash dishes. Charles liked gardening and raised mostly potatoes.

My brother Doug helped Charles build a new house in 1976 through 1978. On the south side they built a big greenhouse full of small boulders to keep it warm. His tomatoes grew like small trees. An underground stream supplied his house with fresh, clean, cold water most of the year. His garden benefitted from the excellent water supply.

Charles worked for Wim Vos through seeding and harvest and then trapped during the winter. Occasionally a mountain lion wandered across his trapline. He felt more comfortable with the wolverines which he sometimes caught. Charles even felt more comfortable with the bears! He cooked up a variety of his catches. Of them all, he said lynx was by far the most delicious.

Charles generously offered his home and helpful advice to neighbors, friends and strangers alike. One of his favorite sayings was, ''Money can't buy happiness but it can buy a mighty fine ship to go in search of it''!

Charles never married. Pete and Barb Chartrand stayed with Charles during his long battle with cancer. He passed away at home on January 2, 1989. He was buried in Peace River.

Charles Dovey.

Success is a journey not a destination.

Elmer and Hepsey Dovey
by Eugenie Tupper and Patsy Lindberg

Charles Elmer Dovey was born March 1, 1884, to Edwin and Rose Dovey in Denver, Colorado. He had twin sisters, Ida and Carrie, born in 1899. Ida died in infancy of pneumonia.

Ed drove streetcars in Denver for 10 years, then bought a dairy herd and moved into the Colorado Blue Mountains. They sold milk, butter, and vegetables to their neighbors. Rose was often ill; her doctor said that she would feel better in a drier climate. When they moved to southern Alberta her health improved considerably.

Elmer never had much opportunity to go to school. While in Denver he walked to school for the few years he went. He was very shy and nervous. When his teacher asked him to go to the front of the class and read aloud, he would get nervous and his knees would shake so hard he would fall down. The class would laugh, breaking the tension, then he would read without further difficulty. The bigger boys liked to play pranks and rough him up after school. He always found a way to make them regret it!

Elmer's dad was granted Canadian citizenship before Elmer came of age, giving him citizenship privileges in both countries for the rest of his life. Whenever anyone asked about his nationality, he always chuckled and exclaimed, ''Just call me a bloomin' Canadian!'' He was still proud of his Colorado Blue Mountains, where he had so many fond memories.

On September 3, 1919, Elmer married a school teacher, Hepsey Wilhemina Giberson from Bristol, New Brunswick. For several years they lived in Calgary. I (Eugenie) was born to them on February 5, 1921, and my brother Charles was born on October 26, 1922.

Mom and Dad lived with Dad's parents in Vulcan in 1929, milking cows and hauling cream and vegetables. I went to school at Dairy School, northwest of Vulcan.

The hard times that came in the early 30's threatened to ruin my parents. Dad worked at anything he could find, sometimes peddling vegetables, milk, cream, butter, chickens and anything else that he could get people to buy. Dad made regular deliveries to some stores with his cranky old truck. The bends in the road would give a snake a backache and the hills often looked like Mount Everest and were just as easy to climb, especially after the rain.

On November 11, 1933, my parents were told that things were better in the north, a land with great potential. Packing everything they thought they needed to start their new farm, they started on their way. Their outfit included a home on wheels: two wagons hooked together and pulled by five teams of horses. About 50 cattle, 20 horses, 25 sheep, 10 hens, and four geese were included.

During the next four years they would travel all summer, renting a vacant farm for the winter when the weather turned cold. Our travelling home was not insulated. It had a plant in the window, a cream separator in the corner and even a folding rocking chair that our ancestors had carried across the United States from Illinois to Colorado in a covered wagon.

Nests for the hens were built into the wagon where they always stayed. The geese were turned loose when we weren't moving. When we were travelling, the geese were put in a pen under one of the wagons. As we travelled we milked cows, churned butter, made cheddar cheese, and canned fruits and vegetables. All winter Mom spun wool on her spinning wheel and knit it into scarves, socks, mitts, and underwear. She had a sewing machine with which to make clothes, as well.

The winters were spent in different locations as we moved north: 1933-34 at Olds, 1934-35 at Stony Plain, 1935-36 in Grimshaw. By 1936 we reached Hotchkiss. Here my parents leased a small farm and stayed for 18 months.

In November 1937, we moved further north to Keg River to live for a few years on a farm that was later owned by Steve Kelemen. My parents made their living by hunting and trapping.

Coming to Keg River was like entering a new land. There was a small flat prairie about one mile wide and five miles long. To the north were poplar trees, muskeg, and sandy ridges. The south was bordered by the Keg River and heavy timber that stretched far to the south.

It was here that we first noticed how long the days were in the summer and how short they were in the winter. The weather was different, too. It wasn't something we could describe, it just felt different. Here we encountered our first chinook since leaving the prairies. We couldn't believe how the temperature could soar to 40 degrees Fahrenheit from well below zero and how strong the accompanying winds were.

We soon moved again, this time to High Camp. This is still in the Keg River area, close to where Mabel Omoth lives now. There were a lot of wolves and coyotes in the area then and our livestock were always in danger. I spent many hours herding and hunting for our 40 sheep. If a wolf drew blood

on a woolly, and they often did, the sheep would appear healthy but would soon die.

I often saw larger timber wolves, sometimes with a Siberian wolf among them. Sometimes they travelled alone, but more often they were seen in packs. The colors of the wolves varied from snowy white to rusty black or even grey, like oversized coyotes.

When we moved to High Camp, Mom and Dad built a new home, a barn and a chicken house which was built in an excavation in the side of the hill close to the Keg River.

On December 1, 1941, I married Louis Tupper and in 1945 we, along with my parents, bought Rankin Holdings from Max Rankin and moved into Carcajou. Together we had approximately 60 cattle, 20 horses, 500 sheep, 20 chickens, two geese, two dogs and a cat.

Meeting the boats every other week as they brought supplies and visitors was an exciting, fun time in our monotonous little world. The Hudson's Bay had a river boat and the other boat we often met belonged to O'Sullivan and Stigsen. A boat would usually make a round trip from Fort Vermilion in two weeks. The boats ran all summer. In the winter, travel was by sleighs pulled by horses or dogs.

Our local forest ranger, Frank Lafoy, often came to visit, bringing pink popcorn for the children. They liked to sit on his knee eating popcorn and listening to his wild stories.

Our two families lived together for a short while, working to get our new home ready. Later, Mom, Dad and Charles Dovey lived in a small house two miles from our two-story log house.

Dad built a watering system for his livestock. His home was built on the rise where Wim Vos now lives. He set up troughs leading from the pump down the slope to the animal watering tanks. All he had to do was pump the water. It worked really well until the wooden troughs rotted!

Mom helped a lot when the Tupper children were born because getting in and out of the valley was difficult.

Mom and Dad left Carcajou in the summer of 1959. They moved on to live in Calgary for two years, then bought a home in Westerose, very close to Pigeon Lake. Two miles west of their home they rented a small farm. Dad bought cattle at the auctions to feed out, then sell in the fall.

In 1978 Mom and Dad came to Manning to live in Del-Air Lodge until Mom had a stroke in November 1980. She was moved to the Auxiliary Hospital in Peace River in March 1981. Dad went

Rankin's log house at Carcajou, 1947.

Hepsy and Elmer Dovey, 1976.

to stay in the Sutherland Nursing Home until she passed away in June 1981.

After her death Dad returned briefly to Carcajou to stay with his son Charles. In August, he moved to Deadwood to stay with his granddaughter and her family (Patsy and Verner Lindberg). Two years later he came to stay with me, Eugenie, in Manning. A year after that he passed away in the Peace River Auxiliary Hospital.

There is so much good in the worst of us
And so much bad in the best of us
That it behooves all of us
Not to talk about the rest of us.

Jean Marie and Bertha Ducharme Family
as told by Bertha Ducharme

Jean Marie's parents were Octave (Fred) and Elizabeth (Roberts) Ducharme. Jean Marie was born at Fort Vermilion. The family moved to Keg River in 1928. Emile, Helen, Manny, and Sammy were older than Jean Marie and John, Malcolm, Alphonse and Tommy were younger.

Mr. and Mrs. Octave Ducharme.

While the family lived at Keg River they had some stock, horses and cows. In the summertime they stayed at Chinchaga where they had a big garden and plenty of meat. They used to ride horses in the summer or go with team and wagon.

In the winter they travelled with team and sleighs or dog teams. If a person had a good dog it was common to travel with one dog pulling a small toboggan with the driver standing. He required good balancing skills!

There was no school in Keg River so some of Fred's family went to school at the Catholic Mission in Fort Vermilion. Life was not too good there and they were glad to come home in the spring.

My parents were travelling on a raft on the Peace River when I, Bertha was born! I still can't swim! Hilare Minault and his wife were with my parents. Our families were coming from Cadotte Lake to our Carcajou home. We moved to Paddle Prairie 52 years ago in March 1942. Our two families travelled together, with teams and sleighs, Ed Wanuch and Roger Wanuch. I remember camping at "Frying Pan Creek" (Keg River Crossing was the usual name).

When we got to Paddle Prairie we had no place to live, so we stayed with Paulis Bottle. We then found a place close to where the Ridsdales now live. Dad built a log house and we all helped to peel the logs and pull them into place one at a time, with big ropes. It was a big house in those days. The chunks of spruce bark were laid over poles on the roof and then covered with sod.

We had no furniture at first, then some things were homemade. One other thing about those days, we never heard the word groceries! We had just plain "grub". Everyone grew a big garden and canned fruit for the winter. We liked to go picking berries and made pickles, too. We had a pit to keep carrots and turnips. They were covered with sand and stayed fresh all winter.

My brothers and sisters were Jimmy, Albert, George, Tommy and Stella. Charles, Fred, Ralph, Susie, Barbara and Hank were our step family.

Sammy and Jean Marie Ducharme joined the army along with "Chiboy" Garbet. Their brother John joined up later. Sammy and Jean Marie served in England and John went on to mainland Europe as an army sniper. John died in Belgium on the Leopold Canal. Jean Marie was in the army for four years.

During the war I remember seeing Jean Marie's picture in the Peace River paper the police were trying to find him. They said he had run away from the army! When that was settled, he was promoted to the Military Police. That way he could stay out all night legally, while he checked on the other fellows! After returning from the war, Jean Marie got a trapline down on the British Columbia

John Ducharme.

border. He also worked on pipelines and pumping stations near Prince George.

I started working at the New Manning Cafe when I was 17 years old and continued there for two and a half years. The wages for dish washing were nine dollars a week -that was good money. Tobacco and cigarettes were 10 cents per package, jeans one dollar and a good dress was two dollars!

Jean Marie came to borrow my nine-dollar wage to pay his fine and I didn't ever get it back! As of April 10, 1994, we have been married for 45 years. There have been many changes here and all over.

Jean Marie and I had 11 children but we lost three sons Billy, Kelly and Fabian. The others are: Dorothy, who has been a nurse in Fort Vermilion for 21 years; Frankie, Donnie, Georgina, Joanne, Ruby, Eldon and Dean. They all live in Paddle. Georgina is the school principal there.

Sunday trip to Chinchaga.

When I was younger, I could remember anything, whether it happened or not. *Mark Twain*

167

Thomas and Ellen Ducharme and Family
by Verna Hamelin (nee Ducharme)

My dad Tommy was born on June 15, 1928. His parents were Octave (Fred) Ducharme and Elizabeth (Roberts) Ducharme. Dad was the youngest of nine; eight boys and a girl, Emil, John, Sammy, Malcolm, Roderick, Jean Marie, Alphonse, Tommy and Helen. Grandpa Fred raised his family between Chinchaga and Keg River. There was always stock to look after and a large garden to tend. Some of the boys went to school at the mission in Fort Vermilion because there was no school in Keg River. When the Keg River school was built in 1937 the children were sent there.

Charlie Nooskey daughters – Ellen, Emma and Mary.

Dad married Ellen Nooskey, daughter of Charlie and Maria (Stoney) Nooskey of Keg River. Mom and Dad's first child, Elmer, died of leukemia when he was only seven years old. Their second son, Ernest, was born on March 8, 1950. He contracted tuberculous meningitis and spent several years in hospital before returning home. Edwin arrived on July 30, 1952. I was born next on April 26, 1954. Bernice came along in November, 1956, John on February 9, 1958, Darlene on September 22, 1959, Derwin on March 4, 1961, and Maureen in 1962.

Dad worked for Frank Jackson looking after cattle and making and hauling hay. When asked one day by Frank if he had fed the cows that morning dad answered, "Well no, not exactly but I gave them a hell of a good feed yesterday!" Dad also dug potatoes for Johnny Vos during harvest time.

Dad was a trapper in the winter. He was a good hunter and did his best to provide a home and decent living for his family.

One year he took us to Lethbridge to work in the sugar beet fields. He worked for Charles Bartha who was a sugar beet farmer. Charles really liked Dad's work and offered him some land and a house if he would stay.

Alphonse and Tommy Ducharme.

Dad didn't want to leave Keg River forever so he didn't take the offer and we moved back. He was a family man and a great tease. As we remember, Dad was always happy. His tragic death from a beating was very hard on our family. He died on November 8, 1962, at 35 years. Mom was pregnant with Maureen at the time.

Our family has also had to deal with the death of Ernest on July 28, 1990, and John's death in Edmonton on November 13, 1990.

Edwin was married to Hazel Parenteau and they had four children, Morgan (deceased), Carmela, Merle (deceased), and Mark.

I married Cyril Hamelin of Keg River and we have three children: Sheldon, born on March 23, 1971; Charlene born September 8, 1972; and Jamie born June 5, 1974.

Verna and Cyril Hamelin at their farewell party.

Bernice has two girls – Shawna and Larraine – they live in Edmonton.

Darlene was adopted by the Schwindts and lives in Hamiota, Ontario.

Derwin lives in Edmonton and has four children.

Patricia Jones (Hague)
by Patricia Jones

In 1940 my brother John and I left our home in Somerset, England, to escape the war. Our parents had arranged for us to stay with Dr. Mary and Frank Jackson in Keg River. I was just nine and my brother had his seventh birthday on the ship as we were sailing to Canada. We travelled completely on our own, first by ship to Montreal, then train to Edmonton, where we were met by Dr.

Pat and John Hague with the Jackson children, Anne and John, 1940.

Brander. From there we went by boat on the Peace River to Tompkins Landing where Dr. Mary met us and we went by truck to Keg River.

Everything about Keg River was completely different from Somerset. I had been in a school with 400 girls, so imagine the change going to a one-room schoolhouse. Living on a farm was also new to us. I loved milking the cows by hand and squirting frothy, creamy milk into my mouth. I also loved riding Canadian style; in fact, I loved it all. Quite often we had no light and had to use well water, all novel experiences.

Pat Hague at the Jackson Farm, 1941.

We were all expected to do chores. Those who didn't work didn't eat. One morning John did not do his chores -getting wood for the kitchen stove. So no breakfast, lunch or supper. His chores were done the next day!

Keg River felt very wild to me; I thought there were wolves waiting behind every tree. I remember being impressed by a grizzly bear pelt, shot by a man who was suddenly charged by the bear. He only had a .22 and two shells. He sat up in a tree for an hour or so afterwards in case the bear came to again.

A doctor in the house made for some memorable events. I remember watching a gangrenous thumb being cut off and popped in the stove. Another time a man with an axe in his back was brought in and the kitchen table was cleared for the operation! Dr. Jackson also extracted teeth and had a bag of sweets waiting for the patient after.

John Hague and John Robert Jackson at the swimming hole.

We had been in Keg River one and a half years, when Dr. Mary took us to Peace River to the dentist. We went in January and there was lots of snow. It was very cold as we travelled by caboose to Notikewin and then on by truck. In the caboose we slept on straw and were covered with rabbit robes. Dr. Mary was so wonderful making us feel part of the family but I realize now how much I missed my mother and father. My brother was so little that it was even worse for him. We kept in touch with our parents by writing letters and enclosing photos Dr. Mary had taken. Letters took months to travel either way.

My brother returned to England first as they could take boys more easily for some reason. He had all his money and little presents stolen from him on the ship. I went back some time later. On the way to the Peace River I was hoping very hard we'd break down so I would miss the boat and have to stay! I felt Canadian after nearly four years with the Jacksons.

Living in Canada, so far from home, helped me become independent and made me keen to travel and see more countries and meet different people. I have a very special feeling indeed for Canada and Canadians.

(Editor's Note: Pat is now married, has a daughter and a son and lives in England.)

You know what's wrong with kids today? Drugs, sex and rock and-roll. Whatever happened to the traditional values like wine, women, and song?

Dwight (Sam) and Evelyn Evans
by Evelyn Evans

Dwight was born and raised near Lethbridge, Alberta. He was employed for a seismic company on Prince Edward Island when we met. I was born in Charlottetown, P.E.I. We got married in Hobbema in 1969 where I was teaching at the time. We have two children, Clay, our son, is married to Tara. They live in Texas. Carol, our daughter, and her husband Bob live in Calgary.

In the fall of 1984, Dwight's name was picked out of a hat for a section of land in Carcajou. There were about seventy participants hoping to receive one of the seventeen parcels of land. The sixth draw gave Dwight the choice of section nine.

We spent the summer of 1985 in Carcajou. We lived in our small holiday trailer. My first encounter with a bear occurred that summer. Dwight, Clay and Carol were testing their skills with the 22. After an hour they set the gun aside, and all was quiet. I looked down the cut line and there, only 50 feet away, stood a huge black bear. I screamed and climbed to the roof of the truck. Needless to say, the bear took off and everyone laughed at my reaction.

Dwight, Clay and Carol toil away picking and burning roots.

That first summer was one long camping trip. We ate by the camp fire and bathed in the dugout. Carol learned to use a scrub board. Dwight and Clay cleared a three acre site for our house. The children and I returned to Medicine Hat in the fall. Dwight stayed on to build our home. He lasted until mid-November. The cold weather drove him south to a warmer climate.

In July 1986, we sold our home in Medicine

Hat and made the big trek north. We hired a Ryder truck and had a U-Haul trailer attached to move our belongings.

Over the years, we found that there was never a dull moment. There were lots of new families moving into our area. The card games and dances were entertaining. There was church once a month. Lots of meetings were held to keep us busy – meetings about the hall, recreation board, St. Judes church, Home and School Association, Ladies Club and the Carcajou Recreation Association.

There were new challenges and unexpected happenings each day. The list goes on – vehicles in the ditch, trees falling on the power line causing fires, home burning, children ill, farm accidents, peat moss fires, beavers dam after dam, wild geese devouring the grain, floods on the flats, bringing horses to Carcajou, wolves and moose running through the yard and company coming by wheelbarrow.

Life is good here.

Evelyn and Dwight Evans.

Fedorchuk Family
Martha Allain (nee Fedorchuk)

I was the eldest daughter of Luke and Nellie Fedorchuk. I was born in Keg River on April 23, 1932. My parents along with my grandparents Nick and Mary Shemeluik came to Keg River in 1929. My parents and grandparents worked very hard; in those days you cleared the land by hand and horses. Dad packed water from a well that we dug near the house. Our water was very good, clear and ice cold. We didn't have real roads in those days. Someone just cleared some bush and a path soon became a roadway.

We went to a one-room schoolhouse which had grades one to eight. Most of us could not speak a word of English when we started school. We had to walk three and a half miles to school in the summertime. In the winter we had a horse and a

caboose sled, where we were nice and warm under the blankets.

At an early age we were encouraged to plant a large garden, then we helped with the weeding and hoeing. We made our own soap. using wood ashes to make lye water and pork or beef fat. Our neighbors were Mike and Annie Michalchuk, John Pawlowich, and the Rudy family. Doctor Jackson was our doctor.

Mrs. Nellie Fedorchuk and daughters Martha and Daisy, 1943.

Terry and Andy Fedorchuk.

My sister Daisy and husband Gabe now live in Vernon, British Columbia. Our brother Andy and his wife Terry live near Manning with their family: Kimberly, Shaun and Robert. They have a welding business. Sister Pat works and lives in Elk Point. I married George Allain on November 18, 1949. We live in Peace River. We both like to garden and grow a lot of flowers, which I start from seed. We also both volunteer at the Food Bank, are members of the Sagitawa Friendship Centre and I like to visit and do volunteer work at the Sutherland Nursing Home. I am glad to have lived and learned in the 1930's. I would not like to be a teenager today.

Frank and Madeline Ferguson Family
by Violet Ferguson

Frank Ferguson moved north from Grouard when he was 13 years old. Madeline Desjarlais was raised in Peace River.

Frank and Madeline (Dad and Mom) were married in Notikewin where Dad was working on the Peace River-to-North Star road construction. He had worked on the Falher-McLennan road, clearing by hand with an axe.

The four oldest children were born in Notikewin. Doris, the oldest, died of pneumonia when she was just eight months old. Clarence, Ernie and Alma were born next. Alma was just a baby when the family moved to Keg River in about 1935. The other children were Susan, Emma, Teddy, Bobby and I.

Dad trapped south of the village in the Naylor Hills and worked for local farmers.

When the school required a janitor, Mom got the job and over 13 years she worked for three different school divisions -Peace River, Fort Vermilion and Northland, but she was only at one school! There never was any running water in the school. It needed to be hauled from the river. When the new school was opened, Mom and Dad got a house at the Cabins and moved down there. Dad worked with Mom as janitors, they won many goodhousekeeping awards. When my parents' home was destroyed by fire in 1968 they retired to Manning. The family stayed with me for a while until they found a house.

The event Clarence remembers most was the large fire of 1949-50 that came in from British Columbia. He and Larone Ferguson were out hunting towards the Chinchaga along the Haro River (also called Big Creek). The wind came up and there had been no rain for some time so it was really dry. The fire swept in very quickly.

Clarence and Larone released their saddle horses and got into the Haro River. The first wave of the fire was in the tops of the trees, then came the second that was much closer and lasted longer. The fire was extremely hot and ate up all the air so it was hard to breathe. The whole time they had to stay in the water with not much more than their faces sticking out. They never saw their horses again. They were finally able to walk home through the ashes and still-burning bushes.

In our family of nine, six are surviving. Doris, Susan and Emma are deceased. Grandma raised two grandsons, Frankie and George. Frankie drowned in 1980. Clarence lives with Mom. Ernie

Violet and Alma Ferguson had just completed their Nurses Aid Program.

Frank Ferguson Family. Back, L-R: Teddy, Bobby, Violet, Alma. Front: Ernie, Clarence.

THE POST

Serving The North Peace River Country

Volume 17, No. 14   THE POST, FAIRVIEW, ALBERTA   Thursday, April 5, 1956

MANY ATTEND LITTLE ROYAL AND ACHIEVEMENT DAY AT F.S.A.

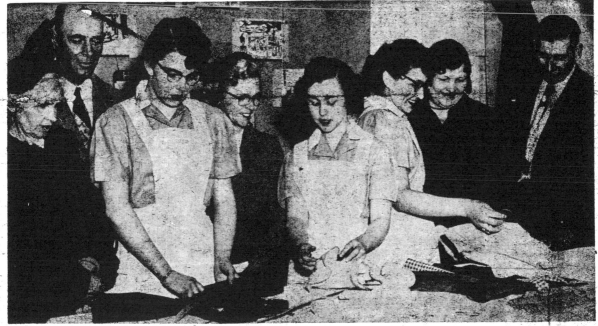

Three Home Economic graduates and their parents admire the girls' sewing projects on display at the Fairview School of Agriculture Little Royal and Achievement Day. Left, Dorothy White, second year student and her parents from Blueberry Mountain inspect the third prize child's garment Dorothy had sewn; Janet Frederickson of Berwyn shows her mother the child's frock which won her second and Mr. and Mrs. Ferguson of Keg River are very pleased with their daughter Violet's exhibit. Violet's parents have, despite the distance, attended almost all public occasions at the school and have shown that people of that area have a growing interest in the Agricultural field and the work done at the Fairview school. —Photo by Ziggie, Fairview Photo Studios

and Kathy operate the Chinook Valley Service Station. Ernie and his first wife Mary had nine children: Veryl, Carol, Susan, Brian, Rebecca, Dale, Marilyn, Barry and Roberta. Roberta is one of Alberta's missing children. She vanished from a Bible Camp near Vancouver.

Madeline Ferguson with daughters Alma and Violet.

Alma married Bill Perdue, they have Carol, Michael, Donna, Billy, Rita and Charlene, and live in Edmonton.

Teddy married Irene. Their family consists of Beverly, Susan, Teddy and Cindy and Wally who has passed away.

I am divorced, but enjoy my children George, Jaqueline, Pearl, Emmerson, and Derwyn.

Bobby and Evelyn have Craig, Wanda, Nelson and Sandy. Dad passed away in 1983 and is buried at Keg River.

Larone Ferguson family
by Margaret Lambert

Larone Paul Ferguson was my father. He married Albertine Chalifoux on August 31, 1919. They had one daughter named Vina. Albertine passed away, leaving Larone a widower.

Dad remarried, exchanging vows with Helen Ducharme, daughter of Elizabeth and Octave Ducharme, on August 14, 1929. Dad and Mom

Vina and Freddie Ferguson and Great Grandma Richards, 1944.

had 13 children together. Their first son, Henry, died as an infant.

Dad was known as Larry by all his friends. People remember him as a great tease and a practical joker, always playing tricks on whoever was close by. He was a great community person who helped organize Sports Days in the summer, and people would come from near and far for those events. Dad and Mom had a fairly large house and they often volunteered their home for dances. Those were hard times with no modern things like power and running water. We had a wood cookstove and heater. The water was carried from the river in the summer. In the winter we melted the snow, but were careful where we got it! In the summer the cookstove was moved outside to keep the house cooler. Getting up a good supply of wood for winter was a big job with no power saws. They used just a Swede saw and an axe. This was a good way for the boys to build their muscles and learn to work together. There was no time to get bored.

To travel anywhere, we had to walk or go by dog sled in the winter. In the summer we travelled by horse or walked.

When the chores were done and we were not at school, we used to slide on the river banks with homemade sleighs or play fox and goose. If it was hot in the summer, we swam in the river. Hopscotch was another favorite game.

Dad trapped, usually leaving late in the fall with pack horses or pack dogs and returning by New Year's Day. Then the second trip would be made on the snow so he travelled by dog toboggan. The spring hunt for beaver and rats would be in all kinds of weather, but often it was cold and wet. Dad was the first hunter in the area to kill a cougar. Frank Jackson bought it and had it tanned. Only one other cougar was around Keg River.

Dad's favorite pastime was reading. He read everything he could get his hands on. One time he was reading "Watch Tower" after we had been visited by a religious group. He came to Mom and said "Helen, did you know that Jesus is coming to town?" Mom was busy making bannock and she told him that she was going to burn all his reading material! Dad just looked at her and walked away chuckling.

Harry Minault was one of Dad's trapping partners. They had quite a time playing tricks on each other but Dad usually won!

Dad was born on April 15, 1898, and died of a heart attack on December 6, 1978.

Dad's daughter Vina had a son, Freddie. They lived with her grandmother, Mrs. Moise Richards, here in Keg River. Vina later married Charlie Gives and they lived on the farm near Deadwood. They had eight children. Vina passed away suddenly in 1961 at the age of 41.

Mom's nickname was "old Helen" because she and her mother had helped as midwives for so many babies born in the district before Dr. Jackson came.

My grandmother was Mrs. Elizabeth Ducharme and she and mom were a great help when Dr. Jackson first arrived in Keg River. Their ability to translate from the native languages was also invaluable.

Mom was the only girl in a family with 8 brothers. Her family spent a lot of time at the Chinchaga where my grandfather raised cows and horses. They also had a large garden. Mom's father, Octave, had worked at the government experimental farm in Fort Vermilion in the earlier days.

Mom was happy to help anyone she could. Her favorite pastime, though, was gambling. She loved poker, and claimed she never lost money!

Mom grew a big garden, too. We picked all kinds of berries and canned them for winter.

People remember Mom's broken English. She never went to school but she made sure she was understood. One phone call to a local farm lady went like this "Hello, Mrs. Kelemen, does your chickens have eggs?"

Cleaning and stretching beaver pelts and making moccasins were other ways that Mom kept busy. She also worked for some of the farmers in the area.

Mom died of cancer in Grande Prairie on September 17, 1976, at the age of 64. She has many descendants in the Peace River district.

Larone and Helen Ferguson and family.

Many of my brothers and sisters have moved away from the Keg River area. Louisa married Dan House. They have seven children and live in Keg River. Wilfred has six children and lives in Grande Prairie as do Octave and Evelyn Ferguson with their four children.

Choosing to live in Paddle Prairie are Helen and George Christian with ten children, and Roderick and Pat Ferguson with their two.

Irene and Malcom McDonald are divorced but have five children in Grande Prairie. I married William Lambert and have four children. We live in Grande Prairie, too.

Leo and Priscilla (now deceased) Ferguson of Paddle Prairie have five children. Allan and Madeline Ferguson, also of Paddle Prairie, have three children.

Hubert Ferguson lives in Grande Prairie as do Gerthie Ferguson with her two children and Edward and Margaret Ferguson.

Donald and Anna (now deceased) Ferguson have five children. Their family lives in Keg River.

(We now include another story about Larone which has been passed on to us by family members who enjoyed his sense of fun.)

Larry supported his family by trapping fur. In the 1930's, one of his partners was Harry Minualt.

They used to play tricks on each other. Larry was often the cook when they camped out along the trapline or in the spring during the hunt. He would cook bannock on the open fire.

Once when he was tired of being the cook, he didn't do a very good job of making the bannock. It was raw and lumpy. This caused a change in who did the cooking. Harry took over the job.

One day they were moving camp. Larry finished packing his three dogs first and Harry was still putting packs on his dogs when Larry took an empty tobacco can and said to his partner, "I'm going for a drink of water." Harry hollered at Larry to bring him some water, too.

Larry got his drink and relieved himself into the tobacco can! He set the can down by a log so the dogs wouldn't spill it. It was after Harry started to drink that his friend told him what he had done!

Larry and Harry were passing by a grave another time and he told his friend that people have good luck when they make a fence around a grave. He got a big kick out of telling Harry that as long as they cut down the tree the dead would make their own fences.

The partnership and the practical jokes continued for a long time.

Lloyd Fischer Family
by Lloyd Fischer

I was born on April 8th, 1932, in Lac La Biche, Alberta. In 1948 I moved to Manning, Alberta, to work for my brother Ken in the sawmills doing bookkeeping. I also drove the school bus while going to high school.

From 1947 to 1953 I was involved in amateur boxing, capturing the Golden Gloves and Provincial Championship in 1953 as the middleweight champion. I was also the chairman of three boxing clubs around the Peace River Country from 1948 to 1978.

In 1950, I set up a homestead in Keg River, Alberta. In 1954, I married Myrna Halabisky and nine years later we had three lovely children, Randy, Richard and Laurie.

In 1963 the lights went out; I had a head-on car collision, which changed my occupation from farmer to life underwriter with GreatWest Life Assurance.

I am a self-taught insurance innovator who believes that everyone should have life insurance because it costs more money to leave the world than to come into it. Believing this, I was able to achieve my goals and was recognized in a South African paper for my outstanding sales record. As a national leader, I also achieved the highest awards Great-West Life offered. I believe in making things happen and getting things done.

During the years from 1963 to 1976, I had eight accidents, three of these very severe. Twenty-eight operations were the result of these accidents.

Some of my happiest days were when my family came into the life insurance business. My youngest son Rick joined the business in 1983. Rick's wife DeeDee also obtained her insurance license. My eldest son Randy joined in 1984. When my daughter Laurie joined in 1985 I was a very happy man!

In 1988, Rick and DeeDee bought out my block of the business. Laurie is currently working as Rick's office manager. I am semiretired and doing a little consulting work for Rick.

This reminds us of the saying "Make it happen; each opportunity is worth exactly what you are prepared to make it."

Craig Fischer and Annette Conway
by Karen Michalchuk

Craig, my brother, was born in Peace River on January 24, 1959. Our parents are Susie Parenteau and Kenneth Fischer. Craig went to school in Manning, Peace River and Keg River and graduated in High Level. Craig then went to Fairview College and took a course in agriculture. After that he started farming and raising cattle in Paddle Prairie.

Annette was born in Wembly, London, England, on May 1, 1963. Her parents are Anne and Thomas Conway. She went to school in London, then moved to Peace River in April 1974. Annette took correspondence courses and graduated with a Bachelor of Arts in 1990.

Craig and Annette were the last ones to live in the old Hudson's Bay house in Keg River. They bought more land, a trailer and moved to Paddle Prairie.

Craig worked for different companies in the Keg River community and worked for the government on the snowplow or grader in the winter months. Craig now works for the Paddle Prairie Colony. His job description is Economic Development. He helped arrange financing for the new mill in 1993 and got the project in operation. Annette works at the school as a special aide. They bought a new home in 1992.

Craig and Annette have three children who were all born in Peace River. Jenna was born on January 27, 1985, Siobhan born June 5, 1988, and Tristan born May 31, 1990.

Annette Conway, Craig Fischer and Karen Michalchuk.

Les and Janice Freeman
by Janice Freeman

I was born in Dawson Creek in 1946, daughter of Hans and Marjorie Ludvigsen, and younger sister of Bruce. I completed my high school in Dawson Creek and went to college in Prince George. In 1965 I married Les Freeman, son of George and Poppy Freeman.

Les was born in New Westminster, British Columbia, the fourth oldest in a family of 10, and moved to Dawson Creek in 1945. Our daughter

Les and Janice Freeman.

Brenda was born in Prince George on December 5, 1965, and our son David was born in Dawson Creek on January 27, 1969.

Les worked for P.G.E. (now British Columbia Rail) when we married, then worked on the W.A.C. Bennett Dam. In 1971 he went to work for United Grain Growers and was transferred to Keg River on the Easter weekend in April 1973. The drive here seemed to take forever and we arrived to find the former tenants' (B. Meashaw family) furniture all on the lawn. This was done so the movers could move us in and them out all at one time!

Brenda started at Doctor Mary Jackson School in the middle of grade two with Margaret Befus as her teacher. David would not start until the following year in the first Early Childhood (kindergarten) class with Doreen Batchelor as his teacher.

In 1975 we purchased NW-15-101-23-W5 from Dave Befus and started farming that land and Lovlin's which now belonged to my father, Hans Ludvigsen. In 1977 we homesteaded the NE-15-101-23-W5 and SE-22-101-23-W5. In 1978 we purchased three quarters of land on the northwest corner of Keg River (NE-4-102-24-W5, SW-3-102-24-W5 and NW-5-102-24-W5).

Brenda graduated from grade nine at Doctor Mary Jackson School in 1980, then took two years in Edmonton at Concordia before transferring to Grande Prairie. After graduating from high school in Grande Prairie she went to the regional college there for four years. On August 6, 1988, she married Kevin Nilsson of Grande Prairie, born to Darren and Tillie Nilsson in 1965 while living in Manning, Alberta. On December 15, 1990, Brenda and Kevin had a son, Jeremy Daniel.

David graduated from grade nine at Doctor Mary Jackson School in 1983. He took his high school in Dawson Creek, graduating from grade twelve in 1986. From there he took one year at Fairview College and then went to work for Canadian National Railways in Keg River. Later he transferred to High Level when C.N. pulled out of Keg River.

In 1990 David bought the Robertson place (SW-29-101-23-W5) from Henry Vos. It was too difficult to farm in Keg River and live in High Level, so in 1991 he quit C. N. and went to work for the United Grain Growers at the Keg River Elevator as second man.

On August 20, 1993, David's girlfriend, Theresa Russell of Dixonville, had a baby boy, Jorden Kyneath Nathanial Russell, and on September 1st they moved in with David. At this time they are living on the Pete Rudy homestead (SW-3-102-24-W5).

Kevin, Brenda and Jeremy Nilsson.

Theresa and David Freeman and Jorden.

In 1993 Les purchased Mel Sherry's place (section-26-101-23-W5) from AADC. Today Les is still farming and managing the United Grain Growers elevator.

We will never forget some of the great times and friends we had and have in Keg River – fishing with Doris and Dave Weber, holidaying and honeymooning with Stan and Gladys Rudy, New Year's parties, bonfires, barbecues, and skating birthday parties on the elevator dugout.

We snowmobiled many a weekend in the Naylor Hills, sometimes getting stuck and unstuck while almost freezing. We played volleyball, baseball, broomball, and flooded the ice rink many a time. We played whist and indoor discing and darts with good friends like the Bricks, MacDougalls and Dezalls.

One of the most recent experiences we had was January 6, 1994, when the train hit a logging truck as it crossed the Keg River road less than one-half mile from our house! Four engines and two lumber cars were derailed and the logging truck was beyond repair. Luckily no one was seriously hurt, as answering the door to someone with a minor head cut and blood all over his face was bad enough. This all happened in -40 degree temperatures.

Some of the organizations I belonged to and helped with are the Keg River Library, the Keg River Hall and Recreation Society, Ladies Club, ECS Parent Committee, Keg River History Book Committee and Manning and District Further Education Council. I have also worked at various places while living here. I was the secretary at the school, secretary at the Keg River Forestry Station, did various jobs at the Twin Lakes Lodge, and have been the bookkeeper at the Keg River Cabins, where I am presently employed. I also do the weather for the Forestry.

Peter I. Friesen
by Peter Friesen

My parents, Maria and Isabrand, moved to Carcajou in the spring of 1934 from Saskatoon. At Peace River they made a raft that was about 10 feet by 70 feet. We travelled down river on it to Carcajou, where there was still a lot of water on the Carcajou flat because of the devastating flood that had hit Carcajou earlier in the spring.

They were offered Dick McGrane's land as he wished to leave the Carcajou area. (It was located on what is now known as the Armstrong flat.) They had to buy his sheep, horses and some belongings that had been in the water. Dick had dug a drainage ditch which helped drain the flat. When the Peace River rose again in July of 1934, it flooded McGrane's flat through the ditch.

The family moved onto the bank of the McGrane flat and lived there until 1939.

Winter time in Carcajou was always a time of chores because cows and other animals had to be in the barn. Barn cleaning was a daily chore and our father insisted that the manure be loaded on a stone-boat and hauled away rather than being pitched out the door or window. This was a tedious process of loading and unloading by hand with a five-tined fork.

We decided to make the task simpler so that we only needed to load. Cow hides were plentiful, so we tied a brace between the front legs of the hide, put the hair side down and hitched the horse to it. To unload, the horse was hooked up to the tail of the hide and the load was dumped off.

Thinking of those years brings to mind the cutter used in winter travel. It was pulled by one or two horses. The seating area was partially boxed in so travellers could be more comfortable.

I built a cutter one winter. We had a very meager supply of tools and money but time was plentiful. We used split spruce poles for runners and two 5-inch spruce poles for the frame. I spent many hours drilling holes and fitting my cutter together. To make it lighter I decided not to use heavy lumber to enclose the seating area. Instead I chose cowhide.

We wanted to show off the cutter as soon as it was completed, so we hitched up the horse and drove off to the Stigsen's Store, crossing the river ice -a distance of about six miles. It was nice to go in, warm up and visit at the store. When we returned to our cutter, to our dismay we found the lining in tatters! A number of dogs had torn up the cowhide of our beautiful cutter!

My father, Isabrand Friesen, passed away on February 5, 1937, and is buried in the Carcajou graveyard.

The Unrahs and the Wielers, who also lived on the McGrane flat, moved to Buffalo Head Prairie in 1936. Thus my mother and we four boys were left alone, except for Abe and Susie Wieler, who lived part time on the upper end of the flat. They made their living trapping.

My oldest brother Abe took out a homestead where the town of La Crete is today. In 1938 our mother also bought a quarter section of land in La Crete. We still reside on that land in 1993.

In the spring of 1939 we walked the cattle and some horses along the ice of the river down to the

La Crete Landing, then overland to Buffalo Head Prairie. The weather was mild and we didn't lose any animals. My brother Abe came upriver to Carcajou, and to McGrane's flat to help make the move. I was on horseback. We had teams with loads of feed going along, too. This was partly to feed the livestock and partly to entice them along the way. I helped with the cattle, and we had told our mother someone would be back as soon as the cattle were settled.

In a couple of days I left Buffalo Head Prairie and went back to the Peace River to find the ice had risen a foot. I couldn't get on the main ice, and if I did, I didn't know how I would be able to get off a day later. If the river kept rising, it would cancel the trip until a boat went upriver. There was absolutely no way of letting Mother and the two boys know we were all right.

When the ice melted and a boat finally did come, I finished my journey. I rode horseback onto the boat at the La Crete Landing and off at the north end of the McGrane flat at about 4 A.M. so I'd be home when Mother got up. I reached home and not a soul was in sight, except one horse and one cow.

I wondered if my mother could have heard the boat coming up the river and had walked the one and three-quarter miles to the upper landing. She had and to her surprise the boat didn't stop. It just blew the whistle and kept on going.

I found that the stove was still warm, so I figured out where she had gone and rode toward the upper landing. She could think of nothing else but that I must have drowned trying to come home. Halfway there I met my weeping mother. She was grieving for a son she thought she had lost!

Two weeks later we loaded what was left of our belongings on a barge, drifted down to La Crete Landing and then travelled on to Buffalo Head Prairie. It was our responsibility to carry on the farming. We were of the age to have fun and be silly, not to build a house and to make hay.

There was a big demand for dog food, so we made our living making dog food from ground wheat and some tallow. In 1943 we sold the steel wheel tractor that we had brought on the barge.

I bought a 22 gas Caterpillar at Claresholm. It was the first Cat in our part of the country. We brought it by train to Peace River, then by truck to Paddle Prairie. There Fred Lambert and I built a stone-boat, loaded enough grub, gas and oil, and put on enough clothes to keep alive in the cold. Our speed was four miles per hour. I had never driven a Cat before, but we made it in three nights and two days.

George, Pete and Billy Friesen in front of house in Buffalo Head Prairie, 1939.

Peter and Mary Friesen.

179

I did custom work for neighbors with the Cat. I also did some commercial trucking.

I married Mary Gunther in Saskatchewan in 1944. We were blessed with seven children: Edna, Philip, Raymond, Erna, Elvira, Vern and Melvin.

(Editor's note: Peter I. Friesen and Mary are well-known community minded people. They are always willing to help their neighbors. Peter acted as La Crete's representative on the Agriculture Service board, High Level Improvement District Council, Keg River Grain Growers Elevator Local and other boards. He is now retired.)

Frank and Joe Gardon
by Joe Gardon

My Dad left Poland in 1928 to homestead in Keg River in 1929. He filed on the SW-4-102-24-W5. This land was in the farthest northwest corner of the Keg River prairie. The land was flat and partly treed. When Dad dug a well, he was lucky to hit an artesian one. There was never any shortage of good water.

Dad tried to save up enough money to bring Mother to Canada, but the Depression and the war made that impossible.

All the farm buildings were built of logs. He raised cows, pigs and a few chickens.

I came to Keg River from Poland in 1949 with my brother John and took a homestead adjacent to my father. We continued to raise animals and grow grain. After two years John returned to Poland because he felt life was too hard here.

In 1950 a big fire came in from British Columbia. It burned our straw stack and some granaries. Dad suffered a heart attack at that time, went to the hospital and never returned to Keg River.

I married and continued to farm until our first son was one year old. We then moved to Radway, where we still live.

John Gabriel and Mary Agnes Gaucher
as told to Anne Vos

John and Mary were married in 1934 in the Eureka River area. They moved around the Peace River country from north to south, finally leaving Valleyview for Paddle Prairie in 1944.

John and Mary had a family of nine children – three girls and six boys: Alice, Florence, Irene, Pat, Walter, John, Wilson, Norman and Russell. They also raised their grandson Gordon.

John had cows and a number of horses when they started farming at Paddle. Mary was elected to the position of Trustee to the Northland School

Mary Gaucher and four of her children, 1955.

Gaucher brothers, Pat, Walter, John, Wilson, Norman and Russell.

Division representing the Paddle Prairie and Keg River schools. She held this position for nine years. John passed away in 1973 and Mary in 1989. They are interred in the Paddle Prairie Cemetery.

Alice lives in Ottawa.

Florence's home is St. Albert.

Irene makes her home in Fort McMurray.

Walter lives in Paddle Prairie.

John died in a plane crash in Inuvik.

Wilson lives in Grande Prairie.

Norman is in Edmonton.

Russell lives in Prince George.

Grandson Gordon lives in Dawson Creek.

Pat lives in Paddle with Mary Cardinal, who was

raised in Fort Vermilion and stayed in Keg River with her aunt to begin grade one. She returned to Fort Vermilion the following spring. Now, years later, Mary lives at Paddle where she is the head of the school janitorial staff.

John Gaucher with daughters, Florence and Irene.

Adolphus (Richard) and Elsie Ghostkeeper

by Ivy Simone Long

My dad, Adolphus, was born in July, 1893, at the St. Bernard Mission in Grouard, which was in the Northwest Territories at that time. He married Elsie Jean and together had a family of 15.

We left High Prairie in 1938 to travel north. We spent one year in the Battle River area before moving north to Paddle Prairie. The family was loaded into two big wagons and we travelled caravan style. We had six horses, four cows, two dogs and some chickens. We must have looked just like Ma and Pa Kettle!

We travelled for five long days in the mosquitoes, rain and bush before finally arriving at the prairie in the spring of 1939. There were only a couple of families living there then. There were no schools, stores or churches.

Dad set to work to build a house and as soon as we had a place to live, he began to plow the land. Dad did many days of long hard plowing for the neighbors, at 50 cents a day.

Our medical care was provided by Dr. Jackson in Keg River 20 miles away, which could be covered in a day by horse and wagon. We call the doctor our medical savior.

In the next year, Dad, Mr. Houle and Sam Johnson went to Joussard to formally set up the Metis Colony.

Dad died on November 29, 1990. He and Mom were married for 60 years. Mom is still planting her own garden and doing her own housework. She loves to travel and visit her children, who are married and scattered over Canada and the United States:

Dolly and her son live in Vancouver.

Annie and Pete House are both deceased. Their family of nine include: Freddie, who lives in

Elsie and Adolphus Ghostkeeper and children. Names are in no particular order. Ivy (Simone) Long, Margarete Campbell, Ralph Richard, Norman Ghostkeeper, Mary Friedel, Donald Richard, Myrtle Burns, Elmer Ghostkeeper, Yvonne Rey, Joseph Richard, Tommy Ghostkeeper, Al Ghostkeeper, Annie House, Sully Ghostkeeper.

Edmonton; Jimmy and Beatrice who live in Grande Prairie; Raymond, Clyde, Rosemarie and Jerry who all reside in Dawson Creek; Ivy who lives in Beaverlodge; and Margaret who lives in Drayton Valley.

Sullivan has died. Ruby lives in Edmonton with their family of four: Brian, Karen, Floyd and Lawrence.

I live in Las Vegas. My sons, Kevin and Michael live in California.

Margarete Campbell and her husband Ken reside in Grimshaw. Their family includes: Faye, Leslie, Dennis and Kenny Joe.

Norman and Florence live in Paddle Prairie with their family: Wayne, Dennis, Sandy, Angie and Dale.

Mary and Art Frediel live in Kamloops with their children: Yvonne, Allen, Gwen, Gale, Tim and Tracy.

Ralph and Mary Richard live in Paddle with Dean, Ralphie, Sonya, Noela and Dawn.

Yvonne Rey and her daughter Jackie live in Vancouver.

Donald and Eleanor live in Paddle Prairie.

Elmer and Kim reside in Edmonton with their children: Winter, Jonathan and Joel.

Myrtle and Bill also live in Edmonton with children: Dennis and Robbie.

Joseph and Dawn live in Manning with Jodel and Dustin.

Tommy and Martha reside in Edmonton and their children are Marla, Shannon and Desiree.

Mrs. Christian and Mr. Ghostkeeper with medals presented on Alberta's 75th Birthday. Mrs. Ghostkeeper is also pictured.

Larry and Diane Giesbrecht and Family
by Diane Giesbrecht

On December 4th, 1989, we moved to Carcajou, Alberta, and by an unusual twist of fate, on December 5th I was asked to substitute teach at Dr. Mary Jackson School. So amidst the boxes and mess of the move, Tamara, who was in grade three, and poor Crystal, who was in grade two, and I headed to school. I say "poor Crystal" because she had to have her mom as her teacher on her first day at a new school, as I was asked to teach in the grade one and two classroom. I think we comforted each other in our confusion.

We came to try to develop our homestead. We rented Charles Dovey's old cabin and moved in just in time for Christmas. That Christmas was very cold and had lots of snow. Larry and I worked on the homestead side by side that first winter. With the help of Laune Budd from Dixonville and Dale Vos of Carcajou, we managed to clear off a portion of our homestead.

By the end of March I had been hired on at the school as an assistant to the elementary teachers.

Larry and Brad Villeneuve started logging together during the winter of 1990 and are still at it. They are contractors for Daishowa Pulp Mill at Peace River.

In the summer of 1991 we moved to Ted and Nora Petersen's place at Keg River and into our own trailer. This brought us closer to our jobs.

Dan Grey
by Anne Vos

Dan was born in Peace River in 1903. His parents were Marie Kate McKenzie and Alex (Whitebear) Grey. Dan lived in many places but always in the Peace country. In his early days he was well known as "Danny Boy". It has been written about him, "he got to be one of the best bronc riders under the sun". Dan participated in Sports Days every year in small towns all over northern Alberta.

Dan married Madeleine Pacquette. They had three sons, Billy, George and Joey. Dan had a homestead near High Camp at NE-8-101-23-W5. He also had a good team of horses that were his pride and joy. The white one was also a saddle horse. He left them with Dave Befus the year he worked in Prince George on the West Coast Transmission Line.

Dan was a member of many fire-fighting crews. He worked on the big fire at Worsley in 1957. He and Roderick Ferguson trapped together in 1958-59. They went to the trapline in October, travelling part of the way with horses. The horses were then let go to return on their own. In their spare time they made their own snowshoes and toboggan. The snowshoes were strung with babiche (raw moose hide cut into strips).

Dan Grey in front of his trappers cabin at Want Lake, 1970.

In the summertime Dan worked for local farmers, especially John Pawlowich. He lived in a cabin next door to Harry Bowe in the Keg River Village.

He moved to Hotel Dieu in Whitelaw after suffering a stroke. He passed away in 1989.

Dan and Harry in front of his house, Keg River.

Bill and Elsie Halabisky
by Elsie Halabisky

Bill Halabisky and I (Yurkowski is my maiden name) were married in 1930 in the town of Vegreville, Alberta, on our way from Garland, Manitoba, to the Peace River country. We filed on some land SW-28-101-24-W5, then built a house. The Bricks (Allie and his daughter Emma) filed on land next to ours and they became our good friends.

Things were tough in the 30's, but we had some cows, hogs, chickens, and a large garden, that helped a lot. Bill went trapping, which brought in some cash for the extras.

We didn't have to pay for entertainment – we had house dances with free music. We had some very good musicians, native boys who were willing to play for free. The ladies brought the lunch. We

had picnics, mostly at the Chinchaga, ball games and a lot of horseback riding.

Bill and I had five children: Edward (Ed) born in 1930, Myrna – 1936, Norma (Laurie) – 1938, James (Jim) – 1945, and Dennis – 1950.

The children all went to school in Keg River until the eighth grade; then because there was no high school offered here, we had to send them away from home for further education. It was heartbreaking for us as well as the children. They were young and we didn't get to see them very often, only on holidays and summer vacation. We were not the only ones to have that problem; there were many others.

Our community was lucky in one respect, though, and that was because we had Dr. Mary Percy Jackson as our doctor since 1930. We may all have died if it had not been for her, as at first there were no roads to get to a doctor in an emergency. She saved many lives.

Bill Grey, Emma Brick and myself rode horseback to Battle River in 1935. We travelled southwest from the village of Keg River to the sixth meridian as we followed the pack trail. It was on higher ground than the trail under the telegraph line. We passed on the west side of Swan Lake. The leaves were turning color as we made the three-day trip.

Back Row, L-R: Lloyd Fischer, Louis and George Hrytcuik, Bill, Eddie and Trudy, Jimmy. Front Row, L-R: Norma, Elsie, Grandma Yurkowski, Myrna, Dennis and numerous grandchildren.

When Emma and I returned, we were alone. Many of the leaves had fallen and obscured the trail. We got lost and decided to leave the horses to find their own way home. At night when we camped, we took turns keeping a good fire going to keep the wild animals away. The third day, our horses started to whinny and not long after we met Carl Norquist with his horses. How nice to know we were on the right trail!

Our roads were just pack trails in the summer and winter roads after freeze-up. People travelled with horse and sleigh; that was the way freight was hauled from Grimshaw and Peace River. Things improved as time went by; a highway was built, then the railroad. Now we have paved roads and we don't mind travelling long distances.

We still live on our original homestead here. We have enjoyed life in Keg River, we have made some good friends and have some very good memories. Most of our family doesn't live too far away, so we are able to get together often.

Bill Halabisky's Story
as told to Myrna Halabisky

My grandfather, Daniel Halabisky, came to Canada in 1897 from Austria-Hungary. He came alone as his wife had passed away earlier. My father, his wife, their daughter Katie, his brother Metro and his sister Feska followed in 1898.

They landed in Halifax, then travelled by train to Winnipeg and on to the little town of Garland, where they took a homestead. Another daughter, Nellie, was born there. Shortly after my father's first wife died. He then married Maria Dzumaga, and from this marriage came eight children – John, Nick, Bill (me), Harry, Emily, Annie, Jean and Joe.

I attended three different schools – Garland, Hague, and Gonta. The greatest distance I had to walk was five miles. I finished grade eight and then had to go to work as times were very hard. My first job at about age 15 was working on the railroad between La Pas and Flin Flon. I worked at any job I could find including harvesting and working in sawmills.

There were dances in different communities and at one of these I met a pretty little blue-eyed girl, Elsie Yurkowski. She lived eight miles from our farm, so there were a lot of long walks between my place and hers.

Elsie's father decided to move to northern Alberta, so I went along, too. We were married in 1930 in Vegreville on the way to Keg River.

I got a homestead in Keg River and built a log

house on it and then had to find a way to support my family. The first year we were here I worked on installing the telegraph line, going to Fort Vermilion. There was no easy way at that time; everything was done by axe. The crews stayed in tents and we fought the mosquitoes.

The next summer John Pawlowich, Yaroslow Romanchuk and I set out walking to look for work. We walked to Triangle and then we beat the roads to Edmonton and on to Hardisty and Hayter. At Hayter I obtained a job threshing for one dollar a day. I worked for eight days and then the rains came.

John went to Smoky Lake, Romanchuk went to Edmonton and I tried to wait out the rain. After three days I gave up and hopped the rails toward home. At Peace River I bought 100 pounds of flour and put it on one of the river boats to Carcajou. I didn't have enough money to buy a fare for myself on the boat, so I walked home from Peace River.

In 1933 I decided to try trapping. I arranged to meet Dan Gray at Buffalo River (about 125 miles from home). I travelled the first part with Louis Bourassa and from there I was on my own. I had never been in that country before and there were only old summer pack trails. After about 15 miles these old trails ran out, but I was able to find my way anyway.

Halabisky's first home.

I trapped for about 55 years and farmed in the summertime. One day as I was beaver hunting, I was sitting by the creek checking to see how fresh the beaver cuttings were when I heard a growl behind me. I quickly turned with my 30-30 in my hands. There was a huge wolf about 10 feet from me. I just pointed the gun and pulled the trigger.

I always had my rifle ready. There were lots of tough times on the trapline, but I loved every minute of it.

Farming was difficult. Our nearest town was 60 miles away, with only a winding trail through the bush. In later years after the MacKenzie Highway was built, our nearest elevator was in Grimshaw. It was a long old haul to take out a load of grain.

Bill and Elsie Halabisky with their 20 pound turnip, 1993.

Dennis and Donna Halabisky
by Donna Halabisky

Dennis grew up in Keg River and went to the one-room school by horse, then later to Dr. Mary Jackson School. He went on to Peace River High School after grade nine.

Dennis brought me to Keg River in 1968. Then the highway was paved only to Manning and the rest of the road was so rough that I spent most of the trip with my hands on the roof of the car so I wouldn't hit my head on the roof! The holes in the main road were big enough to allow a transport truck to get stuck.

I was originally from Claresholm and then from Peace River. We were married in Peace River on August 7, 1970. Dennis spent the next seven years working on the oil rigs. Dennis and I worked out of Keg River in the winter months, but returned in the summer to help on the farm and to get our homestead land and yard ready to move on to.

We spent two winters on the trapline west of Keg River. Dennis still goes to the trapline for part of the winter.

Kimberly was born in Peace River on July 17, 1983. She is now attending Dr. Mary Jackson School. One of our most frightening surprises was the morning of the flood in 1987. The neighbor phoned at 6 A.M. and asked if we could use the D-8 Cat to dig out her road so that the water could flow faster past her house as it was right up to her door! We looked out our door and found our yard and field were under water also!

We warned the Keg River Cabins that a lot of water was coming in their direction. They had about 12 hours to prepare for the high water to reach them.

Keg River manages to hold everyone in its spell, one way or another and we are enjoying our life here!

Jim and Linda Halabisky and Family
by Linda Halabisky

Jim was born in Keg River at his parents home with Dr. Jackson, Mrs. Harrington, and his dad, Bill Halabisky in attendance. He had an older brother Ed and two sisters Myrna and Norma. Dennis was born seven years later.

Jim went to school in the village, then to Fairview for grade 10. While going to school he was in a very bad accident with his brother-in-law Lloyd Fischer, who was giving Jim a ride back to school. Dr. Jackson feared for Jim's life as he had a nasty head wound, but he survived. He went on to work in the oil patch for 25 years.

I met Jim in Edmonton in June 1966. I was there with a friend of mine, Glynis Hodgekinson who was going out with Jim's friend Ken Minard. They introduced us and we were married three years later on June 30th, 1969.

Our son Shawn was born on January 4, 1970, in Peace River where we were living. We then moved to Keg River and lived in Jim's grandparents' (Yurkowski's) house for the summer

Jim and Linda Halabisky.

Sherry, Shawn, Stanton and Shelly Halabisky.

and back to Peace River for the winter. This process was repeated the following year.

In 1972 Mom Halabisky cut her hand with a lawn mower. I'll never forget it as Lillie came and got me. We took a truck to help her. When we got there, Mom was waiting with her hand wrapped up. I then got Dave McDonald to drive us to Manning. Even with all the road construction Dave drove the 70 miles in 45 minutes. Mom lost part of one finger.

On November 14th our first daughter, dark-haired Sheri was born. We stayed with Jim's folks that winter. In the summer we moved into Dennis and Donna's house trailer.

In the spring of 1973 we just about lost our tractor as we had left it on dad's homemade bridge. Overnight the river rose lifting the bridge and tractor. What a sight!

Two years later our blonde, blue-eyed Shelly was born on June 28th, 1975. In the meantime we moved into Mom and Dad's old house next to their new doublewide home. We lived there until 1981.

We moved to Australia and stayed there until Christmas 1983. We had a lovely time there and made friends with some wonderful people who have visited us here.

We came back with a little surprise for us all. Stanton was born nine years after Shelly on May 10th, 1984. It was quite a change.

Now we are quite active in our community. I am a member of the Keg River Ladies Club and the local school board. Jim is on the Agricultural

Service Board. It seems funny but in 1928, when my dad, Charlie Nousek came up on the *D. A. Thomas* looking for land, he got out at Carcajou Landing and took pictures. Now Jim and I reside where those pictures were taken! It is such a small world!

So much has happened to us while we have lived here. We have had many good times. We have enjoyed playing cards with neighbors in the winter. Some of those people were Steve and Mary Kelemen, Vic and Delores Zatko, Linda and Steve Pawlowich, Garry and Colleen, Paul and Jean Galandy. I chased Stan Rudy around the car with a baseball bat. Remember, Stan?!

I guess when we start to think back the good times outweigh the bad!

Myrna Halabisky
by Myrna Halabisky

I was born in Keg River in 1936, the second child to Bill and Elsie Halabisky.

We all attended the little log schoolhouse with the big wood heater in the corner. Some of the families lived as far as four miles from the school and would drive a horse and sleigh to school.

We had to leave home at age 13 or 14 to finish school. (The Keg River school taught only to grade eight.) I went to Manning for one year. The next year I went to Fairview College. When I got back in the spring, I went to work for Mrs. Harrington

Myrna and Norma Halabisky, Allene Brick and Pat Ross.

at Keg River Cabins earning $18 per week. The next spring, 1954, I married Lloyd Fischer. We lived on our homestead and tried to make a living raising cattle, sheep and pigs.

In 1963 Lloyd was involved in a very bad car accident and was in an Edmonton hospital for several months. The doctors told him he would not be able to do much manual labor and suggested he try something different from farming. We then sold the cattle and farm and moved to Edmonton.

Lloyd went back to school with the idea of becoming a teacher. Somehow along the way he got involved in the insurance business. He began working for Great West Life, at which time we moved to Peace River. By this time we had three children – Randy, Rick and Laurie. The boys became very involved in snowmobile racing and dirt bike racing and have a lot of trophies for their efforts.

Randy married Tara Brennan in 1985 and he has two girls – Jessica and Keely. Randy is assistant manager at Westborne Electric in Edmonton.

Rick married Dianne Aihoshi. They have two girls – Kelsey, who is 12, and Shana, who is nine. Rick purchased the insurance business from his Dad and lives in Peace River.

Laurie married Jim Hand. They have one daughter, Emily, and live in Peace River.

Lloyd and I were divorced in 1975.

Bill and Elsie with their 4 children, Emma MacDonald and Don, Mr. and Mrs. Yurkowski and George Hrytciuk.

Jim and Isobel Hamelin
by Gladys Rudy

Jim, my Dad, was born in Keg River on January 23, 1927, and my mom, Isobel, was born in Fort Vermilion on February 20, 1929. They were married in Keg River on January 7, 1950. Dad walked in his father's and grandfather's footsteps, becoming a well-known trapper who used dogs, horses, and later snowmobiles to get to his trapline. Dad also worked for Alberta Forestry for 21 years in many different roles. He passed away in February, 1986.

Jim Hamelin and his horse.

Mom and Dad had nine children: myself, Cyril, Lorraine, Donald, Gerald, Donna, Noela, Vera, and Lorna. Mother was very musical and she passed her talents and abilities on to the family.

All of us either play an instrument or sing or both.

Mom and Dad lived in Keg River for 36 years. All of the children went to school there. We always had a happy home and Mom was always there to guide us with a strict hand and firm beliefs.

Mom moved to Manning after Dad died and she still lives there.

Olivier and Charlotte Hamelin
by Donald Hamelin

Olivier and Charlotte Hamelin were my grandparents. Olivier's father, Chal Hamelin, came to Carcajou from the Rocky Mountain House area in the early 1900's. Charlotte and Mrs. Paulis Bottle were Michelle Sowan's daughters and were raised in Carcajou.

Olivier and Charlotte came to Keg River long before the 1916 survey and lived along the river, close to where Bill Halabisky now lives. When the land was surveyed, they moved to NE-14-10123-W5 where I still live.

My grandfather and his brother Ed went to Yellowknife to get licenses to trap beaver in the Northwest Territories, because at that time there were no beaver here. During that trip Olivier and Ed were advised in Hay River to take firewood with them because crossing Great Slave Lake would take more than one day by dog team.

These brothers were well known for their hunting skills. The Hudson's Bay hired them to provide meat for the store managers. This was how Olivier managed to buy a 44.40, one of the first carbines in the area. Muzzle loaders or bow and arrows were used before this time.

Charlotte was a well-known midwife in the early years. There is a record of her delivering a baby for Mrs. Clement Paul as early as 1910.

Olivier died in October, 1952, in an accident. Charlotte died in January, 1972.

I was raised by my grandparents here in Keg River. Arthur Bowe and I lived close to each other, so we walked the 3 miles to school together each day. We hurried home after school in the winter to check our squirrel snares. We put the snares in the spruce trees across the river from our houses, where the squirrels lived. If we were lucky enough to catch some, we rushed to skin and stretch them so we could sell them to the Bay for twenty cents each. We spent ALL the money on candy!

Arthur and I have shared many memories, especially on the trapline. We travelled south into the Naylor Hills. There had been rumors of a cougar in the hills and we kept thinking about this as we went about setting up the squirrel snares. Suddenly there was this weird noise much farther ahead. We continued on towards our cabin not finding or hearing anything again. Darkness was falling, so we camped for the night in the cabin. We made supper by the light of the coal oil lantern and we played cards. A couple of times during the evening we heard some strange noises that we didn't recognize.

The next morning we travelled together for safety, still hearing the same odd noises. We knew we were getting closer to whatever it was. Finally we came across a young owl that had caught one leg in our trap. So much for the cougar we had feared!

From 1950 to 1952 I worked for Alaska Fisheries on Great Slave Lake. Late in the fall of 1953, I filed on the land my grandpa and the family had been living on for all those years. It was finally classed as eligible for homesteading. Mr. Gilliland, our Member of the Legislature, wrote a letter confirming I had been born and raised on that land. Mr. Allie Brick was at the land office and we were finally given title to the land we had lived on and already considered our home.

Isobel Borbridge and Oliver Hamelin.

Donald Hamelin, Raymond and Rita Cardinal with Coosta Hamelin and Lila Cardinal, 1992.

When Mr. L'Heureux was teaching in Keg River in 1957-60 I hauled wood for the school. For a few years I rented out my land. Then I decided to farm it myself. In 1990 I sold the land to Steve Pawlowich. I still live here part-time and also have a trailer home in North Star.

Adam and Isobelle Harapnuk
by Isobelle Harapnuk

Adam and I owned Frontanac Construction, a company that built houses in Calgary. After many years in the business we began spending part of the winter at our home on the Sunshine Coast of British Columbia at Sechelt. We commuted back and forth for eight years before Adam became totally bored. He was much too active a man to retire.

Adam had had a lifelong dream of owning a farm, so for a complete change we decided to go homesteading! A nice quiet farm in the northern bush sounded just right!

Adam's name was on the government mailing list of people interested in homestead land and we received a notice in the mail of land coming open near Keg River. In June of 1986 we travelled to Keg River for a draw for homestead land.

A draw occurs when the Provincial Department of Lands divides up a surveyed area of land into viable parcels, calls for interested parties to submit their names and then draws one name at a time until all the parcels are taken. Each parcel has a price assigned to it and the first person whose name is drawn gets the first choice of which parcel he or she wants. All normal homesteading rules apply. For the draw we attended there were only 15 people interested in the 17 parcels available!

We were lucky (or unlucky) to get a whole section each – Adam, our son Dale and I. We chose the land that was priced at $58 per acre, thinking it was the best land. It was virgin bush – timber was an even better description.

When we drove in to look at this land, I could not help thinking, "What in the world are we doing here?" Roads had been built in to this new homestead land, but NO other improvements had been made. This land (11-99-20-W5) was in the Scully Creek area near Carcajou, 25 kilometres east off the MacKenzie Highway, then 17 kilometres south and two more east on Homestead Road. In other words, a long way from anywhere and a very long way from my lovely home in Calgary!

Bears were one of my biggest fears! When we built our first cabin (eight feet by 16 feet), I wouldn't have any windows in the place because people told me that the bears could climb in during the night. Instead we put on a clear fibreglass roof which allowed the light in. We also added a screened-in porch where we ate our meals.

Soon homesteading got under way. In order to farm the land we had to get rid of the trees. What a task that was! We hired a man with a Caterpillar and brush cutter to cut and pile these large trees so we could burn them. That was a two-year job.

The day we burnt the brush rows, was an EVENT. We lit only a couple of rows but the next thing we knew, a west wind had sprung up and we had the whole country on fire. All the rows caught fire, several hundred acres and then the forest. We didn't win any friends with the forest service that day! There was plenty of action from them, with water bombers, helicopters and dozens of fire fighters.

Once the land was cleared and all the wood burnt, there was the dirty job of repiling, but that was nothing compared to the root picking. That was a job that never seemed to end!

It was a happy day for me, one and a half years after we moved to the homestead, when we finally got our telephone installed. The telephone became my lifeline to family and friends, and I no longer felt so isolated.

The gasoline-powered washing machine was the same as the one we had at our cabin at Kananaskis so I didn't have to learn to operate it. The propane-powered refrigerator we got from Charles Dovey created a new experience but it was really nice to be able to keep meat and vegetables. We travelled to town, Manning or High Level, both 150 kilometres away, every couple of weeks to obtain supplies. This was quite a change from the 10-minute drive to the Calgary Co-op.

Water has been a problem ever since we started homesteading. There are places in the fields where it has been much too wet and other spots much too dry. Then the water problems for the house are something else. We haul drinking water from the community water supply at Carcajou about 30 kilometres away. We have running water now for the bathroom and kitchen providing we run out and haul it with the truck from a dugout, and then pump it into the holding tank. We can't use this system when it is cold, but we enjoy it in the summer.

We moved a house trailer in several years ago – it was nice to have room for all those conveniences again. The summer after we got the trailer, we had the power line completed to our yard and trailer. Adam had to clear the right of way from here to the last farm that had been connected. That was a big job as well as being expensive, but it is really nice to have power.

We enjoy the country, especially the wild animals.We have seen cougars, moose, deer, foxes and of course bears! Last fall when we were swathing on Dale's land, a cougar decided the whine of the swather's hydrostatic drive was a "friend" calling ... or something! The cougar followed the swather or lurked nearby for several days. We could see a hole up in a high bank and assumed that it was the entrance to the family den.

The bear stories never end. It seems that some years there are lots of bears and others there are only a few. Two-year-old males seem the most inquisitive and destructive. A person must always be on the lookout when the yard is surrounded by trees. The smell of food cooking or garbage, even grain in the granaries, brings them into human company. They cannot resist oats or wheat growing in the field.

The soil here is very good – sandy loam – and my garden has produced well. I have had all sorts of animals wander through, sampling things. The perennial flowers and tulips have wintered well and given me hours of enjoyment.

Daishowa is now taking some of our poplar logs, so maybe we won't have to cut and burn any more. I look forward to the day when the road is cut through to Hawk Hills. It will save us about 100 kilometres every time we go to Manning.

Now it is eight years since we bought this land, and Adam doesn't talk much about boredom! The farm has kept both of us busy. I learned to keep a house that didn't have electricity and survived without a phone. Our home here is comfortable, the farm continues to provide work for both of us and I think we have become quite good farmers in our retirement!

Glady and Eva Harrington
by George Chadwick Watkins (nephew of Eva)

Though never a resident, I did visit Keg River on three different occasions. I was born in Grande Prairie, Alberta, in 1922 and lived in Spirit River until about 10 years of age.

I know nothing of Glady's family background except that he had a brother, Cyril, who was the druggist in Spirit River at that time. Glady was the lineman in Spirit River, I presume for the Alberta Government, and perhaps he was in the same capacity in Dunvegan, as his mailing address

in 1921 was Dunvegan. In the late 1920's it was Keg River.

My mother's oldest sister Eva was born in India, where her father served in the British Army. The family came to the east coast of Canada in 1914 and her father subsequently joined the Canadian Army. At the end of World War I, he took up land in Spirit River under the Soldier's Settlement Board. As I understood it, Eva was married some time between 1914 and 1918 but her first husband did not return from the war. Where and when she met and married Glady, I do not know. Eva never had any children.

R.C. Fitton Family, Eva Harrington standing in centre, 1903.

Glady and Eva were living in a small log cabin near the Hudson's Bay store at the time of my first visit in 1930-31. My next visit was by unpaved road in 1948, with my wife. They were then operating a "roadhouse" on the road to Yellowknife.

They made periodic visits to us in Victoria en route to overseas, Hawaii or the rest of the U.S.A. This would happen every two or three years after "staying in" as they called it.

Glady passed away in 1958, Eva in 1959. They are buried in the North Star Cemetery.

My third visit was in 1975, this time crossing super bridges and on blacktop. We visited Glady's and Eva's graves in North Star and then drove on

Eva and Glady Harrington.

Eva Harrington and nephew, George Watkins in Victoria, B.C., 1932.

to Keg River. The roadhouse had burned down and across from its former site was a new Forest Services Building and various trailers. Then we stopped in to see Dr. Jackson, whom neither my wife nor I had previously met. A most enjoyable afternoon was spent talking of old times. We were then invited to a splendid dinner of wild meat and fruit.

How Glady and Eva arrived at Keg River from Spirit River, I do not know – perhaps the same way that my cousin Jim Harrington and I did around 1930 or 1931.

We were invited for the school summer holidays. The first crossing of the Peace River was at Dunvegan by reaction ferry, thence to Peace River. From Peace River we were loaded, bag and baggage, aboard a barge pushed by a wood-burning river boat. Travelling down the Peace River was made very interesting to us young lads by various stops to unload freight and pick up wood. After at least two days and perhaps more, we stopped at some predetermined place (unknown to me) where a large wagonload of freight was off-loaded and we boys climbed on top. This horse-and-wagon trip took two days with one overnight stop before arriving at Keg River.

My recollections of people and events in Keg River are mainly centered on riding our ponies for miles around or hunting with Glady for grouse and fishing. I can only recall seeing two other non-native women, Dr. Jackson and a woman whose horse killed her father in the barn. Apparently it had been previously abused.

Something that was standard equipment in Glady's house and in many others, no doubt, was a five-gallon crock behind the stove with raisins floating in it and a ladle hung on the lid. Good it was, too!

The most amazing thing to happen while we were there, and never seen before or since by me, was a plague of locusts (grasshoppers). They were large, on the whole – one to two inches in size – and brown and green. They were everywhere and ate everything in sight. It was not possible to walk without squelching them underfoot. The tent we stayed in and the whitewashed building were plastered with them. Dr. Jackson recalled they even ate a rubber ball. This, combined with millions of nosee-ems (sand flies), made for busy days!

(Editor's Note: Eva and Glady were generous community-minded people. They would do anything to be of help to their neighbors or the community. We thought you should also know the following.

Eva held sewing classes in her home for any of the young girls who wanted to learn. Theirs was the only piano in the district and anyone wishing to learn to play was welcome to come by for free lessons. The piano was carefully moved to the school for Christmas concerts.

Bridge playing was a favorite pastime whenever partners were available.

Glady had his homestead (SW-19-23-101-W5) or retreat where "Keg" parties were often held. The Elsons lived on the homestead for a while and looked after the horses that were used for telegraph line maintenance. Later, Jim Hunter and his boys stayed there, making hay and looking after things.) The land was sold to Harold Patterson in 1945.

Glady and Eva had one of the first cars in Keg River.

During World War II, Eva worked diligently for the Red Cross. She taught knitting to anyone interested, so socks and mitts could be knitted for the soldiers.

To have something to do when they retired, Glady built a stopping place on the MacKenzie Highway known as Keg River Cabins. Originally there was a two-story log building. Glady then had Fred Martineau build five log cabins. They were one large room with a wood heater. Glady and Eva rented the rooms, and sold groceries, meals and fuel.

Their retirement was not enjoyed for long. Glady became ill with emphysema, followed by pneumonia. Eva's loneliness led to her early death only a year after Glady.

Hasenack Family
by Betty Hasenack

Originally from St. Catherines, Ontario, we moved to Keg River in the summer of 1978. Tom taught one year in the Dr. Mary Jackson School, then transferred to Paddle Prairie where he still teaches.

We like the area and the people so much that we decided to settle here. Tom and I built our own log house in Keg River and moved into it in the summer of 1990. We have a son James and a daughter Lisa.

Owen and Ruth Hinder Family
by Ruth Hinder

Owen and I arrived in Canada in 1969 from Wales. Northland School Division had hired us to teach in the remote native schools. We went to Cadotte Lake first and stayed there for two years.

Paddle Prairie Settlement, 1971. Colony Manager, Mr. and Mrs. Olsen. Store Manager, Mr. and Mrs. Kjenner. Teachers, Allan MacDonald, Owen and Ruth Hinder.

In 1971 we moved to Paddle Prairie – what a change we experienced! Our teacherage (number three) was a mobile home, which we shared with a weasel on one occasion. What a treat to have hot and cold running water and a washing machine and tumble dryer. Our neighbors were kind and friendly and we were welcome for coffee any evening.

The school at Paddle was bigger than the one at Cadotte Lake and we enjoyed working there. Joyce Parenteau was the teacher-aide in the grade one classroom with me.

We drove to High Level for groceries and to attend the Catholic church. Many times we saw bears and moose beside or on the highway. The snowy owls were abundant one winter we were there. Seeing a wildcat was interesting, especially when we heard that this was unusual.

Our son Darren was born in Peace River in March 1972 and Daniel arrived in March 1975.

We left Alberta reluctantly at the end of June 1972 and have lived in East Anglia, Great Britain, ever since.

Originality is the art of concealing your source.

Pete and Allene Hodgsen
by Allene Hodgsen (nee Brick)

Mom, Dad, my two brothers and Sue and Ernie Brick were living in Keg River with Auntie Emma and Uncle Dave McDonald when I arrived on April 6, 1941. My brothers are William and Laurie.

We moved into a small house just north of the Hudson's Bay store and lived there until I was five. We then moved to North Star so that we could go to school, since Keg River didn't always have teachers.

Sue Brick and daughter Allene, 1941.

We were back in Keg River to homestead on NW-19-101-23-W5 in 1959. I did grade seven and eight in Keg River with Miss Paul for my teacher. There were 33 students in nine grades – a full school! We were now living in the Catholic church house.

Mother was the organist for the church and played whenever possible. She taught me to play and I also played whenever and wherever I could. I played for the church and sang in the choir. I also played in dance bands and at private parties. I still play whenever I can.

I taught correspondence at the new portable school from September 1959 to May 1960. A

Pete and Allene Hodgson's Wedding, June 30th, 1961.

teacher who had just finished university arrived to teach for May and June.

I met and married Pete Hodgsen in Keg River in June, 1961. We have three children – Joan, Bob and Maureen – and now have eight wonderful grandchildren! We have lived in Grande Prairie since August 1971.

Karen and Brian Hohner
by Karen Hohner (nee Nash)

In July, 1980, a team of interviewers from Northland School Division came to Halifax to hire teachers for Northern Alberta. It had been a year since I had graduated and no one was hiring in the province of Nova Scotia.

A week before school was to go in I got a phone call from Don Weaver, the superintendent, that I had a job teaching grades three and four at Dr. Mary Jackson School in Keg River. In one week I had to finish my job as a Red Cross consultant, get together everything I could for a split class of grade three and four students, pack, and get to Grouard for an orientation. Since the secretary for Northland couldn't tell me about Keg

River and accommodations I came prepared with a tent, sleeping bag and all my camping gear.

In Grouard they informed us that Northland provided teacherages and that I and Barb Forbes, the other new teacher, would be sharing a trailer. What a relief! Also, I had been given the grade one and two classroom. So much for all my packing! As I had lived in a city all my life, Keg River came as quite a change. In the city, people don't have the time or the interest to know who you are. It felt strange to have everyone know who I was, but not know them.

The school had nice sized classes, high open-ceiling classrooms and a skating rink outside. Christmas concerts in Keg River were a very important social gathering in the community.

My own childhood experience with these had been very different. We had at least three classes for every grade level, so at Christmas time your class marched to the gym, sang your one song and returned to your room so the next class could have their turn.

When spring approached in Keg River it was time to have a field trip somewhere. Without travelling too far there weren't many places to go. The grade two's insisted we go to the Hawk Hills Forestry tower. Little did I know I had a room full of match-makers!

After our trip they insisted I hand-deliver their thank-you cards as the tower man didn't get mail delivered. Wow, did those kids produce cards and letters. The tower man, Brian Hohner, spent his next winter living in the Keg River Forestry Complex.

We spent many evenings that winter skating and cross country skiing down the Keg River. The river meandered so much that you could go a long way, without being too far from your starting point.

Alfred, the Cabins dog, accompanied us on many of our outings. He seemed to like his organized hikes. After being shot at once skiing north along the highway, we kept our skiing to the river. Alfred was a frequent visitor to school, especially at lunch time. The kids never got tired of seeing Alfred eating everything from mandarin oranges in their green wrappers to the wax paper from their lunches; he wasn't fussy.

Brian moved to Sunny Valley to work on his land the next spring. I got a job teaching at the high school in Manning and we were married that year. Keg River surprised us with a reception at the hall. We ended up with a community quilt that would be suitable for any art gallery.

Surprize party for Karen and Brian Hohner.

I still teach school in Manning. Brian and I have two children, Marie and David.

Amy B. Holmes (nee Weatherup)
by Amy Holmes

My mother (Rachel Weatherup) was born in Salt Point, Michigan. Her growing-up years were spent in Craik, Saskatchewan. She married, and together with my father, settled in the Peace River area. My father died there, leaving Mom with my brother, Bill, and myself. Bill and I were both born in Wembley, Alberta.

Rachel Weatherup.

We first came to Keg River in 1943-1944 - Mother, my brother Bill, and I. Mother came to teach at the school. I was in grade three. Bill was in grade five.

In October of 1943 we left Beaverlodge to travel by train to Grimshaw. Here we met our guide, Mr Ernest Brick. I remember the weather being clear and sunny. We travelled to Keg River via horse and wagon. It took about a week. The first night in Keg River we spent with Mr and Mrs. Ferguson.

Amy and Bill Weatherup.

Mother went on to teach in Calgary, where she lived until her passing in September, 1987. She lies in the Elnora Cemetery. Bill lives in Ottawa. He works for Bell Telephones. He is married, with two children, Cheryl and Shawn.

I am living in Red Deer, Alberta. I have two daughters: Marion, who is teaching in Edmonton; and Elizabeth, who attends Red Deer College in the Office Administration Program and works in the College.

I still remember going to Jackson's farm around Halloween. We had a lunch and carved these pumpkins (is this not a work of art?). We were to go to the home of one of the older Jackson sons for a prank. I can't remember what happened, but we did not carry out our purpose.

I remember the Christmas concert that year. The hall was packed. Everyone seemed so happy. I can also remember the dances on a Saturday night, including the one after the Christmas concert. The lanterns seemed to swing from side to side. Everyone came and had a good time. The ladies brought lunch. Babies slept on the benches. This is something you do not see very often today. Those times should come back, I think.

I used to enjoy going to the Hudson's Bay Post. It was a square building...white, I think. They had everything in it. One counter seemed to hold nothing but furs. The ski-plane in winter or the boat on the Peace River in summer came regularly to pick up the products of the area and to drop off freight.

I also remember the Trading Post owned and operated by the Jackson family. It was the first time I had heard of a "Free Trader". I remember Dr. Jackson very well.

We attended the church regularly. I was glad to see that it had not changed over the years.

It was a good year spent with very friendly people.

My daughter Elizabeth and I, accompanied by my friend Adele, visited the area last summer (1993). Things and the area have changed, but not the people. They are as friendly as they ever were.

Louie and Emilie Houle and Family
by Jeannette Houle

Louie and Emilie Houle (my parents) were married on January 13, 1914, in Athabasca, Alberta. There was no courtship; my Dad had seen my mother and he said, "I want to marry that girl," so he asked about her and found she was an orphan living with her grandmother. He went to their house and spoke with her grandmother, who gave her consent. They got married within two weeks and left Grouard with a load of freight, then on to Peace River. They made this their honeymoon. Whenever Mother told us this story she was so excited, for strangely enough they fell in love and this love affair lasted 59 years!

Wedding Picture of Emilie and Louis Houle, 1914.

Although not all the years were good, Mother and Dad always pulled in the same direction. They raised 14 children. Their first daughter Josephine Hitz was born October 18, 1914, in Clear Hills and 31 years later their youngest daughter Connie was born in Peace River on June 17, 1945.

Josephine, Flavien, Agnes, Margaret, Bertha, Betsy and Stella were all gone from home at an early age to find work and eventually to marry. They all did very well, Betsy was adventurous; she married an Australian and has lived in Australia since 1945. Florence, Raymond, Thelma and Velma (twins) Clarence, myself and Connie were the second half of the family.

Our home in Paddle Prairie was a big house and it was often used for church, community dances and many feasts. Our mother played a strong role in the community, helping wherever she could. She assisted the sick and helped the family if someone died. She was always called to bring new babies into the world. She received no awards and was never paid for anything she ever did in the community. Let's hope she received a gold medal when she got to heaven.

Mom and Dad spent the last few years of their lives in Manning. Dad's greatest pleasure was going to the hockey games and watching his grandsons Terry and Raymond Houle play. Dad passed away in Manning in July, 1972. Mother left us in October, 1978. Since then our oldest brother Flavien died in November 1978. Two sisters passed away – Florence Brown in January 1993 and Thelma Sanford in January 1994.

Jeannette Emilie Houle
by Jeannette Houle

On a cold winter day in 1940 (I know it was cold because Raymond said it was and anyway it is always cold in January), I was born in Battle River Hospital in Notikewin, Alberta. Mrs. Cowie was my mother's nurse and 23 years later, she was my nurse when my son Robert was born. I was named Jeannette Emilie Houle.

In the spring of 1942, we moved to Paddle Prairie. My thoughts often drift back to my childhood. We were very well-taken-care-of, with lots of good home-cooked meals, a clean home and Mom and Dad always there. We never ate at a McDonalds restaurant! I believe that our Dad brought his family to Paddle Prairie because times were very tough and because there was a promise here for the necessities of life. I cannot honestly say why they came; perhaps it was the lure of land

Clarence and Jeannette Houle, ages 6 and 2.

that had never known a plow, or just another dream of a pioneer family.

I believe my mother was a brave woman, for she told us many stories of her hardships. There was no certainty, no regularity in her life. There was often a heavy curtain of silence and Mother would look off into the distance. Someday I, too, would know the anguish of having my family far away.

Lawrence Lariviere, Connie, Velma and Jeannette Houle with Clifford McGillvary going for a sleigh ride.

My three oldest sisters were married and our brother Flavien was working on the Alaska Highway. My sisters Bertha and Betsy had joined the air force. Betsy married an Australian and went to Australia in 1945. I met her for the first time at the Vancouver airport in 1967. Stella, Raymond and Florence went to Grande Prairie to go to school. Raymond came home more often, but the girls stayed in school. The twins, Thelma and Velma, also left home. They all graduated and went on to business college. Don't ask me how they made it, because there was no money given to them - they had to earn their own.

Mom and Dad worried about the twins when they went away to school. The mail was slow and we had no phones. Today we slip on a light coat, jump into a warm luxurious car or on a plane. In a matter of hours we can reach our destination. For our parents it was not so. On my automatic dial telephone I can talk to my daughter in Quesnel, British Columbia, whenever I wish. My parents didn't have that luxury.

All, rich or poor, now have electric lights in their homes and most precious of all - running water. Gone are the days when we depended on wood for our fuel; now we have abundant supplies of fuel oil, propane, and natural gas. One wonders if it will last.

We were taught to have strong attitudes, high values and to always believe in God and I do. I remember Dad saying to Clarence and me, "Think, get involved, and use your judgement. A person who doesn't think for himself doesn't think at all." Our Dad was an uneducated but intelligent man.

My sister Connie was born in 1945 in Peace River. When she and Mom came home, we went to pick them up at the river and I thought Mom had brought me a doll. I loved her at first sight. We grew up together and I guess because we were the youngest, Mom and Dad had more time for us.

There were many incidents at our house. When we were growing up in Paddle Prairie everything seemed to revolve around that little church. I loved the music and always thought it was to be enjoyed. At a very early age I shocked the congregation one Sunday morning when after Elsie and Adolphus Ghostkeeper had sung "Ave Maria" I cheered and clapped very loudly. My sister Thelma was my babysitter that day and she was not impressed with my behavior. The story was told many times by the old folks and apparently Mrs. Flora Parenteau could not stop laughing for the rest of the service.

I hold a great deal of admiration and respect for my parents and the families that I grew with in Paddle Prairie, and the long bond of friendship should carry on into each generation. From them I learnt to be proud of my Metis heritage, but to never make it an issue.

When I was 12 years old we moved to Grande Prairie. I cried all the way to Bluesky. Clarence stayed on the farm and we came home whenever we could. Connie and I went to St. Joseph's school.

In 1955 we moved to Parksville, British Columbia. My sister Connie and I were happy there. We loved the beach and made friends easily. I always took my guitar to the beach and I sang, so we attracted a crowd and had fun.

I got my first job when I was 15. I became a telephone operator for B.C. Telephones. I worked after school and on weekends and I studied hard. My sister Thelma came to Parksville and got a job with McMillan and Bloedel at the Sarita River logging camp on Long Beach. I went there some weekends with my books and I studied and wrote my essays. She had her own cabin and Long Beach was very beautiful for a little girl from Paddle Prairie in 1955.

I married Murray Shaw in Parksville, British Columbia. His family was from Little Qualicum. We had three sons - all born in Manning, Alberta. In 1965 we moved to Quesnel, where Murray worked for the Department of Highways. We were also stationed in Wells, B.C. for two years. My daughter Colleen was born there.

Murray and I separated during our stay in Wells and I stayed there with my four children. When they finished school in June, we moved back to Quesnel. The Wells-Barkerville area was a great place to raise the boys. They grew up loving the outdoors and fishing. These years were good years, but there was the constant struggle to raise my children.

My oldest son Douglas Allan drowned when he was 18 years old. Only the strength I gained from my other sons, Dwayne and Robbie, and my daughter Colleen, got me through this darkest time of my life. Our home was filled with flowers - even Douglas' friends got together and each brought me a rose. I was overwhelmed by the number and their beauty. Somehow the flowers gave significance to Doug's life and to mine.

Flowers don't last forever, but their meaning is still fresh in my mind. Anything that can have meaning for this length of time cannot be a waste. Today I still love to grow and find comfort in flowers. Prayer is great in dealing with grief, but nothing takes the place of a warm, caring person living with you in your pain. For me that person was my sister Connie. I could never have carried my load without her.

I would also like to pay tribute to my brother Raymond (Pasquali). Thank you, Ray, for being who you are to me and all your sisters. Thanks for sharing the good times and our own personal tragedies. From you I learnt how to be tolerant and forgiving. As a little girl I remember the treats and the happiness you brought to our home. Whenever you went away we missed you.

It is no wonder that when our mother was dying of cancer, she waited until Raymond arrived home from his job in the Arctic. Only a few hours after he arrived, she left us. There is a saying that suits Pasquali: "We try not to sing songs about ourselves."

Life is a journey and we are always starting out and then coming home. My oldest sister Josephine Hitz was born and raised and worked her entire life in one place. The same is not true for me. I travelled to many places including all across Canada and spent much time in Ottawa. There I gained a wealth of knowledge and met with many people, such as our Prime Minister Pierre Elliot Trudeau.

I was lucky enough to go full circle and I now live in Carcajou, where the mighty Peace courses through a valley that I call Paradise! Nothing can touch the lonely beauty of the flowers that grow wild here. The long summer days make for good wheat and vegetables and the saskatoons are plentiful most years. The black bear is also a common resident, but I have never seen a grizzly bear here.

The rainbows here are beautiful in the early summer. In the fall Carcajou is home to the ducks and geese – I still look forward to their yearly visit. I'm sure that it is also for a purpose. In the winter, the sky is fascinating, constantly a show with a million stars and the northern lights. When you turn off the lights in the house at night it is very dark for there are no street lights in Carcajou and I love it.

My oldest son Dwayne and Rénee Shaw live in Quesnel and have two children: Skyler, eight years old; and Kristen, four years old. Robbie lives in High Level, works for Computalog and is engaged to Heather Lizotte from Rocky Lane. Colleen also lives in Quesnel. She is married and has two children, Crandell is 10 and Dustin is seven years old.

This is my greatest enjoyment in Carcajou, when holiday time comes and my grandchildren come to visit. I would like to end with this – for go I must – for love will be lost if you sit too long at a friend's fire.

A Mother's Love
submitted by Jeannette Houle

I wanted these included in this book because they reflect values instilled in me by my mother. Our Metis heritage is also reflected in these tidbits of wisdom.

----0---

Because She Is a Mother
She broke the bread into two fragments and gave them to the children, who ate them avidly. "She hath kept none for herself," grumbled the Sergeant. "Because she is not hungry," said the soldier. "No, because she is a mother," said the Sergeant.

Victor Hugo

----0---

Mothers are inclined to feel limp at 50. This is because the children have taken most of her stuffing to build their nests.

----0---

People may admire you for your achievements as a business woman;
I know that my greatest achievement was being an ordinary mom.

----0---

When the son leaves home to start his freshman year at college, his doting mother gives him two cashmere sweaters as going-away presents. Wanting to show his appreciation, the boy comes home for Thanksgiving wearing one of the sweaters. The mother greets him at the door. She takes a long anxious look and says, "What's the matter -the other sweater you don't like?"

----0---

No matter how old a mother is, she watches her middle-aged children for improvement.

----0---

Things that seemed important often suffer a sea of change when one becomes a mother - one would destroy a Leonardo Da Vinci to save one's child pain.

----0---

Fifty-four years of love and tenderness and crossness and devotion and unswerving loyalty. Without her I could only have achieved a quarter of what I have achieved, not only in terms of success and career but in terms of personal happiness. She has never stood between me and my life, never tried to hold me too tightly, always let me go free.

––––0–––

A mother and her daughter grow closer every time they have a successful shopping spree!

––––0–––

One's mom is, to a large extent, a product of one's own imagination – that is why it is so unnerving when they behave like themselves.

––––0–––

Whether you like it or not, your mother goes with you – forever.

Dan and Louisa House
as told by Louisa House

Dan House moved to the North Star district with his family in 1934. He worked for area farmers in the summer and trapped in the winter. He spent several years working for Frank Jackson. In 1950 he married Louisa Ferguson, who was born and raised in Keg River, the oldest child of Helen and Larone.

Dan worked on the Alberta Forestry fire crews for years after they were married. Together Dan and Louisa had a family of four boys and three girls.

Their oldest son Stanley and Marlene have two sons, Byron and Christopher.

Freddie married Linda. They have a daughter Tracy and a son Dustin.

Mary Jane and David Calliou have four children: Curtis, Delaney, Clint and Shannon. They also had one boy who died as a baby.

Noreen and Ed Laboucan have three children: Dakota, Nevada and Ricko. Dakota stars in the Canadian television series called *"North of 60"*.

Valerie and Ron Gaucher have two children, Ronnie and Austin.

Leslie lives with Mona Campbell. They have a daughter Kelly Kirsten Campbell and a son little Leslie House.

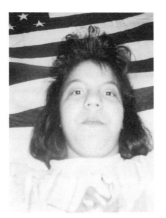

Terry House.

Vern married Judy Strong and their daughter Terry House lives with Dan and Louisa. Vern died in 1985.

Louisa House and Helen Christian, 1992.

L-R: Alphonse Ducharme, Dan House, Charlie Christian, George Christian and Bill.

199

Elizabeth and Jerome House
by Jerome House

Our family moved from Athabasca to North Star and took land just west of Charlie Plavine's. I had four brothers: Joe passed away in 1993; Pete is also deceased; Henry, who is 78; and Dan, the youngest. We have a stepsister, too, in Dawson Creek.

The first time I saw Keg River was in 1934 when I was 15 years old. I have travelled from Vancouver on one side of Canada to Halifax on the other side and like the Peace River country the best.

When war broke out, I had a home in Paddle Prairie. In the fall I worked on some farms in the Notikewin area to help with the harvest. Some of the young fellows out there decided to enlist. I joined up in October, 1941. July 1942 we were trained and on our way overseas. I spent three and one-half years in England. We moved from end to end of the country. I returned to Canada in 1946.

Jerome House.

Frank Jackson of Keg River needed a hired man, so I began working for him shortly after my discharge. Nearly all the farming was done with horses. We rode horses if we went to check on the cows pastured on the Chinchaga River prairie in the summer.

Once when we took Miss van der Mark, a teacher, along out to Chalifoux's prairie, we had a laugh. We showed her where the high water had partially washed away some ancient graves; she was so shocked she nearly backed into the river!

Elizabeth Calliou and I were married in 1948. Her parents were Louis and Betsy (Belcourt) Calliou. They were farming at Paddle Prairie. Elizabeth had been working for the Jacksons in their trading post for a number of years through the war.

We took land on the Metis Settlement along the Paddle Creek for our homestead. We moved there in 1950 after leaving the Jacksons.

Our daughter Eileen and son-in-law work at Foothills John Deere in Fort St. John. Raymond lives in Paddle Prairie. Elizabeth passed away in May,1991. I am retired and live in Paddle Prairie.

Going blueberry picking. L-R: Anne Jackson, Nancy Nykolyshyn, Betty House, June Jackson on Betty's horse Bob and Leonard Hunter.

Jim Hunter Family
as told to Anne Vos

Jim arrived in Paddle Prairie with his father and a dozen heavy horses, Clydesdales, from the Beaverlodge area when he was about 25 years old. They had come down on steamboat to Tompkins Landing, then overland to the prairie and their homestead.

Here Jim met and married Annie Christian. Her folks were farming on the Paddle prairie, too. Jim and Annie had three sons Leonard, Norman and Earl.

Jim's dad was working for the summer on the Hudson's Bay boat when he drowned in the Peace River in an accident.

In 1939 when the Metis Settlement was formed, Jim was forced to move off the land on which he had been living. His children were quite young – Earl was only one year old. They moved to Keg River to Rose McLeod's land. Annie had left.

Jim worked for Glady Harrington looking after the horses that were used on telegraph line maintenance as well as his own horses. He still had a team of Clydes that the boys could do anything with, they were so gentle.

When the Pattersons bought the Harrington's farm Jim worked for them. The boys and their dad also worked for Lonnie Root and Harry Wilson doing a variety of jobs. School was three miles from home and the boys walked or rode saddle horses.

Leonard worked at a number of places but he

Harvesting ice on the Keg River to store for summer drinking water. Leonard and Earl Hunter, Ethelyn Stup and daughter Paulette, Norman Hunter, Lonnie Root with saw and Jim Hunter, 1946.

Baseball game with Jim Hunter catching and Harry Borbridge batting.

always made time for rodeos. Calf roping and wild cow milking were some of the events in which he got trophies.

Leonard married Leona McKenzie of Peace River. They had a family of three boys and two girls. Allen (Rocky) lives in Kelowna. Gordon (Gordy) lives in High Level. Edward (Eddie), Patsy (Tweedy) Johnson and Lois Garnet all live in Grimshaw.

Leonard works in logging at a sawmill with his brother Earl in Manning.

Norman spent a few years with Harry and Pete Wilson, even travelling to the United States with them and going to school there one winter. He also spent one winter with the Arthur Jackson family in Aldergrove, British Columbia. He started working for the B.C. Department of Transportation in Aldergrove and stayed on until his retirement many years later. He married Alma and they have one daughter, Sheri, who is married to Ron Westman. Sheri and Ron have a son Garrett.

Earl was also a rodeo rider, taking part in many

events all over the country. He married Jenny Sharp and they live close to Manning where they log and own and operate a sawmill. They have two daughters, Sherri and Lisa, and a son Todd.

Norman and Alma Hunter in Aldergrove, B.C.

Frank Jackson
by the History Book Committee

Frank Jackson was born in Southend, England, in 1892. He came to Canada with his father on March 10, 1904. His mother and three sisters followed that May, settling in Medicine Hat. At the age of 14 Frank began working on a ranch, where he first hurt his knee. He had surgery on it but it never completely healed. He walked with a limp for the rest of his life.

Later Frank bought a section of land on Red Deer Lake, about 30 miles east of Wetaskiwin. His parents moved from Medicine Hat to a half-section near him, where they retired. At Red Deer Lake Frank became the secretary of the local school board and a councillor for the Municipal District. He was not allowed to join the army in 1918 because of his bad leg.

Frank first married Louise Barr. She had been born in Wisconsin and came to Alberta with her mother, sister and stepfather when she was two or three. She had been raised on a farm in the Wetaskiwin area.

Frank and Louise had two sons: Louis Albert, born on October 30, 1918, and Arthur Carl, born on October 6, 1919.

After losing about 50 head of cattle in the extremely harsh winter of 1919-20 at Red Deer Lake, Frank considered moving. He looked at the Keg River Prairie in May of 1920, after which he and Louise decided that this would be their new home.

Frank and a hired hand put some of the haying

Frank and Louise Jackson, sons Arthur and Louis.

machinery and horses in boxcars which transported them to Judah, 12 miles out of Peace River – the end of the rails at that time. The machinery was then hauled into the town of Peace River and taken by boat to Carcajou.

As they transported the equipment overland from Carcajou to Keg River they discovered something that Frank had been warned about, but was not a problem when he had visited in May - the flies, mosquitoes, bulldog flies and no-see-ums (sand flies). They darkened the sky around any living thing and were very bothersome for the horses. The first trip from Carcajou to the prairie at Keg River took two days. They made two more trips bringing in the equipment. (Over the years many more trips were to be made over that trail.)

Before Frank returned to Red Deer Lake for his family he did some haying and hired some natives to continue haying while he was gone. This trip, Frank and Louise brought everything they owned. They brought furniture, chickens, milk cows and horses. The calves were sold when they got to Edmonton.

Again they travelled by train, then boat; even the cows got on the boat. At the Keg River Landing across from Carcajou they disembarked and began the trek overland to Keg River. They camped along the trail. Once at Keg River they moved into a cabin built by Dick Hutchings. He had come to Keg River as part of the survey crew and had stayed. He planned to be away from Keg River and had loaned his cabin to the Jackson family.

The trip from south of Edmonton took about two weeks and all the animals survived, but the adjustment to Keg River was not to be so uneventful. Frank eventually lost many of these animals to swamp fever at Keg River.

More animals were purchased, a three-room house and barn built, and Frank and Louise settled into life at Keg River. Corrals were built for the cattle, Frank applied for a grazing lease on the prairie and Louise started growing a garden and preserving the harvest.

In the 20's Frank got together with John Brown and formed the Keg River Trading Company. They built a store and warehouse, brought in supplies from Edmonton, grubstaked trappers and bought their fur.

Frank bought supplies for his new store. The tea came in 100-pound chests, coffee beans in 100-pound barrels, white beans in 100-pound sacks, dried fruit in 25-pound boxes, and jam and syrup in cans. There were no cigarettes but Old Chum tobacco and cigarette papers were stocked, as was chewing tobacco which came twisted like rope in 10-pound wooden caddies. Gunpowder, shot, and shells were also stocked. Eventually a warehouse was built on the bank of the Peace River where the boat dropped off the supplies. They were then freighted overland to Keg River.

Allie Brick operated a trading post for Keg River Trading Company at Rainbow Lake for two years. After it lost money both years, it was sold to Revillon Freres.

When the Depression hit in 1929, fur prices fell and never recovered. The Keg River Trading Company was shut down in 1949.

In 1929 tragedy struck Frank's family. After giving birth to their third son in Keg River in October, Louise became ill. Dr. Hamman arrived from Fort Vermilion and decided that she should go out to Edmonton. A plane was sent from Peace River, after word was sent by a messenger who travelled overland as no telephones or two-way radios existed. Louise was flown to Edmonton where she died in hospital. Her newest son, also named Frank, went to live with his mother's parents near Wetaskiwin.

Frank Sr. and his two older boys carried on. He filed for homestead land when it opened up and began breaking the land with an 18-inch walking plow. His first crop – in fact the first crop in the district – was five acres of oats.

Frank developed a friendship with Dr. Mary Percy in Battle River and they were married in 1931. She left Battle River when her contract with the government was up and moved north to Keg River. Together they watched more people move to the Keg River area. Mary carried on practising medicine whether her patients could pay her or not.

Frank and his new wife moved onto the homestead and Frank built an office and waiting room in the basement of the house in which Mary practised. Frank built a successful farm. The farm was called Keweteno, meaning "north" in Cree. The yard around their house reminds everyone of an English garden.

Frank and Mary had two children, Lesley Anne and John Robert. They experienced many hardships caused by the weather and remoteness of the area in which they made their home, but they laughed, made many friends, and carried on as well.

Frank was a handyman and did many things very well. He ran his own farm, and had a large, well-equipped repair shop where he fixed his own and many of his neighbors' machinery. He installed the electrical wiring, heating and water systems in his house. Over the years he tried his hand at wood-carving and produced many of the pieces of furniture in his home, and even tried sculpting. He did a fine job of the pieces that can still be found in the yard of his home.

Frank and his family were given the Master Farm Family Award in 1953 after being nominated by their neighbors. It was awarded after the farm scored well in the areas of farm operation, farm life, community work, and business management. The Peace River Record Gazette of October 1, 1953, announced the award and described the farm:

"Mr. Jackson is a general farmer, with grain his major crop but with a livestock and poultry sideline which gives his farm operation the flexibility to meet the sudden market changes. He keeps an average of 200 acres in Garnet wheat, 150 acres in Victory oats, 250 acres in Olli barley and about 30 acres each in flax and alsike. His oat yield averages 80 bushels to the acre while he reaps about 30 bushels of both wheat and barley to the acre. His livestock is made up of 10 purebred Angus beef cows and a splendid purebred bull, two dairy cows which are a cross between Shorthorn and Holstein, nine first-grade Yorkshire sows, and a small herd of Suffolk sheep."

Other awards went to Frank and Mary Jackson, such as the Alberta Achievement Award in 1976, given "in recognition of outstanding service in the community".

In 1974 Frank became ill and Mary retired from medicine to look after one special patient. Frank died in 1979 at the age of 87. Dr. Mary still lives on their farm.

In 1986 a variety of barley developed in Beaverlodge at the experimental farm by Dr. Wolfe was named "Jackson", to commemorate Frank's contribution to the development of agriculture in the Peace. The barley is a high-yielding, six-row variety. It was developed with the hardiness and resistance necessary to thrive in northern Alberta. It seems fitting that this barley be named for a man who had those characteristics.

Frank's story was published in the form of two books, "A Candle in the Grub Box" (1977) and "Jam in the Bedroll" (1979).

Frank and Vera Jackson and family.

Dr. Mary Percy Jackson
by Dr. Jackson

I came to Canada from England in 1929. I had graduated with a Batchelor of Medicine and a Batchelor of Surgery from the University of Birmingham and had also been to London and passed the Member of Royal College of Surgery of England and the Licentiate of Royal College of Physicians of London exams in 1927.

After that I did two years of hospital work in Birmingham as House Physician in the General Hospital, House Surgeon in the Maternity Hospital, and Casualty House Surgeon in the Children's Hospital.

In 1929 I applied for the position the Alberta Government was advertising in the British Medical Journal. They wanted English women doctors with postgraduate obstetrics to work in outlying areas without hospitals, where the ability to ride a saddle horse would be an advantage. I was accepted and the Alberta Government sent me to the Battle River district, where Manning is now.

After working with a nurse in the Jarvie area to learn about the conditions under which I would practice, I travelled to Peace River by train and then on the *D. A. Thomas* and overland to Battle River. I brought all the medical supplies I was to have with me as well as my personal belongings. In Battle River I was provided with a three-room house where I would see patients who were well enough to visit me. A few weeks after I arrived the settlers bought a horse for me. I rode "Dan" to see many of my patients.

There were about 500 people in the Battle River area then, but large numbers of immigrant settlers were coming in from Europe, and by 1931 there were about 2000 people.

The Battle River Highway was being built from Grimshaw north, but the old trail went round by Clear Hills, and it was nearly 100 miles to Peace River, which had the nearest hospital. The new highway was just a dirt road, and was bottomless mud after rain.

In that first year, as I adjusted to the isolated conditions of northern Alberta, I saw many patients with different afflictions. Saw-wounds, complicated pregnancies, tuberculosis, shot-gun wounds were among my case load. I also practised my teeth-pulling techniques which I had studied briefly before leaving England.

In January 1930, Frank Jackson came from Keg River to Battle River by dog team. He had a septic hand. Those days, before sulpha drugs, penicillin or other antibiotics, infections were much more serious than they are now. His wife had died after their third son was born.

Frank found other reasons to visit and he and I were married in 1931. I moved to Keg River, which was even more isolated than Battle River had been, except that the telegraph line had just been cut through so that we could communicate with the "outside".

It was possible to ride out to Battle River along the telegraph line when it was dry enough in the fall, after Frank had cut detours around the worst swamps, and after it was frozen in winter, one could drive out with team and sleighs; but most of the time we went to Carcajou and then to Peace River by boat – the *D. A. Thomas* in 1930, and after that the *Weenusk*, and the *O'Sullivan Stigsen* boat in 1932.

Frank Jackson's sons, Louis Albert (born October 30, 1918; died in 1975) and Arthur Carl (born October 6, 1919; died in 1983), grew up in Keg River. The third son, Frank, born on October 9, 1929, was brought up by his grandparents in Ferintosh.

Louis and Arthur were 12 and 13 when I arrived in Keg River and they had some fun teaching me about farming. I in turn tried to teach them some of the things I thought they should have learned through school. Keg River had no school and the boys were quite capable with their math skills but weaker with their spelling and writing skills. In some ways I may have been the wicked step-mother!

Frank and I had a daughter, Lesley Anne, born November 5, 1931, in England. I travelled back to England to visit with my family and have my baby there. Then I returned with my daughter. We travelled from Peace River to Keg River in a small plane. Our pilot had never made the trip before but was given directions by someone who had flown to Keg River. He also had a map which had been drawn on the back of an envelope! We nearly got to Keg River and I could even see the village, just as a storm closed in and we turned back to Peace River. We tried the trip the next day and arrived safely.

The birth of our son, John Robert, on January 16, 1935, was no less eventful. I had planned to travel to Grande Prairie for his birth, but we were suffering through an extremely cold spell and travel was impossible. Bob was born at home, with Frank and our neighbor and friend, Eva Harrington, attending to the breech birth. The temperature the date of his birth reached -70°F!

Years later when Bob needed to have his tonsils removed I decided to take him to Peace River for the procedure. When we were returning home, we travelled on the Peace River by boat. It was in May and we experienced a wicked spring snowstorm. Bob was recovering from his surgery, so he was in bed in the only cabin aboard, and because of the cold, the other item – 1000 day-old chicks – were in there, too. It was the only place on the boat that was suitably warm. I was very concerned about Bob being exposed to all the germs that accompany chickens but my choices were limited. He and the chicks did fine. That was the beginning of Rumble Hatcheries that operated out of Peace River for many years.

During the war years Pat and John Hague came from England to stay with us. Their parents, Donald and Edwina Hague, were friends of mine. They were both medical doctors with whom I had trained and who were concerned about their children while London was being bombed. We gladly had Pat and John live with us, although we didn't have many luxuries in life to offer them.

Keg River has been home to me since 1931. I still live on our farm and enjoy my plants and garden. Frank and I travelled some, before and after I retired from my medical practice in 1974. I have met people from around the world and keep in touch by writing many letters. Frank died in 1979.

Frank Jackson Jr. still lives in Ferintosh with his wife Vera. Their children and grandchildren also live in the Ferintosh area.

Anne and her husband, Johnny, live in Keg River where they have farmed for 42 years.

Bob and his wife Doreen live in Calgary as do their two boys, Brian and Dale.

(Editor's Note: Dr. Jackson has been honored for her outstanding service to our community.)

1967   Centennial Medal of Canada "On the occasion of the 100th anniversary of the Confederation of Canada, the Centennial Medal is conferred on Dr. Mary E. Percy Jackson, in recognition of valuable service to the nation."
1967   Alberta Centennial Award 1969 Senior Life Membership in the Alberta Medical Association. "Mary E. Percy Jackson has been elected to this honor by colleagues in the Association because of contributions and long service to the public and the Profession."
1971   Senior Membership in the Canadian Medical Association 1974 Life Membership in the College of Family Physicians 1975 Woman of the Year for the Voice of Native Women
1975   Alberta Achievement Award (also given to her husband Frank) "In recognition of outstanding service in the community with best wishes and congratulations of the people and government of the Province of Alberta."
1976   Honorary Doctor of Laws degree from the University of Alberta
1983   Membership in the Alberta Order of Excellence "In recognition of service of the greatest distinction and of singular excellence for and on behalf of the residents of Alberta."
1985   Honorary Life Membership in the Geriatric Medical Society of Alberta
1985   Honorary Diploma from Fairview College
1989   Named Officer in the Order of Canada

Dr. Jackson wrote many letters to England, particularly in the early days. These were printed and circulated to family and friends. Her story, as told to Cornelia Lehn, has also been published in a book called "*The Homemade Brass Plate*" (1988).

Dr. Mary Jackson with brother and sister-in-law, Leslie and Cicely Percy from England.

Multiple Generations of Jackson Family. Dr. Mary Jackson, Natasha Jackson, June Jackson, Benjamin McLean, Margaret Matheson and Colby Dechant, 1994.

Farewell Song

by students of Dr. Mary Jackson School for Frank and Mary Jackson Sung November 24, 1968, to the tune of *Away in a Manger*

Away fly these people
Whom all deem the best
To taste in the south lands
Their sweet winter rest.

May they both enjoy now
The fruits of their deeds
As long as together
Their "golden heart" beats.

And later on...later,
When years will have passed
May both taste forever
God's home rest at last!

Farewell do we wish now;
May sweet be your rest,
And sweeter returning
To your summer nest!!

Louis and June Jackson

by June Jackson

The first visit I made to Keg River was in 1939, I believe. Accompanied by John Voiriel and my sister Mae, we were going to visit our older sister, Margaret. Margaret was married to Arthur Jackson and was living in Keg River. The trip was via saddle horse over a bush trail which took two days. This meant fording rivers camping overnight along the trail and wondering what lay ahead in the way of weather and wild animals.

Old Dan, a famous horse who knew his way better than we did, took many detours, especially if the grass was greener. After riding two days, John turned around for home, leaving us to find our own way!

Shortly after leaving what we called the South Keg, the horses stopped with their ears alert, a big black bear and her cubs crossed our path. Once they passed, Dan carried on eating his way home.

After crossing the next river, Dan appeared to be just going through bush and eating. Finally after we used a switch on him a few times, he took us to a sign that read "Keg River" and "Hay River". He then proceeded back the same way, which did bring us out to the Keg River prairie with its millions of mosquitoes. Our destination at last!

My next visit was about 1943 with a girl from Calgary who thought a trip on horseback would be a great experience. We worked together for Revenue Canada. Louis Jackson was in the Air Force, stationed in Calgary at that time. He was on leave, so he joined us.

We left from my parents' home in Hotchkiss, each riding a horse. Marg had a fast horse that liked to be ahead, and of course she was nervous, this being her first time away from home. She kept returning to us to be sure she was on the right road, as though one could ever find another!

We camped the first night at Gravina Creek, a famous spot. It was supposed to be a creek with water; however, it had dried up because of the drought. We started a campfire, let the horses graze, and drank wine as there wasn't any water. We slept on a saddle blanket. Marg, being nervous, heard every twig rattle, she kept us awake.

However, she did get really excited when she said she heard a truck. We of course did not expect anything that modern to arrive in the bush. I just said, "Go to sleep! It's likely some Indian going by." That did it! She thought we were in real trouble.

It turned out that she had heard a truck! It was Louis' dad and brother. They had decided to come and meet us and the country was so dry the drone of that old truck could be heard for miles. Marg, being from the city, had never experienced anything like this before – I'm sure her hair was nearly grey by the time she returned to Calgary!

She returned by catching a ride to Tompkins Landing with Dave Mcdonald and a load of pigs. She then took the boat from there to Peace River. On her return to Calgary and the office, she told these tales and drew a great audience!

I believe I rode that bush trail many times. Sometimes the rivers were high and swift and the saddle horses had to swim. I recall one time, breaking over the Third Battle hill on Darky with my foot over the saddle horn, when the roar of the river frightened the horse so badly that he turned around, caught the gun on Tommy Ducharme's saddle, nearly upsetting him, and we were on our way back north.

Once I got Darky stopped and returned, we camped overnight and swam the horses across the next morning. We drifted away down river. I had green ski pants on and the dye came out, so I was rather green when I got home – only from the waist down!

Louis and I were married in Moose Jaw, Saskatchewan while he was in the Air Force. Ronald, our first son, was born on Victory Day: August 14, 1945. It was a great day for us and for everyone in the Armed Forces as well.

We moved to Keg River in 1946 via horse and wagon. It was still very remote. There were no roads – just bush trails through the muskeg and bogs. Ronnie was a baby and we lived with Gramma Jackson for about a year at the old farmhouse in the village.

As it was very difficult to persuade teachers to come to this area, I taught correspondence at the little log schoolhouse for a year.

"Good Berry Pickers," Ronnie and Donnie Jackson.

Annie Rudy, who was a deaf-mute, babysat. I once looked out to see her lifting Ronnie up to see if he was crying.

It was nearly as cold inside as outside most of the time. We used ice for water and it was piled up outside. We also washed clothes on a scrub board, froze them, and brought them in to dry. That is where freeze-dry came from!

We managed to get a summer teacher about 1948 – Hank Tomison, who boarded with us and worked hard on the farm as well as teaching school. We heard from him for a few years after he went to the U.S.A. to work on secret missions such as the ballistic missile.

Ronald now lives in the Rainbow Lake area, where he has his own business. He has two daughters and two grandchildren.

Donald was born in Edmonton two years after our move to Keg River. He weighed only three pounds. He has grown a bit since! He was an active worker in the oilfield with Kapps Transport. He now lives in Spruce Grove, has his own business and has two sons. His boys are great skiers!

Robert was delivered by Grandma Jackson in the old house in the village. Robert was a great worker and worked in the Arctic. He and Ronald owned Jackson Transport for many years. Robert

lives in Manning and has his own business. He has one daughter.

We moved to our own farm in Naylor Hills in 1951. This area is just south of the Keg River Cabins. The boys went to school in the Naylor Hills school. I got involved in the Naylor Hills Ladies Society. We had a tiny two-bedroom house right on the highway. The road had some gravel and was an encouraging link with the outside world.

Bobby and DeeDee Jackson.

We also had bus service from the north and south to the Cabins. The Greyhound bus often needed help out of the ditch in the middle of the night. Many times a bus driver shone a flash light in our door, asking for help. The bus arrival time was 2 A.M.!

Les was born in December just before Christmas in 1952. I was planning to go to Manning (60 miles south) for the birth, but the night he decided to arrive was a cold one. We didn't own a good car – just an old truck, so Louis went to Keg River to find one.

Bill Halabisky had just returned from some place and his car was a warm roadworthy one. We had a wild ride on the icy roads but made it on time. This is perhaps the reason Les still loves the ice and the great game of hockey. He is the head scout and Director of Player Personnel for the Dallas Stars. He lives in Dallas, Texas, and has three boys.

Margaret, better known as DeeDee, was born April 2, 1954. It was -40°F that day and we were experiencing a major blizzard. All the roads were blocked, George and Alice Robertson lived in our yard and they owned a Caterpillar. George made a road to Grandma Jackson's as we followed close behind. DeeDee now works in the Del Air Lodge in Manning. She has two children and a grandson.

Betty Mae came along seven years later. She was born in the Peace River hospital. Betty Mae is a legal secretary and has worked for various firms and oil companies. She is married, lives in Drayton Valley and has one little boy.

Louis passed away suddenly in 1975. I now live in Invermere, British Columbia.

Louis and June Jackson, Ronnie, Robert, Margaret, Leslie, Bettymae and Donnie.

Arthur and Margaret Jackson family
by Margaret Jackson

Arthur and I were married in Keg River's Catholic Church on October 9th, 1940, in our 20th and 21st years.

We went to live on the Jackson farm in a 16 foot by 24 foot log cabin, meagerly furnished with a bed held together with moose hide straps, wooden benches, a table and a wood burning kitchen stove.

There was a large barn for the work horses. Arthur plowed many acres with the walking plow. With the native help he cut slough grass for winter hay. Horses, hay racks and hired men worked long days as there are nearly twenty hours of daylight in the summer months.

I prepared meals for the hired help, mostly pork, canned moose meat, potatoes and home-made bread. Dessert was prunes or rice pudding. We had our own chickens and eggs. The soil grew beautiful potatoes, cabbage, cauliflower and carrots.

In 1941, I picked and canned 60 quarts of wild strawberries. I would carry tea and lunch to the hay-makers and pick in patches I found along the way.

In August that year Ken, our first son, was born. Dr. Mary Jackson patiently spent hours with me. He was a healthy seven-pound boy. She had to sterilize the one basin we had to bathe him in. In the summer we were dependent on rain, or ice that we had taken from the river in the winter and preserved for water. The well water was hard and unfit for drinking. Washing clothes always posed a problem.

Ken's bed was a plywood tea box from the Keg River Trading Post. In the winter months, Arthur hauled supplies for his father's store. He and helpers with horses and sleighs made the 60-mile trip to Hotchkiss. Often it was so cold the horses could only rest for a few minutes with blankets over them. There were only two or three places to get water by chopping a hole in the ice.

On the cultivated land we grew some flax seed. It was very difficult to harvest, but the price of $8.00 per 100-pound bag at the elevator in Grimshaw was considered worthy of the chore. Arthur's father raised pigs so the horse and sleigh trains had a load of pigs or flax when they went south. They carried flour, sugar, tobacco, lard, tea and other basic supplies back north for the trading post.

Sometimes the spring break-up of the roads and rivers would occur while we were on the trail. We would then have to corduroy the hills with any poles or wood we could find – one sleigh at a time.

Other times we would have to raft the freight across the rivers to a wagon waiting on the other side. The horses would paddle and swim over, harness and all.

The chinooks were always a relief in the winter but they usually made the trails treacherous. There were swarms of mosquitoes and flies in the summer. I kept a mesh net over Ken's box bed.

Life seemed to be taken up with daily chores. We had the odd picnic to Hay River (Chinchaga), going by horse and wagon or on horseback. Sometimes the Hudson's Bay factor Doug Stevens and his wife Ann would join us.

Our second son Bud was born at the Women's Missionary Service hospital in December, 1942, in what is now known as Manning. Dr. Doidge kept me in hospital for two weeks. I returned to Keg River in January during one of our coldest winters.

Ken Jackson 1947.

Bud Jackson as a baby, 1947.

The Americans were building the MacKenzie Highway. I was riding in a truck with Bill Reed and we were held up many times by construction machinery. It was so cold they couldn't keep their trucks running. We all suffered with the cold in what became a 24-hour trip with a new baby.

Our third son Barry came along in January, 1944. Dr. Mary delivered him at home. By this time Revillon Freres store had been moved up to the farm and abutted the log cabin. We had an upstairs, more room and more cold fresh air – the muskeg wadding had come out from between the logs in the moving. To make Bud's bottles in the night I would light the air-tight heater to melt the milk.

In October, 1944, Arthur, I and our sons, aged three, two and nine months, went by wagon to Tompkins Landing, where we waited on the banks of the Peace River for O'Sullivan's river boat coming from Fort Vermilion. We were four days on the boat to Peace River, due to low water and sand bars. We travelled in the daylight hours only.

Arthur and Margaret Jackson, Roberta, Doug, Patti and Hugh.

From Peace River we went via train to Brander in the Fraser Valley of British Columbia. There Miss Lawrence, a former teacher-missionary of Keg River, had rented a house for us. Arthur had numerous odd jobs. Eventually we went to work on a large dairy and poultry farm in Matsqui.

In 1948 we were able to get a 60-acre tract of our own in Aldergrove, where the older three boys started and finished school. From the boys' 4-H calves we developed a herd of pure-bred Ayrshires – we called our farm "Northern Echo". Arthur worked for the Department of Highways to keep up and improve our farmstead.

We had two daughters and six sons by the time we left the Fraser Valley. In 1961, we returned to Keg River, where Arthur farmed his father's land. There was an elevator, a railroad and paved highway to the outside markets – all changes that had been made since we left. We had a house in Peace River for a few years.

As the family grew up and left home and Arthur gave up farming, we settled in Powell River, B.C.

Arthur had 10 years of doing his favorite things – fishing for salmon and cod and gardening. Our home is on the seashore. Arthur passed away in July, 1988, after a courageous struggle with cancer. His ashes are spread on the water he loved – the blue Pacific.

I'm still at home in Powell River, where I welcome any northern visitors.

John Robert (Bob) and Doreen Jackson
by Bob Jackson

I was born in Keg River on January 16, 1935, on the coldest day that Keg River ever had. It was 72° Fahrenheit below zero . I've hated the cold ever since!

The isolation of Keg River never bothered us as children. If there was any energy left for play once the chores were done, we found lots to do, from climbing trees to checking out the birds' nests, to swimming in the river. We had hours of fun in the winter sledding with our friends on the hill at Larone Ferguson's, and building better, faster sleighs.

One thing about living in the country and running around barefoot – I really couldn't see much sense to shoes, although rubbers were okay in the winter. If my feet got cold, I just went and stood in a fresh cow pie until they warmed up.

Our parents always encouraged us to try new things. Mrs. Harrington gave me some duck eggs, I set a hen on the duck eggs, and she stayed

Isobel Borbridge and John Jackson whitewashing, 1938.

Technology in 1952 to take Restaurant Management. I was the executive chef at Beaver's Catering for over 20 years. I became a very good cook, which my mother says is one of my problems! Then, I worked for Adeco Drilling until the company was closed in 1991. I spent quite a bit of time north of the Arctic Circle in gas exploration.

Doreen Ferguson and I were married in 1957. We had two sons: Bryan, born in 1960, and Dale, born in 1961. Our home in Calgary was then in the northwest outskirts, but is well within the city now. We moved to Sherwood Park in 1971. Doreen and I moved to Oklahoma for a year. I loved it there! It was hot and you could grow anything! But it was back to the snow and cold in Sherwood Park. We moved to Calgary when our two sons were transferred here in 1991. I keep busy gardening and selling real estate, when Doreen and I aren't chasing grandkids.

Bryan lives in Cochrane with his wife Barbara. They have two sons: Alex, born in 1989; and Max, born in 1991; and three daughters: Trixie, born in 1983; Jackie, born in 1985; and Andrea, born in 1987. Dale has travelled all over the world and lives in Calgary.

Bryan and Barb Jackson. Children, Jackie, Alex, Andrea, Trixie and Max.

faithfully on the nest for 28 days and hatched them out. But she couldn't understand the little ducks, and when the whole bunch jumped into the river she rushed up and down the bank frantically setting up a terrible commotion. We had to catch the little ducks and bring them back to her. I raised ducks for several years after that.

The next venture was raising geese. Mrs. Shemeluik gave me a "woman" goose and a "man" goose. The geese hated dogs, and made a terrible racket when any came near the yard. Of course with the geese we didn't need a watch dog. The gander was really fierce. When one of the goslings fell into a post-hole in the yard, the gander attacked me when I went to rescue it. One summer, we had so many goslings walking around that it was tricky to walk across the lawn!.

I went to the Southern Alberta Institute of

A woman worries about the future until she gets a husband, while a man never worries about the future until he gets a wife.

210

Robert (Slim) Kemp
by Sarah Price

Mr. Kemp was born in Walla Walla, Washington, U.S.A. He moved to Carcajou in the late 1930's and homesteaded NE-15-101-19-W5, which was right along the Peace River. He worked the land with horses.

I remember Slim Kemp as a tall scary man whom a child had a hard time getting used to, but my sister Benita and I soon learned that he was not scary but a very wise old man. He used to ride his horses through the old Carcajou trail that went past our place (known as High Camp).

The first time he stopped, he startled the whole family as it was very cold and Slim's beard, moustache and long hair were full of icicles and frost. He had ridden his horse out and nearly froze. It took quite some time for him to thaw out. After that he insisted on buying us Christmas presents. Mom always had to order these from the catalogues for him.

I remember one time Slim stayed overnight and got up in the morning to wash. He put the wash basin on the stove to heat the water. The next thing we knew, the basin was melted all over the stove. Slim hadn't noticed that it was plastic instead of the usual galvanized metal or enamel.

When he was ready to retire and move out of

Slim Kemp with Sarah Omoth, Cindy Rogers and Benita Omoth, 1962.

Carcajou, Slim wanted Mom and Dad to move to Carcajou to look after him. After much thinking, Mom and Dad wanted us to go to school and be close to medical facilities and a road. Slim sold his farm and moved closer to us. He built a nice little house on the edge of the Keg River near the Cabins and grew a beautiful garden. He also built a little smoke house as he always cured his own meat.

One time at the old Keg River Cabins, a stranger was eating his dinner. Slim Kemp rode by the restaurant window on his white horse and the stranger said, "I always wondered what had happened to the Lone Ranger!"

Edna May Kiselczuk
by Patsy Lindberg (nee Tupper)

Edna Kiselczuk grew up in Nebraska. Northland School Division hired her to teach in Carcajou. She was a rugged, determined English woman. When she made a promise, very little could stop her. She came over the old Carcajou trail with horse and wagon on August 29, 1960.

Since there was no school building, Edna held her first classes in the upstairs room at our house. At first only a few children were present. Robert Lea Kemp sold his farm to her about a month later. She then moved her teaching to one of the little log houses in her yard and called it a temporary classroom.

The students were of all ages; most had little or no schooling. The first few weeks of school were really hectic with some students getting sick and some fainting. Everything was new and strange to them.

With the farm, Mrs. Kiselczuk got some horses and cattle. Sometimes after school she had students help her haul water from the river for the animals. As one of those students, I remember helping nurse an injured heifer back to health.

Edna had a deep faith and love for the Lord and His people. She passed along Gideon Bibles to anyone who was interested. Evangelical missionaries and ministers were always enthusiastically welcomed.

Frank and Jewel Zurovec and their family were the first to come. They held services in the upper room at our house in November. They came from Texas, arriving in Keg River around the end of October. They borrowed a wagon and horses to get to Carcajou. Sleet and snow were falling and they got very cold. They stayed in Carcajou for only about a month.

A new school was built in January, 1961. Edna

arranged work bees for her students to clean and wax the new school floor. She said the floor wasn't clean enough until you could eat off it. The students cleaned the yard as well.

Every school morning she would get up at 5 A.M. and pull her sleigh full of books to school. Some mornings she would hitch up a team of horses and give some of her students a lift to school. On cold mornings she heated rocks and placed them in the sleigh to keep her feet and the feet of her students warm. It sure felt good.

When she arrived at school she lit a fire in the heater and then made a big pot of cocoa for everyone. To warm up she taught us to do exercises. When we all moved in perfect rhythm, she said the school house danced with us. She also said that if we broke the rhythm we would bring the roof down on us!

Some days some of us had no lunch, because there was nothing at home to bring. On those days, she cut up a pumpkin and roasted it or shared her lunch with us. She said that if we were hungry enough, we would eat anything we could sink our teeth into.

Matt Raey and Len and June Clare came from Manning to hold religious services whenever they could. Gertrude Housten (later Dempsey) often came to play her accordion for the meetings. So few visitors ever came to Carcajou, these visits and meetings drew a lot of interest.

They often taught us new songs. We loved the songs and liked to sing. We would each memorize a line, then get together after they left and put it all together. They were surprised when they returned to find that we all knew the song!

Edna found taking care of livestock and teaching school too difficult, so on March 10, 1961, she hired Alex Stone to do the chores. Alex, his wife Gunhild and their children Georgie, Linnea and Timothy then moved to the farm to stay with Edna. Gunhild played her accordion for services and for fun. She also baked delicious cookies and doughnuts that she shared with anyone who visited. The Stones left in the fall before school started.

On August 26, 1961, six young fellows from the Y.M.C.A. who were travelling down the river in two canoes stopped at Edna's place. She was glad to have them stay the night and provide food and hospitality. As they were ready to leave, she gave them some vegetables from her bountiful garden. She was really impressed by their good manners.

All the folks in the valley went to a Halloween party held at Edna's home on October 31, 1961. She led us in games and bobbing for apples. Howard Price made tongues of fire by blowing over a lit match. Everyone had a lot of fun.

Just as the party was coming to a close, a fierce blizzard hit the district. It was the first storm of the fall and many folks had trouble driving the few miles home. By morning the snow was really deep.

Every spring Edna Kiselczuk took us on a field trip to study nature and sketch what we saw. It was as much fun as a picnic. We got to sit under a spruce or a pine to eat our lunch.

Edna's feet often gave her pain. She rarely missed a day even with this pain and did many hours of extra work and study outside the classroom.

Wilber Crowder, a missionary came in his little Volkswagon Beetle on September 3, 1962. He was able to travel on the new highway that was being built into Carcajou. It was yet without gravel, so it was not an easy trip. He held meetings in the school – one right after school and another at 7:30 P.M. With power created by his car battery, he showed slides on training Sunday School teachers. He also did magic tricks with some toys and ropes he brought along.

Bill and Ivy Mainprize and their children, Blake and Winnie came to stay with Edna that fall. Bill didn't know much about caring for livestock and his ideas often clashed with Edna's. As a result the Mainprizes left in the spring.

After Edna retired from teaching, she moved to Manning. She worked as a substitute teacher in the schools there until ill health forced her to retire completely. She said that children seemed harder to teach every year, due to a lack of respect for authority.

Edna Kiselczuk was a wonderful teacher and made a tremendous, positive impact on our lives.

Son Donald and daughter Mary Kiselczuk.

Mrs. Kiselczuk with daughters Lotty and Della.

Wilma and Trygve Kjenner
by Wilma Kjenner

We were transferred to Paddle Prairie Metis Store in October, 1968. We had been at Fishing Lake Colony. The store had living quarters attached for the manager. Trig managed the store until he was taken ill in January, 1971.

Florence Wanuch in Paddle Prairie Store, 1962.

Wilma and Trig Kjenner, Paddle Prairie, 1970.

We had many good times while in Paddle. We have fond memories of Christmas carolling, good parties, box socials and good friends. We went to a barn dance at Keg River and also spent some interesting times with Dr. Jackson.

While in Paddle, we had three different supervisors: Petersen, Bryan and Olsen.

My husband has passed away now but he lived 15 years after the stroke. He was unable to talk but he loved to travel. I now live in a seniors' manor in Elk Point.

Frank and Ann Lafoy
by Frank Lafoy

I call myself a prairie chicken. I arrived in the Battle River area from the prairies in 1929. Six years later, I bought Bob Bieraugle's trap line running fifty miles from High Mountain to the Fontas.

During the Second World War I served overseas for 3 1/2 years. I landed in Normandy on D-Day (June 6, 1944) with the Third Division Huzzars. While overseas I became friends with a Dutch family and I corresponded with them for years.

After arriving back in Canada in 1946, I applied to the R.C.M.P. but was told I would have to wait six months before I would be accepted. In that time I checked out other opportunities. The Hudson's Bay Company paid only $85 a month while the Alberta Government Forestry Department paid $95, so I joined them and was posted to Keg River as the first full-time forest officer. My new employer provided me with $150 to build a house.

I was required to have a dog team of at least three dogs and two horses for summer use. The trap lines had to be registered in Ottawa in those days. As part of my job, I had to travel with pack horses as far north as Meander River to seal the beaver pelts.

I married Anne Lorencz of Manning in 1947. We have two sons: Eric, who works for the police in Yellowknife, and David, a Calgary banker.

Jack Grant came to Keg River after I left. By that time the pay had increased to $135 a month.

I was to work for the government for the next 26 years in nine different locations. When I was in High Prairie, I decided I was having to deal with too much red tape, so I quit. I then started working with the Alberta Government Wildlife Branch in the Rimbey area and I lived in Ponoka, but the area was much too large. There were so many beaver around Rimbey that farmers were being flooded out. Teddy Bluffton declared open season and I had 175 in less than a month.

The big British Columbia fire in 1950 was caused by an Imperial Oil survey crew working with pack horses. Their camp fire was not doused properly. The fire smouldered in the ground all winter and became a full blown fire with the westerly spring winds. Thousands of acres were destroyed as the fire burned at least one hundred miles to Keg River.

Professor Roane did a study on the effects of the fire on wild animals, especially moose. At the head waters of the First Battle (Notikewin River) I found many dead animals along the banks. The water was tested and found to be so polluted that it was killing the animals almost immediately after they drank it. Many animals of all kinds were killed by the fire itself or the lingering effects of this huge fire.

In 1988 I was inducted into the Order of the Bighorn, honoring my many years of work. Ann and I continue to live in Ponoka. I am retired and Ann works at the hospital.

Frank LaFoy's medal and plaque of merit. The Order of the Bighorn.

Harold and Bethora Larivee
by Gladys Tkachuk

Harold was one of many patriotic citizens who served this country overseas during World War II. He travelled to the Peace Country, working at various jobs to support himself and his wife Bethora. They were camp attendants for George Robertson's bush camp one winter. They also worked in sawmills.

Harold obtained a homestead in Keg River at SW-6-101-24-W5 on the 26th baseline. While Harold was building their house, he and Bethora lived in the shop on George Robertson's farm. They spent a very uncomfortable cold winter there.

Neighbors and friends knew Harold as "Squeaky". He got this nickname because his voice was of a very high pitch. Most of the community then knew his wife, not as Bethora, but as Mrs. Squeaky. She was a tiny soft-spoken lady.

Harold was a crack shot and he was very proud of his army rifle. We also remember the many lovely tomatoes they grew in the special sawdust mixture they had alongside their house.

The Larivees lived the life of normal homesteaders, clearing land and working out in the winter when work was available. This peaceful existence was fine as long as Harold managed to stay sober.

What happened on that spring day in May, 1974 is unknown. Gossip has it that Squeaky showed up at a neighbor's house at a very early hour, clad only in his long-johns and rubber boots and was carrying his rifle. He was very drunk and disoriented. Where he went next or what he did next is not known, but he was NEVER SEEN or HEARD FROM AGAIN! He just vanished!

The RCMP conducted a search, organized by Ken Batchelor. Searchers on horseback scoured the area for several weeks, but not a trace of evidence was found.

Mrs. Larivee was too afraid to stay alone and her health failed shortly after her husband's disappearance. She spent the rest of her life in a nursing home in Camrose.

The disappearance of Harold Larivee remains an unsolved mystery of the Keg River area, and with most of the people who could have been involved also gone from this world, it is unlikely that this mystery will ever be solved.

Tom Lewis
by Tom Lewis

I applied for a government draw for a farm development lease for land in the Carcajou area. I got the first pick and have now lived on my choice of land (S-33-99-20-W5) since 1984. I originally came from Cranford, Alberta, but enjoy living in the northern bush country. I hope to have a ranch/farm combination that is self-sufficient. I am supported in my efforts by my girlfriend Peggy Frank and her daughter Dianna.

Lloyd Lovlin Family
by Laura Lovlin

Lloyd filed on his homestead at S-15-101-23-W5 in 1950. Lloyd and his brother Marvin did some brushing and field work for a couple of summers

In 1954 the kids and I went to the homestead, too. Debbie was two and Trenton was a baby. He was sickly, so we made some visits to Dr. Jackson.

I remember the good old days well! NO water, NO power, NO house, but plenty of work! We have made our home in Manning and Lloyd sold the homestead to Hans Ludvigsen in 1975.

Lloyd and Laura Lovlin, 1993.

Lucille and Norman Lowe
by Norman Lowe

Lucille and I arrived in Keg River, January 2nd, 1969, at – 45°F. We came to operate the United Grain Growers elevator. The United Grain Growers house was just newly built.

We had been living at Blackfalds, Alberta, where we had been farming. In the winter I drove truck in the oilfields and Lucille worked as a Registered Nurse's Aid at Red Deer General Hospital.

We had two boys, Rudy and Glen, when we moved north and Tom, our third son, was born in Manning in 1969. Seven years later in 1977 our daughter Jocelyn arrived and then Rebecca completed our family in 1979. Now we have four grandchildren.

At Keg River I was elevator agent but also drove school bus, so there were some busy times.

There were no hopper cars and no boxcar puller while I worked for United Grain Growers.

Some of the experiences we had were with bears. They loved our yard, especially our chicken pen and chop bin. Lucille chased one out of the chicken house with a broom. Luckily it wanted to go!

Another exciting time was water-skiing at Carcajou. Pete Rudy, Johnny Vos and I were using Wim Vos's boat. Somehow we managed to flip the boat and Pete ended up underneath. He was the one with no life jacket and couldn't swim. Somehow Johnny and I got Peter on top of the upside down boat, and he still had his snuff in his mouth! We got to shore, righted the boat and chased down-river after the water skis that had floated away!

The year of 1971 should have been the year of the rabbit. There were thousands! Our cat used to catch them off the back step.

I served several terms on the recreation board and enjoyed the skating rink parties. Lucille helped with Brownies and Guides as a tester for badges.

We spent three and a half years in Keg River, enjoying the people and the area. The soil is beautiful. One cannot imagine how there is so much surface water and none underneath for a well. There are years when the frost comes too soon.

We sincerely wish for better prices and good luck to all the farmers and everyone else in the district.

Hans and Marjorie Ludvigsen
as told by Hans Ludvigsen

I was born in Nybol, Denmark, on May 3, 1908. I was the eldest of Karl and Ingeborg's three children. My two younger sisters were Katrine and Marie, who are now both deceased. Upon completion of my education as a master baker I came to Halifax, Canada, on March 21, 1927. I came west and worked on farms in Hardisty and Provost, Alberta, for two years, moving to Dawson Creek in 1929.

There I started homesteading in Groundbirch. In 1930 Johnny Temple and I opened a bakery in Dawson Creek. In 1933 I left Johnny in charge of the bakery and travelled north through the Nahanni to Cameron Bay on Great Bear Lake with Bert Neeland. I came back out in 1935 and went back to the bakery. In the winter of 1937 I went back to Denmark, returning to the bakery in the spring of 1938.

On May 15, 1944 I married Marjorie Green,

born in Regina, May 11, 1916, the second oldest in a family of seven. Marj moved to Dawson Creek in 1942 to help her father, Percy Green, in his accounting firm.

We had two children: Bruce, born in 1945, and Janice, born in 1946. Bruce married Sharon Dyke of Squamish, British Columbia, in 1974 and they have three children: Mykle, Bryan and Lisa. They presently live in Port Coquitlam, B.C. Janice married Les Freeman of Dawson Creek in 1965 and they have two grown-up children, Brenda and David. Les and Janice are presently living in Keg River, Alberta.

In 1945 I built a new bakery in Dawson Creek. I supplied bread for the army when they built the Alaska Highway. I expanded and temporarily opened a second bakery in Fort St. John to accommodate the army's need for bread as they travelled north. I sold the Dawson Creek bakery to Toastmaster in 1947 for health reasons.

In 1948 we moved to Groundbirch. In 1952 we moved to farm in Arras, keeping the farm in Groundbirch. In 1954 we moved back to Groundbirch; then in 1955 we moved to Dawson Creek, where I have lived ever since. I sold the farms at Groundbirch and Arras and bought

Mr. & Mrs. Hans Ludvigsen.

another small farm two miles away from my former farm at Arras from my father-in-law.

My daughter and son-in-law moved to Keg River in the spring of 1973. When visiting I enjoyed the country so much I sold my farm at Arras and purchased S-15-101-23-W5, known as Lovlin's, in 1975 under the condition that Les would farm it. I travelled to Keg River quite often and helped farm whenever I could. If I had been younger I certainly would have been tempted to move there and farm.

Marj passed away on March 25, 1991, after a battle with cancer, and I transferred the Lovlin farm to my daughter. I moved into Peace River Haven in Pouce Coupe, B. C., in the fall of 1993 and sold my house in Dawson Creek. (Editor's Note: Hans passed away on May 5, 1994.)

Ernest and Nina Marr
by Nina Marr

We arrived in Keg River with our son Thomas in August, 1963.

We lived in five different dwellings, all in the same school yard! We lived in the little grey teacherage until January. The newly constructed duplex was ready then. The duplex burnt down in January, 1965, during the Christmas holidays, leaving the Cartiers and ourselves homeless. Ken South from the ranger station and others saved a lot of our things.

We lived in an old trailer, then the staff room in the school. Finally we got a new three-bedroom trailer.

KEG RIVER MUD! – Marr and Chorney trailers at Dr. Mary Jackson School.

Originally we came from Lloydminster, Saskatchewan, but were living in Regina prior to moving to Keg River. We were at Dr. Mary Jackson School for five years.

The first year was interesting – the new school was not ready for the first day of school, so classes were held in the old school at the Post, in the new hall and in a portable. We moved into the brand new school in January, 1964 and the extremely cold winter that year was a real test for the new propane furnaces!

Ernest was vice-principal for that first year. He was principal from September, 1964 to June, 1968. I taught for three of the five years we were in Keg River. Timothy was born while we were there. The boys were not old enough for school when I started teaching, so Mrs. June Papirny looked after them. How they loved her!

Keg River was a place to which my Dad advised us not to go! But we quickly made friends and experienced a genuine neighborliness. We formed a friendship with Ken and Janet South which continues today. The Dr. and Frank Jackson family were always there when we needed them.

Losing our home and all our wedding pictures due to the fire is one of our sad memories, but we loved skating on the pond near our trailer. And we fondly remember the Christmas concerts at the hall and the other community events.

Our only school trip was to Manning as part of a Social Studies unit!

The farewell evening at the Community Hall and the smell of the rose petals that were thrown on us is another fond memory of Keg River. Although most didn't know it, we were also celebrating our wedding anniversary that evening!

Tamara was born later in Fort McMurray, where we still live and work.

Fred and Sarah Martineau
as told by Fred Martineau

I arrived in this part of the country on June 17, 1940. Cold Lake is where I was born in 1903. Alberta wasn't a province until 1905, so this was all in the Northwest Territories. In 1980 when the government was giving medals to people who had lived in Alberta for 75 years, my brother got one but I got silver due to someone thinking Cold Lake was in Saskatchewan!

When I came to Paddle Prairie the only people living on the prairie were the John Christian family, Paulis Bottle (Chalifoux), the Antoine Bottle (Chalifoux) family and the Adolphus Ghostkeeper family.

Through the summer and fall I built a log house for my family, (just north of where the big shop is now). Then I went back to Cold Lake to move my wife and children, Mabel, the oldest,

Bertha, Mary, Louis, Norma, Shirley, and Lyle to Paddle Prairie.

It was December when we started north. We travelled with John Herman, his wife and three children. We nailed a tarp over the top of the box of Johnny Arnault's (of Notikewin) truck and both families rode in the back of it. We left Notikewin in the morning and got to Keg Crossing (where the Keg River Cabins are now). As we were crossing the river, the truck broke through the river ice and we were stuck tight!

I went off in search of a team of horses to pull us out. I had heard there was a family with horses living at High Camp. I walked to the Doveys and we had quite a time catching the horses and getting back the three or four miles to the truck, all in the dark on a cold night.

While I had been gone, John Herman and Johnny Arnault had been working on the truck, jacking up one side and then the other and putting logs under the wheels. With the truck up out of the water and the horses hitched on the front and everybody out, we were finally on our way. We got to Keg River Post at 10 A.M., 24 hours after we left Notikewin, a distance of 60 miles. The overland trail to Paddle Prairie of 25 miles was not good but it was passable.

The first project at Paddle Prairie Settlement was to get a sawmill set up and operating. With all the people moving in we needed lumber and shingles for the houses. I was the sawyer for a while and then was carpenter on many of the first buildings built in the area.

John Herman built the first store. It was just a small log building. He, his wife, son and twin daughters stayed for three years selling the necessities.

The sawmill provided lumber for all the new homes, the store, a school roof, the nurse's home and office. The people moving in were happy to get jobs in the mill and in logging, as well as in housebuilding. The first school was built of logs by volunteers. People were glad to help because there were a number of children to go to school. It was ready in 1943 and Mrs. Barker was the first teacher. The teacherage was also built by volunteers. In those days everybody helped one another and got along with everyone and people were happy.

My wife and daughters ran a stopping place from 1942 to 1945. Our two youngest children, David and Allan, were born here. There were always people dropping in, with no place to stay or to eat. Charlie Boyd, the store manager, boarded with us. Father Quémeneur used to stay with us, too. He carried along his papers and the prayer books from church to church. One time when the Father was visiting, Sarah saw bedbugs crawling out of the prayer books!

The bedbugs were impossible for me to live with. The doctor at Keg River said the only way to be sure of cleaning them out was by fumigating. This meant the whole house had to be sealed up airtight. Each window and door had to be papered over inside and out and poison spread on each level of the house and left for 48 hours.

Fleas also plagued us in the 1940's. Where they came from or where they went, we have no idea. While they were here (one summer) they certainly had everybody scratching! There were millions and they were everywhere, down the cellar, all over outside from one end of Keg River to the other end of Paddle Prairie. At times your pant legs were grey with them. When winter came, they left or died and weren't seen again!

The government store opened in 1942 with Charlie Boyd as the first manager. John Friesen was the second store manager and his wife taught school.

I was the first supervisor. We saw many changes in those early days. The American Army set up a base on the Settlement in 1943. They were constructing a passable road to the gas field at Norman Wells in the North West Territories. Along with this base came some good jobs for the locals and a passable road to the south. There were also the problems of disease and booze.

Jack Cahill was the next supervisor. He stayed quite a while. Fred McCully followed him. Then Wayne McCullough and his family came. Wayne was anxious to see the people and the Settlement be selfsupporting. He set up a cold storage building and the settlers had a place to sell their beef from cattle Wayne had butchered. He also encouraged the growing of potatoes to be sold.

My next big job was setting up and operating a large government sawmill at Assumption, especially put in to provide work for the locals. It was very successful for a while.

Since leaving Paddle Prairie, I have travelled a bit and spent time in Cold Lake and Manning. My wife Sarah became crippled with arthritis years ago. She passed away in July of 1977.

I then married Delia Latendre. She passed away in 1993. I still have my home in Manning and hope to get back into my garden each spring. There is nothing as good as veggies you have grown yourself. I like to visit family and friends in Paddle

and when I do, I stay with my son Allan and his wife Emma.

(Editor's Note: the following story was in the *Manning Banner Post* on the occasion of Fred Martineau's 91st birthday.) Wilfred (Fred) Martineau was 91 years old on April 6, 1994. Born in Onion Lake, Saskatchewan, to Adrian and Margaret Martineau, Fred had seven brothers and three sisters. Fred is the oldest in the Martineau family.

Fred has only two sisters living, Eva Dahlseide and Hazel Wheeler of Cold Lake, Alberta.

Fred's first wife, Sarah Martineau, passed away July 1977 and Fred remarried a few years ago. His second wife, Dela Latendre of Manning, passed away in March 1993.

Fred had five daughters and three sons. One son Louis Martineau passed away a few years ago.

Fred Martineau's daughters are Mabel Omoth of Keg River, Bertha Parenteau of Paddle Prairie, Mary Davidson of Manning, Norma Houle of Paddle Prairie and Shirley Rogers of Chilliwack, British Columbia. His sons are Lyle Martineau of St. Paul, Alberta, and David Martineau of Edmonton. Fred Martineau has 35 grandchildren, 49 great-grandchildren, and nine great-great-grand-children.

McBain Family
by Bob McBain

In May, 1980, I was given the opportunity to apply for a transfer to Keg River to look after the Petro-Fina Gas Plant. (Later this plant was bought by Petro Canada.) When my wife Debbie found out, all she said was, "Where the heck is Keg River?" We were told it was north of Peace River, a small community with a school, store, garage, post office and bus depot.

We visited Keg River in July when Debbie was pregnant with our second child. I accepted the position to operate the plant and we moved into our new house next to the plant on October 28, 1980.

We enjoyed the opportunity to grow vegetables in our garden. We were able to supply some of our neighbors with tomatoes that we grew in our greenhouse.

We enjoyed picnics and swimming at the Chinchaga River. We met many people who lived between Peace River and High Level. There is never a day that goes by without us thinking of the good times we had during the five years we spent in Keg River.

In July, 1985, I accepted a position to operate a gas field in southern Alberta near Brooks. We had the urge to move back north to Grande Prairie in January 1991. I accepted a new position with Petro Canada at the Gold Creek Gas Plant.

In Keg River we really enjoyed the company of many people. We found getting to know Dr. Jackson a real pleasure.

One of the great experiences we had was the great grizzly episode! Three idiots went tracking a wounded grizzly and two and one-half idiots came out! End of story.

When Daryn, our youngest, was starting school, he always told everyone he was going to be tall. When asked why, he said it was because he was born at A Higher Level!

Debbie and I have three children: Andrea, Robbie and Daryn. We still enjoy our animals including sheep, chickens and a horse. Debbie still raises Maltese dogs.

Bob and Debbie McBain with children.

Emma and Dave McDonald

by Anne Vos

Emma arrived in Keg River with her dad on April 30, 1926. Her dad, Thomas Allen (Allie) Brick, had ranched on the west side of the Peace River, upriver from the town of Peace River. Nancy, Emma's mom, had died during dental surgery. Emma had two brothers, Fred and Ernie, who were older than she and had already moved away from home.

Emma filed on a homestead at SE-28-101-24-W5. Her father filed on NW-28-101-24-W5, where they built their home and buildings. They had horses and cows. Emma milked several cows and made and sold butter.

A team of dogs were a necessity to travel in the winter time. Dave built a dog pen from heavy mesh wire. It was 20′ by 40′ and 10 feet high. The top and bottom were completely enclosed to make sure the dogs could not get out. They were able to run around and be tended without anyone going into the pen. Sleigh dogs could be very temperamental and could not be trusted, especially if a number of them were together.

Allie Brick ran a trading post for the Keg River Trading Company at Rainbow Lake (Hay Lakes) in the winter. Emma accompanied her father to Hay Lakes for the winter. It was at this post that she met Dave McDonald when he came to trade his furs.

Dave's trapline was on the Buffalo River, 30 miles southwest of Rainbow Lake or 70 miles northwest of Keg River. Dave was originally from the Slave Lake and Grouard area. He had several cabins on his trapline and during the years he had different trapping partners, but Tommy Harris was with him the longest.

Dave was known as one of the best trappers, bringing in both the best quality and the largest quantity every year.

Dave and Emma were married in 1935. They made hay and grew oats for their livestock. When the highway was built in the 1940's, Dave began growing grain for market. He grew mostly flax. Soon he bought a truck to haul the seed to the Grimshaw elevators.

Dave and Emma were good farmers and took great pride in their farm and home. The weather caused them problems in the 1950's with many damaging frosts and heavy early snow.

Emma and Dave were community-minded people who contributed hours of work to improve life for everyone in the district. Emma helped at the school and knitted dozens of pairs of mitts and socks for the Red Cross to be sent to soldiers overseas. They also generously contributed to a community fundraiser called Christmas Roll Call that provided a candy bag and a small gift for the children after the Christmas concert.

The community hall also benefitted from Emma's hard work and secretarial skills. The first thing she always did after arriving at the hall was to grab a broom and attack the cobwebs!

My brother and I were always welcome at Dave and Emma's house when our mom (Dr. Jackson) was called away on a medical emergency. Sometimes she was gone for three to four days at a time and we would stay at the McDonalds' during these times.

Dave and Emma owned the first frame house

in Keg River, built in 1945 by the Daigles from Notikewin. It had a cement basement and a cistern to store rainwater. Dave bought a lighting plant to provide power. It was quite a change from their log house!

Emma loved to know what everyone in the community was doing, where they went and with whom! She kept a pair of field glasses on the window ledge so she could see what was happening at the Post, which was a mile from their home!

Emma and Dave loved children but had none of their own. Don Morrison came to them as a baby and they lavished love on him for years, but he went his own way with little regard for them.

Emma and Dave found a number of arrowheads on their land. The most interesting find was a large piece of jade measuring three inches by six inches by three-fourths of an inch. It had obviously been cut from a larger piece. It is not known how it got to their field or where it came from. Norman Tuck took this piece with him to Fort St. James.

Dave had a piece of flesh missing from his left ear. Many children would ask him about it. He enjoyed telling them stories about the rabbits chewing it off while he was sleeping! However the truth was that it had been badly frozen and dropped off.

The community surprised the McDonalds with a large party to celebrate their 25th anniversary in 1960.

Emma's health failed and she passed away in August, 1969. Dave's love of liquor and smoking finally took his life in 1978. He went to sleep while smoking in bed, which set the mattress on fire, and he died of smoke inhalation.

Dave and Emma McDonald.

Dorothy Marie Cardinal McFeeters
by Dorothy Cardinal McFeeters

My mother is Marilyn Doloras Cardinal Andrews. My grandparents, Mr. and Mrs. Jean Marie Cardinal, raised me in Keg River from 1960 to 1968, I then went to live with my mother.

On September 4, 1982, I married Dennis McFeeters, who is a Treaty Indian from Cold Lake First Nations. Dennis works for the oil rigs, driving a vacuum truck. We have three boys, Darin, Derek and Dennis Jr.

We have lived on the Cold Lake First Nations Reserve for 12 years and are still residing here. My mother lives in Edmonton.

Marilyn Cardinal, 1959.

Darin, Dennis, Dorothy, Derek and Dennis Jr. McFeeter.

May your moccasins make happy tracks in many snows and the rainbow always touch your shoulder.

May and Dick McGrane
by Margaret Befus

The McGranes were the first white settlers on the flat now known as the Armstrong Flat. They lived on the rise in the middle of the flat.

They raised a few cattle, lots of sheep, foxes and horses. They built dipping vats for treatment of mange. Cattle had to swim through the vat, which contained a chemical. Someone had to ensure that each head was submerged at least once.

The McGranes raised horses that were of better quality than the native cayuses, though I do not know how they made out with swamp fever. Each year Dick sheared the sheep. One year he sold all the wool and found he had made enough money to buy one suit of Stanfield long woollen underwear! May was very skilled at washing out the wool.

The sheep ranged free, so the coyotes and wolves must have had a heyday.

The McGranes were enthusiasts for a self-help series of books known as the Little Blue Books. They were put out in the United States and covered many subjects.

The family scratched the ground with rather primitive machinery and each year seeded more of it to brome grass. This brome was killed by the flood of 1934. Dick risked his own life to dig a ditch to drain the flat after the flood and the force of the water cut quite a coulee to the Peace.

In 1935 they decided to leave and sold the remaining sheep to the Friesens, who also took over their buildings which probably had not been flooded.

For many years this land was known as the McGrane Flat. Pat Ambler again seeded some of this flat to brome grass in the 1960's.

The McGranes moved to British Columbia.

Barbara and William Mero
by Barbara Mero

We first saw Carcajou on October 2nd, 1975. We went to Howard Price's with his nephew Ron. We camped where Howard is buried, on the Upper Landing which is also called Howard's Landing. We waited there for an airplane to pick us up on the river and take us across to the trapline.

It snowed for a week, so we made a lean-to. We enjoy laughing about those circumstances now, but we didn't laugh much while we were living through the experience.

Charles Dovey became our friend when we went on a spring hunt with him and we all stayed in a teepee.

Bill and Barb Mero.

The poem that follows is one that Bill wrote on a trip from the trapline to Carcajou. It brings back good memories. Carcajou and the people there certainly have a place in our hearts. Tammy was born in the Manning hospital. We moved back to Quesnel in 1978, where our son Coby was born.

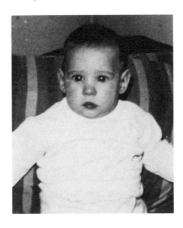

Tammy Mero, age 6 months.

We're heading west to Carcajou
It's twenty below.
The wind is burning our faces,
We're bucking two feet of snow.
The moon is up,
The stars are shining bright.
We hope to hell we'll make it tonight.
Barb said, "Look upon the trail ahead.
Doesn't everything look so dead?"
Nothing is moving, only snow in sight.
We hope to hell we make it all right.
Sixty-four miles of trail like this,
for trees, but little sticks.
Muskeg is lying all over the place,
We hope to hell that we win this race.
Bill yelled, "Look, the river's in sight."
Even though it's awful late at night
We're going to keep moving, for our pace is
    right.

Pulled into Carcajou at the break of day,
Traded our fur for grub and a sleigh,
Turned and headed east toward our shack.
We hope to hell that we make it back.

Michael (Mike) and Annie Michalchuk
by Annie Michalchuk

Mike and I were born and raised in Poland. We were married in 1937. In May, 1939, my brother John Pawlowich wrote my father telling him to bring the families to Canada, where John was homesteading. Dad thought war was surely coming soon. The preparation and the permits took time and it was August before we were ready to leave Poland.

We all travelled by train to Gdvnia. The boys had their heads out of the windows on the train and the sparks and dust caused spots on their faces. The authorities would not let Mom and Dad and the family continue to England until the boy's skin was better. I was very pregnant, so Mike and I were allowed to continue but I was afraid I might never see my family again.

We travelled to England and then on to Canada on a ship which landed in Montreal on August 15th. We then travelled across Canada to Peace River by train. What a huge country! We came from Peace River down the river by barge to Carcajou, where my brother John met us and brought us to Keg River.

John had been here several years and had built a huge log house. Sophie was born shortly after we arrived. I had nothing for my baby. Mary Rudy, her daughter Mary Hartley, and Dr. Jackson were very helpful. They brought me everything I needed.

In 1940 Mike was able to get a homestead (NW-2-102-23-W5). We built a small log house. Times were very challenging. We worked hard. Mike cleared land with an axe. He sold firewood for $5 a load and worked for local farmers for $1.50 a day. Seven of our eight children were born in the original log house. Only Laurie was born in the new house.

Dr. Jackson assisted at all the births and helped with other emergencies.

Water came from a well Mike and I dug by hand. We were happy to finally get power in 1961.

Mike and I along with the children worked on our farm, raising our own food in a large garden. We milked cows and sold eggs. Mike said the children were good root pickers because they were down there close to the roots!

We bought our first 10 cows from someone in Girouxville. Mike trapped weasel, squirrel and other animals for extra money.

Mike was stooking for a neighbor not long after arriving in Keg River. He carried a gun for safety, hearing all these wild animal stories. Mike came face to face with a small black and white striped animal that would not leave. He raised his gun as a club and whacked the animal until he killed it, but as he did he was sprayed with its protective odor!

He carried the skunk to Johnny Yurkowski to find out what it was, only to have the door shut in his face! The odor was terrible. I made him change outside and had to burn the clothes because the smell wouldn't wash out. The $5 we got for the pelt paid for some new clothes!

The children all went to school in Keg River four miles away. They went by horse and buggy in the summer and sleigh in the winter. The children learned to handle the horse themselves with the help of bigger students they picked up along the way. Mike organized the parents of children travelling to school by horse, and they built a barn at the school so the animals wouldn't stand outside in the cold all day.

Sophie did well in school and Superintendent Hooper said she should be a teacher. She assisted Miss Paul by helping the smaller students with their work, as well as doing her grade nine studies. The children all went out after grade nine to continue their education in Peace River, Fairview and Grouard. Fred and Laurie now farm our land with the help of their sons.

During the rabies epidemic in 1951-52, the children's faithful school pony got rabies and had to be put away. This was a very sad time for us all. The priest gave us another horse, but it was not the same.

During harvest, a number of years ago, Mike was sick in bed. A storm was coming up and the wind was blowing hard. I thought I should close the granary lids before it rained, so I quickly climbed the ladder to the top of the 30-foot steel bin and moved on to the roof to close the small opening in the roof. It was then that a huge gust of wind came up and I heard a crash. My ladder! It had blown down and I was now trapped on the roof with the wind and rain battering me.

I prayed that someone would come and help me. There was absolutely no way down. If I were to jump I knew my bones would break. I prayed some more that someone would come, as it was beginning to get dark and I was already cold and wet.

Annie Michalchuk with her sons and daughters and their families, 1992.

Mike woke up and didn't know where I was, so he dressed and came outside looking for me. I called and shouted to him for help. When I got down he was really mad that I had gone up on the roof and he told me to never do it again. But I did, and the same thing happened again!

Annie and her children, Sophie, Helen, Everett, Peter, Fred, Edward and Larry with Lily standing beside her mother, 1992.

It is very hard to believe now in 1993 how we ever managed in those early years with so little. We raised eight healthy, happy children without many of the things people now think are necessary. When Mike and I arrived in 1939, I could never have imagined my life as it is today. It took much hard work by both of us. I am sorry Mike is not with me to enjoy our retirement. I say thank you to Canada.

Mike died of cancer in July, 1979. This is our family now:

Sophie and Vic Dikiatis (Victor and Vincent)
Helen and Lynn Frampton
Everett and Monique Michalchuk (Danny and Cindy)
Edward and Nina (Andrea and Brittany)
Fred and Karen Michalchuk (Wade and Tamara)
Lillian and Jim Nelson (Anthony, Michael, Laurie and Karrie Ann)
Peter and Joan Michalchuk (Nikeae, Paul and Mike)
Laurie and Joann Michalchuk (Kevin, Tanya and David)

Fred and Karen Michalchuk
by Karen Michalchuk

Fred was born in Keg River on May 31, 1945 to Anne and Michael Michalchuk. He went to school in Keg River, bought a homestead, helped his Dad on the farm and worked in Pine Point, North West Territories.

I was born in Edmonton on March 26, 1952. My parents are Susie Parenteau and Kenneth Fischer. I went to school in Manning and graduated from Paul Rowe High School.

Fred and I were married in Manning on July 20, 1970. We lived in High Level for one and one half years and worked for Thompson Construction. Then we moved back to Keg River where we bought the old Hudson's Bay store. My mom ran the store first, then Fred and I had our turn at running it. Eventually we rented out the store and house and finally shut down the non-profit business.

Fred and I bought a quarter of land from Fred's mom, then bought a house trailer and moved onto our new home quarter. We started our own construction company, F. Michalchuk Holdings Ltd. and invested in more land and farm machinery. Years later when the construction business was slowing down in Keg River we started a company in Rainbow Lake, called Rainbow Sand and Gravel, a division of F. Michalchuk Holdings Ltd.

We built a new home in 1992. Most of our time is spent in Rainbow Lake so it is a real treat to get home to Keg River for seeding and harvest.

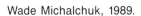

Wade Michalchuk, 1989.

We have two children: Wade born February 1, 1971, and Tamara born April 6, 1974. We also have one granddaughter Alexandra Kara born October 18, 1989.

Fred Michalchuk and granddaughter, Alexandra.

Tamara Michalchuk, 1992.

Peter and Marion Nortcliffe and Family
by Peter Nortcliffe

My family and I arrived at the Keg River Ranger Station in September 1968 and stayed at that location until February 1970. I had emigrated to Canada from England in 1951 and finally settled in Alberta in 1961. I joined the Alberta Forest Service in 1964, being first stationed at Fort Chipewyan, then Embarras on the Athabasca River, then Keg River. We moved from there to the Highwood Station and then on to Blairmore where we remained until my retirement in 1993.

My future wife Marion came from Wales in 1961 and we were married in 1963 at Wetaskiwin. Our children, Richard and Heather, both lived

Peter and Marion Nortcliffe.

with us at Keg River. Richard is now married with one son and lives in Kelowna. Heather is also married and lives in Wetaskiwin with two daughters.

Marion, Richard, Heather and I still have some very fond memories of life at Keg and, yes, we do remember the train wreck of 1968! Like many other former residents we also fondly remember the hospitality of Dr. Mary Jackson and her husband Frank. We spent many hours listening to the "pioneer" stories they lavished on us.

One of my most vivid memories is watching a residence burn to the ground during the winter of 1968 and not being able to help with extinguishing the fire. I saw it start from the front room of the ranger's station. It was only a couple of hundred yards away, across the creek to the south, on the east side of the highway.

With no readily available water supply at that time of the year, there was little anyone could have done to save the residence. It was consumed within a matter of minutes.

Our two children learned to skate on the dugout somewhere in the vicinity of the grain elevator. We also spent more than one day tobogganing with the Johnny Vos family.

Going for a sleigh ride at Tompkins Landing. L-R: Heather and Richard Nortcliffe, Sheila Douglass and Penny Vos.

Harry Bowe stands out in my mind as another teller of tall tales! The early days of "Wop" May and "Punch" Dickens flying through the country were two of his favorites! He also told us of how that chesterfield in his cabin would convert into his coffin when he died. "It's all ready to go when I need it," he would proclaim!

The Pattersons were also great pioneer people. Harold and his wife "Sug" (his way of saying "sugar") were always good for some conversation. We spent many a happy evening being indoctrinated into the art of cheating at a crib game! Their homemade ice cream was always a treat!

Fredrick Noskey
as told by Fredrick Noskey

Fredrick was born in Peace River 84 years ago. He grew up in Grouard, but his family travelled all over the Peace River country. Fredrick had two brothers – Ambrose and Joe – a stepbrother, Charlie, and three stepsisters.

Fredrick has lived in Paddle Prairie, Manning and Keg River. He trapped along the headwaters of the Chinchaga River years ago. Fredrick is now retired and lives in Keg River in a tiny, humble cabin. It is a peaceful, quiet place where deer come right up to his door. He has no modern conveniences and his nearest neighbor is two miles away.

Fredrick Noskey and Len deHaan.

John and Olive Okerholm
by Patsy Lindberg (nee Tupper)

John Okerholm was a short, plump, cheery Norwegian. His wife Olive was also short but very skinny and energetic. They lived on the east side of the Peace River in the old Carcajou settlement. Behind their neat little log house was dense forest. Their back yard was a thick stand of pine and spruce. They loved the wildlife and feeding the birds every winter. They attracted a number of birds, even the shy ones, like the nuthatch and thrushes that I didn't even know lived in Carcajou. The birds sensed their love and became very tame.

The Okerholms were friendly, fun-loving folks who often visited their neighbors. John owned a little button accordion on which he played his lively little Norwegian songs! It was the first accordion that I had ever seen. Another hobby of John's was writing poetry.

Okerholm house, 1990.

We don't know when the Okerholms came to the Carcajou area but he wrote a poem in Peace River around 1924 and built a cabin on the Buffalo River before 1934, so it was probably some time during that period.

Dad once asked John and Olive what they had had for breakfast. Food was sometimes very difficult to get. Mrs. Okerholm said with a smile, "Oh, we always have a good breakfast. I just find a magpie's nest and some tender little mice." (Not exactly my idea of bacon and eggs!) She was always the one to climb the tree to get the magpie eggs, too. If you have ever tried to get into these nests, you know what a difficult task that is!

John liked hunting big game with his friends. One fall John and a friend went moose hunting. They really needed the meat. Through many miles of rugged terrain they walked, finding nothing. Three days later they returned exhausted, hungry and discouraged.

A delicious aroma of supper met them as they came near the cabin. They were embarrassed as they entered the cabin. Mrs. Okerholm had grown tired, waiting for them to return. She shot a moose near home, dressed it and brought it home by herself! John later remarked to Dad, "I don't have to go hunting, I can just send the Missus!"

Olive and John Okerholm, 1940.

Almer and Mabel Omoth
by Sarah Price (nee Omoth)

My father, Almer, was born in Camrose, Alberta, on March 7, 1923, where his parents farmed. Dad joined the armed forces and fought in the second world war. After the war, he worked on road construction where he met Mabel Martineau who cooked for road crew camps. Mom and Dad were married October 10, 1950.

At first they lived in Camrose where Dad worked in the coal mine. They then homesteaded

Lance Corporal Almer Omoth, 4th Bn. Regina Rifles Regiment.

Fred Martineau children, Mary, Louis, Bertha, Mable at their confirmation and sponsors, Mr. & Mrs. Jacknife, 1943.

in Keg River on W-8-101-22-W5. Mom and Dad moved onto the homestead in March 1952, when I was a baby. We lived in a tent until they were able to build a house.

I was born on February 2, 1952, then Benita on September 15, 1953 and finally Chester born on July 7, 1965. All three of us attended school in Keg River until grade 10 and then went to Manning to finish our high school. I worked as a teacher's aide for five years and then attended the University of Alberta where I earned a Bachelor of Education degree. I have been teaching in Keg River ever since. I married Keith Price in 1976.

Benita attended the Northern Alberta Institute of Technology and earned a diploma in Commercial Cooking. She married Terry Price in 1973 and is now divorced. Chester attended Fairview College where he studied heavy duty mechanics and is now a journeyman.

Besides homesteading and farming, Dad worked as grader operator for the Department of Highways for many years until his death in August, 1969. After Dad passed away, Mom still had Chester to raise and Benita to put through school so she worked at Dr. Mary Jackson School as the janitor for 21 years. Mom retired in 1991 and still lives on the original homestead.

Mom has six grandchildren: Bernadette and George (Sarah), Terry Almer (Benita), and Theresa, Karleen, and Chester James (Chester).

A dog teaches a boy fidelity, perseverance, and to turn around three times before lying down!

Jim and Janet Omoth
by Janet Omoth

We were married in 1955 in Robinhood, Saskatchewan. We have five children: Bonnie (1955), Doris (1956), David (1959), Lynne (1960) and Robert (1963).

Bonnie married Larry Berg in 1972. They have one son, Jim, born in 1980 and they live in Toronto.

Doris married John Oxton in 1978 and they have three children: Daniel (1975), Sarah (1980) and Rebecca (1983). Doris is a constable in St. Albert and John works for Husky Oil in Rocky Mt. House.

David married Pam Norman in 1977. They have three children: Mike (1977), Norman (1981) and Ashley (1984). Dave works for Oregon Steel in Camrose and Pam works at the Drop In Centre in Edberg.

Lynne married Merlyn Knutson in 1987. They have two children and were divorced in 1991. Lynne and the two children, Jason (1987) and Patricia (1989), live in Camrose.

Robert is single and works for Oregon Steel in Camrose.

We moved to Keg River in 1965 into the Kemp house. It was a little 20-foot by 24-foot house for seven people, one dog and one cat! Our running water was the Keg River that ran near the back door.

Jim drove school bus and worked in the garage

Janet and Jim with their children.

at the Keg River Cabins for Charlie Isaac. I worked at the cafe in the Keg River Cabins. We moved to a house behind the ranger station across the highway from the cabins and by the Keg River.

What a cold winter 1965 had! In January, the kids only went to school for five days as the bus couldn't run if it was below -40°F.

In the spring of 1966 we moved back to Camrose. Jim has had to take early retirement due to illness. I continue to work at St. Mary's Hospital in Camrose.

(Editor's Note: Jim passed away in May, 1994.)

Jim Omoth grandchildren.

Tina Onstine family

by Tina Onstine (nee Pawlowich)

I came to Canada from Poland with my parents, brothers and younger sister. My older sister Annie and her husband had come earlier. On our trip over, we spent some time in London, then got on a boat for Canada. After a day and a half at sea we had to turn back because of the war. Later the boat was given permission to make the trip. My parents said we had to go to Canada because they were afraid the children would be taken or killed in the war.

Crossing Canada took a long time on the old train that ran on coal. We travelled by train as far as Peace River and then on a freight boat from Peace River to Carcajou Crossing. My brother John and Nick Tomilou met us. This was the first time we had seen my brother in 15 years.

We got to Keg River on August 18, 1929. I was very lonely in this new place, my brother's home. There was nothing to look at but bush! I cried for many days. Finally I got used to the bush and then came the -40° winter weather. We got used to that, too.

We stayed at John's place and that is where our mother died. We had to go on without her. Every day we went to school about three miles away.

Dad got a piece of land and he and my brothers cut and hauled logs to build a house, barn and chicken coop.

That log house caught fire and burned down and we were not able to save anything except the clothes on our backs. We didn't have any chickens then, so we moved into the chicken coop! We lived there for some time while Dad got another log house built. One time when I came home for a visit, the new log house caught fire and also burned down! At that time my brother Adam's son, Carl, suffered third degree burns and Dr. Jackson had to take him out to Manning.

In 1934 or 1935, Frank Gardon thought I would make a good wife. He came to John's to see me but I said, "You could be my Grandpa!" He got mad and went home to get his gun – he was going to shoot me. He stayed around the house for a week and I couldn't even go outside. Finally the R.C.M.P. came and told him to go away.

After mother died it was very hard for us without her. I learned most of my cooking from *Western Producer* recipes. We got used to things in Keg River by going to school, dances and sports days. I began to feel much better about living in Keg River.

Within a year and a half, four of us got married – Adam, Bill, Mary and myself. My sister Mary had met her husband Steve Kelemen when she went to school in Manning. I met Norman Onstine when he worked on building the MacKenzie Highway. Adam and Barbara stayed on the farm with Dad. Bill and Margaret went to farm in Manning. Norman and I built a log house in the bush on our homestead at N23-101-24-W5.

We had a few of everything – pigs, cows and chickens. Our daughters Judy and Pat were born on the farm with Dr. Jackson's and my sister Annie's help. We moved to Kinuso for a while and Donna was born in the High Prairie Hospital. Then we moved back to Keg River.

Norman was not a good farmer and he wanted to move back to Kinuso where his family lived. We did make the move to Kinuso but things were worse, so once again we moved back to Keg River. I hoped he would change.

My son Terry was born in Manning where I had to stay in hospital for several months. Sister Annie and brother John looked after the kids for me. Norman was getting lazier and lazier – he was not a farmer. I talked my brother Steve into buying

Onstine children (1958): Terry, Donna, Pat and Judy

Tina Onstine and her grandchildren, 1975

our land (he paid us $500), and once more we moved to Kinuso. Then Norman promised me that he would work if we moved to Wetaskiwin. We moved but things didn't improve.

After all of this I came to my senses and decided I must divorce him. I went back to Kinuso, gathered up my children who were scattered all over town and we moved into a rented house.

I cooked for a number of years at the Kodiak Lodge Hotel until the children finished school.

Judy married Kenny Olsen and they settled in Widewater.

Pat married Alvin Kugbert. They travelled to Greece and Australia to work on oil rigs.

I moved to Edmonton in 1972 to an apartment with Donna and Terry, who were still in school. Donna married Dennis Huckaluk.

Terry went to work on oil rigs, mainly in Libya, where he met his wife Shelly.

With all my family gone, I met Pierre and we lived together for 10 years until he died of cancer.

I had a job with Canada Packers in the poultry plant for years until I retired. After that I found it difficult to sit around without doing anything, so I bought two houses and I rent rooms to young, recovering alcoholics and drug addicts and I keep quite busy every day.

Jim and Sandy Oster
by Sandy Oster

We left Huntsville, Ontario, in October 1981 with our two little girls; Amanda was three and Melinda was one. We arrived in the Red Deer area just before Halloween and stayed there while Jim worked for Case Power and Equipment. He did other odd jobs until we left in October 1983. While we lived near Red Deer we had two more children, Kristen and Richard (Tony). In October 1983, we moved north to Paddle Prairie where we lived while waiting to get some homestead property. In 1984 we got property in the Carcajou area. We had another addition to our family when Samantha

Taylor's front yard on the homestead.

229

arrived that winter. In 1985 after our oldest daughter finished school for the year, we moved to Carcajou to start homesteading. In 1987 we had another girl, Glori-anne. In July 1990, my father and mother, Richard and Isabel Taylor, moved out to live near us and help out with the homesteading.

Rick and Isobel Taylor with grandchildren.

Jim and Sandi Oster with children, Mandy, Mindy, Tony, Samantha, GloriAnne, Chrissy.

Mike Papirny Family
by Mike Papirny

I was born in Rife, Alberta. It is now called Glendon. Our family then moved to Bonnyville onto land purchased from the Soldier Settlement Board in 1928.

There was hay land, bush and several lakes on this land. We made and sold hay and caught rats to put groceries on the table. We were three miles from school. My five sisters and five brothers walked through blizzards in winter and mud and water in the summer in order to get to school.

Our father died of cancer in 1940. A week before he died, our two-year-old brother died, leaving the family with two burials in a week of -30°F weather. At the age of 17, I was left without

a father, and being the oldest, needed to provide for the family. I wasn't afraid of work. I was exempted from the army to work the farm and help mother with the family.

In the winter I went to work for a fish camp at Winnifred Lake. It was bitterly cold as we travelled by dog team, leaving camp in the morning darkness and returning after a hard day's work in the darkness of evening.

I met and married June Walters in 1944. Since my brothers and sisters had grown up, I left the farm.

June and Mike Papirny.

We then began working for Swanson Lumber at Wildwood, I was a sawyer and made $1.25 per hour. In the spring I decided to go to Whitehorse and bought a 1943 Dodge truck. I built a hip roof tent over the back to keep the rain out and we started out for the Alaska Highway.

Then at Peace River we heard a rumor that Manning was a great farming area. At Manning it was said that Keg River was opening up homestead land. We went to Keg River Post but one trip over those nine miles of "road", if you could call it that, made up my mind. I was moving on!

We went to Dawson Creek and found nothing but mud there as the United States Army was packing up and moving out. On to Fort St. John and then to Trutch, where we hit heavy rain and the road turned into a river.

I camped and happened to talk to an old gentleman. He wanted to know where I was going. He said if I wanted advice, I should turn back south because if I got up north, I might go broke and wouldn't be able to get back. "You do what you like, young fella, but that's God's fact," he told me. His convincing eyes and voice made me believe him.

I turned back and started checking for jobs on the way. At Calling Lake I met a fellow who knew I could weld, so he hired me to weld his Cat. If the weld held, he said, I would have a job.

I was able to rent a house, so I moved my family, June and the children, Geraldine and Dave to Calling Lake. George Rowe and his wife were there, too. We had a wonderful summer. We moved to a sawyer job at Drift Pile for the winter.

The next job was in a garage as a mechanic and welder in Faust. There I met Ken Fischer, who needed a sawyer in Notikewin. I was happy with the job I had but every time I saw Ken, he offered me more money. Finally when he said I could have a house for my family, I agreed, providing I could see his operation first.

I bought an Indian Chief motorcycle, for which I paid $250, to ride to Notikewin. I filled the leather saddlebags with tools and a lunch and got on the way. I couldn't drive right into camp because the ruts were so deep, so I walked the last half mile.

The mill seemed to be in good shape, so I began sawing right away. Two weeks later I borrowed Ken's truck and went to move my family. Since this mill worked summer and winter I thought we were all set.

We bought a truck and fixed it up as a school van and June began hauling the 14 kids from the mill to the Notikewin school.

I had always loved airplanes from my earliest reading of books, and watching Grant McConachie hauling fish off Cold Lake in 1931. Now here in Manning were two airplanes belonging to Raymond Bissette and Larry Clarahan. Once again my interest was revved up. I began to scheme and save my money to get into flying.

When Fischer's mill burnt down I again was reminded of homesteading at Keg River. Vincent Rosypal convinced me that working for others was not the best way to make a living, so in the summer of 1951 the family and I drove to the homestead. We borrowed a tent from Octave Parenteau, and I took a couple of weeks off from the mill job. Rosypal had cut 65 acres of bush for me and I had to pile it and start breaking. I made a deal with Bud Bouma to do some repiling.

The family decided they were never ever going to stay in a tent again! On weekends we came and picked roots and worked up the land, getting it ready for seeding in the spring.

The next year, 1952, I seeded wheat and it grew to a very heavy crop that was five feet tall, had long heads and yielded 36 bushels per acre. I had visions of becoming rich farming! We were struck with reality in 1953 when we had a very poor crop.

I worked on several sawmills, usually as a millwright, to keep the homestead going.

In the spring of 1955 we moved back to the homestead and planned never to work out again. I bought a welding machine and planned to do welding to make a few extra dollars.

Hank Thompson found me in 1956. There was a big fire northwest of Hay Lakes and he needed a cat skinner to take a crew out to work on the fire. What an experience we had!

After I got the crop planted, I sent $150 to a company in Winnipeg for a correspondence course that would prepare me to be a pilot. When I was finished with the course, the company would arrange for me to take flying lessons in Peace River. Johnny Johnson, the forest ranger, was a big help to me by typing my lessons, but before I finished the course the company closed down and vanished!

Next I saw in the paper that I could train as a pilot with Stan Reynolds of Wetaskiwin for $350. My friend Bert Tackaberry in Grimshaw helped me with all my "dumb" questions. He also gave me an armful of books to study and explained how the radio, the navigation system, and Morse code worked.

In February 1958 I enroled in flying lessons with Stan Reynolds. The instructors and maintenance engineers all worked with me and helped me understand how everything worked. My written exam was seven hours, then there was a flying test. I passed! When that license arrived in the mail I was ready to fly a Fleet Canuck.

Ken Fischer thought we should buy a plane that would be good for bush flying. My friends at Wetaskiwin thought we needed a Piper Super Cub. Ken wired down the money. I took some more lessons from a good pilot. He accompanied me to Peace River, then to Keg River. Then I took him back to Peace River.

I was studying map-reading and getting used to landing on my own strip. The family were all thrilled when I took them on short circle trips. I then made a long trip with Ken Fischer to High Level and along the Chinchaga River to look at timber. My friend Johnny Johnson would go up with me to check on fires. I could not charge anyone because it was a private plane.

I kept flying any chance I got and worked at

Ken Fischer's mill again. Then the mill was destroyed in a fire that caused a million dollars in damage. It was started by an electrical short. I got a job with Forestry, working on a Cat.

Ken Fischer began taking flying lessons so he could fly himself but he got in a wreck at the airstrip in Manning. When the plane was repaired we put on the skis and I helped Ken learn how to handle the plane in deep snow. There were many things to learn about flying in the bush, from landing on the river ice to dealing with cracked oil lines and getting fuel at remote spots.

When I left Forestry in 1961 I went to work running Cat for Hank Thompson again. He had a Super Cub and he got me to fly with him in High Level. I got plenty of bush experience flying out to forestry towers and various other places.

Once I went to rescue Ken Fischer who had had to land on a lake between his camp and Dixonville. Ken had no idea where he was, so I was on my own. We found the plane right away and all was O.K.

When there was no flying I ran a small welding shop in High Level. One day I got a piece of hot flux in my eye. The closest medical help was a nurse at Paddle Prairie. My eye got terribly painful after her treatment, so I rushed to Dr. Jackson in Keg River. She looked after it for me. It turned out very well and I will never forget what the doctor did for me. I passed my pilot's medical later with no trouble.

Now the oil business was beginning to pick up in the Rainbow Lake area. Small planes were being used much more. I was advised to go for my commercial license. This was another new field of courses. I spent the winter of 1965-66 getting my commercial license. I then began hauling people and freight all over the High Level – Fort Vermilion area. Emergency medical flights were also becoming important, with injuries and accidents from the oil patch, Fox Lake and John D'Or.

My wife didn't move to High Level because she had a job babysitting for the Marrs, who taught in Keg River, and our son Bradley was going to school in Keg River. She used to drive up to visit me some weekends. On one of those visits June fell and broke her leg. We took her to Manning hospital. They sent her on to Edmonton, her health began to fail and she remained in Edmonton. Bradley stayed with my sister in Edmonton to continue school.

Toward the end of April, Peace Air bought out Fort Vermilion Air Service and they wanted me to fly for them. Next I had word from Edmonton

that June was fading fast, so I went to stay with her. She passed away on May 13, 1969.

Bradley and I moved our trailer to Peace River and I began flying for Peace Air. The next thing, Peace Air needed someone to look after High Level base, so we moved back there.

Flying up there was never dull. All types of weather from blizzards to spring mud were encountered with many close calls.

Mike Papirny and Ranger Johnny Johnson with Mike's plane at Keg River, 1959.

Mike Papirny's medals.

(Editor's Note: Mike has been decorated for his heroic efforts. We recall one of those events for you.)

Mike Papirny was flying a Cessna at Trophy Lodge, providing guests with charter flights of the surrounding area. The drama began when the Peace Air base on Great Bear Lake received a message requesting a portable generator be brought to Douglas Bay, 90 miles away to help start a DeHavilland plane. The request was received at 11:30 P.M. Papirny and a mechanic arrived on site at 12:45 A.M. In the north it remains light most of the night.

By this time, storms were moving in rapidly, causing rough air, big swells and strong winds. Papirny made a skilful landing on the lake and taxied to shore, where the disabled plane was docked. The DeHavilland was finally ready for takeoff at 3:30 A.M. Now the wind velocity had increased and both aircraft were in danger of being bashed on the rocks.

Just when the DeHavilland started its takeoff run, two miles off shore a huge squall and driving rain struck and the left float crumpled. The plane began sinking on that side and the pilot was forced to jump into the 38° water and inflate his life jacket. The seven-foot swells soon swept him clear of the plane and he was submerged a number of times.

The passenger meantime had climbed out on the other float and the plane was upside down with only the floats were above water. After five minutes in the water, the pilot's legs and arms were numb. The two had no idea if Mike and the others had seen the accident or what they could do if they had.

Moments after Mike and the others saw what happened he decided to attempt a rescue...alone! With the other people holding the plane to steady it as he started the motor, he knew there would be a disaster if the wing or prop touched the water. The maneuvers took 30 minutes before Mike managed to reach the downed plane. When he arrived he could see the man on the float but only at the last minute did he see the pilot floating in the rough water. The swells were at least seven feet high and the troughs were just as deep.

It was dangerous to get too close because the Cessna could become entangled in the downed plane. It took a second pass to reach out to the pilot and catch his hand, which Mike then tied to the strut. Mike eased himself to the other end of the float and grabbed the pilot by the seat of the pants and heaved him onto the float, all 200 pounds plus of the man and his waterlogged clothing! The wind struck the fellow and he summoned up energy to climb aboard after one hour in the icy water!

Now Mike had to convince the passenger, who was still clinging to the wreck, that he too must jump into the water and come to the Cessna, even though he could not swim.

Mike could not reach him, so Mike turned the plane to maneuver the tail and water rudder as close to him as possible. Then Mike managed to grab him and drag him onto the float and into the cabin.

Their takeoff was uneventful even though the weather was worsening. They reached Trophy Lodge at 5:55 A.M. The men were rushed in and rubbed with warm bath towels until their circulation was restored.

This was an all-night ordeal that none of those involved will ever forget. "An act of raw heroism by a bush pilot in the true tradition of his rare breed" is one of the descriptions of Mike Papirny's feat of saving the two men.

Mike did receive several tributes and numerous medals for this incident and in recognition of a career of distinguished flying. These include:
- Life of Alberta Gold Medal
  Presented by Grant MacEwan, Lieutenant Governor of the Province of Alberta, January 5, 1971
- Bronze Medal from Carnegie Hero Fund U.S.A.
- Federal Star of Courage from the Queen
  Presented in Ottawa on June 22, 1973, by Governor General Michener
- The Royal Canadian Humane Society Honorary Testimonial August 6, 1971
- $4000 scholarship for Bradley from Atlantic Richfield Oil Company
- Pilot's watch, from Ron Austin, Atlantic Richfield Pilot
- Plaque from the Peace River Flying Club
- Plaque from Indian Affairs, High Level, Alberta
  Inscribed: "Our life was in your hands"
- Trophy from Pacific Western Airlines and Associates, 1966-1975
  High Level Medical Centre,
  Air Radio Manager and Staff,
  Airport Manager and Staff,
  Footner Lake Aviation and Staff
  --------O-------
I treasure the medals and awards I have received and I am glad that people appreciated my services.

All I plan on doing is to try, the good Lord permitting, to stay above ground as long as I can. See you at the fishing hole!

Parenteau Family
by Susie Parenteau Fischer
My grandparents were Joseph Parenteau and Julia (Delorme) Ross. They were married in Duck Lake, Saskatchewan, in 1892. Joseph is buried in Lewiston, Montana, and Julia is buried in Paddle Prairie. There were six children: Sam; Dave, and four girls – Marion, Elmer, Blanche and Clara.

Sam Peter (my father) Parenteau was born at Duck Lake, Saskatchewan on October 1, 1898. Flora Anderson was born at Onion Lake, Saskatchewan, in September 1897. They were married in Kitscoty, Alberta.

Sam Parenteau, age 12 and younger brother Dave, age 3.

Mrs. Flora Parenteau.

Those were horse-and-buggy days. Papa and Mom were living in Chinook, Montana, a year later, working on a ranch, when my brother Octave was born November 13, 1932. Uncle Oliver worked with Papa and they stayed there for four years.

Mom and Dad went back to Duck Lake, Saskatchewan, where Ambrose was born on February 4, 1925.

Papa went where the work was, cattle and sheep ranches mostly. Uncle Dave worked for Mr. Coon, one of the biggest ranchers in Montana. At shearing time, Papa worked with his brother Dave. Haying was a big operation as field after field was hay in the very rolling country and the summers were very hot.

On December 22, 1926, I was born at home on the Crow reservation, in Little Horn, Montana. I was baptized in the Roman Catholic Church on the tenth day of February, 1927, by the Reverend Charles L. Owens. Uncle Dave was my sponsor in the church of St. Francis Xavier Mission in St Xavier, Montana.

When I think of Mama, I remember how she was always there, at home, cooking, sewing, gardening, nursing and loving us. She wore cotton dresses, long stockings and moccasin slippers and always had an apron on. Her long black curly hair was combed and twirled from left hand to right hand, then up it would go making a huge bun at the back of her head, held in place with three long hairpins.

My earliest recollections are of her always being near, seemingly never out of my sight. When we travelled, Mama drove a team of horses hitched to a covered buggy that kept the sun off and the rain out. My bed was at Mama's feet on the floorboards. Mom's covered wagon was led by Papa's and Octave wrangled the loose horses and kept them with us. Sometimes they raced ahead but were never far away. Being anemic, I was raised on goats' milk. When the covered wagon was near, I would reach out my hands and say, "Tohtos sapay nata eke we minekewen" meaning I wanted a drink of milk. That was the only way I would pull through.

Ambrose rode in Papa's covered wagon. At times, I would see Ambrose stand up but soon he'd disappear – he was probably sleeping.

Papa would stop the team he was driving and we would tie up for dinner. Papa looked after his teams, and Octave would care for the loose horses. Mama would make dinner over the open fire. Everyone was hungry and ate heartily; that's eating out in the wide open space. Suppertime was the same, only the goats were taken down from the wagon and tethered out and the horses were unharnessed for the night. Tents were pitched and bedrolls spread out. As soon as the dishes were done, we hit the sack – the tent was our home.

Morning came and once more Mama was cooking and Papa was harnessing up so we could hit the dusty trail again. Mama kept a sharp eye.

out for bits of wood and cow dung that could be used for the next campfire. We travelled on and on from Great Falls, Montana, to Cold Lake, where Grandma and Grandpa Anderson lived. We did not see Grandpa Parenteau again. Grandma Marie Rose and Grandpa Charlie Anderson had not laid eyes on Ambrose or me before.

Now we lived in a one-room log cabin where Mama was always working. She was washing clothes by hand in the round washtub and on the scrub board or heating water on the wood stove in the 10-gallon boiler. Mama also made her own soap. The memory is vivid of her scrubbing on the board and hanging the clothes on the clothesline. It was darn hard work.

Mama always made me nap in the afternoon. One time when I woke up, Mom wasn't there. Grandma Anderson was there to look after us. I cried for my mom, so Grandma talked Cree to us and she called me "muchis skweesis" (a bad girl). Mama was gone to the hospital at Le Goff where she had an operation. After Leo was born, he also had complications, so they were quite a while getting back. Mama spent much time with this new baby, nursing, bathing, changing his diaper or moss bag. I really wanted Papa to give this baby Leo away. At least that was my version. Papa was no help. He said, "Look, this baby has white skin and you, my baby, have nice brown skin". (1929)

The next thing that comes to mind is my new playmate. I had to keep an eye on him because he could disappear so fast! He was so small back then!

Our Mama left us again but this time it wasn't so bad because I had a playmate. One heals and forgives easily when little. Mama came home with a baby girl, Ernestine, in 1931. Mama was really busy then. Papa was a good man, always working hard to bring home the bacon. There were more mouths to fill. It reminds me now of baby birds with their mouths open, waiting for food.

On a beautiful summer day, Leo and I were playing outside. We heard a horse sneeze to clear the dust from its nose, then there was the noise of trace chains and the rumble of the covered wagon. The children's voices rang out with joy and laughter – Grandma and Grandpa Anderson had come to visit! Grandpa pitched his tent a couple of hundred yards from our house by the white poplars in the horse pasture.

Papa was busy outside repairing the wagon box. He was in and out of the barn, probably feeding the horses or shovelling manure. We children ran into the cabin where Mama was making supper and cooking dark raisin pies in the old cook stove that had travelled all over with us. Mama said, "Out! Out!" so we went back out to play.

Papa called loudly to tell Octave to come right away. He was pointing southward. Then we saw this huge twister, funnel-shaped, reaching high up to the heavens. Wrangler Octave was riding Mexican, his horse, to get the milk cow. He and Papa put the cow and horse in the barn. They came dashing to the house just as the high wind reached us.

Through the south window we saw the twister dancing to and fro, cutting a wide swath heading for the cabin. Mama was still taking her raisin pies out of the oven. Our house went dark, Mama screamed, then with just a quick snap, the roof was gone. Rain, dust, mud, grass, and leaves all struck us. It only seems like yesterday – one never forgets such a frightful encounter!

Grandpa Anderson said, "Sam, the baby!" All eyes went to the corner of the room where Ernestine's hammock hung. The baby and the hammock were gone! Mama dashed to the door, but when her father blocked the way, Grandma fainted and fell in a heap on the floor. Grandpa told everyone to stay in the house but Octave and Ambrose ran out. I went out, too, around the house to the back and there was Ernestine still in her hammock hanging upright. Grandpa was six feet two inches and he reached up and put his arms around her. She was all right and didn't even cry. She just cooed at Grandpa. Mama dashed to Grandpa to see her baby. Grandpa reassured her, "The baby's just fine, she's just fine."

The storm was over, leaving us behind. We had supper and went to Grandpa's tent for a good night's sleep. Native people call Ernestine "wa paston" or "kakee wa pas sit" that tornado baby.

In July 1932 we attended the Lac St. Anne Pilgrimage with team and covered wagon and stayed in a tent at the pilgrimage site on the south shore of Lac St. Anne.

One day the covered wagon and the buggy were ready to roll. Grub box, trunks, tents, bedrolls and clothing were loaded. The wrangler rode Mexican again and Ambrose had a pony called Molly. We were northbound as it was harvest time. Papa worked for several farmers pitching bundles into the threshing machine. When the job was done we moved on to Lesser Slave Lake.

It was cold, late in the fall, when we arrived at Lesser Slave Lake. We set up camp on the outskirts of the village. The hill was covered with white spruce and Papa began felling spruce to build a cabin and a barn. It never took long to build. Papa worked quickly with the horses pulling the logs into place. Mama helped, too, by slinging mud to chink the logs, using her bare hands. The door and windows were in place when we moved in. It was heaven with a warm fire burning.

Octave and Ambrose were going to school and they brought a big hard tack (naval rations – biscuits) for each of us – Leo, Ernestine and me. The hard tack was hard to chew, but we loved them.

Papa had a job hauling railroad ties across the lake with "four up" (four horses pulling a sleigh). He left early in the morning and came home late. We rarely saw him.

Bocky Slew used to come to saw and chop wood for us. He also packed snow in a gunny sack and dumped it into the big water barrel. We used snow water for bathing and washing clothes.

Mama was gone again, but this time a special friend of hers stayed with us. Mrs. Cunningham took care of us. This time Mama brought home a baby boy, Eddie, born on November 20, 1932.

Papa started hauling in the new year. In March Papa had an accident. The sleigh reach broke; he got under the load and as he lifted with his legs, his hip came out of joint. We had to find a good doctor, so now we were southbound to Edmonton. We arrived at Dunvegan Stockyards at the first snowfall. Papa was hopping around on one leg, looking after the horses. We camped in a willow shelter for a short time until Papa rented a place, a house with an upstairs. We had lots of room in it.

Papa was in and out of hospital and had to use crutches. The doctors told him he had sciatica rheumatism. Johnny Flaman took Papa to a chiropractor, Dr. Watson. Papa left his crutches there and walked home. How thankful Mama was. As she embraced him, she was crying tears of joy.

We stayed on in Edmonton for five years. During the summer Papa worked on the Jasper-Banff highway with his horses pulling a fresno (a machine for moving dirt). In the winter Papa cut and hauled wood to the city. He was then reunited with his old friend, Mr. Klyne. They had ridden together in Montana. We visited the Klynes and their two sons, Gabe and Clarence, and daughter Helen a lot. We moved to the Calder community by the airport and we went to a Catholic school.

Papa came home with a tall black milk cow that he bought for 10 dollars from two young cowboys. The cow walked all the way from Dawson Creek, British Columbia. She had shoes all around

and was very willowy. I would be thin too, if I walked all those miles!

Mr. Klyne gave Leo the nickname Buckskin because he had blondish hair. He has been called Buckskin ever since. Tommy was born in Edmonton on October 27, 1935. His godmother, Helen Klyne, often babysat for Mama.

When school was out in 1936 we went out to where Papa was brushing for a farmer. He used a brush hook and axe pulling the bigger trees with a team and a chain. We lived in two tents. The milk cow gave milk for the whole family.

Robert was born in May, 1938. He is the youngest and was born in Rocky Mountain House. On the night of Halloween we were camped on the banks of the North Saskatchewan. It was a beautiful camping spot near the railroad bridge. We went trick-or-treating and had a lot of fun. We attended school at Buster Creek.

In the spring of 1940 we moved to Baptise River where Papa built a large log house. We used to have people stopping by all the time. There was a big kitchen and the boys slept there. Mama and Papa had their own cabin and the girls stayed with them. Papa built a big log barn for the stock and a chicken coop.

Wild game was plentiful, we picked lots of berries and Mama had a big garden. There was no end to her canning. At harvest time there was a wagon box full of white Netted Gem and red Norland potatoes. There was never a day that anyone in our family was hungry.

In the winter months Papa logged with the horse. As the boys got older, they walked in his footsteps, logging with horses, too.

We were having supper when Papa said the halfbreeds were now being given land in Keg River. We realized that Papa still longed for the north and had not given up hope of moving there.

In the early spring of 1943 Papa, Ambrose and Uncle Oliver left for Keg River. They logged near Paddle Prairie to make enough money for the move north. Finally as spring sprung, the three men arrived back. Ambrose was home a few days, then had to go to his war job. He worked for a big farmer, John Williams, at Ponoka.

Mama loved her home on Baptise River and never wanted to move again. Papa got his wish, however, and by July 1943 we were ready to go again. The haying equipment, wagon, buggy, and tents were gathered to be loaded onto boxcars on the railroad. Leo, Eddie and I came up in the boxcar. The stock was in another car. We arrived two days ahead of our parents. We unloaded the stock and led them down to the stockyards on the banks of the Peace River. Those animals were glad to get out of that mess, which was now four inches deep all over the car.

The Peace River and its banks were the most beautiful scenery anyone could wish for. It was July and hot and very dry. The passenger train rolled in two days later carrying Mama, Papa, Ernestine, Tommy, Robert, the Lariviere family (Marion, Louis and their children: Marion, Jimmy and Lawrence "Papoose"). Louis had ridden in the boxcar so he could care for his stock. We helped unload the stock and took them to where ours were grazing. This was my first encounter with the Lariviere family, Papa's relatives.

We waited and waited to board the *O'Sullivan Stigsen* boat to take us north. Finally the loading began and by evening we were ready to drift downstream on the Mighty Peace. Our parents made sure to tuck us in our bedrolls. We were up at dawn as the scenery was breathtaking and the winding river seemed endless.

The boat made many stops delivering goods and picking up freight. One other place the boat docked was where black tar was pouring out of the bank. The crew filled barrels with the stuff for some northern villages.

However, I got seasick from that endless rocking and swishing around. I lost my energy and I couldn't lift my head off my pillow. Papa carried me off the boat and when he let go I went down like a lifeless being. We were then at Tompkins Landing, so everything was unloaded.

This seemed to be the end of the world. Parenteau tents and Lariviere tents were pitched and we camped there for two weeks. Papa was the scout. He rode Slim, his black horse, to the mouth of the Keg and came back to tell us the saskatoon bushes were loaded with berries. Papa hitched the horses to the wagon and joined Mama, Robert, and me along with our pails and Aunt Marion and Cousin Marion as we headed for the saskatoons! What a rough ride, as there was no road!

Papa had a big campfire going as the day came to a close. We slept in the wagon box under the stars. The next day we filled up all our pails with berries and went back to Tompkins Landing.

One early morning Mama was worried. She said Papa was up at 3 A.M. and the horses were gone! He left carrying a riding bridle. Mama was very unhappy. She was afraid of bears and crazy people and was worried we might not see him again. I now know she loved him dearly. We were the only two awake. Mama went for a walk to say

her rosary, saying she wouldn't be gone long. I got a fire going so we could have coffee when she got back. It was a long day, Mama kept looking south saying, "The horses will always find their way back." It was a long day for me, too.

Finally late in the evening, we heard the rush of horse hoofs. They were back! Papa was riding bareback in the midst of the horses. We rejoiced! Papa was tired and hungry. He had walked a long way before catching them.

Again everything was loaded and we were ready to roll to the promised land of milk and honey – Paddle Prairie. We kids were all riding our own ponies now. When we reached our destination we were really surprised that the only way to get around was with horses. Oh, my goodness! My prayers were, "Lord Jesus, please get me out of this forsaken country!"

July 1943 was dry and very hot. Papa, Leo, and Eddie made hay south of the village, near Lucy and Henry Calliou's. Fall came early but there was no snow until November. Ambrose joined us and Mama was glad. When the snow did come, Papa and Ambrose logged with horses. Mama and the kids took care of the stock and cutting wood. It was a cold tough winter.

Ernestine and I hauled hay with a team and hayrack. We left early in the morning. It was -30°F. The trip was 11 miles one way. We loaded all the hay the rack would carry. Because it was cold, the load pulled very heavy. The sleigh runners made a terrible screech (like the brakes were on). Every mile or so the ponies had to stop and rest. I was worried and thought maybe we should leave the load and ride home.

Ernestine was curled up in the bedroll on the top of the load. A mile from home they stopped again and I tied up the lines and took off ahead on the run. I looked back several times and they were still standing there. When I ran in the kitchen door, Mama said, "I told you not to load them too heavy." It was now -40, and I tried to warm up. The horses finally made it home an hour later. I ran out to unhitch them and put them in the barn. My heart went out to this little team for the job they had done. I could have hugged and kissed them.

During the summer of 1944 we hayed on the flats down river from Carcajou. The tame hay was abundant and there was plenty of water. Once again the wagon was loaded up with tent, bedrolls, clothes, pot and pans and the grub box. Early in the morning we left for the flats. Papa was in the lead, driving Tom and Dick on the wagon. I was riding Papa's saddle horse, Slim. Leo was driving Babe and Beauty on the mower. Eddie was riding saddle horse, too.

Frances Poitras had a team and wagon. Crossing the Keg River they had to roughlock the wheels with chains as the hills were so steep. Frances and his son Elizer made hay with us.

We cut across country from Paddle Prairie to the hay flats. It was a long tiring day when we stopped. Papa motioned for me to come quickly. I climbed into the wagon and Papa pointed at two moose grazing down a very steep hill. He picked up his 30-30 and went quickly on his horse. He had told me to hang on to the lines. We were right in front of two pines and Papa was out of sight in no time. Then I heard three shots and the moose dropped like rags. Papa ran down the hill with his rifle and his hunting knife.

We had a beautiful spot to camp. All the cooking was done on the camp fire. Papa was worried when he said, "I'll have to get Mama to make dried meat," then his eyes caught mine and he added, "...unless you can do it?" I said, "Oh sure, Mama taught me, but, Papa you'll have to help me." His smiling eyes told me how proud he was of me. The tripods were set up – willow poles for hanging the meat.

The men and the boys worked long hours. They all had breakfast together but dinner and supper time came at various times. We slept in the tents while they made hay. Then they cut white spruce to build a cabin and a barn. Luckily they finished building these before the snow fell.

The cattle and horses were all moved to the flats for winter. The milk cows were left at home. Papa, Octave, Ambrose and Leo went logging for Clarence Williamson. Eddie was my right-hand man when it came to cleaning the barn or watering the stock. Once a day we would fetch a load of hay. When my hands got cold, Eddie would switch mittens with me, because his hands were always warm. Eddie was only 12 years old, but he worked hard no matter what the task. I was wishing we were back in Central Alberta. This cold country was surely for sinners, not for good people!

Evening came and we were on the crosscut saw, getting wood for our stoves. My thoughts were, "When I'm old enough I'll be gone like the Canada goose southbound!"

Every weekend a dance was held in different homes. Margaret and Peter Bottle, Grace and Joe McGillivray, Maryann and Roger Wanuch or Helen and Ed Wanuch offered their homes. New Year's was special, as the dancing was at Emile and Louis Houle's.

Our violinist was the great George Sinclair. George was a great friend of Papa's. Dad played the violin, too. Joe McGillivray was also a great violinist. There were many others who played guitar. Those days dances were dry, we had a lot of fun, and never did I see young people staggering and falling. We usually got home in time to start the fire in the stove, make breakfast and then do the chores!

In March 1945, Ambrose and I both went to work for John Williams. He was a mixed farmer with grain, cattle, pigs, and chickens. Everyone had a job. On the radio the news was always about the war. May 8, 1945, the German army capitulated. People were celebrating, telephones were ringing, the radio was playing *O Canada* and *There's a Boy Coming Home on Leave*. We got a letter from home telling us Octave and Bertha were getting married. Ambrose and I came home, there was snow, but the folks were glad to have us back.

I went to work for Eva Harrington at Keg River Cabins in February 1946. It was a fairly busy place, a truckstop with rooms and a cafe. Louis Jackson was the right-hand man. He hauled wood, cooked and took care of Eva's business. I was Louis' helper until one day he found out I could sling hash. He then had me cooking and I spent less time cleaning rooms. Mary Martineau worked there, too. Dave Lariviere was driving truck and we saw quite a bit of him. He had several 26-ounce bottles of whisky.

For the summer I went back to help Papa and Mama and in August I left again as I longed for the South. When I got, to Notikewin, I went to work for Violet and Jim Gordon at Faulkners sawmill. That is where I met Ken Fischer. We were married on August 23, 1948, in Paddle Prairie. The dance was held at Emile and Louis Houle's home.

Ken had a timber berth west of Notikewin where he, Oliver Auger, Peter Lawrence and Leo Parenteau built a log cabin. When I arrived, the mudding hadn't been done, Leo mixed the mud and straw and I did the mudding with bare hands, of course. We were too poor to buy rubber gloves. Oliver and Lawrence commenced to build their log cabins and barns. Leo and Ken felled a lot of spruce trees for stockpiling.

Metro and George Predy set up their sawmill. They contracted the sawing of the logs on shares. Bob McCracken financed the first mill for Fischer. Bob was a wonderful man. We all loved him. Often he came out to camp bringing mail. He usually had one of his kids along. Fischer and Leo Parenteau set up a Coutts sawmill. Fischer cut the first log and was the first sawyer. Leo was canter, but was sawing before long.

Fischer was millwright and boss. They logged with horses. Many sleigh loads of logs and heavy trees were rolled off at mill site with a loud rumble.

From the kitchen window, one could see most of the operation – the sawmill was 300 yards down the hill. The sawyer quickly lifts the logs into place. One pull on that long arm as he sets the width of the board, then comes the shrill piercing whine of the head saw and the motors revving up with the heavy pull.

Times were tough and in the cookhouse, nothing was easy; chores involved cooking on a wood stove, hauling wood, scrubbing clothes on a washboard, baking bread, and biscuits or bannock and making a huge pot of soup.

Next came the double shift (24 hours a day), more bunk houses and more men. This was all in place by the fall of 1950. The new sawyer, Mike Papirny, came, riding his motorcycle, from Faust. The road to the mill was badly rutted, so he pushed his "Indian motorcycle" into the bush and walked to camp.

Most of my family have worked for Fischer, including Bertha and Octave, Evelyn and Ambrose, Leo, Ernestine, Eddie and Robert. Camp One was nine miles off the MacKenzie Highway. When the timber berth was finished, the whole operation was moved west eight miles (17 miles to Fischerville).

The double shift continued, and they were long, hard hours. Many a good man came and

Susie Fischer and daughter Karen.

went. Many truckloads of lumber were hauled to Grimshaw and hand loaded into boxcars.

Karen Ann Fischer came into our lives on March 26, 1952. She was born in Edmonton. We came back to camp when she was six weeks old. Karen changed my lifestyle for the better. I spent less time in the kitchen.

Davey Samuel Fischer came into our lives in 1956. He was two years old, a blue-eyed blonde boy, and a handful.

The spring of 1957 plans changed for setting up the sawmill as Fischer had acquired another piece of timber, north of Notikewin. It was along the MacKenzie Highway, about two miles north of Williamson hill, east of Boucher's sawmill. Fischer started to set up camp there.

In the fall of 1957 the sawmill began to turn its head saw, rollers, chains and carriage. Bob Woods was one of the sawyers and Leo Parenteau was the other. We ran a double shift and we had good men – they just don't come any better. Eddie Parenteau and Al Opsahl were the millwrights. The cook house was open 24 hours a day, all week long. Delphine Parenteau was the day shift cook and Rita Cardinal (Woods) took the night shift.

In January of the new year (1958) I lost my best friend, Papa. In my sorrow, not once did I think of how others were hurting, only of Mom. My heart went out to her, then I began spending more time with her. It was around that time when those thieves tied up Harry Bowe and robbed him of what little money was in the post office at Keg River.

Tommy Parenteau and Walter Martinuk drove the lumber trucks for the company. Robert Schmidt had a fleet and hauled lumber by the foot or thousand. Ambrose Parenteau was the first trucker to haul for Fischer. In March 1958 the berth was cleaned up and we moved back west of Notikewin, 51 miles off the highway, to Camp Three.

This was the biggest operation Fischer owned. Many families moved out to Camp Three. We had men from all over North America, even a few criminals. While working with them, feeding them and handing them a pay cheque, I never feared them. My heart went out to them, especially when one said, "You are the first woman I have talked to in 18 years." It made me count my blessings.

In January 1959 Craig Lee was born. He was a blessing! Now I had more time in the home to spend with my three children.

At this time I give recognition to the people who worked hard in the lumber business: the

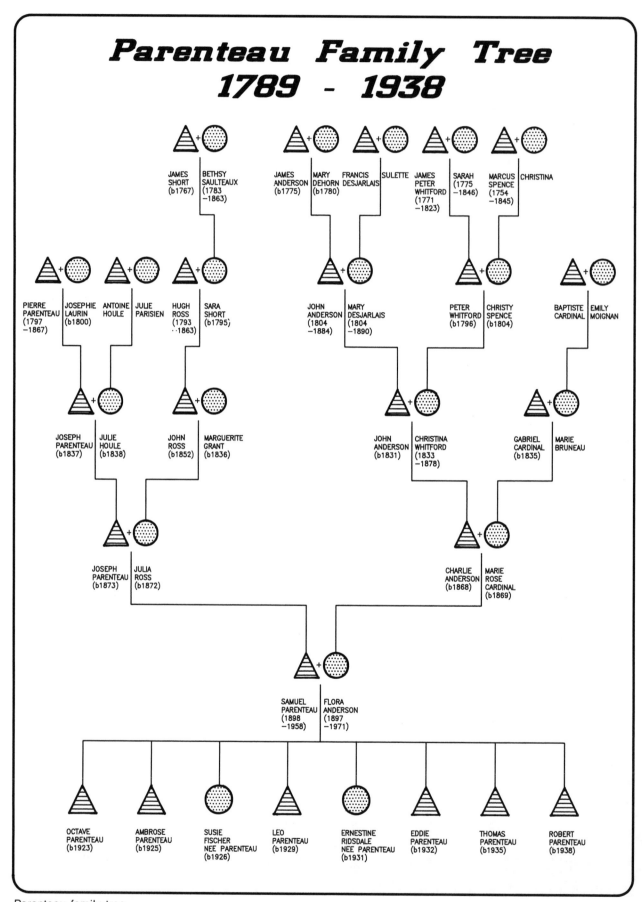

Parenteau Family Tree
1789 — 1938

JAMES SHORT (b1767)
BETHSY SAULTEAUX (1783 −1863)

JAMES ANDERSON (b1775)
MARY DEHORN (b1780)

FRANCIS DESJARLAIS
SULETTE

JAMES PETER WHITFORD (1771 −1823)
SARAH (1775 −1846)

MARCUS SPENCE (1754 −1845)
CHRISTINA

PIERRE PARENTEAU (1797 −1867)
JOSEPHIE LAURIN (b1800)

ANTOINE HOULE
JULIE PARISIEN

HUGH ROSS (1793 ··1863)
SARA SHORT (b1795)

JOHN ANDERSON (1804 −1884)
MARY DESJARLAIS (1804 −1890)

PETER WHITFORD (b1796)
CHRISTY SPENCE (b1804)

BAPTISTE CARDINAL
EMILY MOIGNAN

JOSEPH PARENTEAU (b1837)
JULIE HOULE (b1838)

JOHN ROSS (b1852)
MARGUERITE GRANT (b1836)

JOHN ANDERSON (b1831)
CHRISTINA WHITFORD (1833 −1878)

GABRIEL CARDINAL (b1835)
MARIE BRUNEAU

JOSEPH PARENTEAU (b1873)
JULIA ROSS (b1872)

CHARLIE ANDERSON (b1868)
MARIE ROSE CARDINAL (b1869)

SAMUEL PARENTEAU (1898 −1958)
FLORA ANDERSON (1897 −1971)

OCTAVE PARENTEAU (b1923)

AMBROSE PARENTEAU (b1925)

SUSIE FISCHER NEE PARENTEAU (b1926)

LEO PARENTEAU (b1929)

ERNESTINE RIDSDALE NEE PARENTEAU (b1931)

EDDIE PARENTEAU (b1932)

THOMAS PARENTEAU (b1935)

ROBERT PARENTEAU (b1938)

Parenteau family tree.

Parenteaus of Paddle Prairie, Harry Smith of Dixonville, Alfred Snyder, the guy who developed the gang saw, and Bob McCracken, who gave us a generous loan when we started!

In July 1970 Karen married Fred Michalchuk of Keg River in Manning. In August of that year I moved to Paddle Prairie with Craig who was 11 years old. We got land halfway between Keg River Cabins and the Paddle Prairie village so we could farm. I set up a little grocery store where people could purchase cigarettes, pop, and groceries. We worked hard. Craig ran the tractor or worked in the store.

When Craig was 14 he bought a black heifer from Bill Tkachuk that was the start of his herd. In 1975 he bought three Hereford cows from Ralph Ressler of Manning. The cows were wild and when we tried to get near them, over the fence they would go! Now in 1994 we have an electric fence and the cows are fairly gentle.

The family are all away from home and I'm on my own. Thankfully Karen and Craig are near. I also have my grandchildren to keep me busy.

Just a Thought
by Leo Parenteau
(Submitted by Sarah Price)

Paddle Prairie's pulled out so I am told.
To protect our land from ever being sold.
Federation is mad Government, too.
Until we get a better deal, there is nothing
    they can do.

Three hundred and ten million is the name of
    the game.
But money is nothing when our land is in
    vain.
General Council will take and take they will.
And leave us settlers holding the bill.

With money all gone, no money in hand.
General council will take and take they will.
No matter how much we fuss and fight.
General council will laugh and say that's all
    right.

With trapping, fishing and hunting rights
    gone.
We sit in our chairs and wonder where we
    went wrong.
With hope all gone and deep in pain.
We will sit on some road allowance in the
    falling rain.

It is now in the fall and getting very cold.
We feel so bad about our land that was sold.
At this point in time, things come to a stall
As we sit here and wonder why our forefathers
    did this at all.

Ambrose Parenteau
by Ambrose Parenteau

I was born on February 4, 1925, in Meadow Lake, Saskatchewan.

I first came to Paddle Prairie from Rocky Mountain House in the winter of 1943 to work with my dad, Sam Parenteau. We logged in Paddle Prairie for the winter to pay for the move my family was planning.

Later, in the summer of 1943, my parents (Sam and Flora Parenteau) and the rest of the family moved to Paddle Prairie. They came by train from Rocky Mountain House to Peace River, then by barge to Tompkins Landing. From there they travelled into Paddle by horse and wagon.

I came later in the fall by train from Lacombe to Grimshaw. Then I caught a ride to Notikewin and was supposed to catch a ride from there to Keg River with Frank and Louis Jackson, but somehow I missed them, so I went to the store and bought some food to make sandwiches. I walked from Hotchkiss to North Keg, where I caught the Jacksons. One truck was stuck in the Keg River. Then Uncle Louie Lariviere came to buy groceries and I went to Paddle Prairie with him. We lived northeast of today's location of the Paddle Prairie Store.

Our family had six boys and two girls. My father was born in 1898 and passed away in the winter of 1958. My mother Flora (Anderson) was born in 1897 and passed away in 1971.

From 1939 to 1945 I worked in the summer for John Williams in Ponoka. I remember making $40 a month and sending $30 home to my parents! Mom and Dad always had cows, chickens, pigs, horses and a garden.

I bought my first truck (a second-hand International) in the fall of 1945. I lived in Paddle Prairie permanently then. In the fall I ran a double shift hauling grain to Grimshaw for different farmers. I drove night shift and Jimmy Lariviere drove the day shift. In the winter I hauled lumber for Clarence Williams at South Keg. In 1947 I bought my first NEW truck, a GMC. After that there were several more trucks purchased.

On July 19, 1950, I married Evelyn Price in Manning. She had a set of twins, Daryl and Derwin. I adopted these boys and over the next

Ambrose Parenteau family. Back, L-R: Derwin, Calvin, Daryl, Heather, Wendy. Front, L-R: Lawrence, Trevor, Ambrose, Evelyn, Linda, Corrine.

11 years we had seven children together: Calvin, Wendy, Heather, Lawrence, Linda, Corrine and Trevor.

After Evelyn and I married, we lived for the next six months in the Paddle Prairie Settlement. Then I built our own house on NW 35-102-23-W5. We lived there in the summer and worked at Fischer's sawmill, west of Notikewin, in the winter from 1948 to 1950. I hauled lumber and Evelyn worked in the office at the mill.

The summer of 1955 we moved to west Peace River and were there approximately two and one-half years until we moved back to Paddle Prairie in the spring of 1958. We moved the house from the farm to SW-13-103-23-W5 in 1960. The land was previously owned by Lawrence Lariviere. Here we built onto the house, as our family was growing.

Our door was never locked. One night we heard the lid on the wood stove bang! When I got up to check what was happening, I found a trucker from Fort Vermilion in my kitchen, stoking the stove so he could warm up!

Evelyn opened the Rite Spot Cafe in the early 60's and operated it for about two years. It later became the Rite Spot Confectionery. She also ran the Coachways Bus Depot and the post office. I had the BA gas station and garage and I continued to truck and farm. We also had a sawmill from 1964 to 1967. Our children and hired help were kept as busy as we were!

During our years in Paddle Prairie we required many hired hands. Although it is impossible to mention everyone's name, these are some of the people who worked for us: Sam and Rose Johnston, Agnes Strong, Marjorie Bellerose, Vera Bellerose, Lyle Martineau, Flavian Houle, Jimmy Lariviere, Clifford McGillivray, George Auger, Milton Metz, Lawrence Holliwass, Dick Strong and Henry Mitchell.

When the younger children were small, Father John used to come to our place just before the mail would arrive, and he would play with them and tell them stories while Evelyn sorted the mail. He was a wonderful person and a good babysitter!

In 1959 and 1960 while Jock Shannon and his crew were rebuilding the MacKenzie Highway, they boarded at our place. Evelyn then cooked for 40 men as well as doing all her other jobs.

In the winter of 1964 a Coachways bus ran into the front of our house as it pulled into the yard. The yard was very slippery and the bus driver, Clyde Berryman, could not stop the bus. Luckily no one was hurt, but Corrine and Trevor, who were only five and three at the time, witnessed it all from the living room window!

In 1966 and '67 Evelyn cooked for another crew of 40 men. Belcourt Construction was constructing the power line from Keg River to High Level and Rainbow Lake. By this time Wendy and Heather were old enough to help and they took turns getting up at five in the morning to help their mother cook breakfast.

First truck owned by Ambrose, hauling timbers to Hay River.

Over the years we were able to take holiday trips with the children, which included trips to Smith, Edmonton, Montana, part of British Columbia and a stop at the Calgary Stampede in 1966.

Between 1968 and 1972 I took on another job driving a bus. I also hauled lumber to High Level from the Paddle Prairie sawmill.

Evelyn suffered from high blood pressure for many years. After we raised nine children and saw one daughter, Wendy, get married, Evelyn passed away on February 1, 1973. She had suffered five strokes in four days. She is laid to rest in the Keg River cemetery.

During our years in Paddle Prairie, Evelyn served on the colony council, the Alberta Metis Association and the school board. We both belonged to the Paddle Prairie Rodeo Association. Daryl, Derwin, Calvin, Lawrence and Corrine all tried their hands at riding broncs and steers. Later on, Trevor got into the rodeo spirit by riding bulls and being a bullfighter. Today he is still involved in rodeo by outriding for his cousin, Glen Ridsdale's, chuckwagon.

Our place was a real stopping place because we had the bus depot, post office, cafe and later the confectionery, service station and garage. We had many good times at Paddle and Keg River ball tournaments, sports days, dances and Sunday picnics.

On October 28, 1978, I married Elsie (Smith) Ressler from Manning. Because she had no children, she was quite excited about becoming a stepmother, mother-in-law and grandmother all in one day!!

We bought a house in Peace River and I continued in the trucking business. In the fall of 1980 I bought a Western Star truck and hauled logs for Boucher Brothers for four winters. Elsie was my bookkeeper and helped run the business. Summers were spent hauling gravel and asphalt for paving all over the province of Alberta. One year we finished paving at Strathmore on the Trans-Canada Highway on November 8.

Ambrose Parenteau hauling logs to Boucher's Mill, 1980.

Through the years we have enjoyed trips to Montana, Mexico, Scotland (twice) and England.

August 1st, 1982, we bought 10 acres west of Peace River in the Weberville area. I continued trucking until 1990, when I retired after 45 years in the trucking business.

Since retiring we have done some more travelling which has included two winters in Arizona and California. We have two horses, Sam and Paul, and an American Eskimo dog named Prince.

My children are:
Daryl m. Christine Elter – February 17, 1979
Derwin m. Valerie Parenteau – September 4, 1976 (divorced); m. Lily Smith – April 10, 1993
Calvin m. Beverly Hominiuk – July 6, 1973
Wendy m. Joe Patton – October 9, 1971
Heather m. Leonard Scott – August 11, 1979
Lawrence m. Doris Belanger – May 21, 1983
Linda m. Glen Paul – June 9, 1979
Corrine m. Wes Hoover – December 18, 1977 (divorced); m. Rick Card – June 29, 1985
Trevor – Not married yet!
We have 18 grandchildren and are awaiting the great-grandchildren, hopefully they won't arrive too soon!!

Heather Parenteau
by Heather (Parenteau) Scott

I was born on June 13 1955, in Manning, the second daughter to Ambrose and Evelyn Parenteau. My family lived in Paddle Prairie for a short time after I was born, but then moved to Peace River for approximately two and one-half years. We moved back to Paddle Prairie in the spring of 1958 when I was three years old.

I went to school in Paddle Prairie from grades one to six. My first teacher was Mr. Borley, followed by Miss Mott, Miss Kitchen, Mr. Jenkins and Mr. Davies. Mr. Jenkins used to bring his guitar to school and we would sing. What a treat that was!! He also had a team of husky dogs and after school hours or on weekends he would drive them. Sometimes we were lucky enough to get a ride.

Mr. Davies taught us to square dance in grade six. Because we didn't have a gymnasium, we used to dance in the hallway. This was a really nice change from having to do school work!

I went to Dr. Mary Jackson School in Keg River for grade seven and eight. My teachers there were Mr. and Mrs. Chorney.

The highlights for any school year for me were the Christmas concert and the track meet. The whole community would come out to watch these events. Joe McGillivray (Doggie) made an excellent Santa Claus! After the Christmas concert all the children would receive a gift from Santa.

My parents were very hardworking people. When we were very young they always had hired help, but as we grew we had to learn to help as well. I remember when I was in grade five and my sister Wendy was in grade six, we had to take turns getting up at 5 A.M. to help Mom cook breakfast for 40 men. They were the Belcourt construction crew who put the power line in from Keg River to High Level and Rainbow Lake.

Although there was lots of work to be done, we had time for entertainment, too. Some of that consisted of skating on the dugout, swimming in the dugout, playing ball, going to catechism, listening to hockey games on the radio, and in later years going to rodeos. In the 1960's we got a television set. What a miracle!

My mother was excellent at organizing parties for us. Our door was always open and we seemed to have extra people at our house all the time. With three older brothers, there were always kids around visiting and Mom and Dad treated them like their own. I remember the whist drives we used to have at the different houses.

Christmas was always real special at our house. Mom baked for weeks beforehand. Every year we would have a sleep before going to midnight Mass. After Mass we always went to Grandma Parenteau's for a big dinner. Then by the time we got home, Santa had usually been to our house already.

I remember a couple of years when Santa was still on the roof as we were driving in the yard! We thought he had just climbed out of the chimney! We found out in later years that Santa was my older brother, Derwin.

I have many fond memories of my days in Paddle Prairie. I enjoyed school and growing up there.

Although I went to Peace River for grades nine to 12 (1969 – 1973), I would go home some weekends and in the summer. In the summer of 1970, I worked at the colony office in Paddle Prairie for Terry Petersen. The summer of 1971 I worked in the post office for my mother while she and my dad took the younger children on a holiday to Montana.

Unfortunately, on February 1, 1973, my mother passed away after suffering five strokes in four days. Prior to her passing away she suffered with high blood pressure for 11 years. I miss her dearly to this day, even though we have a wonderful stepmother, Elsie.

I graduated in 1973. My first job was with Horne and Pitfield Foods in Peace River. I worked on the order desk there for two months.

Then I went to work at CKYL radio. That fall, I bought my first car, a 1973 Ford Pinto, for $3500. I worked as a secretary at CKYL for four years. I really liked that job and met many interesting people.

In 1977 I went to work for Murray Nelson at Gateway Optical. This was also an interesting job. I was there for two years.

On August 11, 1979, I married Leonard Scott from Nampa, Alberta. He worked on a drilling rig off the shore of Scotland, so off I went to Scotland two weeks after our wedding.

I missed my family but some of them did come to visit. My father, Ambrose, and stepmother, Elsie, visited twice and two sisters, Linda and Corrine, visited at different times. We also came home quite often and it was wonderful to see all our family and friends.

We lived in a small town called Ellon, just 16 miles north of Aberdeen. Life in Scotland was very good to us. We made many friends in the seven years we lived there.

We were also blessed with two wonderful boys. James William arrived on Wednesday, February 4, 1981. He shares Grandpa Parteneau's birthday and Grandpa Scott's name. Kelly Ryan was born on Saturday, October 16, 1882. He doesn't share his birthdate with anyone – he picked his own!

Scott family, Leonard and Heather with sons James and Kelly, 1990.

Leonard worked for Santa Fe Drilling in the North Sea until July 1986, when the oil business went downhill. Many people were shipped home at that time. We moved to Peace River for two years, then on September 1, 1988, we moved to Beaumont, Alberta.

Leonard has been working for Santa Fe Drilling again since November 1987. He works a 28-days-in and 28-days-out schedule in Nigeria. Our boys are now 11 and 12. James is a basketball player and Kelly is a hockey player. I am a domestic engineer and do volunteer work at the boys' schools. I enjoy what I do and we all love living in Beaumont.

Linda Parenteau
by Linda (Parenteau) Paul

I was born in Peace River on October 21, 1958, to Ambrose and Evelyn Parenteau, the seventh child in a family of nine. I was raised in Paddle Prairie until the age of 14. I attended grade one at the Paddle Prairie School and the following year my parents sent us to Dr. Mary Jackson School in Keg River, where I attended grades two through eight.

While I was in school there, my teacher, Miss Margaret Bolton, formed the First Girl Guide Company of Keg River and I became a member. I thoroughly enjoyed being a Girl Guide. I specifically remember our trip to Edmonton, which included a tour of the legislature buildings, swimming in an indoor pool for the first time and eating pizza for the first time! It was quite an exciting trip for me and one I will never forget.

The last couple of days of our trip, I got really sick and had to stay in bed while the other girls went on the planned outings. I was so sick that I didn't even care! I had to ride in the back seat of Miss Cherpanick's car (she was one of our chaperons) on the way home as I had to lie down.

We attended church most Sundays at Christ the King Catholic Church in Paddle Prairie. We often had the Father over for dinner after Mass on Sundays.

When I turned 14 and was going into grade nine, my family purchased a mobile home and set it up in Terrace Park Trailer Court in Peace River because there were three of us out going to school by this time. We lived in Peace River during the week and went back home on the weekends or our Dad would come to Peace River.

My mother passed away that winter on February 1, 1973. This was very tragic for all of us and a big adjustment as Dad was busy driving

The Parenteau girls, Corrine, Linda, Heather and Wendy, 1984.

truck. He was with us as often as he could be, and while he was away, our older brother Calvin was our guardian. We all had to pitch in with Corrine and I doing the majority of the cooking and cleaning.

I finished high school without a hitch in January, 1976, after two and one-half years. I got a job with the Peace River School Division in February and a month later moved into my own apartment. I worked there for three years and had a few other jobs before joining Northwestern Utilities Ltd. in July 1980. I still work for the company today.

I married Glen Paul from Peace River on June 9, 1979. We have two lovely children: Deiter, born

Linda and Glen Paul with son Deiter and daughter Nadine, 1992.

245

on Mother's Day, May 13, 1984, and Nadine, born on New Year's Day, 1987.

We built our home in 1983 on an acreage (3.3 acres) approximately seven miles north of Grimshaw. We have been here for 10 years and love the country. There is a golf course about one-half mile from our home which we use a lot because we all golf in the summer.

The kids both swim and play ball and in the winter Deiter plays hockey (Glen coaches his team) and Nadine figure skates. The kids attend school at Kennedy Elementary in Grimshaw and Glen works for the Town of Grimshaw. We are blessed with a good life and family and friends who love us.

Harold and Ellen Patterson
by Pete Ristesund

My sister Ellen and her husband saw Keg River for the first time in the spring of 1948. They had travelled with us to help us move to our new homestead.

Harold (Pat to everyone) had just been discharged from the United States Army. He had spent time on various islands in the Pacific fighting the Japanese.

Keg River was such a peaceful place, he decided they should live here, too. They bought Glady Harrington's farm. During the next twenty years Pat and his "Sug" grew grain and hay and raised cattle, pigs, and chickens. They milked cows and

my sister made many pounds of butter which she sold locally.

The Patterson farm was a favorite with local children. The small hills in their driveway gave the feeling of a roller coaster ride and were always fun but the treats upon reaching the farm were even more wonderful. It was a pity Pat and Ellen didn't have children.

Gathering at Patterson's farm, Mrs. Harrington, Manilla and Lonnie Root, Harold and Ellen Patterson, Glady Harrington and Bobby Jackson in doorway.

They sold their farm, held an auction sale to sell all the farm equipment and moved to Salmon Arm, British Columbia, where they again raised cattle. They later moved on to Vernon. Ellen died in Vancouver during heart surgery on February 14, 1980. Pat died several years later. They are both buried in the Pleasant Valley Cemetery in Vernon.

Annie and Mike Michalchuk, Ellen and Harold Patterson in Vernon, B.C.

Opportunity is missed by most people because it is dressed in overalls and looks like work. *Thomas Edison*

Pat Patterson (Harold) with his prize calf.

Clement Paul
by Clement Paul

(Editor's Note: Clement Paul told this story to Pat O'Connor in 1950; it was then left with Mrs. Emma McDonald. It was later found among her papers.)

In October, 1894, I arrived at the mouth of the Keg as we rafted down the Peace River. Here we met Mr. Whitebear and Pat Wesley with three black bears in a dugout. They tasted good. At this time I thought I would never go back home.

My home had been in Clarence Creek, Russell County, about 28 miles from Ottawa. I was born in January, 1863, of French Canadian origin.

Before I came to the Peace area, I worked for the Canadian Pacific Railway from North Bay to Sault Ste. Marie from 1880 to 1881. Then I spiked on the railroad from Red Deer to Edmonton and saw Donald Ross drive the Golden Spike.

During the first winter I spent in Carcajou, I was hired by old trader, Bernard Lariviere, to go to Grouard with furs for Revillon. On the return trip I travelled with Father Falher to Peace River. Oliver Courtrielle and I then came down the river on a big raft, I went ashore at the mouth of the Keg with 1200 pounds of grub and one dog.

In 1898 at Keg River I met Hanna Eliza Chalifoux and we were married by Father Joussard. We lived in Keg River for twelve years. The Hudson's Bay Company hired me to build a trading post house, store and barn of hewn logs. (Editor's Note: The store building is still in use and is 97 years old!) Later, Revillon Freres hired me to build their post.

During these years there were no roads – just pack trails. Anything required was brought in by boat and then on horseback from the river. I brought in a three-foot Massey Harris mower, a rake, harrows, a 12-inch breaker, wagon wheels to build a wagon, four cows and calves and three horses! I raised barley, oats, wheat and potatoes, all first-quality. They couldn't be beat!

When asked about interesting incidents, I could fill a book! Several incidents of special interest were about wolves. George Carter was my partner and he took pictures. A female wolf with five young ones sneaked up on me at the foot of the Caribou Mountains. I shot her at ten feet, then the male pounced on me, I shot him at six feet. We took the five pups home in a pack sack.

Another time I killed 17 wolves one mile east of the Keg River Post after they killed a horse I had bought from another old-timer, Thomas Allen

Brick. I poisoned these wolves and had to walk backwards to protect myself from the pack.

When we left Keg we moved to Fort Vermilion where we had the rest of our children. In all we had 12: Louis, David, Henry, Patrice, Medesle, Margaret, John, Flora, Napoleon, Elizabeth, Agnes and Nora. We ran sawmills for many years.

(Clement died in 1954 and his Eliza died six months later in Fort Vermilion. They were widely known and respected.)

Theadora May Paul
by Anne Vos

Miss Paul came to Keg River from London, England. In October, 1949, she took the train into Peace River, the bus from Peace River to Manning and then caught a ride with the mail car to Keg River. Seven miles out of Keg River the car got stuck in the muskeg. The driver had to walk three and a half miles before he found a farmer who could bring his tractor to pull them out. It was three hours before they were safely on the road again!

Miss Paul came to Keg River to teach school. It was a school of 40 children of many ethnic backgrounds in grades one through eight.

She started teaching on November 1st, 1949. The school was heated by a large round four-foot wood heater that had to be filled many times a day, including the evenings and late at night on very cold nights. Part of a teacher's job was to keep the school warm!

She wrote in an early letter "When harvesting is over, a farmer will saw me a load of logs, but until then I have to chop what wood I can get. Fortunately I learnt how to chop at Girl Guide camps!" She also had to learn about kerosene lamps as they provided the light for the school.

She quickly started hours for a library at the school. Young adults were encouraged to come in and look through magazines and books at the school on Friday evenings and the children were invited on Saturday mornings. Miss Paul had asked her friends in Canada and England to send her any magazines they were finished with.

The students did very well, winning many provincial prizes. In 1950 they won $65.00 for an Alberta Tuberculosis essay contest. They won the same prize again in 1951. In 1952, Larone "Bigman" Ferguson won $50 in a poster contest sponsored for the three western provinces by the Canadian Forestry Association. There were a total of 947 entries in this contest, so he didn't win easily!

Farewell gathering for Miss Paul, 1954.

Miss Paul taught a well-rounded curriculum with students doing crafts as well as learning all the basics. This teaching enabled them to cope well with grade nine when they had to leave Keg River.

The students travelled to school by saddle horse, horse and cutter, horse and cart or by walking. Many travelled several miles at extreme temperatures day after day. Yet the records show that the attendance rate was around 90% each year she taught in Keg River. She made the lessons so interesting that the kids didn't want to miss a day!

In the summer of 1950, Miss Paul went to Edmonton to take a summer school course. She returned in the fall to teach, but the school was closed from September 5th to 8th because of a polio outbreak in the district. In the remaining four years she was in Keg River the school was closed again in 1953 for nine days because of an epidemic in the district.

In 1955, Miss Paul became ill and was diagnosed with a cancerous brain tumor. The operation left her unable to teach and she spent the rest of her life in Central Park Lodge in Edmonton. She passed away in July, 1990.

Carl and Barbara Pawlowich
by Margaret and Bill Pawlowich

In the village of Wielka Glusoza, Poland, Carl and Barbara lived on a small acreage. Their family lived with them, daughters Annie, Tina and Mary; sons Bill, Adam and Steve; and Annie's husband, Mike Michalchuk. Their eldest son John had emigrated to Canada a decade earlier with his wife Tillie. Second son Mike was married and had a family on a nearby property.

The Pawlowich and Michalchuk families decided the acreage was too small for the growing

Miss Paul, 1986.

Karl Pawlowich family, around 1940.

248

clan. War was also threatening, so in May, 1939, plans were made to join John in that far-off country called Canada.

When all the papers were finally ready the Michalchuks were able to leave first. Then the family was allowed to go to Warsaw and by boat to England. There they boarded the vessel called the *Montrose* to cross the Atlantic Ocean. On September 2, 1939, they arrived at the Port of Quebec. They crossed the country by train and arrived in Peace River, where they took a barge down river to Tompkins Landing. Then finally came the hardest part – a wagon ride of about 50 miles to John's farm at Keg River. Once in Canada the family found that their Polish money was worthless due to the fall of Poland to the Germans.

Times were tough because everything was different here. Barbara was very homesick and lonesome for her friends. She didn't speak English, so she couldn't talk to neighbors here. Carl built a small house for them on their homestead but Barbara passed away in 1942.

With a milk cow, pigs, chickens and horses, the rest of the family survived. The children went to school to learn English but part of the time the school had to be closed because no teacher could be hired. Later, Steve and Mary went to school in North Star and Notikewin. Bill and Steve found work in sawmills.

Tina married Norman Onstine. Adam married Barbara Shaw. Mary married Steve Kelemen in November, 1947. Bill married Margaret Greschner in December, 1948. Steve married Linda Sacilowski in October, 1967.

Carl passed away in 1955 at the age of 73 years.

John Pawlowich and family
by Margaret Pawlowich

John was born in Poland on February 5th, 1909. He came to Canada in 1928 with his wife Tillie, somehow making his way to Keg River where he took up a homestead NE-34-101-24-W5.

The only way to make any money was to go out to work which meant walking overland to Peace River to farms where harvesting help was needed – a distance one way of at least 145 miles. Pay was your grub plus one dollar a day.

John talked of contracting for the clearing of land, which he did by hand with an axe in the Nampa and Falher areas. John was a real pioneer of the challenging isolated north. He saw many changes as the raw virgin land was turned into the rich farmland and oil patch of today.

When the highway right-of-way was cleared, John bought a truck and began hauling anything from livestock to grain into Grimshaw. On the return trips he brought freight for the Hudson's Bay, Keg River Trading or a new bull or boar for

Tina and Norman Onstine.

John and Rose Pawlowich.

the neighbors. Sometimes he even brought a keg of beer for the Saturday night parties!

John's family joined him from Poland in 1939. Rose Grant of Manning married John in October, 1953. They had a family of five sons: Johnny, Louis, Greg, Glen, Joe; and two daughters: Elizabeth and Alice.

Johnny married Mona. They have two girls: Angela and Carmela. Louis married Bonnie Millar. They have two girls: Luticia and Kathleen. Elizabeth married Tom Lozanski. They have three children: Kari, Jessica and Lavanda. Alice married Fred Shultz. They have all divorced. John passed away on April 4, 1982. Rose is living in Cereal, Alberta.

Luticia Pawlowich, aged 10, granddaughter.

Kathleen Pawlowich, aged 9, granddaughter.

Adam and Barbara Pawlowich
by Barbara Pawlowich

Adam came to Keg River with his family from Poland in 1939 to join his brother John, who was already living in Keg River. I was born in Peace River and lived in Manning and Notikewin before I married Adam in 1947. After we were married we lived with Adam's father Carl on the farm where we still live.

Our children are:
Rosemarie, married to Eli Feledichuk. Their children are: Barry (wife Donna, daughter Emily), Zoe (husband Freeman Iwasiuk, daughters – Risa and Dana), Terry, and Eli Jr. Margarit, married to Ginter Schnieder. Their children are: Rhonda (daughter Brenna) and Rod. Carl married Colleen and their son is Josh. Carl died in 1982. Michael married Cheryl and has five children: Rachelle, Ashley, Nicholas, Matthew and Stacy. William married Shelly and has three children: Katheryn, Robin, and Leanne. Mina married Ken Shupenia and has two daughters: Nicole and Kimberly. When Rosemarie, Margarit and Carl started

Adam and Barbara Pawlowich.

school, they had to walk or catch a ride with their cousins in a wagon or sleigh. Later Mr. Schwindt was the first bus driver.

One night when we lived on the homestead and I was alone, I heard the strangest noise. Cows make the funniest slurping noise when they drink out of a washtub! Romanchuk's cows had come to visit and were drinking out of a tub I had by the house!

There was the time I was going to visit at the Rudy's with the team and sleigh. Something spooked the horses, I fell out and they somehow managed to run over me. I was not seriously injured.

Adam Pawlowich Family. Mina, Margaret, Rosemarie, Carl, Michael, William, Barbara and Adam in front.

Adam and I are taking life a little easier now. Michael and William farm with us, so we have time to enjoy our grandchildren. We also have time to reflect on all the changes that have occurred since our children were that small!

William (Bill) and Margaret Pawlowich
by Margaret Pawlowich

Bill was born in Wielka Glusza, Poland, on January 20, 1925, and came to Canada with his parents in 1939 at the age of 14.

Bill lived with his father until he was old enough to go to work and left with his younger brother, Steve to work in the sawmills. They went as far south as Fawcett Lake to work in the mill owned by Swanson's Lumber Company.

In 1948 on December 28th, Bill married me, Margaret Greschner of North Star, Alberta. We lived in Keg River from December, 1948, to April, 1949. We moved to North Star, then filed for a homestead east of Manning. The homestead soon became our home. Our three children were born there, Allan Michael on November 9, 1953; Randolph (Randy) William on March 28, 1957; and Donna Elizabeth on August 1, 1958.

Bill and Margaret Pawlowich on their 40th Wedding Anniversary with granddaughter Kristen. Son Allan and wife Linda and daughter Donna and husband Greg Kuhl.

Our family has visited Keg River many times, especially when Keg River had sports and rodeo days. We can remember many good square dances there. Most of the visits were very happy times: Auntie Annie's garden, picnics by the Chinchaga River, stories by Uncle John, peacocks and greenhouse at Dr. Jackson's, homestead days at Uncle Steve's, pigs and chickens at Uncle Adam's and apple pie at Aunt Mary's.

In 1977 Randy passed away in an accident. Allan, an accountant, is married to Linda Kelemen of Notikewin. They reside in Whitecourt with their daughter Kristen. Donna, who teaches in Grimshaw, married Greg Kuhl and they have a daughter Heidi.

Bill always loved Keg River but admits he sacrificed some of the best farmland in Canada to be near my family who were originally from North Star. Bill had filed on a homestead at the Keg but there was too much muskeg on it and government regulations did not allow a claim on such land at the time.

Bill remembers fondly his nieces and nephews in Keg River. Especially when Lily Michalchuk was born. Aunt Annie was up making dinner for the family before Dr. Jackson could get there to assist with the birth. Such was the way of the pioneers!

Our home in Manning was inspected and approved as a boarding home for Northland

Donna Kuhl and daughter, Christmas, 1992.

School Division students. Keg River school only taught to grade nine, so the students needed to board out to complete high school. From 1961 until we retired the following children boarded with us: Wilbert Hawreliuk, Emma Ferguson, Marjorie Trosky, Louis Pawlowich, Michael Petersen, and Glen Pawlowich.

We are now retired but manage to keep busy with the Battle River Agricultural Society and being grandparents.

Steve and Linda Pawlowich
by Linda Pawlowich

Steve came to Canada from Poland with his mom and dad in 1939. They travelled by boat to Montreal, then by train to Peace River, and by barge down the river to Tompkins Landing, where brother John and Nick Tomilou came to meet them. They arrived in Keg River by team and wagon. The family stayed with John for several years.

Steve's dad Carl homesteaded one quarter of land on which he built their home and raised the family. His mother was ill for an extended period of time.

As a young man, Steve with his brother Bill went to work on the oil rigs and in sawmills. In 1958, Steve went to work in Libya for four years. He then worked in Kuwait for two years.

Steve Pawlowich family. Back, L-R: Scott and Gail Halverson, Steven, Ivy and Mike Dubé, Amy and O.J. Blanchette. Front, L-R: Steve, Linda and grandson Declan.

On October 18th, 1967, Steve married me, Linda Sacilowski of Manning. We have three daughters – Gail, Amy and Ivy – and one son, Steven. Gail married Scot Halvorson on August 15th, 1987, and they have one son Decklin. They live in Manning.

Amy went to college in Grande Prairie and is now married to O.J. Blanchette. They live in High Level.

Ivy married Micheal Dubé on May 4th, 1991, and they live in Manning.

Steven is going to school in Manning.

The most important event we recall in Keg River was when the Keg River flooded on August 7, 1987, after ten inches of rain fell in the Naylor Hills. This was part of the weather pattern that caused a hurricane in Edmonton.

Steve and I continue to raise livestock and grow grain on our farm in Keg River.

Bob and Mona Peel
by Mona Peel

Nineteen fifty eight was a good year! Bob was a self-employed logger in the Chilliwack River area of the Fraser Valley in British Columbia. Log prices were good. His equipment was secondhand but in good shape. His logging operation was small by today's standards but we made a good living and he employed a few of the locals we knew. Life was good and we were happy. We had just finished building our dream home on four acres of land near Sardis, British Columbia.

We had two boys – Lionel, age six and Rodney, age three, – and in October we had our long awaited girl – Susan. What more could a young couple want? Many a time, later on, I would look back on my life to this point.

Bob and I had met ten years before and married soon after. We both liked rural life, although Bob had always lived in small towns. I had been raised on farms, both in Saskatchewan and Alberta. When he was a child, Bob had visited his grandparents, who farmed and somehow got the "farming fever".

Bob liked logging but it was hard and dangerous work and most of all, he didn't like being away from home. He would leave for work before the children were up and often they were in bed again when he'd get home. Sometimes, I'd pack the kids up and go to the bush with Bob on weekends – just so we'd be together.

About this time, we got a letter from my brother, Ken Batchelor, who had moved to Keg River two or three years before. He told us a little about the area, so we decided to take a trip and visit them.

In July, 1959, there was a "fire season" and all the logging operations were closed down in the Chilliwack Forest District, so we took the opportunity to go to Keg River.

I really don't know what I expected it would be like, but it would be an experience!

The trip to northern Alberta seemed endless to me but eventually we got there. It was good to visit, Rose and Ken, and the children all got along well as they were all similar in ages. Susan was just a toddler, and Ken and Rose's daughter Alice was a few months older. Lionel and Rodney, enjoying the freedom of the farm, rode horseback and helped with chores.

Ken showed us around the Keg River district and we liked what we saw. The land was so flat and fertile and there were no stones. I believe we stayed two or three days. On the way home, we talked about farming, and the children had fond memories of their cousins and all the fun they'd had on the farm. Bob went back logging, but he couldn't forget about the north and all that good land. He talked of it a lot and I knew he really wanted to own some of it. Eventually we learned that Teddy Krause wanted to sell his farm. By this time, we'd made a few arrangements about getting machinery if we did decide to buy the land. The John Deere dealer in Chilliwack would take our logging truck and loader as down payment on farm machinery that we'd take delivery of in Manning.

In January, 1961, Bob went to Keg River and bought three half-sections from Teddy Krause Sr., Ted Krause Jr. and Alf Brown. Now we were really going farming!

We couldn't move right away, so in May, we all went to the farm to plant the crop. Most of the machinery was delivered, so Bob got right to work. With a lot of help and advice from my brother Ken, the crop was in. While the men were busy, the kids and I planted the garden in spite of all the mosquitoes, etc. During this time, we lived in our camper. After two or three weeks, we went back to Sardis to prepare for moving.

We sold our logging company and our home, and by mid-July we were ready to move. All our possessions were loaded on two trucks. Bob drove our new grain truck and we hired a truck and driver for the second. I drove the car and Susan rode with me. The boys took turns riding with Bob.

The route we chose was through the Fraser Canyon and north to Prince George, then over the Hart Highway to Dawson Creek then on to Grimshaw and finally up the MacKenzie Highway. The trip went well until we were about 20 miles south of Prince George.

The driver we hired stopped on the shoulder to check something and he pulled off too far. The truck upset. Almost everything fell out. Many things were broken or damaged. This incident caused us to be delayed a couple of days while the truck was repaired and reloaded. In due time, we were on our way again and arrived in Keg River the next day.

When we drove into the yard at our farm, I remember thinking how small the house looked. It seemed even smaller by the time we got all our furniture in place. We were all tired so after unpacking a few things, we went to bed.

The next day when we got up, I felt so out of place I didn't know what to do. There was no power, no running water and a telephone only for local calls. I began to think that coming to this place was not such a good idea. I kept those thoughts pretty much to myself, though, because I knew how enthusiastic Bob was about the whole idea.

I looked at the garden we had planted in May and all I could see was weeds. I knew there must be some sign of vegetables, so I started pulling weeds. Sure enough, the vegetables were there, so I kept on weeding.

Bob and the boys went to look at the crops. Everything was growing well and the hay crop was fantastic. In fact, that year, with Ken's help and some hired hands from the village, we took off three crops of alfalfa.

The garden produced all the vegetables we needed and we bought a milk cow, so we had plenty of milk and cream and I made our own butter. I also baked bread and we got eggs from Ken and Rose the first fall. We hadn't had time to butcher any beef, so we ordered it from Manning to put in the deep freeze. We had a power generator going by then and I was able to use all my appliances – except the television, which became a night table.

By mid-August the beef was ready for us to pick up, so Bob got up early to make the trip to town. He drove the car so he could be home quickly.

About four miles down the road, Bob noticed a man standing beside a stalled car, and when Bob stopped to help, the man asked if he was going to town. Bob said yes and quickly the man got a young woman out of the stalled car and put her into the front seat of our car. He got in the back. They weren't very talkative. Bob tried to make conversation but to no avail.

Before long, it was clear to Bob that this woman was having labor pains as she would clench her fists and gasp from time to time. Eventually they said they were neighbors of ours – John and Rose Pawlowich – and they were on their way to the hospital.

The highway to Manning in 1961 was gravel, and this particular day there was a heap of gravel in the driving lane and it was very rough and dusty. The closer Rose's pains got, the faster Bob drove. The back of the car was swaying from side to side. Suddenly as they were nearing Notikewin, Bob heard a baby cry! He was so alarmed he nearly drove off the road! At this point, John said he could slow down now.

When they reached Manning, Bob drove right up on the hospital lawn as by this time he was a nervous wreck. He left John and Rose and the baby in the care of the nurses before going to pick up the half beef.

I was surprised when he arrived home so early but looked completely beat! He went right to bed and slept a couple of hours and later said that it was harder than a day's work!

Lionel and Rod started school in September. Lionel was in grade three and he settled into the routine easily. Rod was a beginner in grade one and he came home the first day and said he had had to eat soap for talking in class! The boys soon adapted to life in a country school and they formed friendships with the other children.

Our closest neighbors were Marion and Pete Rudy. They made us feel welcome right from the start. Many winter evenings they'd come to visit and we'd play cribbage. Marion and I would always play against Bob and Pete and it was uncanny how often we beat the men. Their daughter Brenda became Susan's good friend and they spent a lot of happy times together.

Margaret and Arthur Jackson were neighbors who lived two miles away and they came over sometimes and we'd play bridge. Their two youngest sons, Hugh and Doug, were close in age to Lionel and Rod. The four of them got along well. We had quite a lot in common with Margaret and Arthur because they, too, had moved to Keg River from the Fraser Valley recently.

Ken and Rose lived nine miles away, so we'd visit them on weekends during the winter. It was always nice to go there. Rose usually had the coffee on, and we'd sit around and talk and learn the latest happenings in the district as other people dropped in. The seven kids, (their four and our three) always found something to do and they also liked to listen to Ken's tales.

We had a lot of livestock that first winter. We bought 30 head of cattle with the farm and we got pigs, chickens, four horses and the milk cow, so there were lots of chores for Bob and the boys.

I was beginning to get used to this different lifestyle but washday was definitely the worst day of the week. Our well water was very hard and contained a lot of rust. Soap just would not lather and the clothes turned brown. Finally I smartened up, and I caught rain water off the roof in the summer and melted snow in the winter. What a slow job that was – but at least the clothes were clean.

Another thing I missed from 'life before' was a big bath tub. How I longed for a good soak in sudsy water, as did Bob – especially when he came in from the field covered in dust.

In the whole picture those were small annoyances, though, and we managed to cope as well as everyone else.

We attended most of the social functions in the district and I joined the Ladies Club and thus met most of the area people.

When we moved to the farm, we had planned to start building a new house the following summer. That did not happen. It was mostly because of the water situation. We couldn't have a dugout because our land wouldn't hold water and the only other solution would have been a cistern. We were on the verge of building a couple of times, but something always stopped us. As things evolved, I'm glad we didn't.

Over the seven years we lived at Keg River, we had fairly good crops, but some years the harvest was delayed due to rain or early snow. I remember one year Bob was out combining on November 28th and the temperature was 25 degrees below zero Fahrenheit! There were no cabs on the combines in those days, and when he came in, he was so cold he could hardly speak. He finally managed to get all the crop off that fall, but the grain had to be dried.

We all worked hard on the farm. The children had their special chores and they learned responsibility. Susan had a great love for horses and from the age of three she was always around the barnyard making friends with two young colts we had. Before long, she was leading them around and within a year she was able to ride horseback as well as anyone. She continued to ride her horse Gypsy for many years after leaving Keg River.

There was no need to go to town for groceries very often because we grew everything on the farm. We always kept the deep freeze full of meat and vegetables. Bob liked to hunt and there was lots of game around. He would often come home with six or eight geese or ducks at one time. There were moose and bear and deer to be had for the taking. Once he shot a grizzly bear right in our back field. The only things we had to buy were the staples like salt, sugar and flour, so we'd get them at the Hudson's Bay post, three miles from our place.

In 1964 Susan started school, and about that time we were beginning to think about junior and senior high school for the future. We wanted the children to get the best education possible and we felt they needed more competition and choices than were available at Keg, so we talked about sending them to Manning or Peace River but the thought of ''boarding them out'' didn't seem to be the answer.

In June 1965, our third son Darcy was born. On the advice of Dr. Jackson, I went out to Peace River to await the birth.

Our little house was even more crowded now. The baby crib had to be at the foot of our bed, over the cellar door. I always had to remember to get the vegetables or canning up before the baby was put down to sleep. Darcy was a very good, healthy baby. We all enjoyed him.

Life went on much as usual. In the long winter evenings the kids did their homework or played cards or board games. Bob would read and I'd do knitting or sewing or mending. During the days when the kids were at school, I'd do a lot of sewing but I always had to put it away when they came home because the house was so small. I really don't know how we all lived so happily in that little house – but we did.

One day in the spring of 1967, we were in Grimshaw and we went to the real estate office. We asked to look at land close to town. We were shown a place and immediately we decided to buy it, so we put a deposit on it. It was a quarter section two miles from town with a lovely new four bedroom house. Everyone was delighted and the kids would all have lots of room and they'd go to school in town.

We moved in August but kept the farm at Keg. Eventually we rented it to John Prochinsky. We stayed at Grimshaw until 1969.

We went back to the Fraser Valley and Bob took up logging again and also built a shake and shingle mill. In 1983 we sold the Keg River farm to two of the Coulter boys and we again moved back to our property at Grimshaw. This is where we still live.

Our children are all happily married and they each have two children. Lionel and Rod both work for Alberta Government Telephones. Lionel is in Lethbridge. Rod works in Peace River and lives on the farm next to us. Susan works in the office of the County of Grande Prairie. Darcy lives at Williams Lake, British Columbia, and works for Environment Canada.

Bob and I have been retired for ten years and we're enjoying it. We spend two or three months in Arizona in the winter while Rod and his family look after our home.

We go to Keg River once or twice a year to see Ken and Rose, and they drop in on us occasionally.

Living in Keg River was a good experience for all of us, but I think the children really benefitted most from our time there. I am very proud of the success Bob made of his farming – considering he had little training or experience for it. We are also proud of our four children and no doubt the farm experience had a lot to do with their later lives. They are all successful and responsible adults and we are enjoying our grandchildren.

Ted and Elnora (Nora) Petersen
by Nora Petersen

Our most unforgettable experience was arriving in Keg River on December 23rd, 1965, at 10 P.M. with the temperature at -48°F. We had just driven up from Edmonton where we had been living, and we were sure we had arrived in Siberia! With our children - Ted, Mike and Tim - we came to Keg

Peterson family, Mike, Ted, Teddy and Elnora.

River to manage the elevator. This elevator was the one farthest north that United Grain Growers had in Canada. It was the first and only one in the Keg River district. Our living quarters were attached.

We bought the Keg River Cabins and managed it for seven years. The boys attended Dr. Mary Jackson School. Many things happened during those years while we operated the cafe, garage, store and post office. The new trailer for a cafe was a great improvement.

Tim Peterson with old cafe in background.

There was the fishing trip to Carcajou with Pete and Fred Rudy. We used a net for fishing. Ted Jr. went along on this trip. The bragging and fish stories later led to an embarrassing moment with Ken South, the forestry ranger at the time.

It was a very frightening evening when David Vos was shot in the yard of the Keg River Cabins by a local man. David was rushed the 60 miles to the High Level hospital by Kevin Coulter. Luckily the bullet had only gone through a part of David's hand as he pushed the gun away from himself.

After 27 years of living in the Keg River area, we now live close to Grimshaw and Ted works for Northland School Division.

George and Gert Price
by Gert (Price) Chate

George was born in Fort Saskatchewan in 1920. I was born in England on the southeast coast near Brighton and came to Canada as a war bride.

In 1939 George joined the 49th Edmonton Regiment, now known as the Loyal Edmonton Regiment, and shortly after was sent to England,

where we met and were married in 1942. A few months after our marriage his regiment was sent into active service in Sicily, Italy, and Holland. He was gone for two and a half years and returned to England in 1945. He was then sent back to Canada to be demobbed.

George and Gert's wedding party, 1942.

He resided with his sister Aleatha in Smith until I was able to join him in 1946, when I came to Canada with the war brides. We resided in Smith for eight months. I was very homesick and we were expecting our first child. We returned to

Gertrude and John Clark, 1955.

256

England and Marlene was born there. We came back to Canada when she was 15 months old and once again resided in Smith until my parents (John and Gertrude Clark) joined us in the spring of 1949.

We had heard so much about the wonderful north country and decided to move there. We purchased four acres on the highway and the 26th baseline along the road to Carcajou. George and my father went ahead to build. As soon as the shell of the house was erected, they returned for my mother, Marlene and me.

George had built a box on the back of the pickup and we packed all we could into this, placing the mattress at the back where Marlene and I were to ride. My parents wouldn't hear of me riding back there, especially because I was then pregnant with our second child, Terry. My parents rode in the back all the way and said they were quite comfy.

I had lived in Canada for a total of 18 months but I still didn't visualize the journey! There were so many miles, miles, and miles of no inhabitants, no houses, just trees, trees, and more trees! My mother and father were overwhelmed, especially my mother, who was born in London and loved the city. It was quite an adjustment for them as they were both 62 years old, quite an age for such a drastic change of lifestyle!

We arrived in Keg River on June 20th, 1949. As soon as we got settled in and had insulated the house, we built an addition on the side which we opened as a cafe. My mother and father soon became known as Ma and Pop to all and were very popular with everyone. They caused a lot of laughs when many English expressions were used and interpreted with totally different meanings in Canada.

Many a night truckers would pull in, have a meal and then ask Pop to bring out his accordion. There was always someone with a bottle of overproof rum from the Territories (which at that time could not be purchased in Alberta) or a case of black beer. The singing would go on to the late hours until the truckers returned to their trucks for a sleep. We ran the cafe for about two years.

The oil activity started up about that time and George went to work for a seismic drilling company. Our third child, Keith, was on the way, so we decided to close shop and Pop also went to work with a Texas company as a mechanic and camp attendant. It was about that time that more homestead land was opening up and we were able

to file on the same half-section that included our four acres.

Louis and June Jackson were our first close neighbors, about a half a mile from us. We visited back and forth and drank many cups of coffee after the children had gone to school.

I remember one morning in particular, I came in after hauling the wood and snow in. I went to the bedroom to take off the extra pair of slacks I was wearing. There was a knock at the door and thinking it was June, I called out, "Come on in, I'm just taking my pants off."

When I came out of the bedroom, there were two RCMP officers standing in my kitchen. Was my face red! They had come to take the census and they didn't even crack a smile!

I could fill many pages with "incidents" that June and I shared. I remember the time we were to look after lunch for a card party at Naylor Hills School. George and Louis were both away at the time, so there was no vehicle to take us. June was not to be outdone, so she said, "We'll pack it in the wheelbarrow." We packed the lunch and dishes in the wheelbarrow and off we went with June leading the way.

Then it was my turn to push the wheelbarrow. Just as I was about to take the handles, a car came along. I immediately dropped the handles. Over went the wheelbarrow into the ditch. We both stared in amazement and then started to laugh. We sat on the edge of the ditch until our sides ached from laughter. Then we sobered up and gathered up what we could. As I recall, there were hardly any broken dishes and we managed to retrieve most of the lunch undamaged.

In 1953 Pop was involved in an accident in a company truck and had to be hospitalized for quite some time. My mother went to Edmonton to be near him. They never returned to Keg River to live. After Pop was discharged from the hospital they went to live at Smith to be closer to Edmonton for him to go for treatments. They only came to Keg River to visit.

John, our fourth child, was born that same year and when he was two years old we decided to move across the highway where Alan and Debbie Godkin now live. We had started to build another house but it was never finished.

George was having health problems, so in 1958 we took up residence once again in Smith and stayed there until 1972 when we moved to Edmonton. There we worked as caretakers in a senior citizens' housing complex for the Greater

Edmonton Foundation. George had a major stroke and passed away in 1975.

I stayed on working for the Greater Edmonton Foundation in different lodges and complexes. I married Jack Chate three years later and was again widowed in 1991. I retired from the Foundation in 1990 and am still living in Edmonton.

Keith and Sarah Price
by Sarah Price

Keith, son of George and Gert Price, was born in Manning on December 2, 1951. He attended grade one at the Naylor Hills School in Keg River. The Price family then moved to Smith, Alberta, where Keith lived until he was 16.

Keith worked at the Smith sawmill, on oil rigs and then apprenticed as a commercial/industrial insulator in Edmonton. He worked in this field for several years until he and I were married in 1976. After our marriage we moved to Keg River and started farming. We bought the John Smith homestead and took up more land along the Carcajou road.

I attended grade one at the Naylor Hills one-room school. Then the school moved to the Keg River Post for grades two, three, four and part of grade five. My sister Benita and I had to ride horses or walk the three miles from the house to the highway to catch the bus into the Post to attend school.

When the Dr. Mary Jackson School was built south of the Cabins in 1962, we got a graded road from the highway toward the house. The school bus was then able to come in two miles, but we still had to walk one mile to catch the bus.

When I was in grade 10, I attended school in Manning with my sister Benita. My friend, Pat Vos, was attending Fairview College, so I moved on to greener pastures for grade 11. At this time my father, Almer became sick and passed away. I quit school to work as a teacher's aide for Northland School Division and to stay with my mother and little brother. I worked as a teacher's aide at the Paddle Prairie School for one year and then as secretary at the Northland School Division Office in Peace River. In 1970, I got a job with the Edmonton Catholic School Board in the Native Culture Program.

After working in the schools for five years, I decided to go to university and become a teacher. I attended the University of Alberta Morning Star Teacher Training Program in St. Paul. After completing this program, I was given a five-year conditional teaching certificate. My daughter

Gert Price and family, Keith, Marlene, John, Terry with DeeDee and Leslie Jackson, 1958.

Bernadette was born in my second year of university in St. Paul.

My first teaching assignment was grade five and six at the Paddle Prairie School. After two years of teaching, I decided to finish my degree and so I attended the University of Alberta for two years. During this time I completed my Bachelor of Education Degree along with an Intercultural Teaching Certificate. My son George was born in April at the end of my fourth year of university.

I returned to the Paddle Prairie School for one year, again teaching grade five and six. The next year I transferred to Dr. Mary Jackson School to teach grade three. Since then I have taught all grade levels and all subject areas. One year was taken off to work in Central Office as area officer.

In 1988 I went on educational leave and completed my fifth year of university. I received my diploma in Early Childhood Education. In 1993-94 I was seconded for the school year to do curriculum development for Northland School Division.

George is presently attending the Dr. Mary Jackson School in grade seven. Bernadette is finishing her grade 12 at Paul Rowe High School in Manning.

Howard Bertram Price
by Margaret Befus, Patsy Lindberg and Dennis Sivertsen

Howard grew up in the Rabbit Lake area, near Prince Albert, Saskatchewan. During World War II he joined the infantry, fought overseas and was wounded. On returning to Canada, he worked in the shipyards of Vancouver but hated it.

Howard came to Carcajou in 1954 to visit his brother Mel and his family. Howard liked the area and the people so much that he soon returned to stay.

He often went hunting and trapping with Lou Tupper. He had been in a war, and if you ever startled him, you quickly found yourself facing a gun! We were warned never to approach him unexpectedly, if we valued our lives! He was quick and accurate with his shots, which helped him a lot with his hunting.

On one of their spring hunts, Howard was having trouble with bears stealing his beaver hides. He said to Lou, "They ain't gonna touch my hides tonight."

He then rolled up the hides and tucked them under his head for a pillow. In the black of the night he heard something moving around camp. Suddenly his roll of beaver hides was rudely snatched from under him. He said that his hair all stood on end but he didn't feel like arguing with an intruder he couldn't even see!

In 1957 Howard hired Authur Bowe and Mervin Rudy to cut bush for him.

Howard raised a few hogs and some grain. He farmed with horses the first year. He then decided to modernize, so he bought a Massey Ferguson tractor. He was unfamiliar with machinery and slow to learn. One day he came to visit Lou. When he came to the gate he was pulling hard on the wheel, shouting "Whoa, Whoa!" The tractor never hesitated. It just went chugging on through, flattening the gate as it went. Sadly, he then said, "Well, giddy-up, then!"

He couldn't carry a tune or play an instrument but he really liked to sing. On a clear day you could hear him all over the flat. He'd never make a hit in Nashville but his singing made one feel good.

Henry Cardinal built him a log house and Howard enjoyed having company stop by. He nearly always had the coffee pot on. He often visited his neighbors to play cards and tell stories until very late.

He celebrated nearly every Christmas with the Tuppers. If he didn't come, they would think something had happened to him.

Howard had a very big sow that had a good batch of piglets every spring. The spring of 1962 Charlie Christian found her trying to defend herself against a large black bear. He scared the bear away by beating a stick on a near-by brush pile. The sow had a big hunk torn out of her neck just behind the ear, but she survived and still had another litter. Lou and Howard tracked the bear down and shot it. It was an old black bear, they said, whose teeth were in bad shape and it was skinny, just hide and bones.

Howard did most of his trapping on foot. In later years, he bought a snowmobile, but he never liked it. Howard had quite a collection of guns, including a 25-35 Winchester.

Howard did his own cooking and some of his mixtures were very strange. He put together cooked potatoes, raw carrots, onions and anything else that happened to appeal to him at the moment. Not everyone cared to try his concoctions! They never bothered his cat, though. If he forgot to put things away, she cleaned up for him!

He liked to walk down to the river. One day he was returning from one of these leisurely strolls just as it was getting dark. He thought he saw a black dog drinking out of his water barrel, which was under the eaves of his house. As he got closer a small black bear, which had been half-way in the barrel, ran into the forest!

Everybody was Howard's friend but he was often the butt of practical jokes. Summertime brought the men folk over to his house to play

Howard Price and Lou Tupper with Dennis Sivertson's ski-doo, late 1960's.

259

horseshoes. He taught all the kids how to play crokinole.

One of his favorite spots was Upper Landing, the place the river boats had stopped at the upper end of the flat, so when he died in 1976 his ashes were buried there. Today it is known as Howard's Landing.

Walter and Mary Prochinsky and Family
by Diana Beck (nee Prochinsky)

The big move of the Prochinsky family to Keg River took place in July 1963, from Craigend, Alberta, which is approximately 15 miles south of Lac La Biche. The move was to homestead land seven miles north of Keg River Cabins along the MacKenzie Highway.

There were 10 children in the family when we moved: Roger, John, myself, Wallace, Helena, Eugene, Grace, Elaine, Viola, and Fay. The youngest, Joanne was born in Manning in July 1964.

For the first month we stayed down by the Cabins with Milton and Mary Rudy, until we set up something to stay in on the homestead. We borrowed an old bunkhouse from Harry Bowe and also set up a couple of granaries to use until we built a house. The house was finished enough to move into in November.

It wasn't a week after we'd moved into the house that we had a chinook like we'd never seen before. The winds were so strong that the bunkhouse we had been staying in rolled over and over to rest against some willow trees alongside the highway. You should have seen the look on all the kids faces. Our eyes were like saucers!

The first year we went to school in the school house at Keg River Post. The following year we moved into the new school (Dr. Mary Jackson School) situated by the Keg River Cabins. The school only went up to grade nine; after that we had to go out to get our high school.

On July 22, 1974, Dad passed away at the young age of 62.

At present, Mom still lives in Keg River. Roger, John, Wallace, and myself are also in Keg River. Eugene lives in High Level, Helena in Edmonton, Grace in Hays, Elaine in Provost, Viola in Athabasca, Fay in Prince George, and Joanne in Grande Prairie.

Work and play are words used to describe the same thing under differing conditions.
Mark Twain

Matt Raey
by Patsy Lindberg (nee Tupper)

Matt came to Carcajou to visit on December 26, 1959, with Len Clare. He stayed on with Mrs. Edna Kiselczuk to help her with her livestock. He later stayed with Howard Price and helped the Tupper family.

He had no home of his own in Carcajou and tried to help out in any way he could. When he wasn't working outside, he helped in the house. He often cooked supper. I remember him cooking roast beaver or bear, which were both quite delicious. Sometimes he cooked a strange milk pudding that no one but he would eat!

He spent his spare time reading his Bible or napping. Often he had strange dreams or even nightmares while he was resting.

Matt Raey.

The Rankin Family
by Kay Hopkins

Malcolm and Isabella Rankin with their children Charlie, Wilfred, Lily, Bessie, Clarence, Mac, John, Ellen, Dorothy and Archie decided to move to Peace River. They left Edmonton on March 4, 1915, travelling by horses and sleigh until the snow gave way and they had to change to wagons.

Cattle were shipped by train from Edmonton to McLennan. Then Wilfred drove the cattle from McLennan to Peace River, along with a fellow from Griffin Creek. This fellow kept the cattle until the Rankin family arrived April 1, 1915 after nearly a month on the road.

One sleigh had a caboose and the other one a tent. When they changed to wagons they just used the caboose on the wagon. When they first arrived in Peace River they lived in the caboose and a tent approximately where the present fire hall is situated. They stayed in Peace River only the summer of 1915.

They then packed up and travelled north to Carcajou on a boat named *The Northern Call*. This boat was a small sternwheeler fuelled by wood. Wood was piled along the Peace River at strategic points. The boat would stop at these points and load up more wood for the journey.

While on the journey to Carcajou *The Northern Call* hit a rock and nearly sank about 12 miles down river from the town of Peace River. The people had to get ashore quickly and everyone camped there for a week to wait for the boat to be repaired. After the boat was fixed, they travelled to a sawmill about 35 miles down river near the Whitemud River. They then loaded the livestock on a scow along with all their other belongings and drifted down river to Carcajou.

After they arrived in Carcajou they acquired a contract to cut wood for the steam boat. Due to a severe winter in 1915-16 when there was very deep snow, very little wood was cut. It was during this winter that many of the livestock died.

By the spring of 1916 about the time of breakup, we found ourselves short of food. Oliver Hamelin came across the river from the Carcajou Settlement and picked up Malcolm to get necessary supplies. Charlie and Wilfred travelled overland to Peace River to purchase more supplies in time to return home on the first boat down the river.

As the years passed, life improved for the family. Isabella traded eggs and butter for other essentials and the men continued to cut cordwood for the steamers. In 1929 the steamers were taken off the Peace River due to low water. This, and the fact that the boats began to be powered by diesel fuel, brought about the end of supplying wood for the steamers.

Malcolm died in 1920 at Peace River as a result of an injury in an accident. Isabella moved to Peace River where she resided until her death in 1960.

Charlie Rankin, born in Dauphin, Manitoba, in 1894, died in 1956. He married Martha Bayes – no family. Charlie farmed in Carcajou up to a short time before his death.

Wilfred Rankin, born in Dauphin, Manitoba, in 1897, married Margaret Wiles in 1926. They had a family of six: Ann (Funnell), Lorna (Stranaghan), Ethel (Cochrane), Marion, Shirley (Cockrane), and Thelma (Bossert). Wilfred and his family lived on a homestead near the home place. They moved to Fort McMurray in 1936. Wilfred piloted in the Athabasca and Clearwater Rivers and was also involved in boat construction. He also worked on the Canol Project near Fort Norman. Margaret later married Ken Cockrane and they had a son Kenneth. Wilfred died in Fairview in 1960.

Mary Elizabeth (Bessie) was born in Dauphin, Manitoba, in 1898. In 1924 she married Charlie McLean, a free trader and homesteader at Carcajou. They had a family of seven: Emily and Ellen, aged five and three, died in 1931 of "summer complaint"; Kathleen (Hopkins), Charles Jr. (died 1989), Warren (Jean), Margie (Whithers), and David (Geneva). In 1933 the family moved to Fort Vermilion, where Charlie operated a general store and was a fur trader. They later moved to Peace River in 1943. Charlie Sr. died in 1956. Mary now resides at the Heritage Towers in Peace River.

Lily, born in 1899 at Dauphin, married Leslie Roberts. She died in childbirth in 1925.

Clarence was born in Dauphin in 1901. Clarence trapped and freighted with his brothers and worked for Revillon Freres for seven years. He then became a free trader and moved to Little Red River. In 1943 he bought out Charlie McLean's general store. He married Gertrude Boire and had a family of two girls, Shirley and Cathy. Clarence died in 1951 in Edmonton.

Mac was born in 1903 in Dauphin. Mac was a trapper and freighter, and carried mail by team and sleigh in the winter. He stayed at home and farmed in the summer. Mac also cooked for forestry crews before he moved to Burton, B.C. He lived there for 28 years before he moved to a seniors apartment in Nakusp. He now resides in Heritage Towers in Peace River.

John Rankin was born in 1905 in Dauphin. He died in Carcajou in 1926.

Ellen was born in Edmonton in 1910. At the age of 13 she went to Margo, Saskatchewan, with her mother, sister Dorothy and brother Archie. The three children stayed in Margo and attended school. Ellen completed grade school and then attended Normal School in Regina. She graduated with her teaching certificate and taught at various schools in and around Margo until she retired and married an old friend, Cas Godfrey. Cas died a few years after they were married. Ellen now resides in the Sutherland Nursing Home in Peace River.

Dorothy was born in 1912 in Edmonton. At the age of 12 she went to Margo, Saskatchewan, and stayed there for two years to attend school. In 1925 Dorothy returned to Carcajou, where she helped at home.

In 1929 Dorothy met Jack O'Sullivan, who homesteaded at Carcajou and Peace River during the summer. Jack O'Sullivan and Ted Stigsen started freighting on the Peace River in 1934. Their outfit was called "O'Sullivan and Stigsen River Transportation". They hauled grain and cattle from the north to Peace River. Their boat was comfortably equipped to carry passengers. It had a dining room where meals were provided. For many years the cook was Dorothy O'Sullivan. The boat was taken off the river about 1950 when the new roads north made trucking possible.

Dorothy and Jack had a family of four: Paddy (Bonnie), Beth (Morton), Doreen (Broughton), and Michael (Betty). Jack died in Peace River in 1992. Dorothy still lives in the family home in Peace River.

Archie was born in 1914 in Edmonton. Archie attended school in Margo for a year, then returned home to Carcajou with his mother. He worked on the farm and trapped. In 1944 he left Carcajou and worked on a farm near Westlock, and later worked on a bridge being built on the Athabasca River. He then moved to Edmonton, where he was employed in the maintenance department of the Hudson's Bay store until he retired in 1979. He married Fern in 1976. Fern died in 1987 and Archie moved to Peace River and now resides in the Heritage Towers.

(Editor's Note: The following poem was written by John Okerholm for Isobella Rankin.)

The Rankin Family: John, Bessie, Wilfred, Margaret, Dorothy, Charlie, Grandma Rankin holding Annie, Clarence

Grandma Rankin

On the banks of the Peace I once knew a
    place –
It was known to all in them early days –
Here Grandma Rankin was tending her home.
And would share it with all who would
    happen to come.

Some of the family were staying at home,
Others were already out on their own.
Grandma was known for a long way around,
For here was a good place where shelter was
    found.

And when men in them days were travelling
    about,
They were heading her way, or were just
    checking out.
At the table she would set a place for them
    all,
And none was too modest to come when she'd
    call.

Few of them paid for the stay and the food,
Others forgot – and she well understood.
Pay or no pay she fed everyone the same
There is no doubt that many still remember
    her name.

In the winter there was time for frolic and
    fun,
And in Grandma's house there was plenty of
    room,
And everyone came from fifty miles around,
And danced until morning when the sun came
    around.

Square-dance and hoe-downs and round
    dances, too,
Chicken dance and sword dance the whole
    night through –
The fiddler was busy laying bow on the string,
His helper beat the drum with sticks till it
    ring.

Many a man and women as well,
Will be telling their children these dances were
    swell,
And Grandma was hostess to all,
When the coffee was made and she gave them
    the call.

Grandma has gone from the place we all know,
And I see her as clearly as it's possible to,
Her memory is good and full of the past,
Now Grandma Rankin is taking a rest.

When the time shall arrive and Grandma must
    leave,
For the Elysian home, in which she steadfastly
    believes,
I hope she is granted a place on some knoll,
With her monument there, to be seen by all.

The Roberts Family
by Margaret Befus

The Roberts family came to Carcajou from the United States in the early 1920's. They homesteaded or squatted on SW-22-101-19-W5 near the river. One can still see where there were buildings and outbuildings as well. They had a large log house. The Dixons and the Madsons, who were somehow related, lived with them.

When our family moved to Carcajou in 1963, there was a log shack north of what became our yard. Charles Dovey said it had also belonged to the Roberts.

We are not sure who broke the first land in the Carcajou area but believe it was the Roberts or the Rankins.

The family consisted of the father (his name is not known), the mother who went by the nickname "Bob" and their children: son Leslie and daughter Ethyl. Leslie married Lily Rankin. Unfortunately Lily died in childbirth when their son Jim was born.

Muriel Stigsen recalls going as a child to the Roberts for a Christmas party. It was a long drive with horses from their farm on Carcajou Point. She got snow in her moccasins and froze her toes on the trip.

The Roberts lost all their cattle in the 1934 flood and left Carcajou soon after that. Mrs. Bob Roberts and Mrs. Martha Rankin corresponded for many years.

George and Alice Robertson
by Francis Sawchuk (nee Robertson)

Dad came to the Battle River area in 1919 from Saskatchewan. He married mom, Alice Weber, on January 1st, 1928.

For years Dad had a trapline which included the area around Twin Lakes. The winter of 1937-38 we all went to the trapline. By this time our family included: Myrtle, Don, Edna, Francis, and Ann. George Jr. arrived on December 4th, 1937, after mom travelled by dog team from the trapline to Dr. Jackson's home. The rest of us stayed at the cabin on the trapline with our Aunt Beth.

Myrtle and Don took correspondence courses all winter. We returned to the homestead south of Notikewin in the spring. The family lived on the farm until 1948 when we moved to a homestead in Keg River. Dad farmed in the summer and worked at construction jobs in the winter. He cut seismic lines with Cats and also spent several winters cutting the 30th baseline.

In 1952 Mom and Dad went on a trip to the

Alice and George Robertson, 1952.

United States that included a visit to New York.

In 1957 Dad started up a Cockshutt dealership. Mom organized the community ladies into an active group as they completed a multitude of projects aimed at building and equipping a new community hall. Bake sales, quilts, and card games were some of the moneymakers.

Dad passed away in 1963, Don in 1985 and Mom in 1991.

1958 Calendar from George Robertson's Cockshutt Dealership.

Jaraslav Romanchuk

by Anne Vos

To many of us, Jaraslav was a hermit or recluse. He homesteaded here after 1930. He was lured to this area from the Ukraine by a booklet produced by the government offering quarters of land for $10.

He was very suspicious of his fellow man but he had learned the barbering trade and would cut hair for anyone.

The white stallion he rode and his army uniform with the shiny leather boots are among our most vivid memories of Mr. Romanchuk.

He was very self-sufficient, growing a large garden each year. He went to the store only to buy a few meager supplies of soap, salt, tea, lard and matches or to pick up some mail. He had a tunnel dug underground to his barn. We can only speculate about his reasons for this.

Being a bachelor with no children, Mr. Romanchuk opposed the establishment of a school district in the Keg River area because it would have been accompanied by a school tax. When the district was founded in the late 1930's, he refused to pay his portion of the taxes and in 1940 he had two cows seized to cover what he owed. He protested by writing letters to government officials.

One winter day there was no smoke coming from his chimney, so Bill Brick, running the highway snow plow, stopped in to check on him. Mr. Romanchuk was found near death with pneumonia. He was taken under protest to the hospital, where he recovered.

The only relative we ever heard about was a niece who lived in New York. Once she drove to Keg River to visit him.

One year I sent my son David over to him with a Christmas cake. Mr. Romanchuk, with his usual distrust of others, dunked the foil-wrapped cake in a pail of water. He feared we had sent him a bomb!

Jaraslav passed away in Manning and is buried in Notikewin.

Hubert Alonzo (Lonnie) and Manilla Dewey Root

by Paulette Freil

Manilla was born April 11, 1898, in Ohlman, Illinois, to Elza Creel Sanders and Alice Belle Settle. Hubert Alonzo (Lonnie) was born January 31, 1893, in Chatfield, Minnesota, to Hubert Eugene Root and Ella May Hesselgrave. Manilla and Lonnie were my grandparents.

Root Family, Alma, Ethelyn, Manilla and Hubert (Lonnie), 1920's.

Both families came to Canada in the late 1890's or early 1900's. The Roots first farmed in the Red River Valley before moving to High River, Alberta.

Childhood sweethearts, Lonnie and Manilla married on May 15, 1915, and had two daughters, Ethelyn and Alma. After farming and ranching in High River for a number of years, they decided to move to northern Alberta.

The family waited in Calgary while Lonnie went north to claim two homesteads -one in his name and one in Manilla's. He filed on the NE-28-101-24-W5 June 24th, 1929. He later filed on the NW-12-102-24-W5 for Manilla. (In 1930, they donated two acres of Lonnie's land to the community for a new cemetery.)

Lonnie returned to Calgary in the spring of

Root's scow built in 1932 by Lonnie Root and Dick Hudson. On board, Dick Hudson, Lonnie, Alma, Ethelyn and Manilla Root and Jack Yurkowski with a years supply of groceries on their way to their homestead in Keg River.

1929. Then the family packed their personal belongings in the Nash car and put their furniture, household and farm supplies on a sled drawn by a caterpillar tractor and headed north.

The trip to Keg River took close to three months. They travelled overland to Peace River and there put all their belongings on the *D.A. Thomas* for Carcajou Crossing. They continued on an overland trail to Keg River. Upon arrival at his homestead, they set to building a sod hut before winter set in. Two years later they built a log house on Manilla's homestead.

In 1932 Lonnie, Dick Hutchison and Jack Yurkowski went to Peace River where they built a 12 foot by 30 foot scow. After loading it with a year's supply of groceries and other necessities, they punted down to Carcajou. The wood from the scow was reused in building their log house. They chose Manilla's homestead as the location for the new house because it was situated by the Keg River and water was readily available.

In 1953, after years of residing in this one-room log house, Lonnie and Manilla moved to a lovely new home they had built one mile west. The Christmas party that year included family and neighbors.

During their time on the farm, Manilla had plenty of preserves on hand which were used with the wonderful meals she loved to prepare for guests or the workmen during threshing season in the fall. As well as vegetables, there were beautiful flowers in the garden. She was especially fond of her sweetpeas which were always planted next to the house. Manilla was also a skilled seamstress and loved crocheting. Lonnie, who was always respected for his honesty and commitment to the welfare of the community, was a hard-working man with a good sense of humor.

Upon retirement in the summer of 1964, they sold their land to Steve Pawlowich and bought a home in Manning. There Lonnie continued to maintain a large garden for their own use. Manilla made hundreds of crocheted poodle puppies, which she sold.

Lonnie died January 3, 1973, after being ill for about three years. Manilla continued to live in their home until 1982 when, because of failing health, she moved to Del-Air Lodge in Manning. In 1988 she became too ill to remain in the lodge and was hospitalized. She passed away on October 18th that same year. Both Lonnie and Manilla are buried in the Vale of Peace Cemetery in Notikewin, Alberta.

Their daughter Ethelyn married Theodore (Ted) Stup in Vancouver, B.C., in 1944. They had one daughter and my name is Paulette. Mom and Dad moved to Hay River, NWT, in 1949. Mom died on April 2, 1988. Dad continues to live in Hay River. Lonnie and Manilla's other daughter Alma married Archie Robb and resides in Vancouver.

I married Raymond Friel and we provided Lonnie and Manilla with three great-grand-children, Diane, Daniel and Mark. We all live in the Ottawa area.

Paulette (nee Stup) Friel holding Patricia Vos, 1954.

Ray and Lin Ross Family
by Lin Ross

Our family spent 12 happy years at Keg River while my husband, Ray Ross, managed the Hudson's Bay store. We spent the first eight years of our marriage in Western Arctic Hudson's Bay posts. When we came outside on furlough during World War II, Wop May was in charge of the Air Observers School in Edmonton, training young pilots from all over the Dominion. The Bay released Ray to act as a Purchasing Agent for the Air Observers School for the duration.

After the war, with two pre-schoolers and a new baby boy, we were reluctant to return to the Arctic and leave the two older children outside to attend school, so we were delighted when the HBC came up with a posting to Keg River, advising there was not only a school, but a hospital and a doctor. It seemed too good to be true.

On arrival at Keg River we found that the school was a log building with no teacher or teacherage, the hospital was another log building which was empty except when prospective mothers camped there to await birth. The doctor was bona fide: a young highly-qualified English doctor had come to northern Alberta for a year to be able to ride horseback to her patients.

Fortunately she met and married Frank Jackson, a Keg River rancher and trader, and remained to doctor three generations of widely scattered patients in addition to helping Frank win Alberta's Master Farming award, and many other honors.

The Correspondence school lessons were excellent until a permanent teacher arrived. Lack of good water brought recycling to an art, with baths followed by washing clothes, then the floor, by which time the water was almost as horrific as the foul smelling stuff pumped from the well! There were many good wells in Keg River but ours wasn't fit for even watering the garden until left standing a day or two.

Raymer and Chuck Ross hauling ice from the Keg River, a half mile away.

Gardening was fun, especially if the wind was blowing all the mosquitoes away! I've never tasted vegetables as flavorful as the huge cauliflower, cabbages, etc. grown there. Competition was keen, involving bragging of digging of the first potatoes (as small as marbles) or children pretending to stagger under the weight of a huge cabbage when a better gardener was passing.

Friendly competition didn't spoil the lasting friendships in a community where people had to rely on each other to help in emergencies, to raise money for a hall, or for the exciting Annual Sports Day, when our native friends showed us how flabby we were. Frank Jackson organized a group to fight for the inclusion of Keg River on the prospective railway, and won to everyone's benefit.

They were good years, developing a resourcefulness in children that would have been hard to gain in a city. I value my memories and the friends made there.

Ross Family. Lillian, Ray Sr., Charles, Pat, Raymer, 1955.

Charles (Chuck) Ross
by Chuck Ross

When my father, Ray Ross, was discharged from military service at the end of World War II, he returned to his former employer, the Hudson's Bay Company. The Keg River Post was available, so he travelled up with my sister Pat and my brother Ray. I had just been born, so a few weeks later when I was deemed old enough to travel, my mother Lin and I flew up in a chartered plane from Edmonton.

We were to live the next 12 years in the Bay house, and although my memories have blurred with time, Keg River seemed a pretty good place to grow up. For one thing, we could wander any place we wanted without fear of being abducted and ending up on the back of a milk carton. There was no television and for the most part we were better off without it. Certainly it led to more imaginative play as we had to provide our own entertainment.

The Ferguson house was on the river bank and I spent hours sliding down the hill with Leo, Allen and Hubert and whoever else showed up. We made little sleighs out of packing crate boards from the store and nailed steel banding on the runners. I remember reaching incredible speeds and it was quite a shock to return as an adult and view the pitiful little slope we had considered such a challenge.

There was a field across the road from the store and a little granary in the far corner. I'm not sure how old we were, but it was before we started school that Ronnie and Donnie Jackson and I were over there trying to catch a squirrel. I was up near the roof and fell, snagging the cuff of my shirt near the wrist on a nail. I don't remember screaming but I likely did. Ronnie and Donnie stood on the ground and cried in sympathy.

Eventually Ronnie thought to go to the store and fetch my Dad. It was one of the few times I remember seeing Dad run but he lifted me down and I got to wear a big bandage for a few days. Strange how that incident would come back to me after 40 years!

The freedom to wander and lots of spare time gave us plenty of opportunity to get into mischief and we often did. Looking back, I'm surprised at how patient the adults were. Glady Harrington and Harry Bowe lived the closest and must have put up with an awful lot!

Glady didn't even get angry when I shot up his long-johns. They were hanging on the clothes line and I discovered they made a satisfying

Ray and Chuck Ross at Hudson's Bay Post, Keg River.

"thwack" when hit with a BB gun from a long way back. I didn't think that I was making holes! Mostly I just didn't think! Anyway, all the copper pellets stuck in the frozen flannel and since I had the only BB gun in Keg, there was no doubt about who was guilty.

The original log school had been replaced by a frame building a year or so before I started school. On the first day of school I got into a fight with Jimmy Yurkowski and he somehow got a little nick on his lip that drew blood, so I was deemed the winner. Miss Paul made all the kids stand around me in a circle and look at me until Jimmy stopped crying. I got a bad start with her and things didn't change much afterwards. However, I'm glad to say that Jimmy and I soon became best friends!

The classroom was very cold on winter mornings. It was worst for the smallest, because we sat in the very front and the wood stove was at the back! Miss Paul's desk was even further from the heat but she was English and would have been used to freezing and being uncomfortable! The big kids (grade seven and eight) were allowed to put wood in the stove. They were very lucky!

Some of my fondest memories are of picnics we'd have out on the Chinchaga River. Word would spread somehow (there were no phones) that Johnny Vos was picking everybody up. Now I know that the population of Keg River didn't fit into Vos' truck but that's the way I remember it! I vaguely remember Dave McDonald's truck there too, so there must have been others. McDonald's truck had the starter button on the floor beside the gas pedal.

It seemed like a long journey and there were mud holes that the truck would creep through in low gear. Once we saw a bear and I was surprised that it wasn't flat. The only one I'd seen before was a rug with a stuffed head and glass eyes. That's what I thought all bears looked like!

The Chinchaga is shallow with no overhanging branches, so the water is warm enough for swimming and the banks are sand or gravel bars. It seemed like heaven. When we got older we could ride out on horseback.

Jimmy Halabisky and I rode our bikes out once and I caught my first fish there – but it got away. For some reason I took a sleeping bag, although we didn't camp overnight. I'd developed a taste for chowder, so we gathered several dozen clams to take home to Mom. I rolled them up in my sleeping bag so they wouldn't get crushed on the way home and then forgot about them until

Mom went looking for the source of the horrible smell a week or two later!

My father retired when I was 12 and that meant moving out to Edmonton. At first I was devastated by culture shock – a big school in a big city and I missed my friends. I soon adjusted, though, and by the time I was in high school, my sister Pat was teaching in Keg River. I then looked forward to the summer visits up there. Somehow Keg River seemed to have changed but in retrospect it was probably I who had changed. About that time Pat married Ray Weber and they moved to Yellowknife.

I heard that summer jobs were plentiful there, so I went to Yellowknife, too. After high school and a couple of years at the Northern Alberta Institute of Technology, it seemed natural to continue working in Yellowknife, so I got a job with a hydro company. I liked the work but liked flying my little planes even more, so I switched careers and started flying commercially.

I liked flying and miss it now that my wife, Marion and I live in Vernon, British Columbia. I do go back to fly some summers but after a few months of battling the bugs and the weather, the Okanagan looks pretty good.

Chuck Ross and his plane.

Rod and Mary Roth
by Mary Roth

Rod and I travelled north in the spring of 1961, looking for our future.

Settling in High Level, we both went to work for Owen and Fanny Jordon, who at that time owned the High Level Esso-Motel-Grocery Store and Cafe.

Rod worked for the Jordons in the service station and I worked in the store. We were later joined by my two sons, Miles and Cary Anstee.

When the Jordons sold the business, Rod took odd jobs, bought a winch truck and started a little trucking business. At that time there was a lot of activity in the bush regarding exploration for oil and gas. Oil had not yet been discovered at Rainbow Lake.

In the early winter of 1963, about time oil was discovered west of High Level, Rod and I took over the cafe part of the newly-built Phillips 66 Service Station. After three months we relocated to Bob and Valle Grey's Blue Top Lodge and operated that for a year. It was at this time that Miles and Cary started school in High Level.

During this time Rod continued his light trucking and had branched into small contracting in the oilfield.

At Easter of 1964 we vacated the Blue Top Lodge and I took up homemaking full time. Rod continued contracting and trucking.

On December 24, 1964, our son Christopher was born in the Manning Hospital.

Rod continued his work in the oilfield and in 1966 became a big game guide and outfitter.

In 1968 the oil boom was slowing down, so Rod and I made plans to relocate. In the spring of 1969 we moved with our three sons to a spot 24 miles south of Keg River. We started a service station and restaurant which became known as Twin Lakes Lodge.

The original coffee shop consisted of a mobile home with a large addition. That served as the coffee shop until 1972 when a new cedar log building was opened as a dining room.

The temporary coffee shop was sold to Bill and Doreen Brick and moved to their farm at Keg River to be used as an addition to their home. At the time of writing they are still using it.

Upon moving to Twin Lakes, Miles and Cary started school and Chris started grade one in the fall of 1970.

Northland School Division would not send a school bus for the three boys, so it was Rod's job to drive the boys to school every morning and pick them up every night. This went on for 10 years. It proved a hardship, but at least Rod knew the boys never played "hooky".

Rod took over the trapline vacated by Jerome House and still traps every winter. He is still operating the outfitting under the name Goffitt River Outfitters.

In 1977 the service station was expanded and an eight-unit motel was added. In 1993 recreational vehicle parking facilities were added.

Miles and Cary continued going to Dr. Mary Jackson School in Keg River until they finished grade nine and then they went to Grande Prairie where they got the balance of their education. Chris finished his grade nine in Keg River and then took his grade 12 in Manning.

At time of writing (early 1994): Miles is

Cafe and Lodge at Twin Lakes.

Cary and Miles Anstee with brother Chris Roth and Major, 1973.

married to Karen Hall. Their children are Desirie (six years) and Darren (two years). They live in Peers, Alberta. Miles is employed as a log truck driver.

Cary took automotive mechanics and got his ticket at Fairview College. He worked for Fountain Tire in Peace River, Falher, and Valleyview before an injury forced him to give up mechanics. He then worked for Canadian Tire in Red Deer for two years and now is at home in Twin Lakes.

Chris married Wendy Mace from Edmonton and is working for Grove Pontiac where he is apprenticing as a partsman. They live in Spruce Grove and have a daughter, Shannon (five years), and a son, Tyler, who is two years old.

I was born in Edson, Alberta. From a previous marriage I had three sons: Miles, Cary, and Bill, who lives with my mother on the farm at Edson. I also had a daughter, Connie, who married Jack Walker and lived for a number of years in Whitehorse, Yukon Territory. They moved to the Manning area in 1980 and both were tragically killed in 1982.

Rod was born in Camrose, Alberta. From a previous marriage he has a son, Dale, who lives in Ryley, Alberta, and a daughter who married Terry Reed and lives in Wetaskiwin, Alberta. They have a daughter, Landon (11 years), and a son, Bryce, age seven.

Rod and I still live at and operate Twin Lakes Lodge.

Rod and Mary Roth.

Michael (Mike) and Mary Rudy
by Anne Vos

The Rudy family arrived in Keg River, like all new settlers at the time, by train across the prairies to Peace River and boat or barge down the Peace River to Carcajou.

Mike, his wife Mary, their daughters Annie and Mary, and their sons Milton, Alex, Pete, Fred, Mike and Billy first lived in an abandoned log cabin. The cabin had previously been occupied by a family who had, with the exception of the father, all died of tuberculosis. When Mike got his homestead NW 34-101-24-W5, they built a log house and moved there. All the buildings had walls made of logs, which were chinked with mud mixed with manure, and had sod roofs.

Mike urged the community to get a petition out to the Department of Education in 1931 asking for a school to be built in the district. When the government refused, three of his children were sent to the Catholic Mission in Fort Vermilion for their education.

Annie became a deaf-mute when she was only two years old after a fall in which she cracked her skull.

Annie was the oldest and helped her father outside a lot. One day in 1933, she and her father were going to harness the horses when one kicked him in the stomach. He died of a ruptured liver shortly after.

Mike's wife, Mary, came down with tuberculosis and diabetes and went to the sanatorium in Edmonton. The disease was probably contracted in the abandoned house that had been their first home in Keg River. Billy also got tuberculosis and went to the sanatorium. Neither of them were cured and they both died in Edmonton.

Alex married Marion Steedsman and they had a daughter, Frances. Pete married Marion Lariviere and they had a son, Stanley, and a daughter, Brenda. Fred is single and has had several strokes. He is the only member of his generation of the family still living. His home is the Sutherland Nursing Home. Mike married Dorothy and lived in Edmonton. They had three children. Mary married Fred Hartley and they had four children; Marylin, who was born in Keg River, Patsy, Eddie and Bryan.

Mary (Rudy) Hartley and baby Marilyn, 1939.

Annie Rudy, Bill Halabisky, Johnny Yurkowski, Elsie Halabisky and Mrs. Mary Rudy.

Forest Ranger, Fred Hartley and H.B.C. Manager, Harry Borbridge, 1938.

Milton and Mary Rudy
by Mary Rudy

Milton went with his parents, looking for a homestead in the famed Peace River Country of Northern Alberta. He left me in Manitoba, with my parents and our two young boys, Mervin and Victor.

In the spring of 1936 I left Grandview with the boys to join Milton in Keg River. I travelled by train to Peace River, where I was met by Mrs. Bourassa. We spent some time at the Bourassas', where I learned about the ways of the north country.

My trip from Peace River was on the *O'Sullivan-Stigsen* riverboat. I earned our passage by cooking and cleaning for the crew and other passengers. When the boat stopped in Carcajou, the captain replenished the meat supplies by getting chickens from Mrs. Rankin and a butchered sheep from the McGranes. The meat was kept on blocks of ice down in the hold.

We left the boat at Carcajou to begin the overland trip to Keg River – about 45 miles. Milton, Frank Ferguson and his daughter met us with a team of horses.

One of the most vivid memories I have of Keg River is the welcoming feast the locals provided when I arrived at Rudy's. Moose, bear, lynx, porcupine and prairie chicken were the varieties of meat served.

Another memory was the log cabin in which we lived. It had one room and tiny windows and was heated by a wood cook stove. The sod roof dripped for days after a rain! Later we moved to the house at Jackson's place, formerly occupied by the teacher.

Milton was a self-taught mechanic and there was always something to fix, but there wasn't much money for payment. In the 40's he also ran a Caterpillar for brush-cutting and road building.

We filed on a homestead NW-11-101-23-W5, built another log house and moved there. Over the years we had six more children: Chester, Edith, Fern, June, Kenny and Sharon. The children went to school at the Naylor Hills School across the river from us. Later they were bused to Keg River.

Mervin and Chester died in accidents. Victor lived in Pine Point with his family for years but now lives in Leduc with his brother Kenny and me. Edith (Eddie) lives in Wetaskiwin. June lives in London, England, and is a librarian. Fern is a design consultant in Calgary. Sharon is married and lives in Peace River.

After Milton died in 1968, I sold the homestead. For years I cooked for oil camps. Augusta Tupper was one of my helpers. I am now at home with my beloved little dog and my sons, enjoying my retirement.

Pete and Marion Rudy
by Gladys Rudy

Pete was born in Duck River, Manitoba, on July 12, 1916, to Michael and Mary Rudy. Marion Lariviere was born in Frog Lake, Alberta, on July 14, 1922. They were married on August 16, 1942. Florence Houle was an attendant. A wedding supper and dance were held at Nick Tomilou's attended by a large crowd of well wishers. They raised two children: Stan, born in 1948, and Brenda, born in 1957.

Pete and Marion homesteaded SW-3-102-24-W5 and also farmed another half-section. In the winter Pete trapped northwest of Keg River along the Chinchaga. Marion clerked at the Hudson's Bay store.

Pete had heart problems and after he suffered a stroke that left him unable to speak, they moved to Manning in 1972. Marion spent five long years looking after Pete until he died on October 25, 1977. Pete will always be remembered for his love of children and the many times he was Santa Claus during the Christmas concerts in the district.

Marion, who passed away in August of 1990, will be remembered for all the times she volunteered to help with different groups such as the St. Judes Altar Society and the Keg River Ladies Club. She also organised a number of card tournaments. She loved to sew and made doll clothes by the dozens for her granddaughters.

Marion Rudy with Peterson children.

271

Lloyd Chorney, Wayne Rutter and Pete Rudy in Rudy's kitchen, 1970. Lesson 1 of how to skin a coyote.

Gladys and Stan Rudy, 1992.

Stan and Gladys Rudy
by Gladys Rudy (nee Hamelin)

Stan was born on August 29, 1948, to Pete and Marion Rudy at Keg River. We were married on October 27, 1976. I was the oldest daughter of Jim and Isobel Hamelin and had grown up in Keg River also. We were married in the Catholic church in Keg River.

Stan completed school in 1964 and worked for his dad in the summer on the farm. In the winter he cut bush on the seismic lines with the Caterpillar for Otto Krause. Stan also worked for Ken Fischer at the sawmill.

Stan took over his parents farm in 1972 when his dad became ill. He also worked for Kelemen Holdings in oilfield construction. He began as a cat skinner and worked his way up to supervisor.

I worked for the Hudson's Bay as a clerk for a while after we were married. Then I took teacher-aide training so I could work for Northland School Division. I worked at the school in Keg River until 1975. Starting in 1976, I drove school bus for the district until 1980.

We sold the farm to Les and Janice Freeman and moved to Manning in July, 1980. Stan got a job with Jackson Transport. In 1985 we moved to Rainbow Lake, where Stan worked for Northern Oilfield. We have moved three more times since then -first, to Clairmont to work for Krause, then to Grande Prairie, then to Sexmith where we still reside.

Stan and I have two children. Claudette was born in Peace River on October 27, 1971, and Michelle was born in Manning on September 7, 1976. They both reside with us. We now have a granddaughter! Kirsten Ashley Rudy was born to Michelle on September 17, 1993.

Stan is remembered in Keg River for his infectious laugh. Some people also remember Stan experimenting with his first 4 by 4. He drove across Steve Pawlowich's home field in mid-winter. The expression on Linda's face when she saw the lights of the truck coming across a field where there was no road was truly priceless!

Stan is a dedicated family man and an avid fisherman. He has always had a knack for telling a tale that could only be told by a fisherman!

I will always have fond memories of Keg River as my old home. While there I served on the recreation board, helped with the Ladies Club and sang in the St. Jude's choir.

Many fun hours were spent with Dave and

Claudette Rudy.

Michelle Rudy.

272

Doris Weber snowmobiling, playing broomball and fishing. Nor will I ever forget some of the encounters we had with wildlife as we drove back and forth to Manning.

Les and Janice Freeman still keep us informed on the happenings in Keg River.

Susan and Terry Russell
by Susan Russell

When we arrived in Keg River in May 1984, knee-deep mud and mosquitoes greeted us. Dana was two and Cody was one year old. There was a lot of rain that year but we didn't realize that was normal for Keg River!

We started on a log house while we lived in our trailer. Peeling all the logs required was an enormous job. Turning the 40-foot logs while peeling them was a task. We also had to keep them out of the mud so that they would be clean.

House building took quite a while before the roof was in place – we had to shovel out the snow a few times! We were finally able to move into the basement. It was another five years before the main house was ready to move into.

Cody's birthday party, Dana Russell, Kassey Zatko, Krissy Oster, Kim Halabisky, Clinton Batchelor, Cody Russell, Dustin House, Stanton Halabisky, Tony Oster.

of the trailer and had bounced and bruised to the point where we were unable to sell them. I began making pies, pies, and more pies, then tried slicing and drying to make apple chips. We made fruit leather of all kinds, using apples as the main ingredient!

The Russell's house in the making, 1984.

Terry started his own welding business in 1986 with an old truck and welder. In 1990 he was able to buy a new diesel truck and get it all customized the way he wanted. Then Terry had the misfortune of losing the truck in a fire.

During the summer of 1991 we built a log shop to use up the rest of those peeled logs. We built pig pens and cattle fences, burnt brush piles, picked roots, tried growing things in the mud and of course we continued to fight mosquitoes!

In the fall of 1993, Terry went to visit his mother in Kelowna and returned with 200 boxes of apples! We planned to sell them around the district, but the Spartan apples were at the back

Terry carrying two weiner pigs through the mud, 1984.

273

I started driving school bus in 1990 with an old bus. Then we bought a new Thomas. The bus is still fine but I'm a little greyer!

We have 12 cows and between 200 and 300 pigs. The feeding and milking and daily chores make for a busy life. Climbing in the pens of sows in knee-deep mud was getting to be scary. I finally REFUSED! Now we have troughs that can be filled from the outside of the pen!

Dana and Cody enjoy being pulled by the snowmobile while they ride on rubber inner tubes. Snow gets down their necks and up their back, and their eyelashes freeze together but they are always willing to go again!

Some city children walk their dogs, but the Russells walk Jersey calves! It keeps the calves trained to lead and provides a job to be done.

Terry's dream is to have a team of heavy horses. As a start we have purchased two colts.

We are living in a dream home and are enjoying life in Keg River!

Wayne and Reine Rutter
by Reine Rutter

My husband Wayne reported for work in Keg River with the Alberta Forest Service in September of 1968. I came up on the Greyhound bus from Edmonton in early October. What a ride that was! I was sure I was going to the end of the world, although the scenery was beautiful at that time of year.

We lived at the Forestry Station right across from the Keg River Cabins and Wayne was the Assistant Ranger. We lived in the second house from the highway. We had been married only 18 months when we moved from Edmonton. Keg River was to be our home until August 1971.

In his job as a forest ranger, Wayne had many duties, including directing fire fighting crews and issuing fire permits before any burning could be done. He also spent some of his time being a medic (you might say) on the MacKenzie Highway whenever there was an accident nearby. He was in his glory, of course, because he enjoys taking risks.

Wayne went hunting during hunting season, to ensure that we could at least have food on the table as the income from his job was very poor.

My thrill for extra income during the summer months was to wash blankets after there had been a forest fire. These were the blankets the men used while fighting the forest fire. It kept me busy for a couple of days as I did this on my wringer washing machine.

Wayne, Dena Rutter and their dog Butch.

I helped at school with the Brownie pack and quite enjoyed that. Otherwise I was busy being a home maker.

Our oldest daughter Dena was born while we lived in Keg River. I went to the Peace River Hospital for her delivery on October 9, 1969. She was almost two years old when we left the Keg. Our second daughter Rhea was born the following May (1972) in Nordegg, which is where we transferred to from Keg River.

One of the funniest times Wayne had at Keg River was when he was trying to teach Lloyd Chorney how to ride a motorcycle! One thing that we enjoyed while we lived in the Keg River area was the many fine people we met there.

One couple we often think of is the Lowes, Norm and Lucille. He was the grain elevator operator for a while. They moved from Keg River to Buck Lake. Pete and Marion Rudy were one of those couples to whom we were ever so grateful. Marion visited us during Expo 1986. I was sorry to hear she has passed away.

One of my fondest memories is the peacock feathers that Frank Jackson delivered to our home the day we were moving. I still have them and they are in excellent shape.

I learned to operate a snowmobile while in Keg River and had so much fun doing that. The MacKenzie Highway was always a challenge to drive while it was gravel.

I really enjoyed reading the book *The Homemade Brass Plate*, written about the life of Dr. Mary Jackson. I have passed it on to several friends and they have all enjoyed it even though they don't have a clue about that northern country.

We met many good people living in the area.

The natives were always most obliging with us. We have felt ever since we left the northern area that those were the best years of our lives, and we still feel the same today.

We now live on Vancouver Island in Qualicum Beach. We have only moved once in 10 years, so we feel settled now. Wayne still works for the Alberta Forest Service fighting fires in the summertime and does different jobs the remainder of the year. I work for the Royal Bank in Parksville.

Our oldest daughter Dena lives in Edmonton and our youngest daughter Rhea lives in Coquitlam, British Columbia.

Wayne Rutter family, 1989.

Floyd and Grace Schwindt and Family
by Grace Schwindt

In mid-August, 1959, Floyd and I moved with our children Phillip and Sally to Keg River. We were pastoring at the Pentecostal Church at Oyen, Alberta, and we heard of the need for someone to open an evangelical church in Keg River. Rev. Harry Nettleton from Peace River had held some services at Keg and he felt that there was a need for a Pentecostal Church there.

Frank and Jewel Zurovec from Texas had spent some months at Keg River ministering and then moved back to Texas.

Our trip north was quite an eventful one. The MacKenzie Highway was under construction, so there were many detours. Many cars and trucks were stuck in the mud and we all had to be pulled out by the Cat. We finally arrived at Keg River about midnight. This was the beginning of a nine-year stay which we enjoyed and will never forget.

We lived in a little house across from the Hudson's Bay store. The house left much to be desired!

One night a man from Peace River stayed overnight with us. He was nicely settling down for the night when a cat joined him. He got up and put the cat out. By the time he got back to the bed the cat was also back! He got up and repeated this a few times, thinking to himself that these people surely had a lot of cats, until he went to the window and found a hole in the screen!

Floyd had a lot of work to do on the building to make it more comfortable. After the house was built, this building became the church. We held services and Sunday school while we were living in the building.

About a week after we arrived at Keg River, Phillip started school. We used to watch the children riding horses to the school, which was less than a half mile from our house. Where we had come from, the children went to school by bus, so Floyd was able to start the bus service for the school children of the district, driving the first school bus in 1961. During our stay the power and telephone lines were put in. We also saw the building of the railroad.

We will always remember the many friends that we made there in Keg River. Mr. Harry Bowe was a good, kind friend and we appreciated being able to go over and visit and talk with him. Dr. Mary Jackson was a big help to us when our children and ourselves needed medical help. We appreciated the Jacksons and the times we were able to visit with them.

The first winter we lived in the Harvey Reid place. Harvey, along with Gordon, Patricia and

Floyd and Grace Schwindt with children, Phillip, Darlene and Sally, 1992.

Bobby, became good friends of our whole family. Space does not allow for us to mention all the people who were close friends. Keg River holds a special place in our hearts.

In 1975 we moved to Spruce Lake, Saskatchewan, and pastored a church there for seven years. In 1982 we moved to Mont Nebo, Saskatchewan, where we now make our home.

Phillip is a Lutheran minister and is a chaplain of a nursing home in Melville, Saskatchewan. It is so nice to have him living closer to home. He is single. Sally is married to Frank Stariha and lives in Osoyoos, British Columbia. They have two children – Jennifer and Aaron. They are quickly growing up. Darlene lives in Hamiota, Manitoba. She is single and works at a bakery.

Floyd and I pastor a small Pentecostal Church at Shell Lake 12 miles from our home.

(Editor's Note: We are sad to add that Mr. Schwindt passed away in 1993.)

Mykola and Maria Shemeluik
by Elsie Halabisky

Mykola (Mike) arrived in Canada from Austria in 1911. He took up homesteading in Garland, Manitoba. Three years later, his wife Maria and daughter Nellie joined him. In 1929, Mike and Maria and Nellie and her husband Luke Fedorchuk moved to a homestead in Keg River (SE-27-101-23-W5). It was hard work turning a patch of bush into a farm. There was little time for pleasure but Maria made the best rhubarb wine in the country!

Maria got to enjoy her grandchildren before she died in 1944. She is buried in Keg River.

Mike moved to Hotchkiss with his daughter and her family and later retired to Manning. He passed away in 1959.

Locals L-R: Annie Michalchuk, Annie Rudy, Mrs. Rudy, Mrs. Shemeluik, Luke Fedorchuk, Tina Pawlowich, Pete Rudy, Mr. Shemeluik, Daisy and Martha Fedorchuk.

John Smith
by Sarah Price

Johnny Smith was Mabel Omoth's (my mom's) uncle who came to Keg River to homestead in about 1957. He homesteaded the NE-8 and NW-9-101-22-W5 where Dan Gray had previously lived. Johnny grew some pretty good crops on this land and was known as a good Catskinner. He worked for several people brush cutting.

After he retired and had a hard time looking after himself, he moved in with my sister and her husband, Benita and Terry Price. While Johnny lived with Benita, he looked after the pigs and he enjoyed that so much he diligently got up every morning at 5 A.M. to feed them. One day Terry and some friends butchered the last pig. The next morning Uncle Johnny got up and took the water pail out to feed the pig. He came back about 15 minutes later. It was obvious that he'd forgotten about the activities of the previous day and was too embarrassed to say anything!

We always had a good laugh when Uncle Johnny lived with us. He used to visit his daughter, Beatrice, in Edmonton about once a month because seniors got a discount from the Greyhound Bus company if they rode on certain days. One day he was feeling his rum when he decided to catch the bus. He packed his suitcase and wouldn't think of taking his cane on the bus with him although he needed it badly. In order to get the cane to Edmonton, he got the saw and cut the cane in half and shoved it in his suitcase. We never ever heard how he made out at the other end with his cane!

Johnny died in May of 1982. My husband, Keith, and I bought his land and are now living on it.

Xavier and Angeline Sowan
by Margaret Befus

Xavier and Angeline were native Indians who lived in the Carcajou area all of their lives. Angeline was a Wanuch before her marriage. They had 13 children.

They owned land (SW-30-101-19-W5) after 1922. This was the quarter where most of the village of Carcajou was in 1916 when the area was surveyed. The Sowans lived there when the survey crew visited.

Xavier still hunted with a bow and arrow he made himself in 1920. He also travelled the river in a handmade dugout canoe.

Xavier Sowan was born in 1853 and knew the area of Carcajou very well. Although he only spoke Cree, he was able to warn many of the newer residents about the dangers of the river in the spring of 1934 when the ice was jamming. What followed was one of the worst floods known to have struck the area. His knowledge and warnings probably saved many animals' and possibly even people's lives.

His knowledge of the river came from living beside it for so many years. He made his living trapping and hunting and did well because he was willing to learn about nature. He was 81 in 1934 when he was giving his warnings about the flood. He was also probably an observer of the flood that had struck the Carcajou area in the 1890's.

Xavier died at the age of 83 in the summer of 1936. He was the second last person to be buried in the Carcajou cemetery. Ten other Sowans are buried in Carcajou. These people are believed to be Xavier and Angeline's children and grandchildren. It is not known where Angeline is buried.

Ted and Muriel Stigsen and Family
by Muriel Stigsen

My mother Martha travelled with my dad Roy on his gold-seeking ventures. They landed at Carcajou in 1920, liked what they saw, and decided this would be home. I was to have no choice in the matter.

Charlie Gram's Trading Post was open at this time, selling the necessities and buying furs. The Hudson's Bay Post was also open periodically.

Dad and his two brothers still had gold fever. With another man, they were off in the spring of 1921, searching along the Hay River. They were to die there. Their raft was found washed up below Alexandra Falls. Their bodies were found on a sand bar just below Lady Evelyn Falls, not too far from one another. Only the man who accompanied them survived, but he left immediately after the accident.

My mom, Martha Bayes, remarried in July 1923. She married Charlie Rankin from Carcajou, in Fort Vermilion.

Mother, a persistent letter-writer, organized a petition to the government for a post office at Carcajou. She was finally granted permission to open and run a post office in 1927. During the next 33 years the mail kept her busy, along with household duties. Since there was no school she was also my teacher.

In early November 1933 the river ice broke up, caused by a chinook upstream. The ice then refroze in chunks that looked like the Rocky Mountains. The old natives told anybody who would listen that this was a bad omen. Xavier Sowan did his best to warn everyone on the flats to move to higher ground. Some people believed him, packed up their belongings and moved with their animals up into the hills. Others were not convinced and stayed in their homes.

I rode horseback with Abe Friesen to look at the river when we heard the water was rising. What we saw made us rush home and start moving the animals. The horses and cattle were driven up the hill but the horses ran away and went back to their barns. The water kept on coming up! It finally stopped with an inch to spare at our house.

The wells were ruined and there was water everywhere but none fit to drink. The sheep pens were high enough and the sheep were O.K. The horses moved to the top of the manure pile!

The ice jam was 30 miles down river from the McGrane's flat (now called Armstrong's flat). Just the McGrane and Carcajou flats flooded in 1934. No lives were lost but it took a long time for it to dry up.

Ted was born in 1913 to Johanna and Nels Stigsen in Calgary's Manchester district. They were raising silver foxes and a steady supply of meat was required to feed these hungry, growing animals. It was decided they would move north to Carcajou where fox food would be plentiful.

The family arrived in Peace River with two box cars of supplies. Mother, Dad, and sister Nellie were all in on the move; they were accompanied by a cousin of Jack O'Sullivan (a Carcajou resident) named Bob Hardy. In Peace River Crossing they built a barge to carry them downstream to Carcajou.

The barge drifted after being pulled into the stream and it was guided by a sweep when necessary. The family hired Charlie Rankin as a pilot since they were not familiar with the river. The trip on the river took several days.

The first winter, the Stigsens lived in a small log cabin. Wilfred Rankin was hired to build a log house before the family arrived. After they arrived, the barge they had travelled on was dismantled and used for the floor in their new home.

Jack O'Sullivan had come to Carcajou in 1927. He trapped to earn a living. The Stigsens had known his family in Calgary. When Jack got an inheritance of $10 000 from his dad, he decided to buy McLean's store. The McLean family sold and moved to open another store in Fort Vermilion.

Jack took Nels Stigsen in as a partner and left him to care for the store while Jack looked into operating a river boat on the Peace. The *O'Sullivan-Stigsen* passenger and freight boats travelled the Peace for many years. The two boats that were operated by this company were *The Wolverine* and *The Beaver*.

In 1935, Nels, Johanna and Nellie left Carcajou for Vancouver. The Okerholms and McGranes left at the same time. Many of them had not recovered from the devastating effects of the 1934 flood. The population of Carcajou dropped dramatically during that time. Shortly after, the population again began to rise as more Mennonite families moved in.

Ted was left to operate the store, so he quit farming. He butchered the livestock and sold the meat through the store for as little as four cents a pound. The foxes were all killed around the same time, pelted out and sold. The 10 pairs of foxes the Stigsen family had brought in had cost them $1500 a pair. The pelts were sold for $50 each.

Trappers in the area travelled in all directions up and down the river and along the tributaries

Summer at Monias Creek.

to the Peace such as the Buffalo, Little Buffalo, Wolverine, Keg, and a number of creeks that flow into the Peace within 50 miles of Carcajou.

Ted's store and the Hudson's Bay bought furs and grubstaked trappers. Some of the trappers were Benjamin Cardinal, Xavier Sowan, the Wanuch family, the Armstrongs, Hudson "Bay" Bruce, Ed Hamelin, Harry Gould, Hans Lou, Jack Costello, and many others. Later a few Mennonite families also bought their supplies in the store.

"A Rose between two trappers." L-R: Hans Leu, Muriel Bayes, Harry Gould.

Ted and I were married in June 1942. We travelled to the west coast on our honeymoon. Ted's sister still lives in Duncan with her husband Jim.

We ran the store and helped with the boats until river transportation stopped in 1952. The boat trip to Peace River (150 miles) took at least two days and often much more. The return trip down river was much faster. In high water there was usually a problem with driftwood. In low water, the sandbars posed such a threat that travelling during the night was impossible.

Midnight Moonlight at Monias Creek. Christmas Eve Hans Leu's Cabin, 1931.

One trip, Ted made the 110 miles to Fort Vermilion in 10 hours. The boat had no load and was therefore able to make a fast trip.

The telephone installation to our place was an event that would change our community. With plenty of persuasion and money, the government put a cable across the river for us on April 9th and 10th, 1974. They had to install 85-foot poles on each bank to hold the line.

The flood of 1974 was also in April. This time the ice jam was right close to the settlement. The ice actually bumped the marking bells hanging on the telephone line, some 30 feet above the river. The ice cut the wire at the base of the pole on the west side of the river, knocking out service. Ted was home by himself on the east side of the river, during the flood, so when the phone went off it was back to the old days of the walkie-talkie. We were lucky the ice jam broke when it did and once again our buildings were spared with only minor flooding.

I had moved to the west side of the river in 1962 with the post office that I began running after my mother retired. Ted closed the store and moved, too, in 1978. He sold what he could of the stock and gave away the rest.

We have a son, Donald. He is married to Theresa and they have four boys and two girls. Their names are Fabian (deceased), Dion, Curtis, Annette, Cort, and Pamela. We also have a daughter Sandra. She is married to Dennis Sivertsen. They have two daughters Rene and Shauna. We all continue to live in Carcajou.

Bill and Gladys Tkachuk
as told by Gladys Tkachuk

We arrived in Keg River from Red Water in 1965. Bill, our son Grant and I came in Pat Ambler's grain truck with the furniture on July 5th. It was an extremely hot, dusty day and we stopped at Twin Lakes to wash our hands and faces.

We then went on to Louis Jackson's house, where we were to look after the place for him. We turned off the highway into the yard, I took one look at the place including the house and said, "I'm not staying here!" Bill said, "Give it a couple of weeks."

The house had not been lived in for quite some time. We ended up living there for over six years, the first year with no power! I had all my appliances with me and there was no way of using them. I switched to a gas iron and gas washing machine. The washing machine would work when Bill was at home but whenever he left the yard it went "kaput!"

In September school started. Our daughter June was in grade nine, Wayne in grade four and Grant in grade two. At that time there were about 110 students, four teachers and one counsellor at the school.

In 1972 we bought a homestead of 160 acres, 88 of which were in crop. At that time I began to help Bill in the field. I had refused to in previous years!

I had a variety of chickens and turkeys when at 4 A.M. I heard them making a terrible noise. I got up and looked out the front window and saw

Muriel and Ted Stigsen at their home in Carcajou.

Wayne Tkachuk with daughters Fershell and Latoya.

a bear chasing the chickens. I woke Bill up and told him about the bear. He got up and started slowly getting dressed, so I said, "Just put your boots on!" Bill raced into the chilly night with his rifle and found out the bear had been right into the chicken coop. Bill shot the bear and proceeded to return to the house.

In the meantime I had locked the door and hid under the covers. Poor Bill was knocking on the door when I yelled, "Is it dead?" He replied "I wouldn't be standing here if it wasn't!" So I got up and let him back in the house! The kids have all moved away. June has one boy named Trent. Wayne married Alice Batchelor from Keg River and they have two girls – Fershell and Latoya. Grant has one daughter Lanelle from his first marriage and got remarried in 1991.

As the years went by we've become more financially secure. Bill bought a claim in the Yukon and he travels there each summer to pan for gold. We live on the farm whenever we are in Keg River.

Bill and Gladys Tkachuk with friend Bill Roder.

Nick Tomilou
by Annie Michalchuk

Nick came to Keg River from Russia in 1930. He took SE-4-102-24-W5 as a homestead. Nick worked very hard, hauling logs to build himself a house. Then he built barns for his animals.

"Big Nick", as he was known around the district, was a bachelor. He was large in stature but also had a big heart, especially for children. We never counted the years he was the jovial Santa Claus at the Christmas concerts.

Nick often volunteered his house for dances after Sports Days or weddings. He also helped organize the annual Sports Days. Nick was an active community booster.

During the rabies epidemic in 1951 Nick lost a number of animals, including some cows and pigs. This broke his heart because he loved each of his animals.

When Nick was diagnosed with diabetes, he struggled with learning to stay on his strict diet. He finally came to live with us and I looked after him for two years, but he was not a very cooperative patient! Nick died in March 1966 at the age of 71.

Nick Tomilou.

Oliver Travers

by Oliver Travers

The first time I saw Carcajou was 40 years ago in the middle of June. Three of my pack horses took off, following the old wagon trail from Keg River. I met Almer Omoth on the old road. He told me my horses were heading down the trail at a fast trot.

A few miles farther on, I met Archie Christian with a team of horses hitched to a wagon. The horses were tired, as they were almost knee deep in the mud on the road. Archie said my horses ran out in the bush and kept heading towards the Peace River and Carcajou.

Mile after mile of mud and fighting off hoards of mosquitoes brought me to Elmer and Hepsey Dovey's ranch. Charles, their son, told me he knew the horses got away from someone and there would be someone looking for them, so he had put them in his corral.

"You look tired and hungry," said Hepsey. "Come in the house. I will make you a meal."

It was late in the day, but it being spring and this far north, there were many hours of daylight before the sun set in the north. Charles saddled his horse and I put my saddle on one of my runaway cayuses. We went on a sightseeing tour of the little farming community. We visited Lou and Eugenie Tupper. They had some children who were afraid of strangers.

Howard Price served us bannock, along with fried partridge meat and coffee strong enough to tan brown saddle leather.

We rode over and met a tall grey-haired fellow who was known as Slim Kemp. Laura and Charlie Christian were living in some log cabins. Charles stopped at every neighbor's place and had a visit.

With the sun still high, we rode to the water's edge of the mighty Peace River. Charles pulled his old 30-30 rifle from his scabbard on his saddle and fired a shot in the air. This was a signal to the people over at the trading post that someone wanted to be hauled across the wide body of water. A boat motor started. With the last rays of sunlight glistening off the metal boat motor, a long wooden boat could be seen riding up and down over the big waves.

Ted Stigsen was the old river rat. He knows every bend in the Peace River for miles on each side of Carcajou. With 50 years of fighting high water waves and sand bars, his lifetime of experiences would fill a big book.

We got across the river just in time to join Ted and his wife Muriel in a big meal she had prepared.

A few trappers' cabins, along with the Stigsen's buildings, were all that were on the east side of the river.

Three big men, all brothers – Vincent, Willie and Louis Armstrong – came paddling a long boat upstream. They had paddled from five miles downstream, where they lived on one of the big river flats. These fellows were trappers. Big Louis asked me if the surveyors I was working for were hiring any men.

I told him to ride one of my horses, but Louis walked so fast he didn't want any horse to get in his way.

He got a job cutting pack trail with an axe he kept so sharp you could shave with the blade.

The survey party had four university students hired to cut trail. All four of them couldn't cut as many trees as Louis . He was a bush man. Our pack trails led from Keg River west to the Alaska Highway.

Our big tent camp was set up in Ma Harrington's yard at Keg River Cabins. She told us she owned the whole damn valley and we better be quiet or she would kick our rear ends down the road!

The sun was just peeping over the hills when I looked up to the old Keg Post road. I saw two young men riding a big brown horse. A cloud of mosquitoes hung just above their heads that made a darker shadow over the sun than the horse did.

"Who are those fellows?" I asked Eva.

"Oh, that's a pair of hooterites. They moved in from the south of Calgary. They won't be here next year," she replied.

"Why won't they be here?" I asked.

"They'll starve out, the same as the 50 homesteaders that came from the south. They ain't tough enough to survive here."

The men who crawled down from the big horse were Ken Batchelor and Dave Befus. They told me the horse belonged to Jim Hunter, a trapper who lived farther up the trail.

"How's things going on the homesteads?" I asked.

They replied, "We are seeing a whole lot more dinner times than we see dinners. We will hang in there for a few years and see what happens. We spent 10 dollars and made a bet with the government that we are tough enough to stay on the homestead for 20 years."

I was hired by the survey crew as the boss horse packer. I couldn't even throw a diamond hitch, the twisting of 50 feet of rope that secures the pack to the back of the horse. I was so embarrassed I took my broncs and tied them to trees where none of my crew could watch me load the packs of those snorting horses.

I threw a half hitch on the pack boxes and just kept wrapping the rope round and round until the rope was all used up. Of course, the packs didn't stay on too well. Yes, I was a greenhorn. I asked Ken and Dave if they knew how to throw a diamond hitch.

A few good lessons from my new friends and I could throw a diamond hitch on a bronc that was lying upside down.

Our pack trails led west from Keg River. I didn't know there was so much swamp and muskeg in Alberta as what we put those poor, heavily-loaded horses through.

Then we had to cross the Chinchaga River, that quite often, after a big rain storm, can rise four feet in one night and make the horses swim. We built enough rafts that we could have supplied the ark with timber.

In the middle of October, the survey party shut down for the winter. They planned on working all winter using dog teams. I put four dog teams together with six dogs in each team. When 20 men arrived in Manning the first day of November, it was 40 below. The whole crew turned their vehicles around and went back to Calgary.

With no job for the winter, I went to visit the Batchelors. Ken was away cutting logs and Rose had just had a baby that weighed two and one half pounds. The girl, Alice, had been delivered with the help of a neighbor whose only experience was having children of her own. Rose's daughters, Shirley and Irene, had the baby lying on a hot water bottle, the baby was so small. I knew she would have a tough time surviving, but survive she did.

I went on to the Befus homestead. Dave was there, batching by himself in a little sugar shack he'd built. He was married to the school ma'am. Margaret was teaching about 30 kids at the village of Keg River where she also stayed. I stayed with Dave for a few days, as the temperature was holding at 50 below zero and my truck refused to start.

Every morning, Dave faithfully milked the old cow while she got a hump in her back and shivered every time his cold hands touched her milk faucets. Seven old white Light Sussex hens sat on their nest boxes. Dave would slip his hand under the hens and finding no eggs he'd say, "Well, it's a little early for breakfast."

"We'll wait till ten o'clock," he said. "There'll be three more eggs then, and we can eat breakfast."

You can call that patience, or faith. Whatever it was, Dave had it. It was so damn cold in that barn, I just figured there'd be no breakfast that day.

We sat there sipping more coffee. I kept one eye on the clock. When it reached the Magic Hour, we checked the nest boxes. Sure enough, three more eggs.

Dave broke them in a bowl and added some milk. It looked kind of gooey to me, but there's nothing worse than a fussy beggar! Turned out, they were the best scrambled eggs I'd ever tasted.

Now, we had a great idea to get my truck started. We put the harness on the milk cow and hitched her to my truck. Maybe she could pull and start it.

Old Red wasn't real impressed with the idea. She was getting madder by the minute, when I got elected to lead the cow. Dave was the engineer. The cow refused to pull.

Dave called his dog and told him to bite the cow. Wow, what an explosion! Old Red took after me, and I made the hundred yard dash toward a big woodpile.

Water well boring machine, Carcajou.

With the cow in hot pursuit, Dave managed to get the truck going. That wasn't good enough for Old Red. She wanted a piece of my hide!

I made another long dash, this time for the barn door. That gentle old bossy was right behind me, complete with the truck! Her horns were tickling my backbone and her tongue was licking the tail of my coat when we piled up in the doorway. Who said crippled cowboys can't run?

We cut the harness from our "tow truck". You'll have to ask Dave how the milking went after the pulling contest.

Dave had a water-well-boring machine powered by one big horse that went round and round while the big auger bored in the ground. Dave gave me a crash course on how to run this machine. We dug a few wells in the Keg River district, striking water at about 30 feet. We got news from Carcajou by moccasin telegraph that a few people there also wanted some wells dug.

My father-in-law, Jim Locke, and I loaded a horse in an old truck, hitched on the well digger and started on the winter road to Carcajou. About halfway there, the old truck died on me. There was nothing we could do but unload the horse and start walking.

This was fine for me, but Jim has a wooden leg. About every five miles, we built a fire and rested a while. A pack of wolves howled from every direction. They seemed to be following us. My big dog followed us for awhile then for some reason, he left us and went back to the truck.

We got tired, but every time the wolves got closer and howled, we found another burst of energy. We got to Dovey's ranch about 2 A.M. This didn't bother these pioneer people. They got out of bed and made us lunch.

Charles and I took a team of horses the next day and went for the well-digging machine. There was nothing left of my big dog but a few bunches of hair. The wolves had taught him the law of the north country, where it is survival of the fittest. We tried digging at Dovey's but we hit gravel and big stones at about ten feet down. This machine wouldn't work in stones.

Charles moved the well-digger to Lou Tupper's. These people had 16 children. When those kids saw Jim and me and that strange-looking machine their uncle was pulling behind a team of horses, they must have thought the end of the world was coming! They ran to a big straw pile, where pigs had big tunnels in the dry yellow straw. Kids of all sizes, with big eyes, were peeking out at us as we drove through their yard.

When Mrs. Tupper yelled, "Dinner is ready!" it was like an army coming on the double to get a place at the long table. I have to wonder how these pioneer people could find enough food for two or three extra people to join them at the table. We have had many fine meals with all the families from Carcajou, as well as at Rose and Ken Batchelor's at Keg River.

Many times Rose saw me come in their yard with a string of pack horses. Somehow, she knew that I hadn't eaten in three days. The kids gathered the eggs while Rose peeled another spud and added a cup of water to the soup pot. I gulped down the good food like a female wolf that was nursing pups.

Oh, for the good old days spent at Keg River and Carcajou. If we could just turn back the years and once more sit down with these great people and have a darn good visit and throw another cup of water in the old stew pot just in case some hungry stranger might stop in for a meal!

Louis and Eugenie Tupper
by Patsy Lindberg (nee Tupper)

Louis (my dad) was born in Scots Bay, Nova Scotia, the third oldest in a family of six. His dad, Harmon Tupper, owned and operated a sawmill. In the late summer of 1926 Dad came west, working in the harvest around North Battleford, Saskatchewan, to pay his travel expenses. His older brother Eldon had a trapline along the Cadotte Lake near Peace River. He invited Dad to come and stay with him a while.

For several years they trapped together using dogs and sleds. During the summer months Dad worked for Scotty Watson on his farm just north of the town of Peace River. Scotty had the first market garden in the Peace River area. He also owned some livestock. After working for Scotty for two summers, Dad wanted to have a farm of his own.

Dad returned to Nova Scotia for a brief visit. When he returned, he continued on to Keg River. He and Glady Harrington had an agreement to farm together. All summer Dad farmed, often working with neighbors. He owned a few cattle and horses. Most of the farming was done with horses.

Dad built a little log cabin on his trapline and trapped all winter. Three friends trapped and stayed with him often, using dogs and sleds to bring in the fur. They caught lynx, coyote, beaver, fisher, marten, weasels and squirrels. Fur prices were mostly low but a little money went a lot further that it does today.

He loved the freedom he felt in the wilderness and the wildlife that lived there. He never let a wounded animal get away if he could help it. He understood the ways of most of the animals he hunted, tracking them for days when they were injured. Wildlife that lived close to his home were never hunted if they caused him no harm. He enjoyed watching them.

On December 1, 1941, Dad married Eugenie Dovey in Peace River. The weather was very cold and a blizzard was blowing as they made their way to Peace River with horse and cutter. They arrived at midnight and aroused the Anglican minister, Spinney. He was the only one that they could find. He was a very generous fellow and after the wedding, offered them a place to rest the night.

The next day they returned to Keg River to start their lives together. To impress his new bride, Dad brought a coyote he had snared into the house. When he had found it, the coyote was still alive, so he knocked it out with a stick. Mom wasn't sure she liked this furry beast and she was sure it was still alive. Suddenly the coyote leaped to its feet and dived out the window. In shock, they watched it disappear into the bush.

Mom and Dad made their home with logs, filling the cracks with a mud-and-straw mix. Poles were used as rafters and insulated with flax straw. For light in the winter they lit their Coleman lamp or lantern. These lamps burned coal oil, their little tanks pumped full of air, with one or two mantles to control the flame. Sometimes the mantles cracked when jarred, allowing fire to escape. One evening the flames repeatedly flared up and the fire caught in the flax straw insulation in the ceiling.

Mom, Dad and their three oldest children – Aurora, Diana and Jackie – who were small at the time, were all home. They were able to put the fire out, but not before the interior of the house was ruined. No one was hurt but the house was unfit to live in.

In 1945 Mom and Dad and their growing family moved to Carcajou, where they had a two-storey log house. It had a large storage room added on, which was used as a blacksmith shop and a garage. Raspberries, grass and weeds grew on the sod roof. A batterypowered wind charger provided power for electric lights and radio. Dad and Mom lived with Grandma and Grandpa (Elmer and Hepsey Dovey) in the old Rankin house for a while as their home was built.

One day while Mom was washing clothes, her baby daughter Jackie (Philipine) wandered down to the river. Dad found her moments later, lying face down in a puddle. She still showed some signs of life but they could not revive her. She died on July 17, 1946.

In the summer Dad hauled water from the river in two 45-gallon barrels on a stone boat. In the winter we melted ice or snow. At spring break-up and fall freeze-up, good water was very hard to get. Mom had an old gas-powered wringer washer to wash clothes. Sometimes her fingers got caught in the wringer. That sure did hurt. Sometimes she was overcome by gas fumes. Dad would help her leave the room and revive her.

Dad raised horses, cattle and hogs. Mom kept a few turkeys and chickens. Around 1954 the turkeys contacted tuberculosis and had to be destroyed. After that, Mom and Dad never kept turkeys. The chickens did not get the disease.

Horses were never Dad's favorite animal. As soon as he could, he bought a tractor and sold his horses. First he bought a small Cat which was super slow and later he bought a W-6 Massey tractor.

Owls were determined to steal chickens from the farm. They slipped through the small windows in the hen house to get them. Dad said that he heard an owl on the roof one night, wringing a chicken's neck the whole night long. The squawking was horrible. I didn't think it took that long for an owl to kill a chicken. Weasels were really plentiful one summer. They killed a lot of chickens, too. They even killed hens as they sat on their nests.

When rabies swept through the area, a sheep and a huge red boar were the only losses we had. We saw animals such as foxes, mice wolves and coyotes that acted very strange and gave us plenty to worry about.

We often picked wild berries with Dad during the summer and early fall. One day we were picking saskatoons on Moore's flat when Dad heard something moving on the other side of the bush that he was picking on. Noviena had been picking beside him and he thought that she had moved around the bush. "How's the berries there, Beanie?" he asked. I looked up just as a startled young black bear took off in fright. We thought it was very funny but Dad was red to the neck.

The grain was cut with a binder in the fall and stooked six bundles per stook. When the grain was dry, the fellows got together to thrash it. The first years horses pulled the hay racks. As the bundles were tossed on the hay racks, mice would run in all directions. Gus and I would catch them and put them in a big coffee jar.

I never knew there were so many different varieties of mice in the area. We found deer mice, kangaroo mice, house mice, field mice, and some we couldn't even find descriptions for. We put our mouse farm under a willow in the cow pasture. One day our mice were all gone when we came with more from the field. Every day after that, our mice disappeared. As we were putting the day's catch in the jar one evening, we heard an owl in a tree nearby. He was watching and waiting for another easy lunch.

Mom got correspondence lessons for us until the school was built in Carcajou. She taught the first lessons in an upstairs room. One spring morning as Mom was teaching Aurora and Diana upstairs, Gus and I played downstairs. We made little teepees in the woodbox and lit a fire under them. Mom started smelling smoke and came to investigate. My rear end was soon hotter than the fire we had started. Gus only got a scolding as Mom said that little kids learn from older ones!

Gramma took over teaching us in 1955. We walked the mile and a half to her house each school day, studied for the regular school hours and then walked home again. Along the way was a red-ant hill that provided hours of amusement. If we did well in our lessons Gramma would count out exactly 15 raisins each. We took some of these and fed our pet ants. We also took fresh milk. They seemed to like both.

We tamed a little saw-whet owl and named her Tweety. She went hunting mice with us, catching them as we scared them out of hiding. Soon she was taking mice from our fingers without touching us. One day Dad offered her a pail of berries. She reacted in anger, screaming and glowering at him!

Somewhere around 1957-58 some of our cattle got pink-eye. One big black cow went completely blind with it. Her eyes glowed white like expresionless pools.

Some years food was plentiful. Others were very lean, even at Christmas. One Christmas was especially poor for us with no promise of anything to eat other than a little wild meat that Dad was able to catch. Ted Stigsen came over to visit from the east side of the river where he lived. He brought several boxes for us. In them was a complete Christmas dinner including a turkey, candy and toys. We were really thankful. It was a very nice Christmas after all!

Dad often cooked for himself before he got married and even sometimes afterward. One year he decided we should make some pies for Christmas. He gave the instructions and we (his girls) made the lemon and chocolate cream pies. We stored them in the outside storage granary. We forgot to bring them in early enough for them to thaw before serving them.

At first we tried to cut them with a knife but it didn't make a dent. Someone got the smart idea that we cut them with an axe. Doug took a swing and the pie went flying. Thank goodness it was frozen! We nearly wrecked the table getting our dessert. Dad scratched his chin and thoughtfully muttered to himself, "I don't think we put enough lard in those crusts. They are a little tough, aren't they?"

Dad and Mom had 16 children – four boys and 12 girls.

Tupper children and Dennis Sivertson.

Aurora was born on May 8, 1942. She married Steve Poch and they have one daughter, Mavis, and live in Tisdale, Saskatchewan.

Diana was born July 8, 1943. She married Dr. Ernie Williams and they have five children: Shirley, Jack, Joyce, Lily and Elliot. They live in Stellerton, Nova Scotia.

Philipine (Jackie) was born October 24, 1944, and died on July 17, 1946.

I **(Patsy)** was born March 16, 1946, and married Verner Lindberg. We live in Deadwood and have four children: Wesley, Sylvia, Philip and Sven.

Noviena was born November 16, 1947, and married Christian Quast. They and their three boys – Roger, Bruce and Steven – live in Westerose.

Augusta (Gus) was born March 30, 1949. Augusta married Gene Kuhn, a building contractor and farmer in Wetaskiwin, Alberta. Michael, LaRene and Karl are their three children.

Douglas was born June 26, 1950, and married Darlene Barboundy. They live in Carcajou, where Doug is a carpenter and farmer. Their children are Darla, Becky and Raymond.

Merry married Larry Grapentine, a dairyman in Millet, Alberta. Their children are Danny, Darryl and Leona. Merry was born on December 24, 1951.

Ida married Loucian Paradis, a caretaker for the Wetaskiwin Hospital. Adrian and Victoria are their children. Ida was born on April 4, 1953

Janette was born on July 22, 1954. She works at the seniors' lodge in Winfield, where she lives with Ken Senft. Teena, Angie and Janelle are her children.

James was born July 22, 1954. He is a laborer and his home is in North Star. His children are Christine (Andy Pyddle), James, and Nicole.

Benjamin was born October 18, 1956. He died on the trapline of hypothermia on January 24, 1972.

Sharon is married to Rodney Baumback, a forester in Prince George, British Columbia. They have three children: Kristen, Tyler and Aaron. Sharon was born on September 22, 1958.

Anne born February 2, 1960, married Arnie Stang. He works as a maintenance man for United Grain Growers in Millet. The names of their four children are Terri, Frank, Chris and Corrina.

Kenneth was born January 21, 1963. He has a daughter, Candy, and farms in Carcajou.

Virginia was born January 31, 1965. She is a nurse and lives with her boys Nathan and Jonathan in Prince George.

(Editor's Note: the following tribute was written for Lou Tupper after his death in 1991. It says so much about this pioneer we wanted to share it with you.)

When Louis was a boy, he loved the sea.
He liked to see the ships come in.
When he became a man, he went across Canada
To a place called Carcajou. He made this place his home,
Louis loved the outdoors,
Loved to go hunting and fishing.
He was a kind man who loved his family and friends and took time for them all.
In the winter he would be on his trapline.
He loved it. Louis lived a full and good life,
Even when he got old he never showed his age.
He just "Loved the Outdoors".

Douglas and Darlene Tupper
by Darlene Tupper and Patsy Lindberg

Douglas Trueman Tupper was born June 26, 1950, to Louis and Eugenie Tupper of Carcajou. With five older sisters to make life interesting, Douglas learned to appreciate the finer things in life, like cooking, sewing, and coping with unexpected little surprises. Six more sisters and three brothers were born later.

The Tuppers lived in a two-story log house with a sod roof. Weeds grew with the grass on the roof.

Lou and Eugenie Tupper.

Back Row, L-R: Patsy, Jim, Dianna, Aurora, Janette. Front Row, L-R: Augusta, Douglas, Noviena, Ida, 1955.

The roof leaked during heavy rainstorms. Every fall Dad mixed mud and straw to fill the cracks between the logs to keep out the cold. On the coldest nights a fire was kept burning all night in the wood cook stove, which was the only source of heat.

Three oldest children, Patsy, Phillipa, Aurora, 1946.

When we were growing up, Dad said that a cat would always land on its feet no matter how it fell. Doug decided to test this theory with a grey tomcat. He took the cat upstairs and tossed it out the window with several curious sisters looking on. The cat landed with ease on all four paws. Next time he held it by the feet and dropped it again. Mom was doing paper work in the room below. She looked up to see the cat sailing by. She went to investigate and put an end to the scientific experiments!

Doug was always interested in mechanics. His grandpa (Elmer Dovey) gave him an old radio to take apart. That was the first of many things that he took apart, some of which he never got back together. Mom said "It's a sure thing that he will learn something," as she surveyed the mess. She was right, as now there are very few things that Doug cannot fix.

Doug enjoyed fishing, hunting, and trapping as he grew up. Dad's hair stood on end (the little hair he had, that is) watching Doug climb the steep banks around the Wolverine River rapids and navigate in gnarly dogwood patches with a gun. Dad was sure that his carelessness would bring him to an early grave.

Doug attended Carcajou school for grades one through eight. Most of the time he walked the mile and a half to get there. Sometimes the teacher, Mrs. Kiselczuk, took the students on field trips. Doug enjoyed these along with the other students. He did grade nine in Falun school while he stayed with his grandparents, Elmer and Hepsey Dovey, in Westerose.

Harry, another student at Falun, persistently tried to pick a quarrel with him. One day they met in the coat room, and again Harry tried to make trouble. Doug was tired of this mischief, so he hung Harry up on one of the coat hooks! After that Harry found someone else to bother.

Doug took one semester of grade 10 at Fairview College. He didn't think his marks were high enough to pass, so he didn't return. He found out later that he had passed.

Doug worked several years for Alberta Forestry in Keg River, fighting fires, timber cruising, and running errands. In 1973 he went to Peace River to work in the forestry warehouse. He met Darlene while attending a Bible study meeting in town. They were married in Grimshaw, her home town, on May 12, 1976. Eva Darlene Verenna Barbondy was born and raised in Grimshaw. Her parents, Steve and Patricia Barbondy lived on a farm close to the town of Grimshaw. Darlene has one sister and three brothers. In the fall they moved to a beautiful home in Grimshaw, which they rented. Doug's job with Forestry took him to many different areas.

Darla was born April 30, 1977, then Ruebeca was born on March 10, 1979. Their son Raymond was born on December 19, 1980.

Doug took a course in carpentry in Fort McMurray. Then on February 3, 1981, he started work at the Gift Lake reserve in High Prairie. He taught some of the Metis people how to build houses. Later he worked with the people in Cadotte Lake. Archie Christian and Joe Whitehead worked with him.

Doug found a lot in Donnelly that they bought from the town. They had a basement dug, then Doug built the house all by himself. Work went slowly because he could work on it only in his spare time.

The basement was finished on July 17th and the family moved in on November 27th. Doug continued to work on the interior of his house in his spare time during the four years they lived there. Darla did kindergarten to grade three and Becky did kindergarten in French immersion classes in the French community of Donnelly.

In the fall of 1985 Doug and Darlene moved into a temporary house – a small trailer in Notikewin belonging to Eugenie Tupper (his mom). The children then went to school in Manning. Darla took grades three through five and Becky, grades one to four in Manning Elementary. Raymond took kindergarten at the Rosary school and grades one and two in Manning Elementary.

In July, 1986, the family moved into their new home in Carcajou. The children went to school in Keg River.

Bears were a real treat to the family that fall. An unusual number of bears were seen over a wide area, indicating an overabundance of the animals. Darlene met a grizzly in the bush when she had the children with her on the trike.

Doug felt that Darlene needed to learn to use a gun for her own safety and also for the children's sake. He told her that if she didn't want to shoot to kill, she should shoot over its head to scare it away.

In the spring of 1988 bears often came into the yard. Darlene met a young black bear coming up the path to the house late in the afternoon. The bear sat down watching her. She shot over its head scaring it away. It returned that night and Doug shot it.

Another bear came into the yard later. When Darlene confronted it the bear stood up. She didn't feel very good about the incident. She worried about the children meeting one of these bruins in the bush when there was no one around to defend them. They had as many as four bears come into their yard in a two-day period.

The following spring they bought some chickens for meat and eggs. They had to watch them like a hawk because a fox was always waiting to snatch a chicken dinner.

Their land had a lot of swamp and heavy timber. Darla, Becky and Raymond liked to play in a nearby slough. They decided to have a contest to see who could catch the most frogs. They filled a lot of jars with little jumpers, which they brought into the house for their mom to enjoy. The house soon looked like they were trying to start a frog farm.

In late May, Becky caught a muskrat and skinned it. She put the hide in a granary to dry. In the dark of night a bear swiped it!

For two years Darlene picked roots for Adam Harapnuk while Doug worked for Hasselfield in Grande Prairie. The children helped Darlene with the root-picking when they could. She travelled to and from work on the trike. The whole family picked roots on their own land many days. This sounds like a fun family outing, right?!

Christine van der Mark
by Christine van der Mark

The following is part of a letter written to Dr. Jackson by Christine Van der Mark. She taught in Keg River just after completing her studies at university. This letter was written from Calgary where she returned after teaching for three months in Keg River. Christine recounts her journey out from of Keg River with Tommy and Malcolm Ducharme.

August 31, 1945

Dear Doctor Jackson,

I hope it won't be Christmas before you get this, as I want to tell you the details of my trip out before it is stale news. I really had a wonderful time and wouldn't have missed it for anything.

We camped at South Keg River for tea, and then went on to the Dobson's where we spent the night. Since it looked like rain, the boys told me to sleep under the wagon so I wouldn't get wet. That was very thoughtful of them, wasn't it?

So I slept under the wagon, or rather, I lay under the wagon, but did not sleep on account of the root stabbing me in the shoulder and a slight precipice under my head and several fleas and ants that kept biting all night. We had a few small showers that did not amount to anything.

At 5 A.M. I got up and coughed discreetly but the inert figures under the tarp and my raincoat did not move. So I rattled things around in the wagon, and two heads shot up in the most unexpected places and the boys grabbed their hats and moccasins, and tightened their belts for the day. I did not tell them the time of day until they were thoroughly awake and out of bed!

We started off about 6 A.M., camping at Two Lakes and then at 14-Mile Corner. I got hay fever from the dust and spent most of my time with a grimy hanky in the crown of my hat. How I did bless that hat for the shade it gave, and I cursed it for the number of times it took to itself wings and flew about a mile behind the wagon in the space of a few minutes.

I changed places with Tommy Ducharme for a while and sat with Malcolm Ducharme on the board in front, where he gave some lessons in tracking. But the board was too hard, and with several calluses I was thankful to return to my seat on the bedroll.

On the way to Landry's, there was a place about two miles long on the road where there were fires on both sides of the road. They were mostly ground fires in the dead fall, but the wind blew up ashes and smoke like a grey mist.

We did not stop at Landry's very long. The gentleman was not at home, so we did not camp there but went on to the Second Battle. Somewhere along the road I told the boys that if they wanted to camp I could maybe get a ride with someone; but they thought I had no confidence in the team and was perhaps insulting the horses, and insisted we would make it in time. So I toughed it out in the wagon to the end.

They had a gun in the wagon, and in the middle of nowhere they informed me that if they happened to see a moose, they were going moose-hunting! Once they stopped the wagon, and stood up, looking very tensely in every direction. Even the horses' ears seemed to be cocked at something extraordinary. Malcolm pointed one way, and Tommy another, and they both scrambled off. When Tommy came back, I said, "See a moose?" But he said in a withering tone, "We're looking for water." That was my worst moment. You see I had moose on my mind!

We washed ourselves in the river at the Second Battle, and we actually made it into Notikewin at 6 P.M. I find I do not make a good covered wagon woman because: (a) I get a stomach ache from the jolting and can't eat; (b) when I arrive, I look as though I had been through something; (c) I cause endless amusement to the drivers, though looking at myself, I can see nothing funny except dirt, which isn't so funny. Anyhow, I managed to stagger into Joe's with my dusty suitcase with strength enough to ask for a room and some water, please.

After having washed and changed, I was having supper with the new bus driver when Tommy and Malcolm came in with some of their friends and sat at a booth across the room. They talked in Cree and howled with laughter. Heads kept popping up over the booth to get a look at this strange thing that had travelled with the boys from Keg River.

I must say though that the boys were certainly very considerate to me all the way and made me feel as comfortable as possible under the circumstances.

My folks were very glad to see me again and when I tell them my adventures, Dad keeps saying, "But don't tell that to anyone!" I got a berth on the train so I was able to rest on the way home. Now it is a matter of getting everything clean! Best wishes to everyone there.

Christine van der Mark

Christine Van der Mark.

Sondra and Marc Viau
by Sondra Viau

My husband Marc and I came to Keg River to run the Keg River Cabins after purchasing the business from Bob Riczu in 1986. The Cabins is virtually the only retail outlet of its type, for approximately 60 miles either north or south. Our business contains the post office, a grocery and convenience store, a cafe (with seating for 45), the Greyhound bus depot, gas pumps (serviced with ESSO gas and oil), a workshop, ICG propane service and a six-unit motel.

We moved here from Fort Nelson, British Columbia, where we had lived for 24 1/2 years. Marc worked for the Department of Transportation and Public Works Canada (Housing Division). I worked for almost 10 years for Canadian National Telecommunications and managed the Sears Catalogue Store for 10 years in Fort Nelson.

Marc was looking for a business to purchase so he could retire from the government. We were told by a friend that Keg River Cabins were available, so while we were on holidays we decided to look at it. It wasn't much, but it looked like it could be home, so we moved.

Then a year later in 1987, disaster struck. The Keg River flooded, leaving our buildings wrecked by the mud and water.

In September, 1988, construction started on new buildings. We were back in business on May 1, 1989. The official grand opening was held on August 3, 1989. Since the new buildings were built, business has increased considerably. Our new building is 40 feet by 100 feet. It contains a residence with an addition in the back.

Sondra Viau.

Johnny Vos
by Johnny Vos

I was born to Willemina and Hendrik Vos in Drongelen, N-Br. Holland, in August 1925. I was the second in a family of six. My sister Nel was the oldest, followed by five boys.

My first 13 years of schooling were in Holland. I attended public school between 1931 and 1938, agricultural school in Andel between 1938 and 1942, then agricultural winter school in Dordrecht in the years 1942-1944.

We had a mixed farm in Holland of about 100 acres in small plots spread over five miles. The largest piece of land was about five acres. The work was done with horses and by hand. We had eight to 10 milk cows. Butter was made on the farm and sold directly to consumers. Some of the other produce like potatoes and eggs were also sold directly.

We also raised hogs, sugar beets, oats, wheat, peas, and during the war, rapeseed. We grew apples, plums, and pears for our own use.

Johnny Vos, far right with sister Nel and brothers, Dirk, Bas, and Marius seated, on their farm in Holland, 1931.

The biggest piece of machinery was a five-foot mower, owned with an uncle. A lot of the plowing was done with a single bottom plow, pulled by two or three horses. In the 30's there was barely enough money to go around but we always had three square meals a day. We used about 20 gallons of diesel fuel a year when the custom thresher came to thresh the stacks of grain and the bundles in the barns.

A few things about Holland really stand out in my memory. Our house and barn burned May 12, 1933. I rescued Dad's shotgun and put it against a hedge, close to the house. The burning thatched roof slid on it and the gun burned anyway!

On May 10, 1940, Holland was invaded by the Germans. The bombing of Rotterdam and total destruction of the inner city on May 15, 1940, saw the capitulation of Holland. The next five years we were under German occupation. Lights were not working or were blacked out. We had a lot of airplanes overhead, first the Germans bombing England and later the Allies bombing Germany.

On June 6, 1944, now known as D-Day, we were thinning beets. There was a lot of activity in the air, mostly Allied planes. The invasion of Normandy and Western Europe was under way. This was the beginning of the end.

"Three million soldiers and 2,727 ships were involved in the largest amphibious military operation in history. On June 6, 1944, the first day of Operation Overlord, 57,500 American and 75,000 British and Canadian soldiers landed on five Normandy beaches by sea and 23,000 dropped onto French soil by parachute or in gliders."

(*Graham Heathcote AP Poole, England*)

On Sept 17, 1944, there were more airplanes flying over than we had ever seen. A lot of them were DC-3's pulling gliders for an airdrop of Allied forces at Arnhem, Holland. Due to cloudy weather, air support was not as good as it should have been. The attack was not successful. There was heavy German resistance.

The period from September 1944 to May 1945 was the worst for us. We were just north of the river Maas and the Allied forces reached the south side in early November, 1944. The Allied attack stalled at the River Maas. Our farm was in the front lines until May 1945. Most of the land in our area was flooded by sea water because the pumps were shut down. The Allied forces had no intention of attacking here and destroying Holland. The main attack went across the Rhine into Germany.

During the Battle of the Ardennes the Germans prepared to counterattack from our area. Our village became the staging area for the Germans to cross the River Maas. We had to evacuate. On December 31, 1944, we loaded our horse-drawn wagon with what we could and herded our 15 head of cattle to our new home about eight miles north of the Maas, where we stayed with a family whose house and stables were already full of other refugees.

By that time we were a family of 10. There were eight immediate family members plus Hans Kraal, an 18-month-old Jewish baby whom my mother raised, and a 20-year-old Dutch boy Chris, who was hiding at our place so he did not have to join the German labour force.

Our area was already under artillery fire when we left. As luck would have it we made the trip in between exploding grenades without any injuries. We had just left our home and were about six miles away when Allied Typhoon dive bombers attacked our village. In the next couple of days the village was 80% destroyed. We would not know this until after the war as no one was allowed into our area.

When we were allowed to return home in the last part of May 1945, we found our house and barn still standing. It had two direct hits by artillery shells but the damage could be repaired.

May 1945, end of war! What a feeling. Free after all. Thanks to all those who helped and gave their lives in the effort. A special thanks to Canadian and Polish troops who liberated Holland.

In 1946 I was drafted into the Dutch army for compulsory service. I spent two years in the army and was discharged in March of 1948 as a sergeant.

Land was scarce and with five boys on the farm I decided to come to Canada after being discharged from the army. My parents agreed with this idea. (Three of my brothers – Dirk, Marius, and Wim emigrated to Canada later).

After getting the right papers and health checks I left Rotterdam on April 8, 1948, on board the *Kota Inten*, a ship that had been hauling troops to Indonesia. I arrived in Halifax 10 days later, not knowing a word of English.

I had a two-day train trip to Hamilton, Ontario. Immigration had arranged a one-year job for me on a dairy farm owned by Charlie and Russell Gage at Ancaster. For three months following that, I worked for a farm supply co-op managed by Lyle Hostein.

On August 1, 1949, I left by train from Hamilton to Lethbridge, Alberta. The employment office found me a job at the Henry Sharples Ranch west of Claresholm on the edge of the foothills. I worked there until early December, 1949, when the job ended.

Someone suggested that I should attend a school of agriculture. I tried Olds, but there was no space. The district agriculturalist at Claresholm found out there was room at Vermilion School of Agriculture. I took a one-year course in Agriculture. I made a lot of friends there – we were like a big family. This is where I met Anne Jackson from Keg River.

In the spring I was offered a job on the Jackson farm at Keg River. Louis Jackson picked me up in Manning with the REO truck. We couldn't leave Manning until midnight because of a road ban. We had to chain up to get in on the Jackson road that was drifting in. We arrived at six in the morning on April 8, 1950.

I worked at the Jackson farm for the summer of 1950. The winter of 1950-51, I worked on a seismic crew exploring for oil in the area. Anne homesteaded the E-20-101-23 in 1951. I filed on another half section but later let it go back to the provincial government because it was too wet.

In August, 1952, Anne and I were married. We had a 12-foot by 14-foot "house" on Anne's homestead. We soon built a piece onto it and started clearing some land.

How did we clear the land in 1952? The days of the axe were gone. There were a few Cats and tractors with brush cutters and if we were lucky we could get a D-4 with an operator for $7.00 an hour. If the bush was not too heavy we could clear for $10 to $15 an acre.

Then after waiting for the bush to dry, we could get a fire permit and burn. The drier the weather, the better the burn. However, with dry weather there was also more danger of the fire getting out of control. After we repiled the leftovers by hand and burned again, the land was ready to plow. A lot of the breaking was done with a 30-35 horsepower tractor on steel wheels with a single bottom breaking plow.

Once the land had been turned over with a plow, it had to be dragged, and disked and the roots picked. If we were lucky and had some money, we could get a local family to pile and burn them for us for $1.50-$2.00 per acre; otherwise, we did it ourselves.

Financing the operation was always a problem. In between working on the homestead I had to find a job to bring in some badly needed cash. In the winter of 1952-53, I got a job with Forestry to control wildlife because of a rabies epidemic. Some of the domestic livestock in the area got rabies. We set poison to get rid of the rabid animals. I got $9.00 per day for myself, a horse, and equipment. I travelled with Louis Jackson and learned how to camp in the bush in the winter.

Louis and June Jackson were our best friends in those days, and we missed them when they moved to Manning in 1961.

On the farm we raised some flax, oats, wheat, and barley. We usually had chickens. Our introduction to hog farming started with a wedding gift of a sow from the Pattersons. We got a pen built in time for the first litter. As our herd grew, we built a farrowing pen and some fences. In the winter the good old straw stack from the threshing machine served the purpose.

We grew potatoes for 10 years between 1956 and 1966 and had the first and only irrigation system in the area. We built a root cellar in which to store the potatoes. We mechanized with a digger, sorter and washer. I delivered the potatoes by truck as far away as Yellowknife to the north and Dawson Creek to the west. We got out of potatoes because farm help became scarce.

In the winter I made some needed money hauling in the oil patch for my brother Dirk. There was a real boom here when the Rainbow Oil Field was first discovered and gave us a chance to make a few dollars that really helped out on the farm.

The arrival of the railroad in 1963 also made a big difference to the community. The United Grain Growers built a modern elevator, and our hauling distance was reduced from 125 miles to less than 10 miles. At about the same time the Mackenzie highway was being improved.

Between the better roads, the railroad and the grain elevator, grain growing became more economically viable. More land was cleared and we started using fertilizers to raise even better crops. We began growing rapeseed and could sell this for a fair price when other grain prices were low.

Anne and I have been farming in Keg River for over 43 years.

Johnny and Anne Vos, Penny, Patricia, Henry, David, Mary Lou and Neil.

If you would know strength and patience, welcome the company of trees.

Anne Vos (nee Jackson)
by Anne Vos

My mother returned to her home in England for the birth of her first child. I arrived November 5, 1931. After being looked over by my English family, we were ready to leave for Canada.

We crossed the Atlantic on board an ocean liner. The voyage took five days. In Montreal we boarded the train to travel across Canada to Peace River. From Peace River a small bush plane was to take us to Keg River. The pilot was given a map drawn on a cigarette package so I guess I was lucky to get here.

My brother, John Robert, was born in Keg River on January 16, 1934, on one of the coldest nights ever recorded. His birth was assisted by our neighbour, Mrs. Harrington, and my Dad.

Chores were a large part of growing up. We raised a lot of pigs and Dad had a herd of purebred Aberdeen Angus cows. We burned wood in two stoves in the house and two in the store as well as one in the work shop. It seemed there was continual wood-hauling and splitting. There were furs to count and bale. Rabbits were terrible to count because they shed and the hair got in my eyes, nose and mouth. Some winters Dad bought thousands!

The first time I went "outside" to town was in the winter when I was 10. We travelled with teams of horses and sleighs. It took two days to get to Notikewin. One sleigh had the caboose on it – a canvas tent stretched over a frame. There was usually a stove, grub boxes, bedrolls, hay bales, and trail necessities in it. We sat on hay and covered up with rabbit robes. The other sleighs hauled pigs to be sold, bales of fur, bags of flax seed, and hay for the 20 steers we were herding. Dad owned Keg River Trading Company, so on the return trip all the sleighs hauled freight for the store.

In 1937 I attended the first school there was in Keg River. The school building wasn't ready in September, so we all went to school in the hospital. Miss Lawrence, an English lady, agreed to teach anybody, any age, providing they really wanted to learn. There were 27 of us between the ages of five and 14. In October the hospital was required, so we moved to the school even though it wasn't quite ready. Miss Lawrence stayed for the first three years of my school life. A number of other teachers followed, staying for shorter terms.

I was eight when the war brought many changes to our quiet country life. A number of young men of the district enlisted in the army. In 1940 my half-brother Louis joined the Air Force at age 21 and became an aircraft mechanic. Arthur stayed behind and ran the farm.

The American Army arrived in 1942 to rush construction of the MacKenzie Highway to the oil fields in the north. The road was passable for trucks in the winter, so grain could be hauled to Grimshaw 120 miles away. Flax was profitable during the war because the oil was used in marine paints.

Two children, Pat and John Hague, came to spend time with us to escape the bombing in England. They ended up staying four years. There was a shortage of teachers during the war. My mother taught all four of us correspondence lessons for a couple of years.

In 1946 I went to Victoria, B.C., to go to high school. I stayed with my Dad's sister (my Aunt Dot), and my Grandfather Jackson. It was an experience never to be forgotten!

Dad closed the trading post and moved to the farm. He began full-time farming when my half-brother Arthur and his wife Margaret moved to Aldergrove, B.C., in 1948.

In 1949 I enrolled in a two-year Home Economics program at Vermilion School of Agriculture. During the second year I met Johnny Vos. In 1951 we filed on homesteads at Keg River. We were married the following year.

The road to our homestead was nearly impassable in rainy weather. We had to corduroy the first quarter mile off the Keg River road to be able to drive in with the truck.

When our first child Patricia was six, there was no school bus and we had no way to take her every day. She stayed with Louis and June Jackson during the week and attended Naylor Hills school. The following year there was a bus that travelled only on the main road and took the children to the school at Keg River Post. Patricia and Henry, our two eldest, had to walk a half mile to the road to catch the bus.

There were always plenty of men to cook for, especially during potato harvest when there were at least 10 at every meal.

Good water was a problem, in the summer we hauled from Blackbirds Creek and strained out the "wrigglers"; in the winter we melted snow or ice. Some winters we put up ice to melt for summer drinking water. The ice was cut in large blocks from the river and stored in sawdust. The biggest chore was to wash off the sawdust.

Our family of three girls and three boys were raised in Keg River. Since the school taught only to grade nine, they all had to leave home early. The oldest five – Patricia, Henry, David, Mary Lou and Penny – boarded in Fairview and attended Fairview High School. Neil, the youngest, was involved in hockey in Manning, so he went to Paul Rowe High School and then Grande Prairie Composite High School.

Pat and Garry Stovin with sons Teddy and J.D.

Patricia is married to Garry Stovin and they have two boys – Teddy and J.D. Pat works at Stetson Motors and Garry is with Investor Group. They live on a ranch near Drayton Valley.

Henry married Anne Marie Tretiak. They have two girls – Sydney and Allison and farm at Three Fox Farm just out of Fairview.

Penny, Tom, Kelsey and Brett Elliot on the bank of the Yukon River.

David married Joyce Ulinder and they live in Keg River on a mixed farm.

Mary Lou married Bobby Ng. They live in Edmonton where Mary Lou teaches mathematics at the Northern Alberta Institute of Technology and where Bobby works with Context Associated.

Penny married Tom Elliot and they have two children – Kelsey and Brett. Tom is a Parks Canada warden and Penny is a laboratory technologist. Their home is Whitehorse, Yukon Territory.

Neil is a heavy duty mechanic. He has worked overseas in various African countries including Kenya, Madagascar, and Nigeria. Neil is now working in Manning where he lives with Mirium Stang.

Johnny and I still live on our farm in Keg River where we are talking about retirement!

Bobby and Mary Lou Ng Wedding. Back: David and wife Joyce. Middle: Henry with daughter Sydney, Johnny and Anne Vos, Bobby and Marylou Ng, Garry Stovin, Neil Vos. Front: Henry's wife Anne with daughter Allison, Dr. Mary Jackson, Garry's wife Patricia with son Teddy, June 1991.

Henry and Anne Vos
by Henry Vos

It is very difficult to sit down and write a history of your life and where you grew up. All sorts of things keep jumping into your memory. I will attempt to do it, though. This will be organized according to topic. The areas in which I have some strong and funny memories are: clearing land and picking roots, raising pigs, things kids do, and school.

It seemed like a never-ending job of clearing land and picking roots while we were growing up. Each year there was another place to clear or a piece we had to pick roots on one more time. Maybe that was why there were six kids in our family. Mr. Dika, who invented the mechanical root picker should get a medal, at least from all the kids of families who would now be picking by hand if it were not for that wonderful machine.

When we were kids, Dad had a hired man who was a black fellow. Ben Hayes was huge as I remember him and always liked his shack hot inside. In the middle of summer he would have the heat on.

He did his fair share of root picking and after school we had to help him. Well, as you can imagine, we kids could be very innovative in thinking of ways to get out of this job. I think at times he would have been much happier to have been left on his own, for he probably would have gotten more done. Ben was a very friendly man as well and would play games with us on Sundays. Hide-and-go-seek was one of our favorites.

Clearing trees was no small task considering that most of the trees were from 50 to 70 feet tall. They had to be cut, then piled in rows and allowed to dry so that they would burn. Usually this was a two year process or more. Then the land was seeded. I can very distinctly remember dad hitting a big stump on Uncle Marius' land and pulling the plow completely in half.

These trees, which were a large annoyance and burden to the land owner, are now quite valuable to the pulp industry. Some day people will be planting trees because they will be more valuable than the crops which we now grow.

When we were kids there were always pigs on our farm. Maybe it was because dad raised potatoes and all the cull potatoes went to the pigs. The most exciting times with these pigs was when we had to do something with them. This was either farrowing time, castrating, shipping, grinding feed or butchering. These were major events and we used to look forward to them as kids.

Shipping pigs was always a big day because these pigs were raised outside in a big pen which didn't have the handling facilities which are engineered into all the modern facilities. It was somewhat like a rodeo, perhaps a little less organized! We would get an early start and usually before lunch we would have most of the pigs that were to be sent, on the truck ready to be shipped. I think there was occasionally one or two which waited for the next shipping date. If they were too big before they got on the truck there was always the next butchering. This was another big event for us kids.

Thinking about this now, butchering seemed so much a fact of life, because back then everybody did it. Can you imagine if you were to kill, string up and butcher a pig in your back yard nowadays?

Pigs were Dad's way of introducing us to business. I remember making deals with Dad. If I fed all the pigs after school each day, I could have three or four pigs. Rest assured whenever there was slop to be fed to the pigs, it went to my pigs first!

I can remember one day when I came home, the pigs had gotten out and were in the chop bin. I thought I would teach these pigs a lesson, so as they were jumping out of the chop bin I laid into one with a two-by-four. It dropped to its knees in the doorway and lay there. I got a little worried about what to with a dead pig and how to get him out of the doorway, then he finally woke up!

After I married Anne Marie, we raised a few pigs mainly to clean up bits of spoiled grain we had around the yard. When they were fattened up, we hauled them to the butcher in Fairview. One time when Anne Marie was eight and a half months pregnant with Sydney, we were on the way to the butcher with five pigs. It was a cool day, so we had a tarp covering some home-built wooden racks on the back of the pickup. Near Kemp Creek we met a chip truck and the wind blast from the truck blew the stock racks completely off the pickup. When we finally got stopped, we found that we were 200 yards down the road from the stock racks, with five pigs sitting up in the truck and looking around. We slowly backed up to the stock racks which were sitting in the middle of the road. Unbelievably they had stayed in one piece. Anne and I gently got out of the pickup and picked up the stock racks and placed them back over the heads of the pigs on the truck! To this day we don't know why those pigs didn't move.

There are some fond memories (and some not so fond) of school. My memories of grade one are rather limited, but I do remember Mr. LeClaire very well. He was very strict and probably struck terror into the heart of every grade one student. We got to watch as he would take the yardstick to the hands of some unruly student at the back of the room. One would not even want to ask him if you could go outside to the bathroom, if even the alternative was even more disastrous!

Another memory from school was the day that Dad came to school with the swather to cut the grass around the school yard. It had grown up over the summer and now with school starting, it was quite high. Dad was making a turn near the well, when he got a little close and knocked the back wheel completely off the swather.

In 1963 we moved to Dr. Mary Jackson School at the Cabins. This school had a lot of difficulties with the furnaces and water in the first few years it was open. I can remember these furnaces making very loud banging noises during the course of the day. I don't know that any of the furnaces actually blew up, but it sure seemed like they were going to.

It was nice having a school named after my grandmother; however, it didn't seem to carry much weight when I got hauled into the principal's office about some altercation!

School was very important to our parents. I can remember times when I would ask if I could stay home and help with either seeding or harvest and Dad would not let me. I understand the significance of this now, with a farm of our own. There are times when a person could sure use an extra hand. We all owe a great deal to our parents for the opportunities they gave us.

Henry Vos with White Fox pelts.

I attended university in Edmonton taking agriculture. After university I spent three years working for Vertec Industries, manufacturers of grain driers. I told them I wanted to work for them because I thought I could help them build a better drier. I am not sure they were impressed, but they hired me!

After that time I moved back to Keg River to start farming where my parents continued to farm. Somehow I managed to convince Anne Marie Tretiak to come up to the Peace River country as well. She was a fellow graduate of the agriculture program at the University of Alberta. She got a job one winter at Fairview College and the next year she became the district agriculturalist in Manning. Anne held that job for four years before moving to Keg River to help out with the farming full-time. Oh, we got married somewhere in there as well!

During our time farming at Keg River, one of the ventures we got into was raising foxes. Anne liked livestock and this seemed like a way to diversify the farm. Like a lot of things, though, we got in when prices were high and it was not long before we had some to sell and the prices had collapsed.

In 1989 we moved to Fairview and bought another farm. Some people have asked why, when we managed to sell one farm, we would buy another one. We wouldn't have it any other way. We now have two girls: Sydney (born January 21, 1989) and Allison (born June 18, 1990).

Marius Vos
by Marius Vos

I came to Canada in 1952. The day I arrived in Peace River the Hawk Hills land rush was in progress.

I worked for the Osborne Lawrence farm when I first arrived. In the winter there were plenty of jobs in the oil patch. I went siesmographing. Later I trucked all over the north and had many experiences, both good and bad.

I filed on a homestead N-26-101-24-W5 in 1962. Daishowa should have been in business then, as a lot of timber went up in smoke as people cleared their land!

Now I work near Hazelton, British Columbia, and Joanne, my wife, works in Public Health in Duncan.

We have three children John, Peter and Dianna. Dianna is married to Bruce Polluck, a lumber broker in Vancouver, and they have one son, Cameron.

Marius and Joanne Vos.

Wim Vos
by Wim Vos

I arrived in Canada in 1957 from Holland. I worked in the Peace River area for farmers, then for Dirk Vos Trucking, hauling to the rigs.

The Doveys at Carcajou wanted to sell out in 1964. The road wasn't much more than a trail in the summer but it was passable in the winter, so I bought their farm and moved here. Back then there was no electrical power so we had our own power generating plants. The soil is good for farming and the river is convenient for recreation and I haven't regretted my decision!

I continue to farm and live in Carcajou in the summer and operate an oilfield hauling business in High Level in the winter.

Wim Vos with brother Bas and wife Toni in Holland.

Vos family and friends, 1992.

Del and Emma Weber
by Ray Weber

When my father, Del Weber, was still in school, he told his teacher that he wanted to become a steam engineer and go west with the harvest crews. Steam engines were what powered the threshing machines at that time. The family was already on its way west, having moved from the Kimberly area of Ontario to Manitoba and later to Saskatchewan. Dad's teacher recognized his determination and suggested that his further education be channelled towards math and science, so that he was able to leave school much above his grade level in those areas.

Dad married Mom, Emma Rands, a farmer's daughter from Saskatchewan. In the early spring of 1925 the Weber clan had moved to Peace River to take up homesteads. The family moved often over the next years and there is a family saying that "Weber Temporary is good for five to seven years".

It is my sister Mary who remembers logs being hauled with teams in the winter to build barns and homes. Some of the families lived together until their own homes were built, which probably went a long way towards keeping the spirit of cooperation alive.

The area came to be known as Weberville because the post office was in grandfather Jack's home. The older kids (Dave, Mary, Veryol, Roy, Jack and Ethel) grew up and went to school in Weberville, going barefoot and riding horseback. The 30's were hard times for Peace River farmers.

In 1939 Dad built a sturdy barge, powered it with the engine from his Model A, and loaded the family, food, cook stove, a few friends and neighbors so we wouldn't get lonely, and – since my sister, Veryol wouldn't go without them – her cat and kittens. We headed for Yellowknife, where there were jobs to be had as steam boilers were used to power the drills in the mines. For the kids it was like a riverboat holiday as they travelled along the mighty Peace. There were fewer chores to be done and the scenery kept changing.

The others still talk about standing on the shore by the Vermilion chutes where the barges were unloaded and handlined (guided through the rapids with ropes) through. Even with the ropes the barge ahead of my family's went down, crushed on the rocks and came up as kindling! Veryol couldn't find her pets and her brothers (probably less than tactfully) explained that they were goners when the water went over the barge. Our barge did come through safe and sound, complete with a very wet and upset cargo!

The trek down the Peace River, the Slave River and through the Jean Channel into Great Slave Lake took weeks. The family camped on the rocks one more night. The next morning while exploring, the kids heard boat kickers and bush planes! That day they arrived in Yellowknife where the family lived a few years before moving to Vancouver, where Dad worked in the shipyards.

Mary was married to Red Hamilton and had a son, Delbert. Another baby came along to Dad and Mom – me! After the war, Dad headed back to Alberta to work in the oilfields. He was on hand when Leduc Number 1 blew in. The farming bug was still in his system, however, because in 1955 they took out one more homestead, this time in Keg River.

For a while it seemed as if the Weberville sign should have been moved to a corner about a mile east of the Keg River Post. Then Dave and his wife Doris (Ferguson) moved to their homestead, closer to the highway; Ethel and her daughter Paula went back to British Columbia; Mary and her family had returned to Yellowknife, Veryol lived with her family in Edmonton; Roy (Burman) and Jack took

Del Weber with his John Deere tractor, 1964.

up homesteads as well but never really lived on them for any length of time. After a while only I, the youngest, lived with my parents on the farm.

Dad enjoyed working with farm machinery and was soon doing repairs all over the neighborhood. He exchanged work on sawmill machinery for lumber.

Mom's first priority was her garden and I think she knew most of her plants by their first names. When the "new" house was finally built, Dad made sure that there was a large front window so Mom could watch the traffic on the Keg River road (and put the kettle on if anyone turned in), but most of the time the view was pretty well obscured by all mom's houseplants. The grandchildren referred to this area as "The Jungle" after a small toy elephant got lost there.

Roy owned a garage in Manning for several years before he moved to Ft. McMurray to work with Suncor. Jack is supposed to be retired from trucking but (as when he retired the first time from Pine Point) he can still be found behind the wheel on occasion. He stops in Keg River and keeps us in touch. Mary and I live in Yellowknife with our families. Veryol lives in Edmonton.

Some of Dad and Mom's grandchildren are grandparents themselves now and several of their descendants inherited Dad's interest and ability in things mechanical, but – sorry, Mom! – except for one of Dave's daughters, Elaine, who lives on a farm near Hotchkiss, there isn't a farmer in the lot!

One Keg River story that has always amused us took place one spring when all of the roads were an impassable sea of mud. Now, those who knew Mom knew how she could talk. She also held strong temperance views and when she got riled on a subject, watch out! Her opinions were as well-known as they were well-exercised.

One spring day, Dad decided to take the tractor and go down to the post for the mail. Nobody could do any farm work in the mud and Dave McDonald was also at loose ends. After a few beers with Glady Harrington at the telegraph office and a few more in the back of the store with Ray Ross, Dave realized that he would be wise to get a ride home with Dad. Mrs. Emma McDonald would hesitate to berate Dave in front of Dad. (Dad knew that wouldn't be true in his house, so he was in no hurry to go home.)

The two started out on the tractor but soon got it stuck, so they had to continue on foot. Right in view of Emma McDonald's window, God and most of Keg River, they slid, slipped and staggered along the road, supporting each other when necessary. Mud-wrestling had nothing on them! By the time they got to the house, Emma was laughing so hard that she couldn't be angry. She put them to bed like a couple of kids while she washed their clothes.

Dad was able to go home clean and cold sober and explained his lateness by saying he had had to help Dave. As far as I know, no one ever told Mom. This in itself was truly amazing, given the strength of the Keg River gossip-line!

Doris and Dave Weber with their children and Grandma Emma.

Dave and Doris Weber and Family
by Elaine Weber

My father, Dave Weber, was born in Weberville on July 18, 1927. Dad spent the first 11 years of his life in the Peace River area and took his schooling in the Weberville school.

His family then moved to Yellowknife, on to Vancouver and later to Leduc. In the early 1950's

Wedding of Dave and Doris Weber.

he moved to Keg River to his father's homestead. He married Doris Ferguson of Peace River on May 29, 1955.

Dad worked for many of his neighbors repairing machinery, cutting brush, or helping in any way he could. He filed on his own homestead S-28-101-23-W5 and moved there. Mom and Dad built a house, barn, and chicken house. They had some pigs, ponies, ducks, geese, and chickens.

Dad was an outdoors man and avid sportsman. He went goose and duck-hunting and fishing summer and winter with his friends. In the fall he was a guide for moose hunters from south of the border. He took part in winter sports such as broomball, and snowmobiling, and helped flood the local hockey rink.

Holidaying in B.C. – Dave Weber and children.

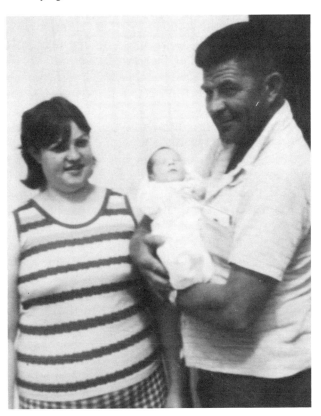

Dave, Elaine and baby Wanda.

Dad sold his homestead to Keith Broadhead and purchased a new trailer and moved it next to Highway 35 on Prochinsky's land. On December 4, 1977, Dad passed away after suffering with cancer. After his death Mom moved away from Keg River and now resides in Rainbow Lake.

Mom and Dad had four children. Sheila was born September 21, 1958, I was born on August 11, 1960, and twins, Dean and Darcy, were born on Mother's Day, May 12, 1961.

Sheila married Fred Hartaway, has two boys Byron and Jason and is expecting her third. They live in Edmonton.

Darcy married Shelly Ressler and they live in Manning with their three children, Robin and twins Randi and Jenna.

Dean married Cheryl Garnet and they reside in Grimshaw with their two children, Tasha and Tyler.

I reside in Manning with my two girls, Wanda and Kim.

Pat Weber

by Pat Weber (nee Ross)

My older brother Raymer, baby brother Chuckles and I travelled to Keg River with our mother in the early spring of 1946. We had moved out from the arctic during the war, but when it was over, my father was ready to go back fur trading with the Hudson's Bay Company. I remember him telling Mom about the new post and assuring her that there was a school!

Chuckles was a baby who liked a lot of rocking and the old Northern Alberta Railway was perfect for him. From Peace River we flew into Keg River on the mail plane and people came out to meet us and say goodbye to the previous post manager with sleighs and teams. They put Raymer and me on a toboggan behind one sleigh, and I promptly fell off into the deep snow. My first impression of Keg River was one of a heck of a lot of snow!

We soon found that while there definitely was a school - a sturdy log building - but there was often no teacher! I started school there, did some of my lessons by correspondence but went out to boarding school in the middle of grade three. I still remember having several teachers in those years at Keg River. Some were better than others.

Those Keg River school children would seem like a dream in today's schools; I recall only one who talked out loud! I suspect I almost made up for the rest, though, as I remember moving from one double desk to another as the teacher tried to put me with someone I couldn't get to talk.

For the same problem, I was frequently sent to stand in the corner and once I decided that since I spent so much time there, I needed a window, so I picked the chinking out from between the logs so I could see out.... It wasn't a cold winter day but my renovations didn't escape notice.

Another time my old horse followed me to school and wandered in during lessons. I was not big enough to make him back out so he had to come right up to the blackboard to get turned around. I tried carrying sugar cubes but I guess he didn't like school because he never came back!

I remember good times, community sports days and occasions when lots of people would go out to the Chinchaga River for a picnic. I remember having more freedom than I was able to allow my children as we rode all over on Old Silver who must have been a great baby sitter. He was so swaybacked we could hardly have fallen off, and when it got late, he always went home.

I remember going to Jackson's farm to help with the harvest one year. The others helped; I'm sorry I forgot the box full of baby mice in the porch, although my mother would probably not have been any happier if I had remembered to take them home.

My liking for mice had a sequel years later. On my first day of teaching I opened my desk after recess to see a pair of little beady black eyes staring at me. The grade four boys turned in some good reports on field mice the next day and at least one parent explained why that trick hadn't caused the excitement they had hoped for!

We must have received a reasonably good education in spite of having a class of 42 students in grades one to eight, because I don't recall struggling too hard in high school in Edmonton. But in all my growing up years away, I always counted the days until I could go home.

Later on, I did come back to teach for a couple of years but I found that years in boarding school didn't prepare me very well to cope with wood stoves, no running water and an oil heater with a tank full of oil that jellied when we had a long spell with 40 below as the day's high.

When we first went to Keg River the road wandered past Harry Bowe's place and Romanchuk's. It was a couple of muddy or dusty tracks that were frequently impassable by either of the two Model A cars or Jackson's Reo truck. Maybe my kids were right about dinosaurs in the backyard because I knew what an REO Speedwagon was before it was a band!

I remember someone telling us that one day

there would be a straight road from the post to the new MacKenzie Highway, and looking at all the big trees and thinking, "No way!" Someone told us there was going to be a new town built between Notikewin and North Star so there would be one big town and I remember our first trip to Manning.

Now when we go back for a visit we always notice changes: farms where there used to be bush; the school, post office and store have gone completely; and there are empty places where my friends used to live. Somehow they managed to shrink the high wind charger in our back yard, we used to pretend it was our pirate ship, mountain or castle; and many of the people I once knew are not there any more, but for those who are left, my very best wishes and thanks for the memories.

(Editor's Note: Pat and Ray Weber still live in Yellowknife. They have two children, daughter Robyn and son Shaun. Robyn was married in 1993. Ray is an airplane pilot for North West Territorial Air.)

Mrs. Lin Ross, daughter Pat with her husband Ray and grandchildren Robyn and Shawn.

Raymond Weber
by Raymond Weber

In July of 1953, my parents and I went to Keg River to visit my dad's sister, Alice. She and her husband, George Robertson, had been living there for some time and had invited us to come and see the country. This visit would change our lives.

It was a beautiful summer, and the crops were doing well. Dad and Mom decided to take a homestead, and I got polio!

Over the few days we were with George and Alice they showed us several open sections of land. The one my parents chose was on the north side of the Keg River Post road and one mile east of the Post.

Emma and Del Weber in front of their house, 1964.

One evening at supper I could not hold my knife to spread butter. There were other symptoms but this one I remember. Early in the evening they took me to see Dr. Jackson. At that time polio was a little known disease in the north, but after a brief examination, I overheard the doctor tell my folks that she thought I had polio. Although she had never encountered it before, she had been reading about it and was probably as familiar with this disease as any doctor in the country.

Dad drove all night over the old Slave Lake

road, and Mom rubbed my back and legs with liniment. The next morning we were in Edmonton and I went to hospital for the rest of the summer holidays!

In the fall of 1955, we moved to Keg River from Leduc, Alberta. On my way to school the first morning, Dave Lariviere stopped and gave me a ride right to the school. He took me in and introduced me to the teacher, Mrs. Befus. For some time after, the kids all thought I was Dave's son!

Mrs. Befus sent two of the bigger boys, Alfred Hamelin and Frank Minault out to find a desk for me – out in the snow drift! The classroom had close to 30 students, from grade four to grade eight. Delores Galandy and I were the whole grade seven class!

In the winter the Michalchuk kids drove to school in a cutter and would go past our place as this route offered the most protection from the wind and the drifted snow. I would watch for them, and their horse, Nigger, would watch and wait for me, but when my foot hit the cutter, he was on his way again.

If it was colder than -40°, we didn't have to go to school, but anything warmer was no excuse. Helen, Everett, Eddy, Freddy, Lillie, and Peter would all be in the cutter in a bed of straw and covered with a huge feather tick if it was really cold. There was no place under there for me so I ran and rode on the back of the cutter. I must say that had there been room under the tick, the girls would not have let me in there anyway, as they would have been teased unmercifully by the whole school.

The horse on the other hand liked my company and would let me run with him, but not pass! If I did, he would break into a gallop and I had to really run to get back on the cutter. All good fun and exercise and it kept me warm in the mile and a bit from our house to the school.

Keg River was a beautiful place to live, from the point of view of a 12-year-old boy. I learned to hunt, trap, drive a tractor and work. I know the neighbours all thought I was the laziest kid in the whole of Keg River, but I did work – not as hard as some but I did work!

I had mostly recovered from polio but after picking roots for a long time I could not hold on to them as my right hand was still weak. My dad would notice when this would happen and suggest I go hunting or some other chore that didn't require strength in my hand.

One of my friends was Chuck Ross, whose father was the Hudson's Bay Post Manager. He and I covered a lot of Keg River on our bicycles, over the years we lived there.

School at the Keg at that time only went to grade eight. After that we had to go out to school, so when I started in grade nine it was in Manning. However, the first Easter at Keg River, I discovered Chuck had a sister who had returned home for the holidays. This summer (1993) Pat and I will have been married for 30 years.

I think if I could have flown for a living and stayed at Keg River, I would have. But in 1959, we moved to Yellowknife, so dad could find work as the farm had not done well. I decided that if I were to fly, then Yellowknife would be the place. In 1961 we moved back to Keg River, and I spent another year and a half there before leaving home to get my flight training, but my parents spent the rest of their lives on the farm.

Emma Weber, Mary Hamilton, Doris, Pat, Ray, and twins, Dean and Darcy Weber.

Later, after I had learned to fly and we had our own airplane, Pat and I returned to Keg River, for a visit. It was quite a thrill for me to land in Bill Halabisky's field west of our farm, and take Mom and Dad for a plane ride around Keg River! There were fields and buildings that they had never seen from the ground. My brother Dave, who also lived at Keg River, was the one who introduced me to flying for my fifth birthday in Vancouver. It was an awful lot of fun to fly with him after all those years.

Later, when I was flying full time, and had to fly over Keg River, I would stop if I could; and if I couldn't land I would buzz the house. Mom thought every plane that went by was me, and she'd give me heck for not stopping!

Pat and I still try to get back to Keg River whenever we can, but that is not all that often any more. As she says, Keg River has changed, it is not home for us any more but it is still nice to go back.

Harry and Ida Wilson
by Ida (Wilson) Ristesund

Harry Wilson was born in the United States and worked both there and in Canada as a driller in the oil fields.

In the early 1930's he heard about the Keg River area while he was working in Calgary. Intrigued by what he heard, he travelled to the area by boat and other means. He liked what he saw so he filed on a homestead before going back to the oil fields.

That homestead was later expropriated to become part of the Metis Settlement which was established north of the Keg River Post. He was offered a different quarter in exchange (but did not take it).

On November 21, 1942, Harry and I were married in Phoenix, Arizona. He warned me at that time to be prepared to move to Canada at some point in the future.

We were living in Utah when Harry received a letter from a friend in Keg River informing him about a half-section farm that was up for sale. It had a log house and some land that was opened out. Harry wrote back, instructing his friend to purchase the land for us.

With the help of my brother-in-law, Harold Patterson, Harry hauled a tractor in a Ford truck to the United States border and left it there for the winter. In the spring of 1948, Harry and I, along with my sister Ellen and husband Harold, started for Keg River. We had the Ford pickup truck loaded down with furniture and the necessities of homestead living. We pulled a small trailer which was full of canned fruit that Ellen and I had spent weeks canning.

Harold and Ellen liked the Keg River area and also decided to make it their home. Harold bought land not far from ours.

The farming was good in those years. We never had a crop failure. Harry and I liked to travel, so we spent the first few winters back in the States.

Norman Hunter, one of Jim Hunter's boys,

Harry Wilson, Norman Hunter, Ida Wilson and Hawk, Harry's seeing eye dog, 1961.

came to live with us when he was under ten. He stayed with us for years and joined us in our travels to Alaska and the lower mainland on different occasions. Norman also attended school in the States while we spent time down there.

It was on one of our winter journeys through British Columbia to the States that Norman decided to stay in Aldergrove. He got a job with the Department of Transportation there, settled down and later married. He still lives there with his family.

In the early years of Harry's career as a driller, he lost an eye while working in Calgary. Years later, on the homestead in Keg River, he hit his head as he was entering the barn and he gradually started to lose the sight in his other eye.

He had his first operation in Edmonton, but with no success. That was the beginning of a long series of doctors and operations all over the States. They were not successful and Harry became completely blind.

We heard about a seeing-eye dog school in California. I drove us to California, where Harry convinced the school that he was physically capable of the training necessary to have a seeing-eye dog.

We bought a small trailer and lived there for

303

a month while Harry went through the training process. Through strong determination Harry graduated with his dog Hawk. Hawk gave Harry his much sought after independence and they functioned well together.

We stayed in Cedar City, Utah, for a year and then came back north. Harry hired some help and continued to run the farm for a few years.

Harry Wilson, holding Patricia Vos, 1954.

During those years Johnny Vos and Harry ventured into potato farming. Even though the potatoes grew very well, they proved to be too labor-intensive to be economically viable.

In later years, Harry and I rented the farm out and went to Peace River, where Harry lived in the Auxiliary Hospital. Harry passed away on July 30th, 1976.

I continued to live in Peace River until October 3rd, 1979, when I married Sam Ristesund and we moved to the Manning area. Today I live in the Del-Air Lodge in Manning.

Labor disgraces no man; unfortunately, you occasionally find men who disgrace labor.
Ulysses S. Grant

Michael and Olena Yurkowski
by Elsie Halabisky

My father, Michael Yurkowski, was born in Austria and moved to Canada in 1905. He settled on a homestead in Garland, Manitoba.

My mother, Olena Demkiw Hrytciuk, was also born in Austria and came to Canada with her first husband, who died some years later. At that time there were no widow's pensions, no welfare, no help whatsoever. She had a difficult time trying to make a living for herself and her three small boys: Louis, Jack and George. Mother's neighbors were very good to her, giving her odd jobs to do. She also took in sewing.

My parents were married in 1911 and had five children – myself (Elizabeth), Anne, Johnny, Mary and Bill. Dad worked for the Canadian National Railway and rented his land to my uncle. We children helped with the chores when we came home from school. We had numerous animals, including cows which we milked, selling the cream and butter.

After 14 years with the C.N.R., Dad decided to quit and stay home to farm. He then heard about the beautiful Peace River country. A friend of Dad's, Mike Rudy, was also interested in the Peace country, so they decided to go and have a look.

They did a lot of travelling by foot and by boat on the Peace River. That year in Keg River everything, the fruit trees and the grass, was beautiful. Frank Jackson had a lovely garden that looked so nice. My Dad and Mike Rudy decided to take land and try homesteading again. They filed on land for themselves and their sons.

They went back to Garland and the following spring (1930) they crated their furniture and shipped it to the Peace River Crossing. They also shipped a carload of cattle, horses, hogs, chickens, a dog, and a cat. They, their families and all their worldly goods came to Carcajou from Peace River on the boat called the *Russian Navy*.

It had flooded that year, so we were stranded at the landing for about three weeks. We still had to cross the Keg River, which was really booming. While we waited for the water to go down, we began to learn the basics of camping out. We found the going very rough, as we had never cooked a meal over a campfire before. Also, the mosquitoes were so bad that you couldn't open your mouth to speak without having at least one fly in! We didn't have mosquito bars – we had never heard of them before. We lived in tents, but there were two or three warehouses where the

Hudson's Bay Post, Revillon Freres, and the Keg River Trading Company stored their freight when it came in on the boat. There were freighters from Keg River at the Carcajou Landing to pick up freight. They were also waiting for the time when they could get their freight across the Keg River. They were a big help, which was lucky for us. They even let us sleep in the warehouses. They showed us how to cook on the campfire, make bannock and a number of other things we didn't know how to do in this north country. If we were to survive, we had to learn fast!

We left the Carcajou Landing and travelled by horse and wagon. The roads were not good at the best of times. This time they were full of ruts and the ruts were full of water. Finally we arrived at Keg River and put up tents since there were no shacks or shelters of any kind. The family settled on SW-27-101-24-W5. We then began our life in Keg River.

The first few years were rough. We were able to get most of our groceries from the three stores that were in Keg River, but a lot of the supplies were freighted in after freeze-up or in the summer, brought up the river by boat to Carcajou Landing, then freighted to Keg River.

Louis Hrytciuk took up a homestead west of us along the Keg River W-30-101-24-W5. He helped with many community projects. He had a part in the United Farmers group getting the recreation lease established.

George Hrytciuk had carpentry skills that were put to good use in the school. He built the desks and the teacher's desk, which is still in use in the hall.

Mom and Dad made Keg River their home for the rest of their lives, as did the rest of our family.

Olena and Michael Yurkowski.

Johnny and Mabel Yurkowski
by Johnny Yurkowski

Keg River has been my home since April, 1930. My parents and brothers, my sister Elsie and her husband Bill Halabisky, the Rudy family, the Shemeluiks and their daughter Nellie all arrived here at the same time. We had travelled from Garland, Manitoba. Bill had a car and some of us came with him. Mother, Mrs. Rudy and the smaller children came on the train to Peace River.

When we reached Slave Lake with the car, there was so much water there that the road was impassable. We left the car and continued on the train. George rode in the boxcar with the settlers' effects so he could tend to the cattle and horses in the stock car. Our machinery and household furniture were included in the settlers' effects. We travelled down the Peace River to Carcajou on the *Russian Navy*, a commercial boat that was working the river that year. We unloaded all our belongings at the Keg River Landing on the west side of the river.

There were other people camped there, too. That's when we found out we could not go on to Keg River because the ice had just gone out and the river was flooded. We spent two weeks camped on the edge of the Peace River until we could travel to our homestead at SW-27-101-23-W5. The mosquitoes were terrible as we lived in our makeshift camp.

Dad and Mr. Rudy had spent the previous year looking for new land to farm. The land we had in Manitoba had been sandy with rocks. They had walked hundreds of miles in the Peace River country from Fort St. John to Fort Vermilion and finally decided the soil here in Keg River was what they were looking for.

In 1932 I was 16 years old and there were no paying jobs in Keg River. I decided that I would walk out and find work. With five dollars in my pocket I started off. There were cabins along the telegraph line about every 15 miles. The trail was very wet, so walking wasn't easy. I worked at any job I could find from stooking wheat for 10 cents an acre to working on a threshing crew for one dollar a day.

My friend and I travelled the rails like hoboes. We went all the way east to the lakehead at Kenora, Ontario. Hoboes were just a bunch of guys travelling and looking for work of any kind. They could ride on the freight trains for free. However, catching the trains while they were moving at 40 miles an hour or jumping off them at the same speed was very dangerous. The roundhouses were a warm place to sleep.

At Kenora my friend and I got a job working on the Trans Canada Highway. We moved crushed and blasted rock by hand into the road bed. I got my hand caught between two rocks and an artery was cut on the back of my hand. The blood shot out! The foreman got me a ride to the hospital in a new V-8 Ford. Those trucks were just being manufactured in 1933-34.

Politicians would stop by our camps and give us speeches about how they would improve things if we would vote for their party in the coming election. Things did improve, we then got 25 cents an hour! We had been getting $9.50 a month moving rock with horses and fresnoes (machines made for moving dirt that were pulled by horses) and push carts.

In January 1942 I volunteered for the army. We were in training for one and a half years. I got embarkation leave for two weeks. While I was home I scalded my foot. I went out to Peace River with Dr. Jackson since she was going anyway. Dr. Casper put me in the hospital in Peace River for a week. Then I was in trouble because my army pass had run out!

When I got back to base in Red Deer I was placed in detention and was hauled up on the carpet even with my sore foot! One of the officers chewed me up and down, then he had a strip torn off him because they finally believed that I had been in the hospital. When I was "absent without leave" my wife Mabel's allowance was cut off. Finally everything was sorted out and I left for Europe. I was behind my regiment, but I caught up to them in Halifax.

We landed in Normandy on day three. The sight of the carnage was unbelievable – broken tanks, boats, and landing barges sunk. We had to walk in chest-deep water to shore through all of this and four inches of oil floating on the water. The beaches were red with blood, covered with broken equipment and piles of guns. Overhead there was wave after wave of bombers and fighter planes.

We had no idea where our regiment was or where the enemy was! The first city we came to was turned to rubble, and we had to use Cats to clear a way through. The local people came out of cellars and bomb shelters.

I was away for three and a half years. My life slowly returned to normal as I returned to live in Keg River on my homestead. I trapped out on the

Johnny Yurkowski with wolf head. Killed to collect the bounty.

Chinchaga in the winter and farmed in the summer.

Mabel and I have a family of two daughters and one son. Alice Jean and Lawrence Budney have two daughters, Dawn and Nicole, and a son, Cory. They live in Fort Saskatchewan. John James has a son, Frank, and a daughter, Terry, and lives in Keg River. Lily and Allan McMillan have two children, Chad and Orleana, and they live in Grimshaw.

Mabel and I continue to live near the Keg River Post on our homestead.

Point of interest developed during construction of speed corner at Keg River Post, Johnny Yurkowski and road foreman.

Frank and Jewel Zurovec Family
by Jewel Zurovec

In 1958, we were called of God to go to Peace River, Alberta, Canada. Our children were ages 12, nine, seven, three, and six months. We searched the maps to see what was in Peace River and found it was a territory. Believing God wanted us to go there, we sold all we had, loaded our car (a 1950 Cadillac with one slick tire) and came to the Peace River territory. We had no church or organization behind us but trusted the Lord.

On arrival in Peace River, the settlement, we came to a little church by the river and told the lady of the house God sent us there from Texas. Her husband, who was the pastor, was praying for God to send someone to the Keg River Post area. He never expected God would send someone from Texas!

I stayed behind in Peace River while my husband Frank and brother Nettleton drove to Keg River. They asked around to find a place for us to live. Anything would have been great.

Well, there was a little trappers cabin by the Keg River that belonged to Mr. Wilson. He said we could stay there. My husband came back to take me to the Keg to show me the cabin. I loved that little cabin and was thankful to God for providing it.

It consisted of one room. Frank built three double bunkbeds for all of us to sleep in. He took some old boards and made a shelf where each person's clothes were kept.

We had only the warmest things we had in Texas, which were not very warm for Canada. Sister Nettleton went through their things and clothed us with proper attire. The Clares of Manning provided us with a stove and an old couch. We had a small little table for two, a log for a chair and we had never been so happy in all our lives.

My thought when I first saw the cabin was Jesus had no place to lay His head but He had given us a beautiful little cabin to lay our heads. What a wonderful God He is.

We told people about Jesus, sang and prayed with anyone who wanted prayer and helped all we could. That first Christmas was the most humble Christmas we ever spent and I will always remember Thanksgiving and Christmas in Keg River.

We held church in the school and community centre and on Thanksgiving after we had held church nearly all day, we came back to the cabin to find a box of food there. All kinds of good things filled the box. We rejoiced that God had led people there to bring us such a wonderful blessing!

The temperature was quite different in Canada from what we were used to, but the children adjusted. They never had colds even though they often ran around the cabin with bare feet.

We had so many amazing experiences. One thing that we were amazed at was when we would wash clothes and run out to hang them on the line. Before they went over the clothesline, they were frozen stiff. We would bring pants in that would stand up by themselves until they thawed out!

We will never forget the beauty of Keg River and the Peace River Territory. It is amazingly beautiful. Frank and Bruce would go to the river, cut ice and haul it in a sleigh pulled by Tarzan, a wonderful horse we will always remember. We melted the ice in a large barrel by the stove.

We slept a lot in the winter time as it was daylight only a short time. We made up for it in the summer when it stayed daylight many hours. We put blankets on the windows so the children would think it was night and go to sleep.

We moved into a granary at the corner of the village across from the Hudson's Bay Company. The village people were across the way and would stop by or come over. We were able to minister to them and help them as much as possible. We love the people of Keg River and thank God for their love and concern. They probably thought we were

Aaron in front of the family cabin with the meat supply close at hand.

crazy for going up there with all those children, six in all, and trusting only in the Lord to provide our means.

We never took up any offerings or passed the plate. We felt God had sent us up there and He would take care of us – which He did. Every family in Keg River, Paddle Prairie and Carcajou was used by God to help us fulfil our calling.

Without the people listening to God (even though they did not know that is what they were doing) the mission could not have been completed. Johnny and Mabel Yurkowski, Margaret and Dave Befus, Del and Emma Weber, Dave and Doris Weber, Anne and Johnny Vos, Barbara and Adam Pawlowich and the Christians of Carcajou and many more were instruments in the carrying out of this Canadian Call.

We had many experiences that we will never forget and will always be treasures in our hearts. One particular experience was going to Carcajou when it was about ten below Fahrenheit. There was ice on the gravel and dirt roads. We travelled all night in a wagon covered by a tarp. My husband was driving a little Ford tractor which we had to winch up, go a little way further and winch up.

At one time we all got out of the wagon and Frank made a large fire. We had Joshua, our newborn son, with us and the other children. I never prayed so hard in my life for some help from God.

All at once, I saw some lights coming and lo and behold, it was two ministering angels, Dave Befus and Dave Weber. They brought us coffee and sandwiches and came to help us. We will always be grateful to them. I will never forget them saying, ''Nobody can tell us there is no gravel in this road, because we felt every rock!'' They sat down and held the wagon on the road with two ropes to keep us from going over the edge into the ravine.

We spent all of that year in Keg River and came back to the States in the summer for a short time. We came back to Canada and stayed until our visas played out. We were unable to stay any longer and said our goodbyes. However, we went back as often as possible through the years. We have always had the dream that some day we will return to Canada. Our hearts will always be there and we still love the people of Keg River, Paddle Prairie and Carcajou. We are still hoping to some day return and never leave.

The children with whom we arrived in Keg River are: Bruce Lynn, Aaron Lane, Cindy Lou, Starlette Rose, Bonnie Dale and Brenda Kay. Frank Joshua was born in October, 1959, in Hay River, North West Territories.

(Frank passed away in January, 1994.)

Zurovec family in Peace River.

INDEX TOPICS

Mrs. Stoney.

D.A. Thomas on the Peace River.

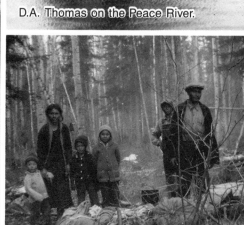
Native camp in the bush.

The Sam Parenteau place, 1940.

Walter Lariviere, Sam Parenteau, Ji

Keg River Native Village.

Mike Papirny and Fischer's Super Cub, 1959.

Ron and Don Jackson.

Charles Dovey and three nieces.